Asking About Prices

Asking About Prices

A New Approach to Understanding Price Stickiness

Alan S. Blinder

Elie R. D. Canetti

David E. Lebow

Jeremy B. Rudd

Russell Sage Foundation
New York

The Russell Sage Foundation

The Russell Sage Foundation, one of the oldest of America's general purpose foundations, was established in 1907 by Mrs. Margaret Olivia Sage for "the improvement of social and living conditions in the United States." The Foundation seeks to fulfill this mandate by fostering the development and dissemination of knowledge about the country's political, social, and economic problems. While the Foundation endeavors to assure the accuracy and objectivity of each book it publishes, the conclusions and interpretations in Russell Sage Foundation publications are those of the authors and not of the Foundation, its Trustees, or its staff. Publication by Russell Sage, therefore, does not imply Foundation endorsement.

Library of Congress Cataloging-in-Publication Data
Asking about prices : a new approach to understanding price stickiness
 / Alan S. Blinder . . . [et al.].
    p. cm.
 Includes bibliographical references and index.
 ISBN 0-87154-121-1
 1. Prices—Mathematical models. 2. Business cycles—
 Mathematical models.
 I. Blinder, Alan S.
 HB221.A76 1998   97-26536
 338.5'2—dc21   CIP

RUSSELL SAGE FOUNDATION
112 East 64th Street, New York, New York 10021
10 9 8 7 6 5 4 3 2 1

To Madeline, with love
A. S. B.

For Beth, without whom nothing would be possible, and for
Chloe and Hannah, for whom everything is possible
E. R. D. C.

To Coletta, Jeremy, and Meg
D. E. L.

For Rochelle and Heineken
J. B. R.

Contents

Preface   xi

PART I   ON LEARNING BY ASKING   1

Chapter 1 Why Study Price Stickiness? Why This Way?   3
Chapter 2 Antecedents   16
Chapter 3 Research Design   47

PART II   THE BASIC FINDINGS   81

Chapter 4 Wouldn't It Be Nice to Know . . . ?
            The Factual Basis for Theories of Price Stickiness   83
Chapter 5 Basic Results on the Twelve Theories   107

PART III   DETAILED FINDINGS ON EACH THEORY   127

Chapter 6 Nominal Contracting   129
Chapter 7 Implicit Contracts   149
Chapter 8 Judging Quality by Price   165
Chapter 9 Psychological Pricing Points   175
Chapter 10 Procyclical Elasticity of Demand   186
Chapter 11 Cost-Based Pricing: Lags from the Chain of
            Production   197
Chapter 12 Constant Marginal Cost   211
Chapter 13 Costs of Adjusting Prices   226
Chapter 14 Hierarchy   253

Chapter 15 Coordination Failure   260

Chapter 16 Inventories   274

Chapter 17 Nonprice Competition   283

PART IV   WRAPPING UP   293

Chapter 18 What Have We Learned?   295

Appendix A Manufacturing Interview   315

Appendix B List of Variable Names   337

Notes   339

Bibliography   361

Index   371

ALAN S. BLINDER is Gordon S. Rentschler Memorial Professor of Economics at Princeton University, where he has taught since 1971. He also founded and directs Princeton's Center for Economic Policy Studies. He has served as vice chairman of the Board of Governors of the Federal Reserve System and as a member of the president's Council of Economic Advisers.

ELIE R. D. CANETTI is an economist for the International Monetary Fund. He previously worked at the World Bank and the United States Treasury.

DAVID E. LEBOW is an economist at the Board of Governors of the Federal Reserve System.

JEREMY B. RUDD is senior economist at the Council of Economic Advisers, Washington, D.C.

Preface

What a long, strange trip this research project has been. The tale needs to be told here, for it explains both the long gestation period since the interviews ended (in March 1992) and the complicated coauthorship of this book. It also gives credit where credit is due.

The idea of assessing the validity of theories of price stickiness by asking actual decisionmakers began percolating in my mind about a decade ago—after more than fifteen years of teaching graduate macroeconomic theory at Princeton. For the longest time, I vacillated over two questions. Could such a survey be done successfully by an academic economist with limited resources at his disposal? (The answer, I now know, is yes.) And would anyone pay attention to the results? (The answer to that question will be determined by readers of this book.) After more than a little prodding from Eric Wanner, president of the Russell Sage Foundation, I decided to give it a try.

My first brilliant tactical decision came in 1988, when I recruited Elie Canetti, then a Princeton graduate student, as the chief research assistant on the project. Working together over the course of about three years, we refined the questionnaire, designed the sample, recruited and trained the interviewers, and conducted the initial interviews—including the pretest and pilot study described in chapter 3. Canetti ably handled literally hundreds of organizational and administrative details, made numerous substantive suggestions about research design, and dug up most of the previous survey research summarized in chapter 2. Importantly, he also managed the team of Princeton graduate students that did the interviewing.

When Canetti left Princeton for the International Monetary Fund, I made my second brilliant move: hiring Jeremy Rudd to take over. Over the course of about nine months in 1992, the two of us completed about two-thirds of the statistical analysis reported in this book—plus some that is not reported. His diligence, care, and subtle suggestions when I was going astray were all invaluable.

By October 1992, I had drafted about a dozen chapters—some essentially complete, others fragmentary. A complete draft manuscript by early 1993 looked like a virtual certainty. Then the roof caved in on this project. Bill Clinton was elected president of the United States, and I soon became involved, first, in the transition, and then in the first Clinton administration as a member of the Council of Economic Advisers. Life on the Clinton CEA left little time for any outside activities, and no time whatever for research. So the manuscript was shelved—both literally and figuratively—for about two years.

In June 1994, I became vice chairman of the Board of Governors of the Federal Reserve System. After a few months of getting my sea legs, I made my third brilliant tactical move. I knew that it would take much prodding and help for me to make any progress on the book while serving as the Fed's vice chairman. Fortunately, staff economists at the Board of Governors are expected to spend a portion of their time on economic research, and my special assistant, David Lebow, was an expert on pricing research. So in the fall of 1994 I asked Lebow to take responsibility for moving the project forward—which he did exceedingly well. He first replicated and then completed the statistical work that Rudd and I had begun a few years earlier, correcting a number of small errors in the process. He also drafted several of the remaining chapters and raised many substantive questions that improved the analysis. Progress was slow while I served on the Fed, but there was clear forward motion.

The final leg of the long journey began shortly after my return to Princeton in February 1996. I once again enlisted the services of Rudd as research assistant. He and Lebow together finished and double-checked the statistical analysis. And the three of us jointly completed writing the few remaining chapters—apart from chapter 18, which I drafted alone. All four coauthors then reviewed the entire draft manuscript, making many small changes.

Thus, while I am the common thread that links the inception of the idea in 1987 to the publication of this book in 1997, and while all final decisions were mine, each of my three coauthors made major and truly indispensable contributions. The work you hold in your hands literally would not be here were it not for their efforts.

With Thanks

I owe three deep debts of gratitude. The first is to the two foundations which generously funded the research. The Russell Sage Foundation graciously provided both seed money to start the project in 1988 and a small grant to complete it in 1996. The Alfred P. Sloan Foundation provided the bulk of the funding under a three-year grant that should have ended in 1993, but was subsequently put into suspended animation. I am grateful to both foundations for their support—and for their patience.

Next, I am indebted to the team of former Princeton graduate students that, along with Canetti and me, conducted the two hundred interviews: David Genesove, Katy Graddy, Dean Jolliffe, Harold Kim, John Leahy, Alec Levenson, Anthony Marcus, John Penrod, Michael Quinn, Stephen Schwartz, Tim Vogelsang, and David Zimmerman. They have all now finished their graduate studies and gone on to bigger and better things. But I must single out Schwartz, Marcus, and Vogelsang for doing an extraordinary number of interviews, and doing them so well.

Finally, I am deeply grateful to the more than two hundred business executives who took the time to talk to us about their pricing practices. Our pledge of anonymity prevents me from naming any of them, but they were the essential—and irreplaceable—ingredient in this study. We learned a great deal from listening to what they had to say, and hope you will, too.

A User's Guide

As a guide to the reader, the book is organized into four parts. Part I, which consists of chapters 1 to 3, deals with the motivation for and the methodology of the study. Why did we opt for the interview approach and how did we implement it? Part II summarizes and highlights the main findings, both on the facts of price stickiness (chapter 4) and on respondents' evaluations of the various theories (chapter 5). Part III is the longest—twelve chapters in all, each presenting the detailed findings on a particular theory. But most of chapters 6 to 17 are quite short. Finally, part IV, which is chapter 18, sums up and draws some conclusions.

The book is structured to cater to diverse tastes. Only readers with the deepest interest in price stickiness will want to read it straight through from beginning to end. Those with less dedication to the subject matter can read parts I and II completely, pick and choose among the theory-specific chapters in part III according to taste, and then finish with chapter 18. Readers who are less interested in the literature and the methodology, and more anxious to find the punch lines, can give chapter 1 a quick read, jump directly to chapters 4 and 5, and finish with chapter 18. Each chapter also concludes with a brief summary, to aid the most casual visitor to the manuscript.

A Note on Data Availability

The data collected for this study constitute a treasure trove of information, much of which cannot be (or at least has not been) obtained in any other way. We have not been able to exploit all the possible uses of these data in this book. In order to make the data available to other researchers, we have created a public-use file (in STATA format) that can be accessed and downloaded over the Internet via anonymous FTP from *princeton.edu*. Except for some identifying information omitted in order to protect the anonymity of respondents, this file is precisely the one we used in our statistical analysis. Both the dataset itself (*pricepub.dta*) and a short description (*pricepub.readme*) reside in the *pub/pribook* directory. The data should be downloaded as a binary file.

Disclaimer

The views expressed herein are those of the four authors and not of any of the institutions with which we are associated. We all thank Anil Kashyap for many helpful comments on the penultimate draft.

ALAN S. BLINDER
Princeton, N.J.
May 1997

Part I
On Learning by Asking

Chapter 1

Why Study Price Stickiness?
Why This Way?

Nothing astonishes men so much as common sense
and plain dealing.
—RALPH WALDO EMERSON

The Importance of Price Stickiness

In recent decades, macroeconomic theorists have devoted enormous amounts of time, thought, and energy to the search for better microtheoretic foundations for macroeconomic behavior. Nowhere has this search borne less fruit than in seeking answers to the following question: Why do nominal wages and prices react so slowly to business cycle developments? In short, why are wages and prices so "sticky"? The abject failure of the standard research methodology to make headway on this critical issue in the microfoundations of macroeconomics motivated the unorthodox approach of the present study.

No one should think the question unimportant. On the contrary, sticky prices are an essential element of Keynesian economics, which is sometimes called the economics of nominal rigidities. (It is called less polite things as well.) The sobriquet is an exaggeration, to be sure, but a forgivable one, for embedding the assumption of short-run price or wage rigidity into almost any macro model will make it produce characteristically Keynesian results—such as that an injection of money raises production. The simplest illustration is the quantity theory of money with fixed velocity:

$$MV = Py.$$

In the absence of nominal rigidities, real output, y, is essentially fixed on the supply side of the economy, so that changes in money must pass directly and proportionately into prices. But if P, the price level, is sticky in the short run, the very same equation implies that part of any change in M must first show up in y. Conversely, if a vertical aggregate supply curve (attributable, say, to instantaneous market clearing) is appended to an otherwise "Keynesian" IS-LM model, the real effects of fiscal and monetary policy disappear.

When a scientific discipline knows next to nothing about a question of paramount importance, it is in some trouble. How did macroeconomics get into such a predicament? Two obvious explanations can be dismissed immediately. First, it is not because macroeconomists have just discovered that wage-price stickiness is a central issue; we have known this since Keynes's *General Theory*, if not before. Second, the failure does not result from lack of effort. Scores, if not hundreds, of theorists have worked on this problem, producing many interesting theoretical explanations; and new ideas keep popping up all the time.[1] Progress has not been hampered by lack of imagination.

Nor, by the way, has it been hampered by lack of observation. Although much time and energy was wasted in the 1970s and 1980s arguing over whether or not the economy should be modeled as a giant auction hall with perfectly flexible prices, a small mountain of empirical evidence testifies to the fact that wages and prices adjust slowly to macroeconomic events. For example, the economist Robert Gordon (1990) summarizes the evidence that aggregate price indexes move sluggishly, while Yoram Weiss (1993) surveys some papers that provide similar evidence for individual prices. The tricky questions are two: How slow is slow? And what factors account for the sluggishness? This book is devoted to the second of these two questions. But a brief word on the first is in order, for it helps explain why conventional methods of economic inquiry—theory and econometrics—have yielded such meager results.

Why So Little Progress So Far?

When we say that wages or prices are "sticky," we generally mean that they move more slowly than would Walrasian market-clearing prices. Two curmudgeonly questions arise, each of which influenced the design of this study: Is the statement operational? And is it something we should care about? We take these up in reverse order.

Is Wage-Price Stickiness an Important Phenomenon?

The question here is basically whether wage-price stickiness has allocative significance. For example, if no one ever borrowed at the credit card interest rate, which remained around 19 percent for years, then the fact that this rate was extremely sticky would hardly have mattered.[2] Ever since the economist Robert Barro's (1977) ingenious paper, macroeconomists have worried that the sticky wages we see in many labor markets may in fact lack allocative significance. Specifically, firms may not equate the real wage to the marginal product of labor and workers may not equate the real wage to the the marginal utility of leisure. Why? Because, it is argued, employees and employers implicitly enter into long-term agreements to exchange labor for money. These contracts clear the labor market in a long-run sense, thereby tying long-run average labor supply closely to long-run average wage payments. But if workers dislike wage variability, the contract may pay steady wages month after month even if both the marginal product of labor and actual hours of work vary considerably over time.

This argument has persuaded many economists that it is hazardous to conclude from the observed stickiness of wages that there is pervasive disequilibrium in labor markets. It also calls into question the allocative significance of the limited variability of real wages over the business cycle. But is the argument empirically important? Do firms and workers actually enter into such agreements? No one really knows. When Alan Blinder and his student Don Choi (1990) asked a small sample of personnel managers what they thought of the implicit contract theory, the results were a bottle half full and half empty.[3] About half thought it "plausible or relevant," the rest did not.[4]

Irrespective of its empirical relevance, the theory has profoundly influenced the thinking of academic economists and has shifted the focus of research from wage stickiness to price stickiness. When Blinder initiated this research, he knew he would be preaching to the unconverted and was anxious to have at least some economists pay at least some attention to the unorthodox research findings. So he decided to study only price stickiness. Of course, the implicit contracts argument can be applied to prices, too. Sticky prices may just be installment payments on long-term agreements, rather than symptoms of non-clearing product markets. But everyone seems to agree that, however important or unimportant the implicit contract theory is in labor markets, it must surely be less important in product markets, where arms'-length, spot transactions are much more common.

Is Wage-Price Stickiness an Operational Concept?

The next question is whether and how we can breathe empirical life into the theoretical notion of price stickiness. In brief, how slow is slow? To state the issue perhaps a bit too boldly, a theory that predicts that prices adjust more slowly than market-clearing prices—*and nothing else*—is basically untestable, and therefore an empty theory. Why? Because economists have no agreed-upon metric to use in assessing the observed speed of adjustment of any particular price, let alone the aggregate price level. So if we find, say, that the price of candy bars changes every six months, how do we know whether this is slower or faster than the Walrasian norm?[5]

If a theory makes no prediction other than that prices move less rapidly than Walrasian prices, econometric testing is almost (but not quite) out of the question. To conduct a test, a complete model of supply, demand, and price adjustment must be specified, estimated, and used to derive a quantitative measure of the speed at which the market-clearing price moves. Then actual price movements can be compared to this norm. This research strategy is not a counsel of perfection; it can be implemented. Indeed, it is one of the ways that econometricians have demonstrated that prices and wages are sticky. But, of course, any such demonstration is conditional on the validity of the many maintained hypotheses used as the framework for estimation. So any such finding is open to dispute.

But the problem goes deeper than this. If we have a wide variety of models, each of which predicts that prices are sticky and nothing else, conventional econometrics will have a hard (if not impossible) time distinguishing among them, for there is no way to test one theory against another. This problem, we think, is the main reason why formal econometrics has made so little progress in weeding out invalid theories of wage-price stickiness. It is one of

the two problems that originally drove Blinder—in desperation!—
to the interview method.

The other problem is that several of the most prominent theories of price stickiness rely on variables that are either unobservable
in principle or unobserved in practice.

One example is a theory that achieved wide popularity in the
1980s, which holds that firms hesitate to cut prices in slumps out
of fear that customers will misinterpret any price cut as a reduction
in quality—*when in fact there has been no such quality reduction.*[6] Notice
that unobservability is crucial to the argument; if quality were easily observed, there would be no possibility of misinterpretation
because everyone would recognize when quality had changed.

Another example is the "menu cost" theory, which says that
firms change prices infrequently because they incur a fixed cost
each time they do so.[7] In principle, such costs can be measured. In
practice, however, we have few such measurements and are
unlikely to get many.[8] It might seem that this particular theory does
at least carry a clear collateral implication—namely, that fixed costs
preclude small price changes, where the precise meaning of "small"
is defined by the size of the menu costs. In principle, that is correct.
But our inability to measure menu costs directly robs this implication of operational significance. Will the firm avoid 1 percent, 5 percent, or 10 percent price changes?

When theories rely on unobservables in essential ways, econometric testing is difficult, to say the least. Thus it is no accident that
new theories of price stickiness have continued to proliferate faster
than applied econometrics has been able to discard old ones. It was
that unsatisfactory state of affairs that first set Blinder thinking
about an alternative approach.

Time for a New Approach?

In pondering this dilemma, a curious "empirical regularity"
emerged. Virtually every theory of price stickiness outlines a
thought process that allegedly leads decisionmakers (generally
modeled as profit maximizers) to conclude that it is against their
best interest to change the price. But if people actually think the
way one of these theories says, then they should be aware that they
do—or so it seemed. Hence an idea: Why not ask them?

This naive idea must be approached with caution. If you confront a price-setter with an open-ended question like, "Why don't you cut your prices more (or more often) when sales sag?" you may get shrugs, blank stares, or incoherent answers. What you hear is unlikely to fit neatly into economists' theoretical boxes. But suppose you ask more pointed questions. Suppose you describe in plain English the chain of reasoning that, according to Theory X, goes through the minds of price-setters. If Theory X really describes their behavior, the decisionmakers ought to recognize and resonate to it. If they do not, then they are probably not behaving as the theory says. At least that was our methodological precept. If the true reasons for price stickiness are buried deep in the subconsciousnesses of decisionmakers, then interviews are unlikely to uncover them.

Here are two examples of the rather pointed way in which we posed questions about the theories.

One very old theory of why prices may be rigid over the business cycle, which enjoyed a strong revival in the 1980s, starts with the premise that profit-maximizing firms with market power set price (P) as a markup over marginal cost (MC), which markup depends on the elasticity of demand ($\epsilon > 1$).[9] Thus:

$$P = MC[\epsilon/(\epsilon - 1)],$$

where ϵ is defined to be a positive number. The theory then asserts that demand curves become less elastic as they shift in so that, even though MC falls as output contracts, the markup rises to compensate. The result may be approximate constancy of the profit-maximizing price over the business cycle.

In principle, this theory can be tested by conventional econometric means; all we need do is measure how the elasticity of demand varies over the business cycle in a variety of industries. In practice, however, any applied econometrician will recognize that as a tall order, unlikely to be filled with the nonexperimental data at our disposal. But now think about using the interview method as an alternative to time-series econometrics. If this theory is the real (or one real) reason for price rigidity, firms must both believe that their demand elasticities are procyclical and act on that belief. In that case, if you ask them about it—eschewing jargon like "elasticity," of course—they ought to recognize the idea and feel comfortable with it.

To test this theory, our questionnaire posed the following plain-English question:[10]

> B5(a). It has been suggested that, when business turns down, a company loses its least loyal customers first and retains its most loyal ones. Since the remaining customers are not very sensitive to price, reducing markups will not stimulate sales very much. Is this idea true in your company?

If the respondent answered yes, we then asked:

> B5. How important is it in explaining the speed of price adjustment in your company?

To preview some results that will be examined in more detail later, almost 60 percent of respondents accepted the premise that the elasticity of demand varies procyclically. But only about half of those (hence, about 30 percent of all firms) rated it a "moderately important" or "very important" source of price stickiness.

Our second example, the Okun (1981) "invisible handshake" theory, is an even more extreme example in that direct econometric testing seems out of the question even on conceptual grounds. The idea behind the theory is that firms have implicit understandings with their regular customers which proscribe price increases in tight markets, presumably in return for stable prices in weak markets. What observable variable can be used to measure the importance, or even the existence, of such implicit agreements? None, we fear—which may be why there has been so little econometric testing to date. But it seems to us that, if such tacit agreements exist, firms ought to know that they do—and should say so when asked.

Our questionnaire therefore "tested" this theory by posing the following question:

> B2(a). Another idea has been suggested for cases in which price increases are not prohibited by explicit contracts. The idea is that firms have implicit understandings with their customers—who expect the firms not to take advantage of the situation by raising prices when the market is tight. Is this idea true in your company?

About two-thirds answered yes. Furthermore, a large majority of those answering yes rated implicit contracts a "moderately important" or "very important" reason why prices adjust slowly in their companies. The theory evidently holds promise in certain sectors of the economy.

But Aren't Interviews Unreliable?

Economists are disposed to be skeptical that you can learn anything about economic behavior by asking people. Most believe you should not even try. Instead, you should observe what they *do* in markets (not what they say), model that behavior theoretically, and test the model econometrically.

The litany of objections to interviews is not without merit. Critics argue that responses may be terribly sensitive to the precise wording of the questions. We agree and hence devoted many hours to the form and structure of the questionnaire. While we do not pretend to have achieved perfection (and will, in fact, mention some problems in subsequent chapters), we invite skeptical readers to inspect the full questionnaire that was used in the field. It is included as appendix A of this book.[11]

Other critics will object that interviewees have no incentive to respond truthfully or thoughtfully, and so may refuse to cooperate or give misleading answers. Where the respondent has reason to conceal the truth or mislead the interviewer, this objection is, to our minds, a show stopper. In such cases, the interview method is simply not a promising mode of inquiry. Thus, for example, interviews may be a poor way to estimate the extent of tax evasion or the prevalence of collusion among businesses. But there are many interesting and important questions about which people have no particular reason to conceal the truth—unless they are pathological liars. In such cases, the interview method might help.

The thoughtfulness problem goes deeper. For example, people may not understand or be able to articulate their own motives or behavior very well. We all know the billiard-ball analogy: A good pool player makes excellent intuitive use of the laws of physics without understanding them intellectually. So if you ask expert players to explain how they shoot so well, they may not give you a coherent answer—and almost certainly will not give an answer that a physicist would mark correct. For this reason, we think, many economists are skeptical that you can learn anything by asking "economic players"—even good ones—about how they play the game.

In part, we agree. We do not, for example, think much is learned by asking corporate executives open-ended questions about the goals of their companies. They may just pick objectives that sound lofty or otherwise appealing. But more pointed questions, posed in plain English, can elicit more useful responses. For example, if you ask skilled billiards players whether they base their shots on the principle that the angle of incidence equals the angle of reflection, they will probably think you strange. But, if you take them to the table and ask about the angles they choose—using elementary physics to tailor your questions—they would probably respond in the affirmative. Closer to home, we should remember that most of our standard data come, in the first instance, from either face-to-face interviews or mailed questionnaires filled out by minor functionaries. How else do you think the Labor Department measures unemployment or the Commerce Department estimates Gross Domestic Product (GDP)?[12]

Thus, while many objections to the interview method have some validity, we should keep them in perspective. Economists above all should evaluate the usefulness of any suggested mode of inquiry—including interviews—by posing the classic question: Relative to what? The imperfect knowledge we pick up from questionnaires should not be compared to some epistemological ideal, but to the imperfect knowledge that nonexperimental scientists can deduce theoretically or glean from econometric investigations.

In doing so, it is important to remember that theory and econometrics also have their limitations, which are often inadequately appreciated. All too often theoretical deductions are untested and/or based on untested premises. Worse yet, either the conclusions or the assumptions may be *untestable*. Econometric evidence is often equivocal and/or subject to methodological dispute. Results may be fragile owing to small samples or multicollinearity. There may have been "regime changes" during the sample period. Appropriate instruments are scarce or nonexistent in time-series applications. And computers make data mining all too easy. Stacked up against competition of this caliber, the interview method may not look so bad after all—especially if viewed as a supplement to, rather than a replacement for, more conventional modes of economic inquiry.

In sum, we are more than willing to accept the methodological precept that economists should rely on the standard tools of inquiry—theory and econometrics—where they bear fruit. In cases where people's observed behavior conflicts with what they say they do, we, like most economists, would stick with the observations.

But we have just argued that conventional research techniques have made virtually no progress in explaining wage-price stickiness. Might we not, therefore, learn something by opening our eyes and ears and listening to the folks who populate the economies we study, the people who actually do the things we theorize about? Yes, it is true that physicists and chemists do not ask their subjects why they behave as they do. But, in our zeal to emulate the hard sciences, economists should not misinterpret that lesson. If molecules could talk, would chemists refuse to listen?

A Bird's Eye View of the Survey Design

Details of how the questionnaire was designed and tested, how the sample was selected, and how the interviews were conducted are provided in chapter 3. Here we offer the reader in a hurry a quick summary of the methodology.

Twelve theories of sticky prices—all but one of them culled from the theoretical literature on the microfoundations of macroeconomics—were selected for testing. The selection process was far from random and not entirely objective. First of all, we took it for granted that almost all firms in our economy (excluding farms) are price makers rather than price takers—an assumption amply justified by the survey responses. Second, the selection of theories for testing reflected Blinder's personal judgments about which of the many theories of price stickiness were most prominent in the academic literature, translatable into plain English, and sensible enough to be explained to business people with a straight face. These choices are justified, to some extent, in chapter 2.

Each theory so selected was turned into a question for part B of the questionnaire; two examples were offered above. Call these the *main questions*. (They are numbered B1 through B12 on the questionnaire.) Each main question was followed by up to ten additional questions tailored to the specifics of each theory. So part B of the questionnaire has twelve sections, one for each theory.[13] Part A requests a variety of factual information about the company, such as its size, how often it changes prices, to whom it sells, whether it has formal contracts, and so on. Even economists who are skeptical that we can learn anything of value by asking business executives their opinions on theories may find the answers to these factual questions enlightening. We certainly did.

Selecting the sample was a delicate task. Our philosophy was simple, though its execution was not. We took the goal to be to explain why the GDP deflator moves sluggishly, and hence sought to create a random sample of the GDP. Well, not quite. The sample was actually limited to the private, unregulated, nonfarm, for-profit GDP. The motives for making these exclusions—which together amount to about 29 percent of GDP—are perhaps obvious; if not, they are explained in chapter 3. That chapter also explains our sampling method in detail—namely, how a computerized "dartboard" was created, with each firm assigned a "slice" proportional to its value added.

Once this was done, a random sample of three hundred and thirty firms was drawn, interviews were requested with each, and two hundred agreed to participate.[14] The stunningly high response rate of 61 percent already suggests that any nonresponse bias is probably small, but some evidence in support of this point is offered in chapter 3. Interviews were conducted in person, generally in the respondent's office. A few were done by Blinder personally, but most were carried out by a team of thirteen Princeton graduate students specially selected and trained for the task. Interviews varied in length, depending mainly on how discursive the respondent was, but generally took forty-five to seventy minutes.

Since the probability that any firm would be selected into the sample was proportional to its value added, all averages and distributions reported in this book are unweighted. The weighting was embodied in the probability of being selected into the sample, so any further weighting of the responses would have amounted to double counting.[15]

Plan of the Book

The book is organized into eighteen chapters, but most of them are blissfully short. Chapter 2 reviews the theoretical, empirical, and survey antecedents to this research.

Chapter 3 offers details on the questionnaire, sample selection, and interview procedures, highlighting some problems that are not mentioned in the brief summary above. It also offers some evidence that there were no serious biases from nonresponse, only minor differences in coding across the fourteen interviewers, few significant effects of interview date (the data collection period included a recession), and almost no differences at all by geographical location.

Chapter 4 summarizes the findings from the "factual" part of the questionnaire (part A). We view these findings as answers to a set of fascinating and important questions that simply cannot be addressed with standard data sources. For example, we offer here what we believe to be the first estimates of the fraction of United States GDP sold under written contracts, the fraction sold to repeat customers, the average lag between a change in demand and the corresponding change in price, and so on. Many of the answers are surprising—both to us and to others.[16]

Chapter 5 provides an overview of the results for the twelve main theories. Which of the theories seem to have the most validity overall and within particular sectors? What do the survey results tell us about specific questions that cut across theories? For example, are prices more sticky downward than upward? Surprisingly, the answer appears to be no. Chapters 6 through 17, most of which are brief, delve into the details of each of the twelve theories. Each chapter explores a theory in detail, gives the survey results on its "popularity," explores which attributes of a firm help explain its affinity for the theory, and discusses the answers to follow-up questions designed to shed light on the validity, applicability, or other aspects of the theory. Because chapter 6 is the first of these chapters, it also includes some methodological discussion that is relevant for the subsequent chapters.

Finally, chapter 18 quickly sums up, assesses what we have and have not learned, points to some policy implications, and offers the inevitable suggestions for future research.

Chapter Summary

This entire book was motivated by a failure—the failure of conventional theoretical and empirical research tools to answer a question of overwhelming importance for macroeconomic theory and policy: Why are prices sticky? One important impediment to progress, we suggest, is that many of the competing theories are epistemologically empty, or nearly so. They may predict nothing other than that prices should move more slowly than some unknown Walrasian norm. Or they may be based on variables which are either unmeasurable in principle or unmeasured in practice.

Is there a way out of this methodological box? Some economists, perhaps most, would answer no. But, since each theory is based on a chain of reasoning that allegedly takes place inside a decision-maker's head, we suggest that an interview approach may hold promise. To be sure, there are many hazards in trying to learn about how economies work by asking participants. But skeptics who raise these (valid) objections to interviews often forget about the many hazards that plague conventional econometric and theoretical research. A pragmatic attitude, not methodological purity, is called for. And since the interview method is virtually uncharted territory, an initial exploration seemed worthwhile—and was made. This book is a report on that expedition.

Chapter 2

Antecedents

An economist is someone who, seeing that something works in practice, asks if it can also work in theory.

—ANONYMOUS

This chapter offers a highly selective summary of previous research on price stickiness. The intent is not to provide a comprehensive survey of all the relevant literature; in particular, scant attention is paid to the mountains of empirical work that support the view that prices are in fact sticky. Rather, the chapter is meant to provide context for the interview study and, to some extent, to justify its form.

The next section presents a fairly complete catalogue of theories of sticky prices, paying careful attention (wherever possible) to the empirical evidence bearing on each. Readers who are already thoroughly conversant with the theoretical literature may safely skim this section; but nonspecialists wishing to acquaint themselves with the literature should find it useful. With a few exceptions (duly noted below), this catalogue can be thought of as the menu of theories available when Blinder decided which ones to include in the survey. The selections were neither random nor entirely objective; nor could they have been. But neither were they helter-skelter nor, we hope, excessively idiosyncratic. Here we try to explain and justify the choices.

Although no one has ever attempted a study quite like this before, we are not the first to use survey techniques to study pricing. So the second part of this chapter summarizes the intellectual precursors in survey research, many of which are quite old by now and pertain to countries other than the United States. Most of the material in this section will be totally unfamiliar to modern research economists since this mode of inquiry has been out of style for a long time. As will be seen, there were good reasons for the change in fashion, for most of the earlier studies suffered from severe methodological deficiencies. Our judgment is that, in total, they shed relatively little light on the validity of alternative theories. (Of course, that was not usually their goal.) Nonetheless, there are some interesting tidbits to be culled.

Theories of Price Stickiness

As mentioned in chapter 1, there is no shortage of theories of sticky prices. Indeed, the problem is precisely the opposite: we have an embarrassingly long list from which to choose. So the first step in designing a survey instrument was to decide which of the many theories to include. We began by scouring the intellectual waterfront to compile a reasonably comprehensive inventory of theories that could lay claim to some significant intellectual support—as evidenced, say, by the attention they had received in academic circles.[1]

Before reviewing the list, it may be useful to share with the reader some of the criteria that guided the selections.

First, we excluded any theory that, in Blinder's judgment (therein some subjectivity), either sounded silly or actually was silly. After all, we were going to present the theories to practical business people, not sell them to the referees of scholarly journals. It was essential that we be taken seriously.

Second, we decided to ban from the questionnaire any theory that might conjure up images of the Antitrust Division of the U.S. Department of Justice, on the grounds that such questions might induce respondents to clam up or give evasive answers. So questions about oligopolistic collusion, limit pricing, and other concerns of industrial organization specialists, legitimate and fascinating though they might be, were nonetheless excluded.

Third, and finally, we had to eliminate theories that were too complicated—another subjective judgment—to be explained crisply in plain English.

Fortunately, these criteria proved not to be very confining. While something was lost by banning questions about collusive behavior, few of the leading theories of sticky prices were eliminated on these grounds.

Theories do not align themselves in any natural order, so any would-be cataloguer must create his or her own Dewey decimal system. Ours classifies each theory into one of five categories, depending on whether it is based on the nature of costs, the nature of demand, the form of contracts, the market structure, or on imperfect (and, especially, asymmetric) information—plus one theory which does not fit naturally into any of these categories. Obviously, these are not mutually exclusive categories since any modestly complete theory must have, at minimum, something to say about both demand and costs. So other authors might catalog things differently. However, nothing hinges on the categorization. Hence, with due indulgence from the reader, we proceed.

Theories Based on the Nature of Costs

Constant Marginal Cost   One extremely simple theory of why prices vary less than quantities over the business cycle is based on the premise that the marginal cost function (MC) is flat over a wide range of possible outputs, as shown in figure 2.1. If MC takes this shape, then a profit-maximizing firm will not wish to change its price much when its demand—and hence marginal revenue (MR)—curve shifts. More concretely, if the firm applies a constant markup to marginal cost, then a flat MC curve will produce a constant price over the business cycle.[2]

This very old idea was revived in the 1980s in a series of interesting and provocative papers by Stanford's Robert Hall (1986, 1988) and has garnered a great deal of attention since. The cost structure depicted in figure 2.1 seems plausible to many people, and the theory is simple and intuitive. So we decided to include it in the questionnaire. (It is theory B7 on the questionnaire; see appendix A.)

In truth, however, the notion that constant MC can account for sticky prices is more subtle than it appears. Discussion of most of these subtleties is reserved for chapter 12, but one point is general enough to put on the table right now. Hall's model explains sticky prices only if the (flat) MC function does not move around much over business cycles as, for example, input prices change. In fact, the fixed-markup model implies that P should react immediately and proportionately to any change in MC. So what the model really explains is stickiness in the ratio of P to MC, which is a relative price, not stickiness in nominal prices. To turn it into a theory of

Figure 2.1   Constant Marginal Cost

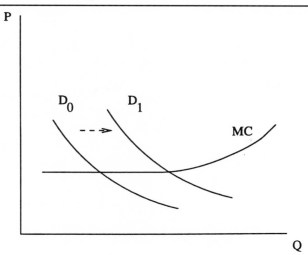

P   = price
Q   = quantity
D   = demand
MC = marginal cost

sticky nominal prices, we must add something else—like a theory
of nominal wage rigidity or some explicit costs of changing nominal prices.

This is a pervasive problem that afflicts most of the theories
devised by economists because models of rational behavior proscribe money illusion. Unfortunately, however, it is not a problem
that can be tackled very easily by the interview method—for a
simple reason. While the distinction between absolute and relative
prices is natural and elementary to economists, it is neither to ordinary business managers. So we cannot easily get respondents to distinguish between factors that rigidify nominal prices and those that
rigidify relative prices; the latter are, to them, unnatural constructs.
We did, however, try to chip away at this problem in various small
ways in the questionnaire. These will be discussed in context, as
they arise.

Cost-Based Pricing with Lags   The next theory maintains the
assumptions that prices depend on marginal cost and that markups
are fixed, but drops the hypothesis that marginal cost is constant

over the business cycle. Instead, it assumes that MC has the usual upward-sloping shape, but that prices of final goods adjust to cost shocks only with a lag.

At first, this hardly sounds like a theory at all. Are we to explain price stickiness by assuming that prices adjust slowly? What turns an apparent tautology into a theory with content is the recognition that most goods pass through several stages of production on their way to the final consumer. Rubber is turned into tires which are sold to automobile manufacturers who turn them (along with many other components) into cars. Copper is extruded into wire which is installed on a memory board which becomes part of a computer. Robert Gordon (1981) observed that, if there are many stages of production, short lags between cost changes and price changes at each individual firm can compound into long lags between (initial) cost changes and (final goods) price changes for the entire economy. He thus called attention to "the role of the input-output table in translating prompt price adjustment at the individual level to gradual price adjustment at the aggregate level."[3] A few years later, Olivier Blanchard (1983) of the Massachusetts Institute of Technology provided the equations, which are summarized in chapter 11.

At some level, of course, this theory must be true. Surely no one doubts that prices depend on costs and that the reaction is not literally instantaneous. But that does not tell us anything about the empirical importance of the idea. If, say, the typical firm changes its price one day after its costs change, the theory will not account for any significant price stickiness in quarterly data. You will note, too, that the input-output theory carries a clear testable implication: Goods that pass through the most stages of production should have the stickiest prices. Saying this is not the same as saying that prices of final goods move more sluggishly than prices of intermediate goods, however. Compare, for example, bananas and electrical generators. So it is a difficult proposition to test empirically. To our knowledge, no one has done so.[4]

Since this theory is intuitively appealing, easy to explain to practitioners, and almost certain to have at least some empirical validity, we included it on the questionnaire as theory B6. It is, of course, a modern wrinkle on a very old Keynesian idea: that prices react to costs with a lag.

Costs of Price Adjustment Prices might be sticky because it is costly to change them. This extremely straightforward idea actually comes in two variants, which have starkly divergent implications.

One variant assumes that the cost of adjusting a price is convex in the price change, say, $C(\Delta p) = c(\Delta p)^2$. Proponents of this theory, such as the economist Julio Rotemberg (1982), appear to have borrowed this assumption uncritically from the literature on the costs of adjusting factor inputs. However, it is far from clear that quadratic adjustment cost is a reasonable assumption for prices.[5] Does it really cost one hundred times as much to change a price by a dollar as it does to change it by a dime? If true, however, the quadratic assumption clearly implies a particular form of price stickiness: A firm wishing to raise its price will do so gradually, in a series of small steps, rather than all at once.

The second variant models the adjustment cost as a fixed "toll" that is paid any time the price is changed. The size of the toll is independent of the size of the price change. Because the cost of printing new menus is the simplest example of such costs, they have come to be called "menu costs." If the costs of changing prices are in fact independent of the size of the change, we should observe that price changes are infrequent but of sizable magnitude. Small price changes should be avoided. At the micro level, we should find price stickiness of a very particular sort: prices should remain constant for periods of time and then jump abruptly. This is precisely the opposite of what quadratic adjustment costs imply. But, at the macro level, aggregation would smooth the adjustments, making the observable implications perhaps not so different.[6]

The menu cost variant has spawned an enormous theoretical literature since the economists N. Gregory Mankiw (1985), Michael Parkin (1986), and, in a different way, George Akerlof and Janet Yellen (1985) first called attention to it.[7] It is by now one of the main strands of New Keynesian theorizing. But direct empirical testing has proven difficult owing to the absence of data on menu costs. However, both Dennis Carlton (1986) and Anil Kashyap (1995) have found a fair number of what appear to be very small changes in actual transactions prices—which seems to be bad news for the menu cost theory.

Given the unknown empirical importance of adjustment costs for prices, and the unknown relative importances of convex versus fixed costs, this theory was an obvious candidate for inclusion on the questionnaire. (It is theory B8.) We first presented the two variants as a single theory: that costs of adjustment deter price changes. Then, if the respondent agreed with this premise, we posed follow-up questions to try to distinguish between the convex cost and menu cost versions.

Inventories   Firms that hold finished goods in inventory can use them to buffer changes in both prices and production, if they so choose.[8] The intuitive idea is clear. When demand spurts, a firm can meet some of this demand out of inventory, thereby augmenting effective supply and limiting the necessary increases in both price and output. Similarly, when sales are weak, firms can accumulate inventories, thereby effectively augmenting demand and mitigating the need for price and output reductions.

A bit of notation may help clarify the argument. Let q be production, s be sales, and I be inventory investment. The three are related by the identity:

$$I = q - s.$$

When there are no inventories, q must equal s at all times. In the presence of inventories, the inverse demand function relates price to sales, not to production, so:

$$p = D(s) + e,$$

where e is a demand shock that varies over time. When e changes, a firm with no inventories must choose among adjustments in price and production that satisfy:

2.1 $$\frac{dp}{de} - D'(s)\frac{dq}{de} = 1.$$

But a firm that can vary its inventories can choose among pairs of adjustments that satisfy:

2.2 $$\frac{dp}{de} - D'(s)\frac{dq}{de} = 1 - D'(s)\frac{dI}{de}.$$

Since $D'(s) < 0$ and dI/de is negative if inventories are used to buffer demand shocks, the weighted average of price and production adjustments is smaller in 2.2 than in 2.1.

We classify this as a cost-based theory because one major determinant of whether a firm makes much use of inventories as buffers is the relative costs of changing inventories versus changing production. This is an arbitrary categorization, however, because another determinant of the degree of buffering is whether demand shocks are permanent or transitory. The intuition here is that the ability to vary inventories enables the firm to postpone the ultimate price and output adjustments—if it wants to. But if the change in demand is permanent, there is no reason to postpone the inevitable; so prices and production should bear most of the burden of adjustment.

Is the theory empirically valid? There is some econometric evidence that, as the theory implies, inventories lessen the variability of production (Fair 1989; Krane and Braun 1991).[9] But we know of no direct evidence on the posited negative effect of inventories on price movements. However, the central implication of the theory vis-à-vis price stickiness is actually more subtle than this. It is *not* that firms with inventories should have less variable prices than firms with no inventories. After all, the two types of firms operate in fundamentally different markets—for example, one type sells goods while the other sells services. We do not really believe that General Motors (which keeps inventory) has stickier prices than, say, the law firms it hires (which do not). What the theory really predicts is that, within the class of goods-producing firms, those which can vary inventories most cheaply should have the stickiest prices. It need hardly be pointed out that this is a difficult implication to test.

That the theory seems plausible, and yet is so difficult to test directly, made it a prime candidate for inclusion on the survey instrument. The inventory-based theory also seems highly intuitive. So this theory was included in the questionnaire as theory B11.

Theories Based on the Nature of Demand

Procyclical Elasticity of Demand We mentioned earlier that constant markups and constant marginal costs will lead to prices that are constant over the business cycle. Another group of theories is based on the idea that, although MC is procyclical, markups are countercyclical, leaving prices roughly acyclical. Marginal cost is procyclical for the usual reason: MC is an increasing function of q. But why should markups be countercyclical? A number of possible explanations have been offered. The first one we will consider is based on the hypothesis that the price elasticity of demand is procyclical.

The mechanics of this argument are trivial. As is well known, the marginal revenue and price of a firm with a downward-sloping demand curve are related by:

2.3 $p/MR = \epsilon/(\epsilon - 1)$,

where ϵ is the elasticity of demand (measured as a positive number). Since a profit-maximizer sets MR equal to MC, the optimal markup is equal to the righthand side of 2.3, which is Lerner's index of market power. Thus the markup moves inversely to ϵ and, therefore, a procyclical elasticity of demand produces a countercyclical markup.

The basic idea that the demand curve becomes less elastic as it shifts in has been around a long time. The question is: Why? One recent answer to this question was suggested by the economist Mark Bils (1989a) for the case of indivisible durable goods. Suppose most durables are luxury goods and that richer people have lower price elasticities of demand—perhaps because their time is so valuable that they will not do much shopping. In a boom, the marginal buyer comes from further down in the income distribution and hence has more elastic demand. In a slump, the marginal buyer comes from higher up in the income distribution, and hence demand is less elastic.

A simpler model—the one used in the questionnaire—posits that firms have different types of customers who differ in their attachment to the firms' products, and therefore in their elasticities of demand. Regular, loyal customers have low price elasticities; occasional, off-the-street customers have much higher price elasticities. As the market shrinks, the least-loyal customers are the first to exit, leaving the firm with an increasingly inelastic demand curve. In a cyclical upswing, the opposite happens: new customers enter the market, raising the elasticity of demand.[10]

There is a fair amount of econometric evidence suggesting that markups are in fact countercyclical—that is, that prices fluctuate less than marginal costs; but none of this evidence points convincingly to procyclical elasticity as the cause.[11] Since there are many alternative explanations of countercyclical markups, we must at this point remain agnostic about any particular one. For this reason, and because the general idea has received so much recent attention, we included procyclical elasticity of demand as one of the theories to be tested in the survey. (It appears as theory B5 in the questionnaire.)

Nonprice Influences on Demand   Dennis Carlton (1989), among others, has suggested that markets may clear along dimensions other than price. In particular, suppose that demand depends not just on prices and incomes, but also on such characteristics as the delivery lag and the quality of service provided with the good: $q^d = d$ (p, y, L, Z, . . .), where L is the delivery lag and Z measures service quality.[12] After a shock, the entire vector (p, L, Z, . . .) will adjust to clear the market. But the shares of the adjustment shouldered by price, delivery lag, and ancillary services will depend on how sensitive the firm's costs and demand are to each. Carlton argues persuasively that there is no a priori reason to think that almost all the burden almost always falls on p.

Notice that this idea is closely related to the inventory-based theory discussed earlier. For goods produced to order, delivery lags play the same buffering role as inventories play for goods produced to stock; indeed, in theoretical models, backlogs are often treated as negative inventories. Carlton's wrinkle is to note that the delivery lag, unlike the inventory stock, is a plausible determinant of quantity demanded. Indeed, Carlton (1984) presents evidence that delivery lags are statistically significant determinants of demand for several manufacturing industries; in fact, they have almost as large an effect on demand as prices do. Unfortunately, there is little empirical evidence beyond Carlton's work. So we included this idea on the questionnaire as theory B12.

Psychological Pricing Points   This is the first theory that was not culled from the theoretical literature, but rather was suggested by practitioners.[13] Many sellers, especially in the retail business, apparently believe that certain threshold prices—such as $29.99 for a shirt or $999 for a home computer—have special psychological significance to consumers. In economists' jargon, the demand curve is thought to be extremely elastic at prices just above those points. (See figure 2.2.)

Figure 2.2   Pricing Points

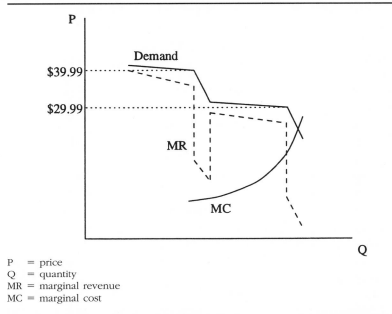

P   = price
Q   = quantity
MR = marginal revenue
MC = marginal cost

Pricing points give rise to price stickiness in the following way. Suppose a store selling shirts for $29.99 experiences a small rise in marginal cost. If it thinks $30 is a psychological barrier, it may prefer to hold the price constant rather than raise it to, say, $30.15. At some later point, after several small cost increases have accumulated into something sizable, the price may be raised to, say, $31.99.

Is there any evidence in favor of this theory? It is known that retail food prices ending in 41 to 50 cents or 75 to 100 cents are more common than prices ending in other digits.[14] But that does not establish that price changes lag systematically behind cost changes; it could be that prices adjust promptly to costs but are always "rounded off." Nor does anyone know how important threshold prices are in practice. Since the belief in pricing points is part of the folklore of pricing, and thus is presumably familiar to many practitioners, it seemed an ideal candidate for inclusion in the survey. (It is theory B4 on the questionnaire.)

Theories Based on the Nature of Contracts

Explicit Nominal Contracts   Certainly the simplest "theory" of price stickiness is the hypothesis that many goods and services (especially labor) are sold under contracts that fix nominal prices for finite periods of time. While the contract is in effect, prices are not free to adjust to either demand or cost shocks. Nominal contracts are, of course, a mainstay of Keynesian macro models.[15] But this is not really a "theory" at all. It is simply a statement about the way things are. To make it a theory, we need to explain why contracts fix nominal prices.

Reasons why buyers and sellers might wish to enter into long-term contracts that stabilize prices are easy to elucidate (see our discussion of the next theory). But neoclassical economic theory strains to rationalize prices that are fixed in nominal, rather than real, terms. There is much confusion on this point. While it is easy to build plausible theoretical models in which partial, rather than complete, indexing is optimal, these models do not lead to the conclusion that the optimal degree of indexing is zero—except under extreme circumstances (such as where there are no nominal shocks).[16] Yet totally unindexed contracts are the rule, not the exception. No one knows why.

Our hunch is that the search for a purely rational theory of nominal contracts is hopeless. After all, demand and supply functions derived from maximizing behavior will always be homogeneous of degree zero in all nominal prices. Menu costs do not really do the trick. Once it has been decided to live with purely nominal contracts, menu costs may indeed explain why prices are adjusted infrequently. But they do not explain why contracting is in nominal terms to begin with. To explain nominal contracting, we may have to admit that commonly held notions of "fairness" incorporate money illusion. This does, after all, seem to be a fairly well-established psychological fact.[17]

In any case, despite the ubiquitous appearance of nominal contracts in Keynesian models, no one knows either what share of United States GDP is sold under nominal contracts or how important these contracts are in rigidifying prices. The survey offers estimates of each. (See questions A8 and B1 on the questionnaire.)

Implicit Contracts   An important variant on this theme is the "invisible handshake" theory, due to the late Arthur Okun (1981). Okun argued that buyers and sellers who value long-term relationships may enter into implicit "contracts" under which, for example, sellers pledge not to exploit the situation by raising prices when markets are tight. In return, buyers agree not to insist on price reductions when markets are slack. Clearly, such implicit contracts will rigidify prices. However, Okun suggested that widely accepted notions of fairness would permit prices to rise whenever costs increase, especially if the cost increases were public knowledge. Hence he posited that prices would be much stickier after demand shocks than after cost shocks.

There are many ways to rationalize the existence of long-term, implicit contracts. One explanation emphasizes the value of relation-specific rents that arise in long-term trading relationships, rents which the two sides can share as long as they stay together. Another explanation focuses on differential attitudes toward risk of firms (which are presumed risk neutral) and consumers (who are risk averse); this is the product-market analog of the implicit contracts theory of the labor market (Azariadis 1975). A third is based on (allegedly) widely accepted notions of "fairness."

An important question is whether the Okun theory applies to nominal or real prices. Versions that are motivated by neoclassical considerations (like risk sharing) will certainly apply only to real prices, implying that implicit contracts should be implicitly indexed. But, as indicated above, versions based on psychological notions of fairness may well contain important elements of money illusion, leading to implicit *nominal* contracts. For those who are willing to accept unconventional data from such sources as experiments and attitudinal surveys, there is accumulating evidence that fairness plays a considerable role in pricing even when there is no long-term relationship, and that the concept of fairness embodies money illusion. This evidence will be discussed more fully in chapter 7.

Implicit contracts strike many economists (including us) as quite plausible. Yet their existence is—almost by definition—not subject to objective verification, at least not from conventional data sources. So this theory seems almost an ideal subject to be studied by the interview method. It appears on the questionnaire as theory B2.

Price Protection We come now to a second theory suggested by a practitioner, rather than by a theorist—one which had an unusual history in this study.

Many firms, especially sellers of high technology products with prices that frequently fall, offer their customers "price protection" against subsequent declines in price.[18] A typical price protection clause in a sales contract might read as follows. Suppose company A sells company B 2000 disk drives for $100 each. Company A then guarantees that, if it cuts the price below $100 while company B still has some of the drives in inventory, it will refund the difference retroactively to company B. Thus if, for example, company B still has 200 drives in stock when company A cuts the price by $20, then company A would pay company B $20 × 200 = $4000. It should be clear that this somewhat dulls the incentive for company A to cut prices![19]

We stumbled onto this theory in a curious and disconcerting way. While the survey was in progress, Blinder (1991) gave a preliminary report on the survey methodology and early results at the December 1990 meetings of the American Economic Association. A reporter from *The Wall Street Journal* was present and, a few days later, an article on the research was prominently displayed in the newspaper (Wessel 1991). This article elicited a number of letters and phone calls from business people and economists, many of whom purported to reveal "the real reason" for price stickiness. Most of their suggestions were already on the questionnaire, but one in particular was not.

An executive from a high-tech company in California claimed that she knew the real reason for sticky prices in her industry and many others. It was, she said, because of price protection. She then not only explained what the term meant but graciously sent several examples of price protection clauses in standard contracts. The idea sounded plausible, and some quick (and nonscientific) inquiries verified that price protection is a common practice. Had we left the most important cause of price stickiness out of the survey? We were sufficiently worried to devise a test. After hurried consultations with a few people, we drafted an addendum to the questionnaire which inquired about price protection. The full text read as follows:

B13. The last idea pertains to "price protection." [NOTE: IF RESPON-
DENT DOESN'T KNOW THE TERM, YOU CAN DEFINE IT: For price
cuts: Seller rebates to buyer the difference in price on some goods
previously purchased. For price hikes: Seller fills outstanding orders
at the old (lower) price.]
(a). Do you offer price protection to your customers? If so, roughly
what portion of your sales are price protected?
    How important is price protection in slowing down price decreases
in your company/division?
(c). Does price protection also discourage you from increasing prices?
(d). When you give price protection to your customers, how often is
it explicitly written into a contract?

We decided to add this question to the end of the questionnaire
(so as not to contaminate the other responses) for the next thirty
interviews. Then, if price protection appeared to be important, we
would make the new question a permanent part of the survey, even
though we had already completed seventy-seven interviews without it. If it seemed unimportant, however, we would remove it. In
the event, only three of the thirty executives to whom we posed
the question thought price protection was at all relevant to the
speed of price adjustment. Most, in fact, did not even have price
protection clauses in their contracts. We breathed easier—and
ignored price protection thereafter.

Theories Based on the Nature of Market Interactions

So far, we have discussed ten theories that were tested in the survey and hardly any that were not. As we move to the next category—theories based on market structure—the tables turn. Most of
the theories under this heading were omitted from the questionnaire for a simple reason. Not surprisingly, theories based on market structure typically involve oligopolistic collusion, limit pricing to
deter entry, and similar phenomena. But recall that we decided
early on not to ask companies any such questions for fear that
merely asking them would put respondents on guard—despite our
guarantee of confidentiality. A particularly clear example is:

The Kinked Demand Curve of Oligopoly Theory Perhaps the
granddaddy of all theories of sticky prices argues that oligopolistic

interdependence leads to a concave kink in the subjective (and, under rational expectations, the objective) demand curve facing an oligopolist. (See demand curve DAd in figure 2.3.) The argument, it will be recalled, is that the oligopoly firm assumes the worst. If it lowers its price, it assumes that its rivals will match the price reduction, producing the rather inelastic demand curve Ad. Hence there is little to gain by cutting price. If, on the other hand, it raises its price, it assumes that rivals will not follow suit, leaving it at the mercy of the more elastic demand curve DA. So price increases might prove disastrous. The upshot is that even substantial changes in marginal cost may not induce any change in price. The oligopolists remain—in cozy if tacit collusion—at point A in the diagram.

The kinked demand curve theory was originated by the Oxford researchers R. L. Hall and C. J. Hitch (1939) and the economist Paul Sweezy (1939) to explain the stickiness of "administered" prices in concentrated industries. As we shall see, Hall and Hitch even based the idea on survey evidence! While the game-theoretic

Figure 2.3   Kinked Demand Curve

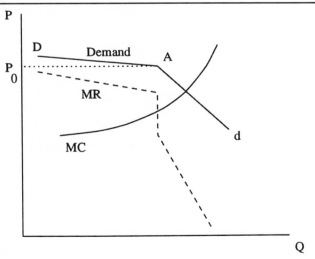

P   = price
Q   = quantity
MR = marginal revenue
MC = marginal cost

foundations of the kinked demand theory have remained elusive, Joseph Stiglitz (1979) suggested an information-theoretic derivation which was nicely formalized and modeled by Geoffrey Woglom (1982).[20] In the Stiglitz-Woglom model, customers are attached to particular firms and are poorly informed about prices elsewhere. A firm that cuts its price will attract relatively few customers at first, for it takes a while for the word to spread. However, a firm that raises its price will lose many customers because its regular customers will assume that prices elsewhere have probably not changed. Hence, imperfect information makes the demand curve more elastic for price increases than for price decreases.

There has long been considerable theoretical interest in the kinked demand model. And, of course, it is enshrined in many textbooks. In addition, there is a substantial body of empirical evidence bearing on its validity—with mixed results.[21] Nonetheless, we did not inquire about the kinked demand curve idea because we did not want to bring up the subject of collusion, even obliquely. The Stiglitz-Woglom version might have been testable, but it is only one possible source of the kink, and probably not the most plausible one. However, the next theory is based on a related idea that applies naturally in competitive markets.

Coordination Failure   Suppose demand in an industry rises, warranting an increase in price. You run one of the firms in the industry. If other firms are going to raise their prices, you certainly want to raise yours. And other firms feel the same way. But you worry that competitors might not raise their prices, thereby leaving you out on a lonely limb. So you wait for others to act first. Absent an effective coordinating mechanism that would enable all the firms in the industry to move in concert, the result may be that prices remain fixed. Similar coordination failures can arise on the down side, or in the case of changes in costs.

One obvious solution to this problem, of course, is to have a price leader. So the theory is closely related to the old idea of price leadership. Another solution is to engage in collusive behavior. But it is almost impossible to sustain collusion in a monopolistically competitive industry with many firms; and it may even be hard for any single firm to remain the price leader for long. The same problems arise in unstable oligopolies. (See the next theory.)

Coordination failure is a very old idea that has recently been revived and modernized by economists such as Russell Cooper and Andrew John (1988) and Laurence Ball and David Romer (1991).[22] Their specific ideas and new wrinkles will be examined in detail in chapter 15. Suffice it to say here that the theory seemed sufficiently intuitive, topical, and interesting to merit inclusion on the survey. (It is theory B10 on the questionnaire.) It is also quite easy to explain to practitioners.

Is there evidence bearing on the validity of the coordination failure theory? For reasons explained in the next section, the economists Julio Rotemberg and Michael Woodford (1991) suggest that their empirical finding that markups are countercyclical is evidence for the sort of tacit collusion that the theory denies. But, as we noted earlier, there are alternative explanations of countercyclical markups. So the case is certainly neither proven nor disproven.

Oligopolistic Price Wars During Booms   It is well understood that an oligopoly would prefer to collude in order to maintain the monopoly price. But it has also been known for a long time that business fluctuations make such collusion difficult to sustain. For years, it was generally supposed that cartels break down most frequently when markets are weak.[23] If so, that would enhance the cyclical sensitivity of prices because price cuts would occur during slumps. But then Julio Rotemberg and Garth Saloner (1986) offered a model of oligopolistic behavior in which price wars break out more frequently in booms. In that case, the ebb and flow of effective collusion during business cycles would reduce the cyclical sensitivity of prices.

The basic idea of the Rotemberg-Saloner model is as follows. Oligopolists normally collude to charge the monopoly price. But there is always an incentive to cheat: By shading the price, you can steal much of the market from your rivals. Hence firms enforce the collusive agreement by relying on a severe punishment scheme: If any firm deviates from the agreement, the others lower the price to the competitive level from then on, thereby eliminating all monopoly profits. Now consider how a positive shock to demand affects the costs and benefits of cheating. The rewards from cheating rise because the market is bigger. But, if the demand shock is not expected to persist, the present discounted value of the punishment remains the same. Hence, Rotemberg and Saloner deduce, cheating should occur more often in booms.

At first, this inference seems exceedingly fragile. In actual business cycles, fluctuations in demand are quite persistent. So the present discounted value of the punishment would appear to rise in booms and fall in slumps, which would destroy the counterintuitive Rotemberg-Saloner result. Surprisingly, the theorist Michihiro Kandori (1991) shows that the basic result goes through in the presence of serially correlated shocks—if the discount factor bears a certain relationship to the number of firms in the industry. If it does not, John Haltiwanger and Joseph Harrington (1991) show that prices are likely to be lower (given the level of demand) when demand is falling and higher when demand is rising.

Rotemberg and Woodford (1991) provide some empirical evidence to support the view that variation in the degree of collusion among oligopolists over the business cycle is an important cause of countercyclical markups. For example, they show that more concentrated industries (for which collusion is likely to be more important) tend to have more cyclical markups. Still, their evidence is far from conclusive, and it would have been interesting to hear what business people think about this theory. However, we did not include it on the survey because of our unwillingness to ask firms (even subtly) about collusion.

Resale Price Maintenance   Resale price maintenance occurs when the manufacturer, rather than the retailer, sets the final retail price of an item. Strictly speaking, it is illegal for anyone to dictate the selling price to a retailer. Nevertheless, many products come with prices stamped right on them, presumably to encourage retailers to charge that price.

The economist Jean Tirole (1988) lists several reasons why manufacturers may want to control the retail price of an item. One major reason is that any market power exercised by the retailer reduces demand to the manufacturer, and so reduces the manufacturer's profits. Setting the final price is one way for the manufacturer to capture the bulk of the profits.

Of course, resale price maintenance need not cause sticky prices. It just pushes the pricing decision back to the manufacturer, and the question is whether a manufacturer has any reason to choose stickier prices than a retailer. In any case, the illegality of this practice (in its pure form) was sufficient to disqualify it as a candidate for the survey.

"Thicker" Markets in Booms Recently, the researchers Elizabeth Warner and Robert Barsky (1995) noted a puzzling fact. Data on the prices of eight very specific commodities sold in fifteen retail stores in Ann Arbor, Michigan, during the winter of 1987 to 1988 showed that "sales" (that is, markdowns from normal retail prices) occurred more often when business was brisk, such as on weekends and holidays, than when business was slack. Since we normally think of peak periods as times when demand curves shift out (Christmas is a case in point), it seems surprising that prices would be lower then. So what is going on?

Warner and Barksy suggest an explanation that produces a procyclical elasticity of demand which, for reasons explained above, would tend to rigidify prices. But they get there via an ingenious route. Search is more efficient, they suggest, in periods when people shop more intensively, such as on Saturdays and at Christmas. Hence it is rational for people to invest more time in search in such "thick" markets. One reason might be economies of scope in search: Once you are out shopping for the lowest price on shirts, it is pretty trivial to shop for the lowest price on ties. If people search more intensively during peak buying periods, the elasticity of demand should be greater then.

The argument is clever, and may even be correct.[24] However, we should not jump to conclusions on the basis of data from a few stores in one college town. For example, we do not know if this phenomenon is observed at business cycle frequencies. In any case, the "thick markets" theory came to our attention much too late to be incorporated in the survey.

Macroeconomic Policy One commonly heard argument that seems to be part of the "oral tradition" of Keynesian economics is that the success of stabilization policy in mitigating the business cycle has itself been a cause of increased price and wage rigidity (Baily 1978). The argument is simply that firms today are less worried that recessions will last long or deteriorate into depressions than they were sixty years ago. The basic idea seems plausible and can probably even be deduced from theoretical first principles—provided those principles explain why firms do not want to cut prices in response to transitory drops in demand. But there are at least two problems.

First, price stickiness is not a new phenomenon. It predates Keynesian demand management policy by a long way. Indeed, Gordon (1990, 1130) has estimated equations for the United States in which "neither prices nor wages were more sticky in 1954 to 1987 than 1873 to 1914." Second, the theory is incomplete. To make it coherent, we need some reason why firms do not want to lower prices—albeit briefly—in slumps and then raise them back in recoveries. Menu costs or implicit contracts are two possibilities.

We did not test the "shallow recessions" theory on the questionnaire for two main reasons. First, as just noted, it is not a complete theory; something else is needed, and that "something else" usually suffices to explain price stickiness on its own. Second, we were wary of asking managers questions about the overall macroeconomy, as opposed to questions about how their own businesses operate. They presumably know much more about the latter than the former.

Theories Based on Imperfect Information

Several theories of price rigidity based on imperfect information, and especially asymmetrically imperfect information, surfaced in the 1980s, most of them due to Joseph Stiglitz, often in collaboration with the economists Bruce Greenwald and/or Andrew Weiss. Since these theories always involve unobservables in an essential way, they defy testing by conventional econometric methods. Hence they seem, on the surface, to be prime candidates for testing by the survey method. Since we wound up including only one member of this group on the questionnaire, we should explain why.

Judging Quality by Price   The one uncertainty-based theory which we did include is actually a modern variation on a very old theme. In some markets, customers probably judge quality by price. For example, would Rolls Royce sell more cars if it lowered the price dramatically? Would Ralph Lauren sell more shirts, or Calvin Klein more jeans? Maybe, but maybe not. The traditional explanation for judging quality by price was snob appeal. But Stiglitz (1987, and elsewhere) suggested an alternative explanation based on the modern theory of imperfect information.

Suppose product quality is unobservable, or at least has some important unobservable aspects, but that high prices and high quality are correlated—and everyone knows that they are. Then a firm contemplating a price cut might fear that consumers might misinterpret the price reduction as a reduction in quality. If so, it will naturally be hesitant to reduce prices when, say, demand falls.

Obviously, this theory cannot be tested in conventional ways because it is based on the premise that quality is not observable by anyone; it is not just the econometrician who is ignorant. And the idea seemed to be intuitive and easily understood by practitioners. So we included it in the questionnaire as theory B3.

Relative Uncertainties in Price Versus Quantity Changes   Greenwald and Stiglitz (1989) offered another explanation for price stickiness that, we thought, was subtle and ingenious. They argued that prices vary less than quantities over business cycles because risk-averse firms are more uncertain about the profit consequences of changing prices than about the profit consequences of changing production. The idea sounded sensible. And, even though it involved comparing the concavities of two profit functions (one in p, the other in q), we thought we could explain it to practitioners in plain English. We were wrong. Several attempts to craft a question during the pretesting stage failed; the business executives who graciously agreed to serve as guinea pigs simply could not understand the idea.[25] Sometimes they furrowed their brows. Sometimes they offered answers, but not to the question we thought we were asking. After several unsuccessful attempts at redrafting, we reluctantly concluded that this particular theory is not suitable for testing by the interview method.

We tell this story to make a simple point: Not all theories are testable by the interview method; some are simply too complicated. That does not necessarily make them bad theories; after all, general relativity is a pretty tough concept, too. It just means that some other method must be employed to test them. Still, one cannot help but wonder about the empirical validity of a theory that is incomprehensible to the people whose behavior it is alleged to model.

Unobserved Variation in the Cost of Capital   Greenwald and Stiglitz (1988) have also offered a new theory of price rigidity that blends imperfect information with an old idea of Edmund Phelps and Sidney Winter (1970). Phelps and Winter suggested that a price reduction can be thought of as an "investment" in a future customer base: The idea is that, if you lower your price today, you will gradually attract new customers and therefore face a more attractive demand curve tomorrow. Greenwald and Stiglitz append to this idea the hypothesis that both credit rationing and equity rationing grow more severe in recessions, thereby raising the implicit cost of capital. If this is so, then firms will invest less at all margins when business conditions deteriorate. Since price reductions are viewed as investments in future customers, Greenwald and Stiglitz deduce that capital market imperfections rigidify prices.

This theory was not included in the survey for the following reason: At least where observables are concerned, it is starkly counterfactual. It is well known that interest rates are procyclical, not countercyclical. For the Greenwald-Stiglitz theory to be true, not only must the *unobservable* component of the cost of capital rise during slumps (perhaps due to rationing) but this increase must overwhelm the observed—and often pronounced—decline in interest rates. It seemed unlikely that practical business people would react positively to, or even understand, this idea.

Finally, there was one last theory which did not come from the theoretical literature and which does not fit neatly into any of the above-mentioned categories.[26] It was nonetheless included in the survey, so we should explain why.

The Hierarchical Structure of Large Firms   As mentioned earlier, six business men and women graciously volunteered to help us pretest the questionnaire. At the conclusion of each such interview, we asked whether we had omitted any factor that was important in slowing down price adjustments.[27] One respondent, who held the unusual title of Vice President for Pricing in a large manufacturing company, suggested what seemed to be a promising idea. In his firm, he told us, price changes are often delayed by the time it takes to get a large hierarchical organization to move. He ventured that this might be true in most large companies.

On hearing this, we thought to ourselves: This is precisely the sort of phenomenon that might be empirically important (for big companies) and yet totally ignored by economic theory. So it was added to our list of theories; see theory B9 on the questionnaire. As it turned out (see chapter 14), it was incorrect to generalize from this one firm; apparently, few executives think that internal hierarchies slow down price adjustments in their firms.[28]

Previous Survey Research on Pricing

As we have noted, economists are accustomed to using conventional research tools, especially econometric methods, to learn about pricing behavior. The portion of that research that bears directly on the validity of the various theories of price stickiness has just been summarized. But this book is motivated by the notion that there is an alternative way to study pricing: by asking the people who set the prices. This idea hardly originates with us. It has a long—though thin—history, dating back at least to the famous interviews of British manufacturers conducted by a team of Oxford economists in the 1930s and reported on by Hall and Hitch (1939). That paper is justly celebrated for its invention of the theory of the kinked demand curve. What is often forgotten is that the idea for the kinked demand curve came from interviews.

The Oxford team interviewed thirty-eight British "entrepreneurs" (their term), thirty-three of whom were in manufacturing enterprises.[29] The questionnaire was submitted in advance and then interviewers visited the firms to discuss the questions and answers in person. Unfortunately, both the questionnaire and the nature of the interviews changed from the early stages of the project to the later stages (p. 33), thereby severely vitiating comparability.[30] And the sample was neither random nor representative since "most firms were approached through personal introductions" (p. 13). Nor is any information given on how many firms refused to cooperate. For all these reasons and more, the data cannot support formal statistical analyses; and Hall and Hitch did not offer any. (They did, however, offer some simple tabulations.)

Their central conclusion, which they viewed as "so nearly unanimous" (p. 13) that it could probably be generalized, is that most firms set prices by adding a markup to full costs (including fixed costs) rather than to marginal costs. Four main theories of pricing emerged from the Oxford interviews.[31] The most famous, of course, was the kinked demand curve. Another was that firms colluded—whether implicitly or explicitly—to create an effective monopoly which faced an inelastic demand curve, and hence did not want to cut prices. A third was that prices were maintained only modestly above "full cost" as a way to deter entry. And the last was what contemporary economists would call costs of price adjustment.

The Hall-Hitch paper was extremely controversial for years. Indeed, the issue it raised—Do firms practice marginal cost pricing, as assumed by economists?—still rages. It appears that this was both the first and the last interview study of pricing to have a major impact on the thinking of economists.

When Blinder first thought about doing this study, however, the first precedent that came to mind was not Hall and Hitch (1939), but rather the researchers A. D. H. Kaplan et al. (1958). But on closer examination it turned out not to be a precedent at all.

Between 1948 and 1951, Kaplan conducted a series of lengthy and detailed interviews (about ten per company) with twenty very large industrial firms in the United States. The interviews ranged over many topics; pricing was just one of them. With the help of colleagues Joel Dirlam and Robert Lanzillotti, follow-up interviews were held with some of the companies later in the 1950s, leading to a well-known book, *Pricing in Big Business*, which was finally published in 1958. The book tells us almost nothing about the survey methodology, but it is clear that the firms were not selected randomly. Nor were they meant to be representative in any sense; Kaplan and colleagues give us twenty case studies, not a systematic survey.

The objectives of the Kaplan et al. study differed markedly from those of this book. First, Kaplan et al. clearly preferred depth to breadth; they exhibited no interest whatever in statistical tabulations. Second, they focused on determination of the level of prices whereas our interest is in price changes. Third, they devoted a great deal of attention to the goals of the firm—a topic we basically ignored—and much less to economists' theories of price behavior. In fact, the most famous finding in the book was probably that many firms (seven out of twenty, to be exact) seek to achieve a target rate of return. In addition, the questionnaire itself suggested two pricing theories to respondents: marking up costs and pricing to market. For all these reasons, the Kaplan et al. study tells us essentially nothing about the validity of alternative theories of pricing.

A subsequent book by Lanzillotti (1964) comes much closer in spirit to our methodology. This study used a structured survey instrument to interview two groups of small manufacturers in or near the state of Washington in 1960. Forty-seven of the firms were participating in a Small Business Administration (SBA) loan program, and a matched group of forty-four companies were not involved in the program. The response rate for the first group was an impressive 69 percent—presumably related to the SBA's imprimatur. In addition, the same questionnaire was mailed to a stratified sample of 468 small manufacturing firms; 35 percent responded.

As the title of Lanzillotti's book suggests, the questions related to firms' pricing (and marketing and production) policies—not on reasons for any putative price stickiness. Roughly half of the respondents stated that they had a target percentage markup of prices over costs (generally actual rather than "standard" costs). When asked what might induce them to change prices, most chose the obvious responses—changes in competitive conditions or changes in costs (or both).

Between 1951 and 1955, the researcher Bjarke Fog conducted a series of interviews, somewhat along the lines of the Oxford study, with Danish manufacturers. Fog (1960) began with a structured questionnaire, but found that "so many difficulties were encountered that it later had to be abandoned and replaced by a modified, flexible form" (p. 10). In so doing, "the interview method was gradually changed into a conversation method" (p. 11). Fog's sample was impressive in size: 139 firms provided reasonably complete information and another 46 provided at least some information. Although he tells us almost nothing about the sample-selection procedure, the firms are clearly not representative of Danish manufacturing. On the contrary, he deliberately concentrated on three specific industries; in fact, fifty-five of his firms were in a single industry (footwear).

Fog's methods clearly do not generate data suitable for statistical analysis. They also make generalization hazardous. Realizing this, Fog offered none of the former and little of the latter. One weak generalization was that marginal cost pricing seemed not to be the norm. However, in contrast to Hall and Hitch, he judged that full-cost pricing based on fixed markups was "very rare" (p. 103). Instead, he suggested, markups were flexible and often procyclical. A few other interesting "findings" were that few firms knew their elasticity of demand and a number had only "a very limited knowledge of their cost conditions" (p. 215).

The economist James Earley (1956) reported on a mailed questionnaire of 203 manufacturing firms chosen from the American Management Institute's list of "excellently managed" companies. The questionnaire was sent from the president of the Institute to the president of the company, with a suggestion that he might have several executives participate in answering it. The response rate was a high 54 percent. Earley's focus was on whether or not these well-managed companies made decisions on "marginalist" criteria; his conclusion was that they probably did. For example, he found that price-cost markups were not fixed, but depended on elasticity of demand and "expected competitive pressures."

In 1962, the researcher Warren Haynes published a book called *Pricing Decisions in Small Business* based on case studies of eighty-eight small American businesses. Of these, thirty-four were in retailing or wholesaling, twenty-eight were in manufacturing, and twenty-eight were in services.[32] Although Haynes mentions Fog (1960) as a precedent, the design of his study seems most similar to that of Kaplan et al. (1958): the sample was neither representative nor random; multiple interviews were conducted with each firm; statistical data were neither sought nor obtained; and the central focus of the study was the goals of the firms. (Conclusion: "Profit maximization is not the single, all-pervasive goal in pricing" [p. 50].) However, in contrast to Kaplan et al., Haynes' case studies were of small firms, not large ones.

The finding that Haynes most emphasizes is that full-cost pricing appears to be rare in small business; instead, demand affects the markup. Another interesting departure from the Hall-Hitch "model" was that Haynes' retailers marked up wholesale prices, not full costs. The former seems to be closer to marginal cost than the latter. Haynes interprets the "trial-and-error" pricing policies that a number of small businesses reported as a kind of rump marginalism, akin to groping their way toward MR = MC.

Sometime in the 1970s (dates are not given), the economists Ewald Nowotny and Herbert Walther (1978) surveyed 187 Austrian industrial enterprises with sales over one hundred million Austrian schillings.[33] Their paper focuses specifically on the validity of the kinked demand curve theory, which they tested by asking firms, separately for price increases and decreases, (a) whether rivals would match their price changes and (b) what their elasticities of demand were. While there is some contradictory evidence, Nowotny and Walther basically found the postulated kink under "normal business conditions" and "in recessions," but not "in booms." In booms, the kink was apparently reversed: more firms expected rivals to match price increases than price decreases. Another interesting finding is that firms' subjective price elasticities were low for price reductions whether or not rivals matched the price cuts!

Of all the studies we found, the one that seems closest to our own was conducted by a team of researchers led by Lawrence Gordon (1981) in both Canada and the United States in 1978. Under the auspices of accounting trade associations in the two countries, the team interviewed twenty-two manufacturing firms in each country—mostly large firms "of the *Fortune 500* type" (p. 7). Each interview was "structured around a detailed questionnaire" (p. 2), which, unfortunately, is not published. Since sixty-six firms were contacted, the response rate was an excellent 67 percent. However, "the samples were not randomly selected in the technical sense" (p. 8), so the authors warn against generalizing the findings.

Nonetheless, a variety of interesting tabulations are offered. For example, the four leading goals of the firms were profits (where the mean score was 4.70 on a 1 to 5 scale), return on investment (4.41), market share (4.13), and sales volume (4.06). Two principal pricing strategies emerged from the study: pricing to market (that is, meeting the competition) and marking up costs. Regarding the latter, Gordon et al. found that markups were generally applied to some concept of full cost, including an allocation of fixed costs. However, the definition of fixed costs varied widely across firms!

In the early 1980s, the researchers D. Jobber and Graham Hooley (1987) conducted a large mail questionnaire survey of manufacturers and service companies in the United Kingdom. Their principal goal was to ascertain the pricing objectives of the firms. Their sampling frame was senior executives drawn from the mailing list of a magazine called *Marketing*, which included the full membership of the Institute of Marketing. They note that the sample is therefore probably biased toward larger and more marketing-oriented companies. While they do not report the original sample size, 1,775 replies were received; so the sample must have been quite large. Jobber and Hooley found profit maximization to be the most popular objective by far, especially among small and medium-sized companies.[34]

Shortly thereafter, the marketing researcher Saeed Samiee (1987) obtained somewhat contradictory results in a mail survey of two randomly selected samples of companies: one was of foreign-based firms and the other was a matched sample of American firms. His main objective was to compare the pricing strategies of the two sets of companies from a marketing point of view. (They looked pretty similar, although U.S. firms emphasized pricing a bit more.) Of a total of 846 questionnaires sent out in the mail (with no follow up), 192 were returned—for a response rate of 23 percent. No statistically significant differences in response rates by industry were detected. His respondents, who were top marketing executives, rated profit maximization a poor fifth out of ten possible pricing objectives. Satisficing goals like "satisfactory return on investment," "specified profit goal," and "maintain market share" all scored higher. One intriguing finding was that the authority to set prices was more centralized in U.S. companies, which may lend some credence to the "hierarchies" theory mentioned earlier.

In another mail survey, though with a quite different focus, Robert Smiley (1988) asked 858 executives some sensitive questions about such matters as limit pricing to deter entry. The sampling frame was all members of the Product Development and Management Association plus all members of the American Marketing Association with the following job titles: product manager, brand manager, director of product management, division manager, vice-president for marketing, and manager of marketing. He received a 34 percent response rate, which was encouraging given the sensitive nature of the questions. Moreover, several statistical tests for selectivity bias failed to detect any.

What do we learn from these previous attempts to use mail questionnaires and face-to-face interviews to study pricing? Regarding the substantive economic issues of interest to us, very little, we are afraid. It is only a slight exaggeration to say that all the previous studies taken together teach us virtually nothing about the relative empirical importance of the various theories of sticky prices. (Of course, that was not their primary purpose.) However, we did pick up several useful pointers about survey methodology:

1. People will indeed respond, whether in writing or verbally, even to questions that appear rather sensitive. Unfortunately, however, the history of surveys of pricing gave us little basis on which to estimate the response rate we might expect.

2. Without a highly structured questionnaire you cannot learn anything that can be generalized—which means that we cannot learn anything we wanted to learn.

3. Only a large, random sample can yield information of a statistical nature. For us, the breadth versus depth debate was thus easily resolved in favor of breadth.

4. It is important to fix the methodology at the outset of the study and stick with it, so that all the data are comparable.

5. Despite all these problems, interesting ideas can and do emerge from interview studies.

The first and last points on this list encouraged us to proceed; the other three guided the design of the survey. But, perhaps the most important lesson we learned from this Cook's tour of the previous literature was that the study we were contemplating would not be superfluous. We had not been scooped. The limited survey evidence on pricing that had been accumulated over half a century told us very little that was generalizable—and even less about the validity of various theories.

Chapter Summary

Being of the nature of a catalogue, this chapter does not lend itself to neat summarization. Suffice it to say that there are many—indeed, too many—theories of price stickiness and that they differ in theoretical coherence, inherent believability, and empirical support—to name just three relevant criteria. While the competing theories are not mutually exclusive, so that virtually all of them could be true in part, the theoretical garden certainly looks in need of some weeding. And yet conventional econometrics has thus far provided little basis for discriminating among alternative models, mainly because they all share the same empirical prediction: that prices are sticky. We therefore think that the interview method is worth a try.

This study is not the first attempt to learn about firms' pricing policies by asking business people. A variety of such studies, using interviews and/or mail questionnaires, have been conducted at various times and places. There is something to be learned from each of them—including the mistakes they made. Yet, in total, they do not add up to a great deal of knowledge about business pricing. And, most important, none of them focused on the question of primary interest here: the validity of alternative theories of sticky prices. The issue seems wide open.

Chapter 3

Research Design

Data is the plural of anecdote.

—GEORGE STIGLER

It is a troublesome truism of survey research that the details of how you ask a question, and to whom, exert a powerful influence on the answers you get. So we take pains in this chapter to spell out precisely how the survey was designed and conducted. Providing such details is particularly important when the survey methodology is as novel as this one's was. To our knowledge, there have been no previous attempts to survey a random sample of the GDP.[1] One of the first things you learn in attempting to do so is that surveying the GDP is quite different from surveying a random sample of the population.

But there is a second reason to spell out the details here, and that is replicability. The ability to replicate research findings is the essence of scientific inquiry; it is how you distinguish a fluke from a fact. And, while it seems unlikely that many scholars would want to replicate this study precisely, if the research is judged a success, others may be inclined to adopt similar methodologies.[2] So, just in case, we provide almost enough information here to permit an exact replication of the "experiment."[3]

This chapter is not for everyone. Readers who are either uninterested in the details of the survey methods or content to trust that we have always made the right choices can skip directly to chapter 4, where analysis of the data begins. But, in presenting the results to many different audiences, we learned that listeners have many questions about how the data were collected. You will find most such questions answered here.

Free-Form Versus Structured Interviews

The study that was actually conducted differed radically from the one that was originally envisioned; and the reasons for the change in strategy are instructive, for they colored every aspect of the research design.

Firms differ greatly in the nature of their products, costs, demands, market structure, corporate philosophies, and so on. So it is a foregone conclusion that different theories of pricing will be relevant to different companies in different degrees. For example, manufacturers of standardized products are unlikely to worry much that their customers judge quality by price. And firms that serve mainly "off the street" customers are unlikely to have implicit contracts with them. So, initially, Blinder believed that the right questions to ask should be tailored to the company that is answering them.[4] It seemed foolish to walk into the headquarters of a giant manufacturing corporation armed with the same questions you would use at the local supermarket.

Furthermore, the theories themselves are somewhat idiosyncratic. On hearing that theory X strikes a responsive chord with a particular firm, economists would follow up with different questions than if they had just heard that the firm behaves according to theory Y. For example, if costs of price adjustment are said to be an important cause of price stickiness, economists would want to know the nature of those costs and whether they are larger than the corresponding costs of changing output. They would also want to know if the firm has some way (such as varying inventories) to avoid adjusting either quantity or price. If, on the other hand, they learn that the firm's elasticity of demand is procyclical, economists would inquire into the sources of that procyclicality.

For these reasons, Blinder was initially skeptical that we could gather the appropriate information via a structured questionnaire with a mechanical skip pattern. Hence the original idea was to conduct free-form interviews with a limited number of companies, somewhat along the lines of Kaplan et al. (1958) and others. In this conception of the study, each interview would have been custom-made on the spot and would have meandered logically down a path dictated by the answers being received. It was just the sort of interview that a team of consultants, called in to advise on pricing strategy, might conduct on their first site visit.

The advantages of such customized interviews are twofold: They economize on time (a very scarce resource in such situations) by avoiding foolish and unnecessary questions, and they can elicit very detailed and pointed information. By contrast, a tightly structured interview that is administered mechanically is a blunt instrument which is limited to generic questions of wide applicability. However, the structured format also has some major advantages, advantages which Blinder ultimately judged to be overwhelming. Most important, it yields statistical information which has some claim to generality and can be analyzed by standard statistical techniques. This is plainly impossible if each firm is asked a different set of questions.

Similarly, it is feasible to survey a much larger number of firms using a structured questionnaire than a free-form interview. The reason, basically, is that a standardized interview procedure allows multiple interviewers to do the job. Thus, the original idea to conduct free-form conversations with executives envisioned, say, twenty interviews—all conducted by Blinder. When the conception was changed to a structured survey, administered mainly by graduate students, the target sample size was raised to two hundred. Our interpretation of the Stiglerian quip that opens this chapter is that anecdotes turn into data when they number in the hundreds. With two hundred firms, you can aspire to mimic the GDP; with twenty, you cannot.

Third, and again related, a sample size of two hundred allows some scope for disaggregation by industry, by firm size, and in other dimensions—options that are simply not available with a sample size of twenty.

Finally, there are the related questions of objectivity and replicability. It requires a gigantic—and almost certainly unwarranted—leap of faith to believe that twenty free-form interviews conducted by Alan Blinder would yield the same findings as twenty free-form interviews conducted by John Smith. (If you don't believe that, change the names to Milton Friedman and John Kenneth Galbraith.) By relying instead on a highly structured questionnaire, we raise the probability (though certainly not to unity) that the findings will be objective and replicable.

Thus, in the end, we have no qualms about the decision to abandon the original conception and plan instead for a large-scale, structured interview study. In saying that, however, we should not lose sight of the limits of a highly structured questionnaire. The survey instrument found in appendix A can (and no doubt will) be criticized for being insufficiently personalized and specific.[5] To cite just one example, we inquire about the firm's elasticity of demand by asking:

A4. If you cut your prices by, say, 10%, by what percent would you expect your unit sales to rise?

A straightforward question, it would seem. But some firms never cut prices, just as others never raise them. And a 10 percent price cut is unimaginably large to some companies, while to others it is a commonplace event. There are also firms, like construction companies, for which every sale is a unique event. Since neither "average price" nor "unit sales" is a particularly natural concept to such firms, the entire question seems strange to them. Alas, the real world is a complicated place. In consequence, something is lost by limiting oneself to a structured questionnaire.

One further issue needs to be addressed here. Once it was decided to use a structured questionnaire and to seek a large sample, there was a further choice among mailed questionnaires, telephone interviews, and face-to-face interviews. We selected the last of these three methods even though it is by far the most expensive. So we should explain the reasons.

Mail surveys, which have been used successfully in many contexts, seemed out of the question here, so the notion was never seriously considered. Why not? There were many reasons.

First, the survey instrument looks frighteningly long (the skip pattern naturally omits many questions), inviting a quick trip to the circular file. What would you do if a thirty-three-page document arrived unannounced and uninvited on your desk?[6]

Second, even if the questionnaire was not discarded, we feared it would be passed to a minor functionary who lacked the requisite knowledge. Part of the art of surveying companies rather than people is to get to the right person in the organization. We wanted some control over that.

Third, many of the questions are complex and need to be paraphrased by the interviewer on the spot. This obviously ruled out a mail survey. But it also made us doubt the efficacy of a telephone survey for, as Don Dillman (1978, 58) notes, "Simplicity is imperative for the telephone interview."

The complexity of the questions also explains why we used Princeton graduate students, not professional pollsters, to do the interviewing. The reader may perhaps have been interviewed by a Gallup or Harris pollster. If you complain that a question is unclear or ill-posed, the interviewer—following strict instructions—normally just repeats it verbatim. That obviously would not do in our context. Several scholars who participated in the Social Science Research Council's (SSRC) Committee on Cognition and Survey Research suggested that the standard injunction against allowing interviewers to paraphrase questions is a mistake. For example, Robert Groves, Nancy Fultz, and Elizabeth Martin (1992, 51) noted "repeated failures of the respondent to comprehend the question as desired by the researcher." And Lucy Suchman and Brigitte Jordan (1992, 259) referred to such misunderstandings as "a hidden source of invalid data." The latter authors specifically recommended "allowing the interviewer to talk about the questions, to offer clarifications and elaborations . . . (p. 263)" as a way to minimize such errors. That is precisely what we did.

Fourth, there are a number of open-ended questions—asking, basically, "why?" in some context—to which the respondent might legitimately offer multiple answers. We did not want to suggest the answers to respondents by writing them down in checklists.

Fifth, experience with mail surveys to corporations suggests a likely response rate in the 5 percent to 35 percent range. Since this unorthodox research was bound to be highly controversial under the best of circumstances, we did not want anyone to be able to dismiss the results by simply chanting the words "response bias" like a mantra. So we decided to do the study only if we had good reason to expect a response rate significantly above 33 percent. That also precluded using the mail.

Having said this, we hasten to point out that the Bank of England recently conducted a survey, which approximately replicated ours (Hall et al. 1996), by mail and obtained a sample more than three times as large as ours with a response rate of 59 percent. That raises a question: Did we make a mistake by ruling out a mailed questionnaire? On balance, we think not.

First, it seems unlikely that a team of private researchers could ever obtain a response rate anywhere near that obtained by a country's central bank. Second, the Bank of England obtained such a high response rate only by employing a rather unusual sampling technique: having its agents contact firms that they knew, and then sending the questionnaire to those who agreed to participate. This method appears to have produced a rather unrepresentative sample.[7] By contrast, we believed from the outset that obtaining a truly representative sample of U.S. industry was absolutely essential to the success—and to the credibility—of the research. So we took great pains (detailed later in this chapter) to create a truly representative sampling frame from which we could select firms randomly.

We could also have used the telephone. And here we are less sure that the right choice was made. A one-hour phone call to Chicago (day rates) may cost about twenty dollars, most of which is the interviewer's hourly wage. Sending a graduate student to Chicago to do the interview might cost six hundred dollars or more. Even if three interviews are accomplished on a single trip, which was not uncommon, the cost per interview is still ten times higher. Is the information really ten times better? Our thought was that it was—although, as just admitted, no one knows for sure.

The biggest concern we had was with the response rate. If you have ever tried to get a top executive of a major corporation on the phone (and you are neither customer nor spouse), you will know what we mean. Phone calls from nosey strangers during business hours are unwelcome intrusions that can easily be dispatched. By contrast, many of our respondents enjoyed the face-to-face interviews and a fair number (not the giant corporations, of course) were actually flattered to be included.[8] The interview also takes about an hour, on average, and it was hard to imagine keeping many business people on the phone for that long amidst the inevitable interruptions. So we judged that item nonresponse in a telephone survey would be much higher than in a face-to-face survey, making the results correspondingly less reliable and less useful in statistical analyses.

But nonresponse was not the only problem. Interviewers necessarily miss things over the telephone that they pick up in person.

Like body language and grimaces. Like looks of puzzlement. Like glances at the wristwatch, or indications of keen interest. These signals tell you when you should speed up or slow down, when you need to repeat or paraphrase a question, and so on. As Suchman and Jordan (1992) note, we often forget that interviews are a form of human conversation. People respond better to other people than to disembodied voices. Finally, and related, when you take the time and trouble to visit someone in his or her office, you give a tangible sign of the importance you attach to his or her answers. That, it seemed to us, would lead to more thoughtful (and, hopefully, accurate) answers than would a phone interview in which the respondent's primary objective would be to get it over with quickly.[9] For these reasons, we also judged that the quality of the data would be far superior if collected in person.

But that does not decide the issue. Even if we grant that face-to-face interviews produce data of higher quality with a higher response rate, there remains the fact that such data are perhaps ten times more expensive per observation than data from telephone interviews. Thus the same research budget would pay for ten times as many observations in a phone survey. That trade-off encapsulates the judgment call that ultimately had to be made. We opted for quality over quantity. Who knows if that was the right choice.

From Journalese to English

The previous section may leave the false impression that the decision to use a structured questionnaire rather than a free-form interview was easy. The truth is that Blinder wavered for a long time out of concern that designing a suitable survey instrument might be impossible. Specifically, three questions were worrisome:

First, could economists' technical theories of price stickiness be translated into crisp, clear prose that is comprehensible to practical business people who, while intelligent, generally understand neither mathematics nor economic jargon?

Second, given the bewildering variety of firms, would it be possible to design a single survey instrument that could be administered to all companies?

Third, would academic economists accept two or three plain-English sentences as a faithful rendering of a theory? Or would they insist that their favorite theory had been misrepresented in the questionnaire?

To decide whether economists' theories could be translated into plain English, Blinder adopted the experimental approach: He sat down at the word processor and tried to do it! Much to his surprise and delight, the task turned out to be relatively easy. After a few evenings, he had a working draft. For approximately the next two years, the original version was revised and improved in hundreds of ways in response to remarks from economists, suggestions by survey specialists, and the reactions of business people. In the end, the amazing thing was not how much the questionnaire changed but how little. The survey instrument that ultimately went into the field in April 1990 closely resembled the original draft devised in the spring of 1988. Translating from technical journalese into plain English simply proved not to be very difficult.

Of the hundreds of changes that were made as successive drafts were refined and improved, only three are important enough to mention here.

First, it quickly became apparent that different language would be needed for different types of firms. For example, a manufacturer has "production," but a retailer does not. So three different versions of the questionnaire were created, each using slightly different prose: one for manufacturers (and mining and construction companies), one for wholesale and retail trade, and one for service companies (which included transportation, communications, and utilities). Other than minor differences in wording, the three variants differ only in that the service questionnaire omits one of the twelve theories (B11 on the manufacturing questionnaire), since that theory applies only to firms that hold inventories of finished goods, and two part A questions about inventories.

Second, as explained in chapter 2, pretesting in the field led to one additional theory (hierarchical delays). It also convinced us that one of the twelve original theories—Bruce Greenwald and Joseph Stiglitz's (1989) idea that price changes create more uncertainty than quantity changes—was too complicated to be explained in plain English. This was, however, an exceptional case. Most theories were easily translated into ordinary prose.

Third, as we explained in chapter 2, the theory based on price protection was added to the questionnaire briefly, and then deleted.

We come now to the hardest question of all: Can we get economists, who are trained to sneer at "anecdotal evidence," to pay attention to the survey results? We do not pretend to have found a perfect solution. Anyone who does this type of research in economics is swimming upstream in a profession which looks upon learning by asking as an activity suitable for the lower classes. The beliefs of some economists cannot be shaken by survey evidence, maybe not by any evidence. But they are a small minority. So we focused our efforts on the persuadable, but certainly not gullible, majority.

Two concrete steps were taken to increase the credibility of the results. First, we wrote letters to those we thought of as either the originators or major proponents of each of the theories on the list. Each letter explained the nature of the study, included a copy of the relevant portion of the questionnaire, invited suggestions for improving the questions, and asked the "theorists" to suggest other implications of their theory that might be tested by the survey. The idea was to guard against ex post criticisms that the questions did not fairly represent their favorite theory. Most responded.[10] Several offered good suggestions for modifying the questionnaire, which were adopted. Interestingly, however, not one person suggested a single additional implication that could be tested in the questionnaire, thus verifying our impression (see chapter 1) that the theories are somewhat lacking in empirical implications.

Second, and much more important, we took great pains to ensure that the sample of firms would be large enough to generate a database suitable for statistical analysis, randomly selected, and representative of the private, for-profit GDP. Later in this chapter we describe in detail how this was done. The intent was to guard against the criticism that the findings are anecdotes rather than data.

When all was said and done, however, the major determinant of how persuasive the results would be was clearly beyond our control. Any type of research is liable to yield definitive answers to some questions but murky results on others; that was almost inevitable here. And given the prevailing skepticism among economists about the validity of interviews, only the most striking results were likely to be persuasive. This was clear in advance. Such research is a high-risk endeavor, not for the faint-hearted.

A Quick Guided Tour of the Questionnaire

The end result of the process of constructing the questionnaire is presented in appendix A, where the full text for manufacturers is offered for those who wish to peruse it. We offer here an abbreviated road map and some interpretive remarks.

The questionnaire is divided into two main parts. Part A (which begins on page 316) is primarily factual and part B (which begins on page 320) deals with the twelve theories.

Although part A is by far the shorter of the two, it normally occupied more than half the interview time because respondents often took this opportunity to tell us about the basic nature of their company and/or industry. We asked firms about their customer base (questions A2, A3, A4, and A6), their cost structure (A11, A12), the contracts they have with their customers (A5, A8), their basic pricing practices (A9, A10, A13), and a few other things. The questions were designed to serve two purposes.

First, they provide a fascinating set of facts that is simply not available in any other data source. For example, no one knows how much price stickiness there is, on average, in the U.S. economy. The answers to question A13 (which comes in four variants) give us the conceptually correct measures, for they indicate the time lag between a shift in either demand or costs and the resulting change in price.[11] Even readers who refuse to believe that we can learn anything about the validity of theories by asking practitioners should find this factual information of interest. Chapter 4 provides the details on what we learned from the answers to these questions.

Second, the data obtained in part A can be thought of as a set of "right-hand variables" to be used in "regressions," either figuratively (such as in cross-tabulations) or literally. That was, in fact, the purpose we had in mind in deciding what questions to ask.[12] Variables from part A are used as both classifiers and regressors in chapters 5 to 17, though with only modest success. It turns out that the objective characteristics of firms do not take us very far in understanding their differing attitudes toward the theories.

Part B turns to the twelve theories explicitly. It is, consequently, divided into twelve sections. Each section starts with a main question which inquires about the relevance of the theory being examined. These "popularity poll" questions follow a prescribed pattern: first the theory is described briefly, then the respondent is asked how important she or he thinks it is in her or his company. For example, the simple idea that nominal contracts rigidify prices was phrased as follows:

> B1. One idea is that many goods are sold under explicit contractual agreements that set prices in advance, so firms are not free to raise prices while contracts remain in force.
>
>   How important is this idea in slowing down price adjustments in your company?

Respondents were free to answer in their own words, and interviewers were instructed to code the responses on the following four-point scale:

1 = totally unimportant

2 = of minor importance

3 = moderately important

4 = very important.

If, for example, interviewers could not decide whether the answer they had heard was a 2 or a 3, they were instructed to code it as a 2.5. Interviewers selected such noninteger responses in only a very small minority of cases.[13]

If a respondent answered the main question "totally unimportant," we skipped immediately to the next section of the questionnaire; no further questions about the rejected theory were asked.[14] That is why part B took less time than part A. But, if we heard any other response, follow-up questions about the theory were posed. Since the follow-up questions are specific to each theory, they defy any short summary. Readers who are curious about the questions asked about any particular theory are referred to appendix A. Most will be discussed in the course of chapters 6 to 17.

Several of the theories rest on a maintained hypothesis that might or might not be true for a particular company. In such cases, we first asked about the validity of the premise. Here is an example:

> B3. Another idea is that firms hesitate to reduce their prices because they fear that customers will interpret a price cut as a signal that the

quality of the product has been reduced.
(a) Is this idea true in your company?

Only if the maintained hypothesis was accepted (that is, if question B3(a) was answered "yes") did we proceed to the main question. ("How important is it in discouraging or delaying price decreases in your company?") If, on the other hand, the maintained hypothesis was rejected, we simply coded the answer 1 ("totally unimportant") to the main question and moved on.

Finally, if you peruse part B of the questionnaire, you will encounter several checklists.[15] These are usually catalogues of candidate answers to a question like "Why is that?" For example, question B10(a), on the reasons for coordination failure, asks: "Why do you not want to be the first firm in your industry to raise its price?" It is important to realize that these choices were not offered to the respondents as suggestions. With only a few exceptions, respondents never saw the written questionnaire.[16] The checklists were provided only to make it easier for interviewers to record quickly the open-ended answers they heard. Multiple answers were possible, and were frequently given.

Estimating the Response Rate: The Pilot Study

A recurrent concern in planning the study was that the response rate might be low, thereby undermining the credibility of the findings—whatever they might be. Of course, a low response rate does not prove that results are biased; after all, refusal to cooperate may be uncorrelated with anything measured in the survey. But it would certainly sow seeds of doubt. And, given economists' general hostility toward interview evidence, we wanted to sow as few seeds as possible.

But how could the response rate be estimated? We began by combing the literature for previous comparable surveys on which to base an estimate. But, as noted in chapter 2, none of the precedents seemed quite germane; the study we were planning was close to unique. Furthermore, few of the studies gave any indication of how many companies had refused to cooperate. We were thus forced to turn to the economic theorist's favorite empirical tool:

armchair introspection. Blinder tried describing the nature of the survey to a small (and certainly not random) sample of economists, business executives, and survey specialists—asking each to guess the likely response rate. But since their guesstimates ranged from 10 percent to 67 percent, this too proved fruitless.

So here was the dilemma: Blinder did not want to make a huge investment of time, money, and effort in a survey that might get a response rate of, say, 25 percent. But he had no estimate of the response rate. What to do? Eric Wanner, president of the Russell Sage Foundation, suggested a way out: Why not conduct a small-scale pilot study? This would not only yield an estimate of the likely response rate in a large-scale study, but would also help us polish the questionnaire and interviewing techniques. A good idea, Blinder thought; so he put together a proposal to do just that, which the Foundation kindly funded.

It was important, of course, for the companies in the pilot study to be selected randomly and to represent the target population of the eventual full-scale study. We therefore created a crude sampling frame of nonfinancial firms located within about five hundred miles of Princeton, New Jersey, and drew a random sample of sixteen companies, stratified by sales.[17] Specifically, we drew 2 firms from among the 100 largest companies (ranked by sales) in Ward's 1987 business directory, 2 from the next 1,295, and 12 from among all the smaller firms. This stratification was based on the fact that the top 100 firms in Ward's directory accounted for about 12.5 percent of total sales, the next 1,295 firms accounted for roughly another 12.5 percent, and all the rest accounted for about 75 percent.[18]

We then wrote each firm an introductory letter requesting an interview and followed up with phone calls and/or further mailings as necessary. After considerable effort, we successfully interviewed eight companies in the spring of 1989. Seven companies refused to participate and, in one case, we were never able to get a response despite repeated contacts. Counting this last company as a "no," the estimated response rate was 50 percent, with standard error 12.5 percent. This struck us as high enough to merit proceeding to the full study, especially since we thought we could raise the response rate in the full study.[19] In the event, 61 percent of the companies we contacted agreed to be interviewed.

Aside from estimating the response rate, we learned a great deal from the pilot study. It led to some changes in the questionnaire and, as will be noted in the following pages, helped us considerably in developing procedures for contacting people and conducting the interviews. When you are traveling in uncharted territory, there is nothing quite like a little reconnaissance mission.

Creating a Random Sample of the GDP

Once the decision to go ahead was made and the questionnaire was finalized, the next step was to create a sampling frame—a figurative "urn" from which company names could be drawn by computer. Assuring random selection was no problem. The difficult part was to ensure that the urn itself was truly representative of the GDP.

Actually, as noted in chapter 1, the goal was to create a sampling frame that represented the private, for-profit, unregulated, nonfarm component of GDP—about 71 percent of the total.[20] The reasons for the four exclusions are perhaps obvious.

First, government and other nonprofit enterprises were excluded because the theories were formulated to explain the behavior of profit-maximizing firms.

Second, firms whose prices are completely regulated were omitted because price rigidity in this sector is either trivial to explain (price flexibility is illegal) or too difficult—requiring a theory of government regulatory behavior. In any case, these last considerations are far afield from the central concerns of this study. However, the sampling frame did include some firms that sell products at both regulated and unregulated prices. In such cases, we inquired only about unregulated prices.[21] It also included a fair number of firms that were subject to some type of nonprice regulation.

Farms were excluded primarily because no one believes farm prices to be sticky.

One other compromise with the notion of a truly representative national sample was made. For reasons of cost, the sampling frame was restricted to the Northeastern United States, which we defined as the following sixteen states plus the District of Columbia: Connecticut, Delaware, Illinois, Indiana, Maine, Maryland, Massachusetts, Michigan, New Hampshire, New Jersey, New York, Ohio,

Pennsylvania, Rhode Island, Vermont, and Virginia.[22] Several things need to be said about this geographic exclusion.

The rationale for limiting the sample in this way was simple: The value of each data point is independent of geographical location, but the cost of obtaining the data depended on travel distance from Princeton. An optimal sample design would presumably have addressed this problem by oversampling nearby locations and undersampling distant ones in just the right way. We crudely approximated this solution by eliminating all companies outside the Northeast and treating the others equally.

The Northeast region accounted for about 43 percent of the nation's GDP in 1986.[23] However, the industrial mix in the Northeast does not quite match that of the nation as a whole. Table 3.1 highlights the differences at the crudest level of aggregation.

When we first looked at these numbers, we were surprised that the differences in industrial structure were not more dramatic than they were. Nonetheless, the nation's GDP is not a blowup of the precise bill of goods and services produced in the Northeast, so geographical truncation would clearly compromise the representativeness of the sample. However, it was easily remedied as follows. Suppose pricing behavior varies across states only because the industrial mix varies, not because, say, California firms are inherently different from New Jersey firms. Then we can (and did) create a synthetic national sample by adjusting the sampling weight of each firm in the Northeast to reflect national, rather than regional, shares in value added. Firms in broad industry groups (defined in terms of two-digit Standard Industrial Classification [SIC] code) that are

Table 3.1   GDP by Industry, Northeast and Overall United States

Industry	(1) Northeast	(2) Overall U.S.
Manufacturing	21.5%	19.7%
Trade	16.5	16.7
Services[a]	35.6	33.3
Construction and mining	4.8	7.0
Transportation, communications, and utilities	9.2	9.3

[a] This category includes financial, insurance, and real estate firms.

overrepresented in the Northeast, like banking and motor vehicles, were given appropriately lower sampling weights; and firms in industries underrepresented in the region, like gas and oil extraction, were assigned higher weights. In this way, the industrial structure of our sampling frame was made to duplicate that of the nation as a whole.

Having designed the sampling frame conceptually, we needed to find a computerized database of companies from which to construct it literally. Five alternatives were available for purchase from commercial sources, of which two (Dun & Bradstreet and Trinet) seemed much more comprehensive than the others. We selected Trinet on the basis of its much lower cost. Our instructions to Trinet asked the company to furnish a computerized listing of all companies in 1986 with sales over $10 million in the seventeen-state area, excluding subsidiaries (so as to avoid double counting) and certain SIC codes that could clearly be identified as government enterprises, farms, and nonprofits.[24]

The exclusion of companies with sales under ten million dollars was, once again, motivated by cost. Because there are so many small businesses, reaching any sizable portion of them would have been prohibitively expensive. Clearly, an optimal experimental design would have balanced the value of the information obtained against the costs of obtaining it and would, therefore, have assigned very small sampling probabilities to very small companies. We approximated this crudely by assigning a zero probability to any company below the ten million dollars threshold. This decision did, however, eliminate between one-quarter and one-half of the GDP from consideration.[25]

Financial companies required special treatment because "sales" is not a natural concept for them. The database gave employment in each firm, so we needed to translate ten million dollars in sales into a corresponding cutoff point for employment. The translation was done as follows, where S is sales, V is value added, and E is employment. To go from S to E, note that:

$$E/S = (V/S)/(V/E).$$

Our approach was to estimate V/S for the whole economy and V/E for banking and insurance, and then divide to get E/S. We obtained

national data on value added and sales for as many two-digit industries as we could and, from that, made a rough eyeball estimate that
the typical V/S ratio was about 0.5.[26] Then, from data on SIC codes
60 (banks) and 63,64 (insurance companies), we estimated that the
typical ratio of value added to employment in banking and insurance was fifty thousand dollars per worker. That led us to estimate
an S/E ratio of a hundred thousand dollars in sales per worker. So
the ten million dollars cutoff point in sales was translated to one
hundred employees for insurance companies.

Banks required a further correction because most of their value
added derives from interest-rate spreads and this study is about
prices (that is, components of the GDP deflator), not interest rates.
We wanted to include the prices of bank service charges but to
exclude spreads between borrowing and lending rates. To estimate
the size of service fees and the like, we examined the annual reports
of four banks chosen arbitrarily from among the files in the Princeton University library. Since these showed non-interest earnings to
be about one-seventh of total revenues, we made seven hundred
employees the cutoff point for banks.[27]

Eliminating small firms from the sample again raises questions of
bias. We partially corrected for this bias in the same way we eliminated the bias from geographical truncation. Any sample that
excludes firms with annual sales under ten million dollars will
underweight certain industries, such as retailing. We therefore
raised the weight of each retail firm in the sampling frame enough
to assign retailing its proper national weight—and similarly for
every other two-digit industry. In this way, we eliminated any
"large-firm bias" that stems from the different industrial structures
of small versus large businesses. However, to the extent that small
firms differ from large firms within the same industry, the bias
remains.

It would be a mistake to think that this truncation by size makes
our study applicable only to "big business." In fact, a firm with ten
million dollars in annual sales is a modest-sized business at best. For
example, a single supermarket can record more than ten million
dollars in annual sales.

In the end, all these exclusions, corrections, and reweightings left
us with a sampling frame of about twenty-five thousand companies, each weighted by its estimated value added.[28] From this com-

puterized "urn," we drew our sample by use of a random number generator. As a test of our procedure, five thousand companies were selected with replacement, keeping track of the order in which each name was drawn.[29] We then grouped these five thousand names by two-digit SIC code and compared the resulting distribution with the distribution of GDP by industry. When we verified that the two distributions matched closely, we were confident that our procedure was correct.

We then focused only on the first nine hundred names that had been drawn. After eliminating duplicate names,[30] we were left with 627 companies. This sample was further culled by eliminating government corporations, nonprofits, and one well-known company which we knew to have gone out of business.[31] That left a working sample of 564 companies. In the event, we never had to go beyond number 420 because our response rate was so high.[32]

Is the Sample Representative?

How successful were we in generating a representative sample of the U.S. GDP—or, more accurately, of the private, for-profit, unregulated, nonfarm GDP? Although our procedures were designed to produce a representative sample, there are at least two places where things could have gone wrong. First, of course, there is sampling variance. Two hundred firms is a relatively small sample (but see below); so our results might be skewed just by chance. Second, and more important, there is always the possibility of bias from nonresponse. Participation in the survey was entirely voluntary, so it is possible that the 61 percent of the sample that agreed to be interviewed differed systematically from the 39 percent that refused.

For example, we designed our procedures on the hypothesis that response rates would be the same in each industry. If they differed, our sample would be nonrepresentative, though not necessarily biased in any important way. Late in the interviewing process, we discovered that the hypothesis of equal response rates was mostly correct. But there was one minor exception and one major one. While most industry-specific response rates were in the 55 to 65 percent range, construction and mining companies (two small sectors) exhibited higher response. More important, though, retailers were less willing to talk to us than firms in other industries; the response rate in retailing was below 50 percent. We tried to remedy this deficiency by oversampling retailers in the last wave of interviews.[33] But this was not entirely successful. As it turned out, retailing comprised 8.5 percent of our sample of two hundred firms, compared to 13.1 percent of the relevant portion of GDP.

Table 3.2 shows the distribution by one-digit SIC code of three groups: the two hundred firms in our sample (column 1), the three hundred and thirty firms that we solicited (column 2),[34] and the entire relevant GDP in 1991. (Given our sample size, any finer breakdown by SIC code would be meaningless.) It also shows, by one-digit SIC code, the response rates we achieved—because differential response rates are the main source of nonrandomness. As can be seen, the sample generally reflects the composition of GDP by industry. But it somewhat overrepresents firms in durable manufacturing, and underrepresents firms in retail trade, finance, and services. As discussed above, the underrepresentation of retail trade stems mostly from a lower response rate in that industry. Differences in other industry groupings may reflect our decision not to sample firms with sales of less than ten million dollars.

We can also check to see whether the geographical distribution is random within the seventeen-state area. Table 3.3 offers the same

Table 3.2   Distribution of Firms, by One-Digit SIC Code

		(1)	(2)	(3)	(4)
Industry	SIC Code	Sample	Sampling Frame	GDP[a]	Response Rate
Agricultural services	0	0.0%	0.3%	0.7%	0.0%
Mining and construction	1	11.0	8.8	7.7	75.9
Nondurable manufaturing	2	13.0	13.3	11.7	61.4
Durable manufacturing	3	21.5	18.8	13.6	69.4
Transportation, communications, and utilities	4	8.5	8.5	6.1	60.7
Wholesale trade	5	10.0	11.5	9.2	52.6
Retail trade	5	8.5	11.8	13.1	43.6
FIRE	6	10.5	11.8	17.0	53.8
Services	7,8	16.5	15.2	20.9	66.0

[a] Private, nonfarm GDP excluding regulated utilities, owners' equivalent rent, household production, and nonprofits, 1991.

Table 3.3   Distribution of Firms, by State

State	(1) Sample	(2) Sampling Frame	(3) GDP[a]	(4) Response Rate
Connecticut	2.5%	2.1	4.1%	71.4%
D.C.	2.0	1.5	1.1	80.0
Delaware	2.5	1.8	0.9	83.3
Illinois	17.0	17.3	11.9	59.6
Indiana	7.0	5.8	4.9	73.7
Mass.	6.5	7.6	6.7	52.0
Maryland	4.0	3.6	4.3	66.7
Maine	0.5	0.9	0.9	33.3
Michigan	6.0	8.2	8.0	44.4
Missouri	0.5	0.3	0.0	100.0
New Hampshire	1.0	0.9	1.1	66.7
New Jersey	8.0	8.2	8.9	59.3
New York	22.5	21.8	20.0	62.5
Ohio	7.5	7.6	9.7	60.0
Pennsylvania	7.0	7.9	10.7	53.8
Rhode Island	0.0	0.0	0.9	—
South Carolina	0.0	0.3	0.0	0.0
Virginia	5.0	3.9	5.4	76.9
Vermont	0.5	0.3	0.5	100.0

[a] Private, nonfarm gross state product in the states surveyed, 1991.

type of information as table 3.2, except that firms are now classified by state rather than by SIC.[35] By and large, the geographic distribution of the sample is very similar to that of GDP, although Illinois looks somewhat overrepresented in the sample.

   Checking on the size distribution of firms is more difficult, since
we lack a good national control. Furthermore, for reasons explained above, we deliberately excluded firms with annual sales
under ten million dollars.[36] Nevertheless, table 3.4 shows a rough
breakdown by firm size, as measured by sales. So as not to mix
sales figures from two different sources, the sales figures reported
in table 3.4 for firms in the sample are based on records from the
Trinet database, not from the interviews.[37] GDP by firm size (column 3) is measured by business receipts based on the Internal Revenue Service's (IRS) Statistics of Income data for 1992; the figures
in parentheses eliminate firms smaller than ten million dollars and

Table 3.4   Distribution of Firms, by Size

Size	(1) Sample[a]	(2) Sampling Frame[a]	(3) GDP[b]	(4) Response Rate
Less than $10 million	0.0%	0.0%	26.4%	n.a.
$10 to $24.99 million	22.5	20.3	7.1 (9.6)[c]	67.2
$25 to $49.99 million	13.5	12.7	5.0 (6.8)[c]	64.3
$50 million or more	64.0	67.0	61.5 (83.6)[c]	57.9

[a] Based on the Trinet database for 1986.
[b] IRS Statistics of Income. Share of 1992 business receipts in each size category, all industries excluding agriculture.
[c] Numbers in parentheses exclude firms with sales below ten million dollars.

show shares in the three largest size categories only. (The small number of size categories displayed in the table was determined by the availability of the IRS data.) According to these data, the sample includes far too many firms with sales between ten million dollars and fifty million dollars: 36 percent versus 16.4 percent in the IRS data. This discrepancy does not owe to differential response rates (see column 4). Rather, the Trinet sampling frame itself overweights these firms relative to the IRS data. The difference may reflect the fact that column 3 measures sales, whereas the sample as reflected in column 1 was chosen by weighting firms by employment. For that explanation to be true, the largest firms would have to have a relatively high ratio of sales to employment. In our sample, this is in fact the case.[38]

This seems an appropriate place to note that our sample is actually a good deal larger than it appears. Two hundred firms sounds like a small number and, by the standards of survey research, it is. But mean sales in our sample are about $3.2 billion. (Median sales are, of course, much smaller: just $200 million.) So the 200 firms account for $637 billion in annual sales. To compare this to the relevant GDP in 1991, we must remember that value added in our economy is roughly half of total sales. Hence our 200 firms account for about $319 billion of GDP, or 7.6 percent of the total value added in the nonfarm, for-profit, unregulated sector. If we recall that our decision to omit all firms with annual sales below ten million dollars eliminated between one-quarter and one-half of the GDP from consideration, the surprising conclusion is that we interviewed an astounding 10 to 15 percent of the target population—a large fraction by any standard. So, while two hundred is a small number in a statistical sense, our survey was unusually broad in an economic sense. In fairness, however, this statement should be tempered by noting that the seven biggest firms in our sample—those with annual sales over twenty billion dollars—accounted for 58 percent of the total.

The final objective characteristic that can be used to compare our sample to the national average is inventory holdings. Just under half of our sample was in manufacturing or trade and reported their ratio of inventories to annual sales.[39] The average of these figures is 0.187. By comparison, the national inventory-to-sales ratio in manufacturing and trade for 1991, expressed on an annual basis, was 0.135. So our firms seem to have too many inventories, on average.

Overall, then, the sample looks to be reasonably representative of the relevant portion of GDP. The distribution of firms by state is very close to that of GDP in the states surveyed, and the distribution by one-digit industry is similar to that of overall GDP. Industry differences that do exist may be due to the exclusion of firms with less than $10 million in sales, as well as to a somewhat lower response rate in retail trade. Our sample does look to be somewhat too inventory-intensive, however.

Interviewing Procedures and Problems

Interviewers

As mentioned previously, we decided early on that the interviews could not be conducted successfully by professional polltakers acting like automatons. The nature of the survey required that interviewers be able to interpret, paraphrase, and improvise on the spot; these criteria pointed to graduate students who understood both the theories and the objectives of the study. Having decided this, another concern arose: Would the interviews be sufficiently uniform to justify the statistical analyses that would follow? Although every interviewer worked from a common "script" (the questionnaire given in appendix A) and normally read it verbatim, interviewers sometimes had to rephrase and explain the questions.[40] Furthermore, respondents were free to answer in their own words, and each interviewer then had to translate this free-form prose into a numerical scale for computerized coding. Anyone who has ever played "telephone" knows that different people have been known to hear the same thing differently. How could we ensure that each interviewer would explain the questions and code the responses in the same way?

The answer, of course, is that it was impossible to be sure. However, we tried to impose as much uniformity as possible with some on-the-job training. Before going out "solo," each student interviewer participated in two or three training interviews, accompanied by either Blinder or Canetti. On the first of these, the trainee would listen as Blinder or Canetti conducted the interview, and both interviewers would code the responses independently. Immediately afterward, Blinder or Canetti would review the interview with the trainee, question by question, discussing any discrepancies in the way responses were coded. On the second interview (or sometimes the third), the roles would be reversed: Blinder or Canetti would listen while the trainee conducted the interview. Both would code the responses, and we would once again compare notes and homogenize coding styles.[41] The objective was to get all the interviewers coding responses in more or less the same way so as to minimize any "interviewer effect" on the way data were recorded.

Did we achieve uniformity? Mostly, but not perfectly. As one test, we sent a team of two trained interviewers on a few of the interviews. In these interviews, one student would ask all the questions, and each would record the responses independently. The recorded responses were nearly identical in each of these cases. This does not prove that each interviewer administered the questionnaire identically, but it does suggest that coding differences were minimal.

To look for possible "interviewer effects" in the data, a series of χ^2 tests was run to see whether the identity of the interviewer was related to the responses to any of the twelve main questions. Of the twelve χ^2 statistics, two were significant at the 10 percent level (theories B6 and B9)—one more than would be expected by chance. Unfortunately, the χ^2 statistic was also significant at beyond the 1 percent level in both cases. As a second test, ordinary least squares regressions were run with (the deviation from the mean of) each of the main theory questions on the left and fourteen dummy variables (one for each interviewer) and no constant on the right. These regressions test whether each interviewer dummy is significantly different from the mean. Of the 168 coefficients in the 12 regressions, 5 were significant at the 5 percent level and 20 were significant at the 10 percent level—about the number that would be expected by chance. Nevertheless, as a precaution, interviewer dummies were included in all regressions that were run. Few were significant. So we conclude that interviewer effects are not much of a problem.

Timing

We began conducting interviews in April 1990. Due to the limited number of interviewers—only fourteen very part-time people to do two hundred interviews—we sent out requests in batches of approximately fifty, figuring to complete about twenty-five interviews in each batch. The last wave of letters was mailed in September 1991. As it turned out, July 1990 was the peak month of the long business expansion that began late in 1982, according to National Bureau of Economic Research dating. The national economy slid downhill from the summer of 1990 until the early spring of 1991, staged a short recovery for a few months, and then sagged again late in 1991 before beginning a lasting recovery in early 1992. Since our interviews took place between April 1990 and March 1992, they were conducted at quite disparate stages of the business cycle.

In principle, this fact should be irrelevant to the answers since we inquired about normal business practices—not, for example, about what firms did the last time they changed prices. But it is certainly possible that recent experience colored the responses of some firms; so companies interviewed at the cyclical peak might have given systematically different answers than companies interviewed at the cyclical trough.

We examine this possibility in several ways. First, we ran χ^2 tests to look, in an unstructured way, for any associations between calendar month and the answers to any of the twelve main questions. Distressingly, the χ^2 statistic was significant at the 10 percent level in four of the twelve cases (theories B1, B6, B7, and B8), which suggested that we should look further. Next, we ran ordinary least squares regressions with (the deviation from the mean of) each of the main questions on the left and twenty-four dummy variables (one for each survey month) and no constant on the right, to test whether each dummy was significantly different from the mean. Of the 288 coefficients in the 12 regressions, 15 were significant at the 5 percent level and 25 were significant at the 10 percent level— about the numbers that would be expected by chance.

To the extent that the results do depend on the timing of the interview, the presumption was that the dependence came from the stage of the business cycle, not from the name of the month. So we added the Commerce Department's index of coincident indicators (ICI) in the month of the interview to the data set. Regressing the answers to the main theory questions against the ICI yielded a significant coefficient in three cases (B1, B8, and B9). So, as a precaution, we experimented with including the ICI in all regressions.

A second aspect of calendar time also demanded some attention. As mentioned in chapter 2, an article on the research project was published in *The Wall Street Journal* on January 2, 1991. It was suggested that some of the executives we interviewed after that date might have read the article and been influenced by it. This struck us as far-fetched, but there is a simple way to test for it.[42] For each of the main theory questions, we ran a conventional t-test for equality of the mean responses before and after January 2, 1991. Again, we were dismayed to find significant differences at the 10 percent level for three questions, and at the 5 percent level for one question. It turns out, however, that the index of coincident indicators was uniformly higher prior to that date than after it. As a result, it is difficult to determine statistically whether the questions are best described as being correlated with the state of the economy or with the date of the newspaper article. Judging that the former was more likely, we decided to control just for the state of the business cycle, not for the date of the newspaper article, in the regressions.

Geographical Truncation

It will be recalled that our sampling frame was limited to the Northeastern United States. On the maintained hypothesis that any systematic differences in responses by state are entirely attributable to differences in states' industrial structures, a synthetic national sample was created. Once the data were collected, however, it became possible to conduct a crude test of the maintained hypothesis that there is no pure geography effect. Specifically, if we could show that virtually none of the responses varied systematically by state within the seventeen-state area, this would bolster confidence that geography did not matter.

To detect any possible association between the seventeen state dummies and the answers to the twelve main questions, we again ran a χ^2 test for each. One question (B6) showed significant state effects at the 1 percent level, and another (B1) showed significant effects at the 10 percent level. Next, as with the interviewers and months, we ran ordinary least squares regressions with (the deviation from the mean of) each of the main theory questions on the left and seventeen dummy variables (one for each state) and no constant on the right. These regressions test whether each state dummy is significantly different from the mean. Of the 204 coefficients in the 12 regressions, only 3 were significant at the 5 percent level and 11 were significant at the 10 percent level—only about half as many as would be expected by chance. Thus, we conclude that the results do not differ by state within our seventeen-state region, which is a strong indication (though not a proof) that geographical truncation is unlikely to be a serious problem in the analysis.

Response Rate

There are at least three distinct aspects to the response rate problem: getting companies to agree to participate, locating the right person in the company, and obtaining answers to the questions. We take these up in turn.

Our procedure for contacting companies was as follows. Once a company name was drawn mechanically from the computerized "urn," we looked up its main officers in Dun & Bradstreet or Standard & Poor's directory, selected a name, and sent a letter on Princeton University stationery requesting an interview. The letter explained the nature of the study, promised confidentiality, noted that economists are often criticized for paying too little attention to the way real businesses operate, and observed that we can remedy this defect only if business men and women cooperate. Where there was some personal contact (such as where Blinder knew someone high up in the company) or a Princeton alumni connection, we did not hesitate to exploit it.

The mailing included a reply card which gave the respondent two ways to say yes and no way to say no.[43] About 38 percent of the cards were returned promptly with one of the "yes" boxes ticked, at which point one of our interviewers would contact the respondent to set up an appointment. Many firms, however, did not respond to the first mailing. In such cases, we contacted the company by telephone and/or additional mailings as often as necessary. It often took many calls and faxes, but roughly another 22 percent of the firms eventually agreed to be interviewed. Thus our overall response rate was a surprisingly high 61 percent—11 percentage points higher than we had estimated in the pilot study.

One major difference between interviewing people and interviewing companies is that, in the latter case, you must find the right person with whom to talk. For small companies (the judgment was subjective), we generally sent the initial letter to someone with a title that sounded like the "boss"—the president, chairman, or whatever. Exceptions were made, however, for companies that listed someone with a title like vice-president for sales or sales manager. For large companies, we clearly did not want the CEO; it seemed pointless to ask the CEO of a giant corporation how some specific product is priced. Instead, we sought someone with a job title like vice-president for sales or marketing, or a product line or division manager. In multidivision companies, we tried to contact the largest division. Table 3.5 summarizes the job titles of our respondents.

Table 3.5 Job Titles of Respondents

President, CEO, COO, owner, partner	51
Vice president	83
Manager, director of...	40
CFO, comptroller	9
Economist	6
Chairman of the board	3
Other	8
Total	200

Note: Some respondents had multiple titles and some companies were represented by more than one person. In such cases, the most senior job title is recorded.

Often the corporate listing did not point to any one clear target.[44] In such cases, we normally sent the letter higher up in the corporate hierarchy than we thought it belonged. The reason was something we learned in the pilot study. As just noted, our reply card offered two ways to say yes. By ticking the first box, the respondent said: Yes, please call us to set up an appointment. By ticking the second box, the respondent declared the company's willingness to participate but referred us to someone else in the company. We invited executives to "pass the buck" in this way for two reasons.[45] First, it helped us locate the person in the company best positioned to answer our questions. Second, it seemed to improve the response rate. Our image of what happened within corporations goes something like this: The letter arrived on Joe's desk. Although Joe saw merit in the request, he was too busy to do it himself. So he passed it along to his subordinate, Ed, with a note saying "Ed, please handle this." To Ed, the note from Joe had the force of law. So, when we contacted his office, Ed was already disposed to cooperate.

Did these procedures get us to the right person? That question cannot be answered definitively; in large firms, for example, there are clearly several "right people." The best evidence we have on this question is that the number of "we don't know" responses was very small, and we almost never heard, "You're asking the wrong person." This made us think that we were reaching the right people.

It should be noted that we did not conduct multiple interviews with the same company to check on the accuracy of the answers we were getting.[46] In principle, this would have been advisable both because of honest mistakes and because many of our questions require subjective judgments that different people may make differently. In addition, the answers to some questions may differ across divisions of a large company.[47] But we decided against performing any such cross-checks for two reasons. One was that we had a limited supply of interviewer time at our disposal. The other was that we did not want to insult respondents by appearing to check up on their answers. We leave it to the reader to decide whether or not these were good reasons. But the choice was certainly a deliberate one.

Getting answers proved to be no problem at all. Once in the door, we found people more than willing to talk frankly—and at length.[48] They usually found the questions interesting, understandable (with some exceptions), and not invasive of privacy.[49] Our experience, in fact, was that people were often eager to tell us things about which we would never have dared ask for fear that we would appear to be prying. (We did, of course, promise and maintain confidentiality.) Many respondents expounded at great length on the details of their businesses. We were, after all, asking about what many of them felt was the most fascinating subject on earth: their own business.

Problematic and Ambiguous Questions

Having said this, we hasten to add that the questionnaire itself fell somewhat short of perfection. Despite the many drafts and extensive pretesting that preceded the actual field survey, a number of questions were—with the magnificent wisdom of hindsight—infelicitously worded. In what follows, we call the reader's attention to every question that we suspect of being "bad" in any respect. Fortunately, there are not many.

While we tried and tried to remove every possible source of ambiguity from the questions, the English language is not quite that precise. Furthermore, the need to write general-purpose questions that were suitable for all types of firms prevented us from pushing the precision of the language to its limits. Fortunately, the interviewers were always present to interpret, clarify, and answer queries, so we do not think ambiguity posed a major problem.[50] Nonetheless, certain ambiguities did arise. Here are two of the most bothersome ones:

In some businesses—nonresidential construction is the clearest example—every sale is unique. Do such companies sell their products under explicit contracts that fix the price? To the business executives' way of thinking, the answer is certainly yes; almost all work in that industry is done under contract, and the contracts normally specify a price. But, by our definition, the answer is probably no. Since our interest is in price stickiness, the appropriate definition of a fixed-price contract is one that covers multiple sales. Contracts in the construction business are rarely of that type. So executives in that industry found it odd when we asked about "formal, written contracts that cover multiple sales" (a quote from question A8 of the questionnaire). Nonetheless, all but one answered the question. (The answers were spread pretty evenly across the five possible responses.)

In another example, to distinguish cyclically sensitive from cyclically insensitive businesses, we posed the following question:

A6. In some firms, sales rise and fall strongly with the ups and downs of the national economy. Sales in other firms are much less sensitive to the state of the economy. How would you characterize the sensitivity of your company's sales to the state of the economy?

That seems straightforward. But a number of companies answered that their business was very sensitive to local, not national, business conditions. How should such a response be coded? Conceptually, the answer is clear: If local business conditions are highly correlated with the national business cycle—as must be the norm—then the response indicates high cyclical sensitivity. If not, the response indicates little cyclical sensitivity. In practice, of course, we did not know the cyclical covariances of local and national output for every locale, so rump judgments had to be made.

Finally, we asked firms about the elasticity of demand that they face as follows:

A4. If you cut your prices by, say, 10%, by what percent would you expect your unit sales to rise?

We have already noted that some firms had problems answering this question, and that these problems could have been mitigated by a free-form interview rather than a structured questionnaire. (For example, some firms never cut prices.) But even in the absence of such problems, question A4 is ambiguous about whether rival firms are also cutting their prices by 10 percent. As a consequence, some firms might have reported their estimate of the elasticity of demand facing the industry, rather than that facing the firm. Phrasing this question ambiguously was a conscious choice. We feared that posing a more complicated hypothetical question ("If you cut your prices by, say, 10 percent, but your rivals held their prices constant, by what percent would you expect your unit sales to rise?") would reduce the number of responses greatly. We therefore decided to allow firms to answer the question as they saw fit. We do not know whether that was a wise choice, but it was a deliberate one.

Unintelligible Questions

Much effort was expended to avoid jargon and render every phrase on the questionnaire in plain, understandable English. Nonetheless, some of the concepts which economists find natural are far from natural to business executives. For example, we were surprised how difficult it was for respondents to distinguish between fixed and variable costs (question A12). A number stumbled over the question and 9 percent never gave an answer, even after rephrasing. Another example is the concept of marginal cost—which we phrased on the questionnaire as "variable costs of producing additional units" (see question B7[a]). This elementary concept often had to be repeated, paraphrased, and/or interpreted for respondents, to whom differential calculus is not second nature. Ten companies (5 percent of the sample) never gave an answer.

Finally, while we eschewed the word "elasticity," even the concept proved to be difficult to understand. As noted in chapter 2, one of our theories is based on procyclical elasticity of demand. We posed the idea as follows:

B5(a). It has been suggested that, when business turns down, a company loses its least loyal customers first and retains its most loyal ones. Since the remaining customers are not very sensitive to price, reducing markups will not stimulate sales very much.
Is this idea true in your company?

In the field interviews, we found that respondents had a surprisingly hard time with this question. Very often, it had to be paraphrased or explained further before we got an answer. But, in the end, 97.5 percent of respondents eventually answered.

We mention these three questions to warn the reader that the answers to questions A12, B5, and B7 may be contaminated with more than the usual amount of measurement error.

Misunderstood Questions

One very important misunderstanding may affect some of the data, and it is incumbent upon us to warn the reader about that, too. The questions always pertained to actual transactions prices—not to posted or contractual prices, if the latter differed from the former. And all the interviewers were absolutely clear about that. Any time the distinction arose during an interview, we told respondents that we cared only about transactions prices. But we did not continually remind them after each question. So it is entirely possible that they occasionally gave answers that pertained to, say, list prices rather than transactions prices. When we suspected that (for instance, "We change our price every January 1st"), we normally asked the respondent if he was telling us about list or transactions prices. But, if there was no obvious reason to question the response, we normally just took it at face value. It is therefore possible that the survey slightly overstates the degree of price stickiness in the U.S. economy.

"Motherhood" Questions

A properly constructed questionnaire will avoid at all cost questions that are phrased in such a way that the respondent feels almost compelled to agree. (These are questions like, "Do you approve of motherhood?") We tried our level best to keep all such motherhood questions out, but at least one crept in accidentally. Actually, it was an "anti-motherhood" question.

Our practice was to pose a symmetry question for each theory, if that was possible. If the main question inquired about price decreases, a follow-up question would ask about price increases. When it came to theory B12, however, this strategy backfired. The basic idea of that theory is that markets can clear by characteristics other than price. For example, if demand shifts down, a firm may think of shorter delivery lags, more aggressive marketing, or better service as alternatives to a price cut. (See question B12 on the questionnaire.) That is all fine. But when you turn the question around, the alternatives to a price increase turn out to be longer delivery lags—which is fine— and giving poorer service—which is not something to which most firms care to admit, even if they do it. So we think the responses to question B12(c) on the questionnaire should be heavily discounted. (In fact, 71 percent of respondents said that this idea was less applicable to increases in demand than to decreases.)

The Ordering of the Questions

Any psychologist with even a modicum of training in survey techniques will warn you that the order in which questions are asked can influence the answers, sometimes dramatically. One or two did, in fact, warn us of this peril and suggest that we randomize the order. We did not follow their advice for three reasons:

First, with a sample as small as two hundred, and ninety-four different questions, randomization was impractical. Even if we randomized only the twelve main questions, there would still have been 12!—or 479,001,600 possible orderings. At most, we could have used five or six. But doing even this seemed inadvisable for the following reason.

Second, the questionnaire has a skip pattern that is complicated enough so that interviewers, moving rapidly in real time, occasionally made mistakes. Thus, some questions that should have been asked were skipped, and vice versa. But the number of such errors was quite small. We feared many more such errors if interviewers had to cope with numerous different forms. We also feared that errors would have crept into the skip patterns on the printed forms if there were multiple versions of the questionnaire.

And third, by the standards of, say, Gallup polls, many of the questions in the survey are "deep" or involved; they require thinking. The survey instrument ordered the questions in a certain logical sequence. Thus, for example, once we got people thinking about the nature of their demand (starting with question B2), we kept them on that subject (through question B5). We thought the quality of the answers would deteriorate if, say, we jumped from a question about demand to one about costs and then to market structure, and so on.

In the end, it is for each reader to judge whether these reasons are good enough to justify the decision to use a single ordering. As a partial (and nearly trivial) check on this decision, we looked to see if the popularity of the twelve theories was at all correlated with the ordering on the questionnaire. The simple correlation of the theory's "score" and its place on the questionnaire was 0.12; the rank correlation was 0.09. Neither is significantly different from zero.

Chapter Summary

There are two versions of the same cliche: "The devil is in the details," and "God is in the details." Take your pick. But either way, the details of sample and questionnaire design are crucial to a study of this sort. So this chapter not only spells out a great many of the details of the research design, but also tries to explain and justify the reasoning behind them.

The most critical decision, we believe, was to opt for a relatively large number of highly structured interviews rather than a relatively small number of free-form interviews. As outlined in this chapter, there are pros and cons associated with either choice. But we judged that the need to produce data that would be amenable to statistical analysis overwhelmed all other considerations. Still, there was a cost: We could not tailor the questions to the circumstances of specific firms; nor could we pursue certain ideas as deeply as we might have liked.

Having decided on a structured interview, the next step was to design an appropriate questionnaire. In this context, at least, the art of questionnaire design was to strike a reasonable balance between fidelity to economic theory and usability in the field. Could the questions pass muster with academic economists and still be intelligible to the people who would be answering them? Fortunately, this balancing act turned out to be one of those rare instances in which a task proves easier in practice than it appears to be in principle. While the job took some fine tuning, and perfection was never achieved, drafting a workable questionnaire proved to be not too difficult. Furthermore, problems in the field proved to be minimal—though not nonexistent (all such problems are discussed in the chapter).

The sample was "stratified" in a very particular way. Since we wanted to "talk to the GDP deflator"—or, more precisely, to the deflator for the private, for-profit, nonfarm, unregulated sector—firms were selected into the sample with probabilities proportional to their value added. No extant sampling frame was available to do this, so we were forced to create our own—which, by and large, appears to replicate the national economy quite well. Once this was done, and a sample was drawn, we expended considerable effort to get firms to cooperate. Fortunately, the response rate was gratifyingly high—61 percent—and there is very little evidence of any sample selection bias.

In the event, two hundred interviews, generally lasting forty-five to seventy minutes each, were conducted between April 1990 and March 1992. The respondents were heads (chairs, presidents) of small companies and appropriate officers (not generally CEOs) of large corporations, all of whom answered in their own words. The interviewers were Princeton graduate students (plus Blinder), who coded the responses into a database that is now publicly available. What we learned from these data is detailed in the rest of the book.

Part II
The Basic Findings

Chapter 4

Wouldn't It Be Nice to Know . . . ?
The Factual Basis for Theories
of Price Stickiness

> It is a capital mistake to theorize before one has data.
> —SIR ARTHUR CONAN DOYLE

This study was motivated by the belief that theories of price rigidity were being generated in an empirical vacuum, insufficiently informed by the facts. What share of United States GDP is sold under nominal contracts? For how long do those contracts normally fix prices? How many firms encounter significant "menu costs" or other costs of adjusting prices? How common is judging quality by price? The list of what we do not know about price stickiness could go on and on.

The list of what we do know is distressingly short.[1] The huge number of times that Stephen Cecchetti's (1986) paper on magazine prices gets cited is ironic testimony to just how thin our knowledge is. The paper is a fine one. But do we really care that much about newsstand prices of magazines?

Part A of the questionnaire (plus a smattering of questions in part B) was designed to lift the veil of empirical ignorance on price stickiness a bit. Since we know so little, the number of questions that might have been asked is vast. But, interview time being a precious resource, we tried to concentrate on variables directly germane to theories of sticky prices. Most questions in part A, therefore, inquire about either the degree of price stickiness or variables that seem relevant to the validity of the various theories discussed in chapter 2. For the convenience of the reader, selected key results are gathered together in a summary at the end of the chapter on page 106.

How Sticky Are Prices?

The survey offers two direct measures of the stickiness of prices. One is the answer to the question:

A10. How often do the prices of your most important products change in a typical year?

Of our 200 firms, 186 answered this question, and gave a median response of 1.4 times per year.[2] As table 4.1 shows, there is a strong mode at 1, meaning that annual price changes are by far the most typical. Perhaps more pertinent for macro models, fully 78 percent of the GDP is apparently repriced quarterly or less often. That certainly seems like enough price stickiness to matter. The most fascinating numbers in the table may be in the tails of the distribution, however. About 10 percent of GDP is apparently repriced less frequently than once a year; and an equal amount is repriced more than once a week. Indeed, 1.6 percent is repriced more than once a day. Yes, Virginia, there is an auction market sector. But it is pretty small.[3]

Firms that answered question A10 were then asked why they do not change prices more frequently than they do.[4] This is not the sort of question we normally like, for it is too abstract and requires a great deal of introspection. It is a bit like asking the proverbial pool player, "Why didn't you shoot that shot differently?" Nonetheless, the question (which is A10[a] on the questionnaire) does have

Table 4.1   Number of Price Changes in a Typical Year (n = 186 Responses)

Frequency	Percentage of Firms	Cumulative Percentage
Less than 1	10.2%	10.2%
1	39.2	49.4
1.01 to 2	15.6	65.0
2.01 to 4	12.9	77.9
4.01 to 12	7.5	85.4
12.01 to 52	4.3	89.7
52.01 to 365	8.6	98.6
More than 365	1.6	100.0
Median = 1.4		

one very great virtue. Coming as early as it did in the interview, it gave respondents a chance to choose their favorite explanation for price stickiness before their minds were contaminated by hearing any of our suggestions. So it behooves us to pay attention to the results.

Because the question was open-ended, the answers defy any neat categorization. One hundred and seventy-one firms answered the question; but some gave two or three replies, and others answered with some variant of "we change prices as often as we please"—suggesting that they should not have been asked the question in the first place. This left us with 196 usable responses, and table 4.2 is our heroic attempt to tabulate them in some coherent, albeit admittedly subjective, way.

The explanation that tops the list—antagonizing customers—is open to various interpretations and does not obviously correspond to any of our theoretical categories. It is, however, the way many business people think about the virtues of price stickiness. Much the same can be said of the catch-all "competitive pressures." After that, however, we can recognize several of our theories. Costs of price adjustment (theory B8) are cited by twenty-eight firms. The twenty-seven firms that tell us that they change prices infrequently because their costs change infrequently are implicitly expressing agreement with theory B6—cost-based pricing. An additional fif-

Table 4.2   A10(a): Why Don't You Change Prices More Frequently Than That? (n = 196 Responses from 151 Firms)

Response	Number of Firms
It would antagonize or cause difficulties for our customers	41
Competitive pressures	28
Costs of changing prices (B8)	28
Our costs do not change more often (B6)	27
Coordination failure, price followership (B10)	15
Explicit contracts fix prices (B1)	14
Custom or habit	11
Regulations	7
Implicit contracts with regular customers (B2)	5
Miscellaneous other reasons	20
Total	196

teen firms gave answers that evoked theory B10: coordination failure. And nineteen companies mentioned explicit or implicit contracts—theories B1 and B2.

To a theorist interested in the concept of price stickiness relevant to macro models, A10 is not really the correct question. If, for example, cost and demand shocks occur infrequently, then Walrasian prices would adjust infrequently, too. We would not want to call that price rigidity. Therefore, another question inquired about the conceptually correct concept of price stickiness by asking how much time elapses between a shock to either demand or cost and the firm's corresponding price adjustment. There were actually four variants of this question, corresponding to positive and negative shocks to both demand and cost. The first of these was:

> A13(a). Firms and industries differ in how rapidly their prices respond to changes in demand and costs. How much time normally elapses after a significant increase in demand before you raise your prices?

The other three questions were similar. Respondents were supposed to decide for themselves the meaning of the adjective "significant." Table 4.3 summarizes the results.

There is much to say about this small table. (The meaning of the last column will be explained.) At the substantive level, the main observations seem to be the following:

1. Lags in price adjustment are fairly long. In round numbers, about three months typically elapse between a shock that would change prices in a Walrasian world and firms' price response. This seems to be good news for simple macro models that assume a "one period" lag in adjusting prices.

Table 4.3   Lags in Price Adjustments, in Months

Type of Shock	Mean Lag	Standard Deviation	Number of Responses	Number of "Never Happens"
Increase in demand	2.9	3.2	128	52
Increase in cost	2.8	3.0	163	23
Decrease in demand	2.9	3.7	132	52
Decrease in cost	3.3	3.9	101	73

2. There is essentially no evidence for the common belief that prices adjust more rapidly upward than downward. For demand shocks, price decreases and increases come with identical average lags. For cost shocks, price decreases do appear to come with about a half-month longer lag than do price increases. But this difference is neither significant in a statistical sense nor very large economically.

3. There is also no evidence for the commonly held view that firms respond more rapidly to cost shocks than to demand shocks. If anything, the data point in the opposite direction.

4. The cross-sectional variances in adjustment lags are huge—larger than the mean itself in all four cases. It would be a mistake, however, to interpret these large standard deviations as reflecting mostly sampling variance—although some is surely present. Rather, these numbers testify to the enormous variation across firms in the speed of adjusting prices. These differences stand out more clearly in table 4.4, which provides the detailed distributions.

In round numbers, one fifth of the firms display no stickiness at all; they adjust prices immediately after a shock. But about an eighth of the firms delay price adjustment for more than six months! The longest reported lags range from one year (for price increases) to two years (for price decreases following cost decreases).

Given all this variety, it is natural to wonder if there are systematic differences by industry. There are. In general, service companies adjust prices most slowly and trade firms do so most rapidly,

Table 4.4 Distributions of Lags in Price Adjustment

Lag (in Months)	A13(a) Demand Up	A13(c) Cost Up	A13(b) Demand Down	A13(d) Cost Down
Zero	22.7%	23.9%	18.9%	22.8%
0.1 to 1.0	19.5	20.9	29.5	22.8
1.1 to 3.0	25.8	22.1	22.0	17.8
3.1 to 6.0	21.1	23.3	16.7	20.8
Above 6	10.9	9.8	12.9	15.8
Median (months)	2.0	1.5	1.2	2.0

with manufacturers somewhere in between. Details are provided in table 4.5. The simpler measure of price stickiness given earlier in table 4.1—frequency of price change—displays the same pattern. The median number of price changes per year is three in trade, but only one in manufacturing and services.

It is also natural to wonder if large firms display more or less price rigidity than small firms. Responses to the four variants of question A13 are modestly positively correlated with (the log of) firm size (question A1); the four correlations range from 0.03 to 0.22. However, firm size is also positively correlated ($p = .24$) with the number of price changes per year (question A10)—meaning that larger firms change prices more frequently. The overall picture, then, is a bit confusing and merits further consideration.

Questions A10 and A13 (in four variants) offer five measures of the degree of price stickiness. Are they different? Or do they all contain roughly the same information? Table 4.6 answers this query by displaying a correlation matrix for the five variables. Quite clearly, the four versions of A13 contain similar, but hardly identical, information. But the answers to A10 have surprisingly little correlation with any of them. (The correlations are, of course, negative.) If we extract the first principal component of these five indicators of price stickiness, using standardized data, we find that it accounts for only 56 percent of the variance. All five variables have nonnegligible factor loadings, meaning that each makes some independent contribution to the first principal component.[5]

An important technical point about item nonresponse must be made at this point. The response rates to the four variants of ques-

Table 4.5   Mean Lags in Price Adjustment, by Industry, in Months

Industry	A13(a) Demand Up	A13(c) Cost Up	A13(b) Demand Down	A13(d) Cost Down
Manufacturing	3.0	3.2	2.5	4.1
Services	3.4	3.6	3.4	4.8
Trade	2.3	0.9	2.0	1.4
Construction and mining	2.4	1.8	3.8	2.0
Transportation, communications, and utilities	3.0	4.2	3.2	5.0

Table 4.6 Correlations Among Alternative Measures of Price Stickiness

	A10	A13(a)	A13(b)	A13(c)	A13(d)
A10	1.00	−.18	−.18	−.14	−.21
A13(a)		1.00	.64	.58	.46
A13(b)			1.00	.42	.50
A13(c)				1.00	.73

tion A13 reported in table 4.3 are among the lowest in the survey. Thus the bad news is that we got fewer responses to the more appropriate (but harder) question about price stickiness. There are two distinct causes of nonresponse. One is that the respondent does not know the answer; this accounted for about a quarter of the nonresponses to question A13 (or about 9 percent of the sample). The other source of nonresponse, accounting for about three-quarters (or about 26 percent of the sample), is that the question was inappropriate for, or could not be comprehended by, the particular firm. For example, when we inquired about delays in cutting prices following a decline in cost, seventy-three firms told us either that they never cut prices or that their costs never decline. As you can see in the last column of table 4.3, positive cost shocks are experienced by the most firms, negative cost shocks by the fewest.

The Nature of Price Adjustments

Modern theories of price adjustment distinguish between two broad classes of strategy: time-dependent rules in which prices are reviewed periodically at fixed calendar dates (such as monthly or annually), and state-dependent rules in which prices are adjusted on no fixed schedule, but whenever they get sufficiently "out of line" (for example, the (S,s) rule). We asked firms whether they have regular, periodic reviews:

A9. Do you have a customary time interval—such as a week, a month, a quarter, or a year—between price reviews for your most important products?

The answers told us that time-dependent rules are twice as common as (S,s)-type rules. Nearly 60 percent of the firms said they do have

Table 4.7   Interval Between Periodic Price Reviews (n = 121 Responses)

Interval	Percentage of Firms
Daily	5.8%
Weekly	5.8
Between a week and a month	14.0
Two to three months	13.2
Six months	16.5
Yearly	44.6

periodic reviews, while 30 percent said they do not. (The remaining 10 percent have periodic reviews for some products but not for others.) The distribution of responses among the 121 firms reporting a numerical time interval between reviews is given in table 4.7. Clearly, annual review is the most common by far. Only a quarter of all prices under periodic review are reviewed as frequently as monthly.

These results on time-dependent and state-dependent rules need to be qualified, however, by noting some apparent inconsistencies between these reported intervals between price reviews and the frequency of price change from question A10. These two variables are strongly negatively correlated, as one would expect.[6] However, twenty-one firms report that they change prices more often than they have price reviews, which seems to indicate an inappropriate definition of "price review period." At the other end of the spectrum, several firms report that they change prices much less frequently than they have price reviews. In fact, seventeen firms change prices less often than every fourth price review. While in a literal sense there is nothing inconsistent about reporting frequent price reviews and infrequent price changes, such firms might more reasonably be viewed as pursuing state-dependent pricing strategies. If we exclude these 38 firms, the fraction with meaningful periodic price reviews declines to about 40 percent of the total.

A related question, prompted by models based on costly price adjustment but perhaps also relevant to issues of fairness, is whether firms change prices all at once or in a series of small steps. The former is predicted by menu cost models (such as, Mankiw 1985) whereas the latter is predicted by models with convex adjustment costs (such as, Rotemberg 1982). As table 4.8 shows, apparently, once-and-for-all adjustments are the norm.

Table 4.8 A10(b): When You Do Raise or Lower Prices, Do You Normally Do It All at Once or in a Series of Smaller Changes? (n = 198 Responses)

Response	Percentage of Firms
Normally all at once	74.0%
It varies	9.6
Normally in small steps	16.4

These results would seem to indicate that relatively few firms have nontrivial convex costs of price adjustment—perhaps one-sixth of GDP. They suggest, instead, that the norm is either negligible adjustment costs or costs that are lump-sum in nature, as assumed in menu cost models. To distinguish between these last two possibilities and elicit further detail, we asked firms if they incur meaningful costs of price adjustment. Specifically:

B8(a). Another idea is that the act of changing prices entails special costs in itself, so firms hesitate to change prices too frequently or by too much. The costs we have in mind are not production costs, but costs like printing new catalogs, price lists, etc. or hidden costs like loss of future sales by antagonizing customers, decision making time of executives, problems with salespeople, and so on.

Does your firm incur such costs when it changes prices?

Of our two hundred firms, eighty-six responded "yes," seventy-two responded "no," and forty-two answered that, while they have such costs, their magnitude is trivial.

We then followed up by asking the firms that reported nontrivial adjustment costs about the nature of those costs:

B8(c). Do these costs of changing prices come mainly from changing prices often or mainly from changing them by large amounts?

The answers were as follows:

Mainly from often	69%
Mainly from large amounts	14
Both	17

Among firms with nonnegligible adjustment costs then, more than three-quarters of the costs appear to be of the "menu cost" variety;

less than one-quarter appear to be convex. Putting these two sets of results together, it appears that 57 percent of prices can be adjusted with zero or negligible costs, 33 percent incur fixed costs of price adjustment, and only about 10 percent incur convex adjustment costs.[7]

It is natural to wonder about the consistency of these responses. Do the firms that report costs from frequent, rather than large, price adjustments normally change prices all at once rather than in small steps? Are firms with significant menu costs more likely to follow (S,s)-type strategies than regular periodic reviews?

Unfortunately, but quite typically for a survey, the data are not as consistent as we would like. For example, there is no significant association between whether adjustment costs attach to large or to frequent price changes (question B8[c]) and whether the price normally changes all at once or in small steps (question A10[b]). A χ_8^2 test of association between the answers to these two questions fails to reject the hypothesis of independence (p = .32 in a sample of eighty-one firms). Similarly, neither of these two variables displays any correlation with the importance of adjustment costs as measured by question B8(a), nor with the existence of periodic price reviews (question A9). The only significant correlation within this set of variables is between the existence of periodic reviews (question A9) and the importance of adjustment costs (question B8[a])— but it has the wrong sign. Large menu costs should presumably push firms away from periodic reviews toward (S,s)-type strategies. Yet firms with meaningful adjustment costs are more likely to have periodic reviews than firms without such costs. Fortunately, though, the customary interval between such reviews does tend to be longer for firms citing meaningful adjustment costs.

The inference seems to be that the nature of adjustment costs has little to do with the way firms change prices, which looks like bad news for theories of price stickiness based on costs of adjustment.

Contracts: Explicit and Implicit

Another prominent family of "theories" is based on the notion that contracts rigidify prices.[8] Surely, there is some truth to these theories; everyone knows of goods and services that are sold under contracts that fix the nominal price for finite periods of time. But this "fact" presents a quintessential example of Hart's Law (named after

A. G. Hart): In a country as large as the United States, you can find fifty examples of anything. So far as we are aware, no one knows how prevalent nominal contracts are in the U.S. economy. The survey gave us a chance to find out. We began by asking:

A8. What fraction of your sales is made under formal, written contracts that cover multiple sales?

The distribution of answers is presented in table 4.9. Notice that the distribution is bimodal, concentrated at the lower end (more than a third of all firms have almost no contracts), and least dense near the middle. By assuming a functional form for the underlying density, it is possible to estimate the fraction of the relevant United States GDP sold under formal, written contracts. For this purpose, we took the density to be uniform within each range in the table—that is, to look exactly like the histogram corresponding to table 4.9. Under this assumption, the answer is that 38 percent of GDP is covered by written contracts. As might be expected, these numbers vary across industrial sectors. But the only sector that really stands out from the others is wholesale and retail trade, where the incidence of written contracts is well below average.

Table 4.9   Share of Sales Under Written Contracts (n = 195 Responses)

	Percentage of Firms				
Type of Customer	All	Manufacturing	Services	Trade	Construction and Mining	Transportation, Communications, and Utilities
None or almost none (0–10%)	37.4%	38.8%	30.2%	67.6%	23.8%	5.9%
A minority (10–40%)	24.4	26.9	17.9	21.6	23.8	41.2
About half (40–60%)	8.2	10.4	6.6	5.4	14.3	2.9
A majority (60–90%)	15.1	13.4	18.9	2.7	19.0	32.4
Almost all (90–100%)	14.9	10.4	26.4	2.7	19.0	17.6

Those who believe that the price-auction model is nevertheless valid as an approximation will immediately enter two objections. First, although contracts exist, they may not really set prices. Second, prices set in contracts may be discounted frequently. Both issues were addressed by follow-up questions on the survey.

To see if contracts typically fix prices, we asked the question tabulated in table 4.10. It is clear that the overwhelming majority of contracts do, in fact, specify the price. (It is, of course, the nominal price that is specified.) Based on these numbers, a conservative estimate is that about 75 percent of contracts actually fix prices.

But are prices set for periods long enough to matter? We asked respondents to tell us for how long prices are normally fixed by contracts. The answers form a highly skewed (and quite dispersed) distribution with a mean of 20.3 months and a median of 12 months.[9] That seems a long time.

So far, it appears that roughly 28 percent (75 percent of 38 percent) of all prices in the U.S. economy are set by nominal contracts, and that these contracts typically last a long time. But this fact would be of limited interest if discounts off the contract price were common. Apparently, they are not, however. More than 80 percent of all firms report that they never or rarely offer discounts.[10] Another 11 percent say they do so only in "a minority of cases." Fewer than 8 percent of all firms say that discounts are given in as many as half the cases. A rough calculation based on these responses suggests that only about one-eighth of contract prices are discounted.

If we put all this information together, the back-of-the-envelope calculation seems to be that about 25 percent (seven-eighths of 28 percent) of all prices in the U.S. GDP (weighted by value added) are literally fixed by contracts—and that these contracts typically last long enough to matter.

Written contracts are not the only form of price setting agreements that firms make with their customers. Since Arthur Okun

Table 4.10 A8(a). Do These Contracts Normally Set Prices for a Stated Period of Time? (n = 127 Responses)

Response	Percentage of Firms
Rarely or never	13.4%
Sometimes	8.3
Most of the time	11.8
Always or almost always	66.5

(1981), if not before, economists have emphasized that tacit agreements between buyers and sellers can rigidify prices even in the absence of explicit contracts. But, once again, no one knows how prevalent these so-called implicit contracts really are. We inquired by posing the following question:

> B2(a). Another idea has been suggested for cases in which price changes are not prohibited by explicit contracts. The idea is that firms have implicit understandings with their customers—who expect the firms not to take advantage of the situation by raising prices when the market is tight.
> Is this idea true in your company?

Among the 197 respondents, 64 percent answered yes and 36 percent answered no. (This includes eleven firms that were not asked this question because they had previously reported that all of their sales were made under explicit contracts.) Thus, in round numbers, implicit contracts exist in about two-thirds of all U.S. companies.[11]

Two other facts seem at least tangentially relevant to the importance of contracts in the U.S. economy and so seem worth mentioning here:

One is rationing. On the basis of his consulting experience, one well-known economist (who shall remain nameless?) suggested to Blinder that firms frequently ration customers in periods of peak demand rather than raise prices. It turns out that such behavior is atypical, however. When we asked firms:

> A5. Do you ever put customers on allocation, that is, limit the amount they can buy?

fully 78 percent told us they never or rarely do; only 6 percent said they do so frequently. Thus quantity rationing does not appear to be common in the U.S. economy. (However, it is common to vary delivery lags; see chapter 17.)

The other relates to regulation. We have mentioned several times already that fully regulated firms were excluded from the study. But partially regulated firms were included. (In these cases, we inquired about unregulated prices.) In total, forty-five of our two hundred firms reported some sort of regulatory limitation on their ability to raise or lower prices. Among these forty-five firms, the mean fraction of sales subject to some kind of regulation was 60 percent.

The Nature of Product Demand

Any theory of pricing must involve, at a minimum, the nature of the firm's demand and cost structures. We begin with what we learned from the survey about demand.

An obvious preliminary question is: To whom do you sell? We actually posed this question in two different ways. First, we asked each company to break down its sales among consumers, other businesses, and "other" customers—presumably meaning government units. Here, naturally enough, some substantial differences emerged across sectors, as table 4.11 attests.[12] But the most salient observation to be made from this table is that the great majority of sales are made not to consumers but to other businesses. This fact may bear on the relative importances of various theories of price stickiness. For example, one suspects that judging quality by price is more relevant to final sales to consumers than to interfirm trade. We next asked:

> A3. Approximately what fraction of your sales go to regular customers with whom you expect to do business again, as opposed to those you do not expect to be repeat customers?

The answers surprised us, as they did many other economists in seminar presentations of these results. Details are given in table 4.12.[13] In the whole economy, the estimated mean percentage of sales going to regular customers is 85 percent, and the median is 93 percent. More than half the sample reported that more than 90 percent of their sales represent repeat business. And only about 10 percent of the sample said this share was 50 percent or less. Even in retail trade, more than 70 percent of sales go to repeat customers. Thus, in the aggregate, sales to nonrepeat customers are almost

Table 4.11   Distribution of Sales Among Customers, by Sector

Type of Customer	Percentage of Sales					
	All	Manufacturing	Services	Trade	Construction and Mining	Transportation, Communications, and Utilities
Consumers	20.8%	6.4%	40.6%	30.5%	13.9%	16.8%
Businesses	70.4	86.7	57.4	62.6	53.6	75.9
Other[a]	8.7	6.9	2.0	6.5	32.1	7.3

[a] Principally government.

Table 4.12 Share of Sales Made to Regular Customers, by Sector

	Percentage of Sales				
Range	All	Manufac- turing	Services	Wholesale Trade	Retail Trade
50% or less	10.7%	4.3%	15.1%	0.0%	23.5%
50.1 to 90%	34.5	28.6	43.4	25.0	52.9
90.1 to 99.9%	24.4	25.7	20.8	40.0	11.8
100%	30.5	41.4	20.8	35.0	11.8
Mean share	85.2	91.6	80.4	93.9	71.2

small enough to be ignored. This finding, once again, would seem to bear on the applicability of several theories. For example, implicit contracts can presumably be made only with regular customers.

Since our chief concern is with how prices do or do not vary over the business cycle, we next asked each respondent:

A6. How would you characterize the sensitivity of your company's sales to the state of the economy?

This variable is mainly used as a cross-classifier and as a right-hand variable in the regressions that come later. At this point, it serves mainly as a consistency check because, in principle, roughly equal numbers of firms should characterize themselves as "relatively sensitive" and "relatively insensitive" to the business cycle. Fortunately, this proved to be the case: about 43 percent of firms classified themselves as "relatively sensitive" while 39 percent said they were "relatively insensitive" to the state of the economy. Differences by sector were surprisingly small, with construction and mining and trade (but not manufacturing) firms somewhat more cyclically sensitive, on average, than others.[14]

Many, if not most, economic theories of pricing are forward-looking. In setting prices, firms are assumed to take into account forecasts of future business conditions and, certainly, forecasts of future inflation. Making use of the latter would seem to be a minimal requirement for any firm seeking to set its real price—which is what virtually all economic theories presume they do. After all, if you are trying to set p_i in order to achieve a target p_i/P, your expectation for P would seem to be highly relevant. The specific question we asked was:

A7(b). Do forecasts of future economy-wide inflation rates ever directly affect the prices you set?

The responses hold bad news for any theory based on the idea that firms seek to set their real price. Half of all respondents told us that they never take economy-wide inflation into account; fewer than a third told us that they do so often. It is important to realize that the answer was prompted. That is, we did not just ask firms to list the factors they take into account in setting prices, and then observe that the expected future price level was often absent from the list. Rather, we specifically put the idea that expected inflation might be relevant into their heads, and then asked them to react. Still, only a minority took the bait.

One explanation for this result might be that our survey was conducted during a period when inflation was relatively low. A businessman who cannot keep infinite amounts of information in his head may worry about a few important things and ignore the rest. And when nationwide inflation is low, it may be a good candidate for being ignored. Indeed, one prominent definition of "price stability" is inflation so low that it ceases to be a factor influencing people's decisions. Under this explanation, this question would have received a more positive response had the survey been conducted ten years earlier.

A second possibility is that the P in the ratio p_i/P for many firms may be, say, the industry-wide average price rather than the economy-wide average price. If an industry's average price change is not highly correlated with the national inflation rate, it may be rational to ignore the latter. Our forward-looking questions—A7(a) and A7(b) on the questionnaire—focused on aggregate variables, and may therefore have been too restrictive.

It is also worth noting that the answers to question A7(b) did differ somewhat by industry.[15] Manufacturers and service companies apparently pay somewhat more attention to inflation forecasts than do other companies; retailers and wholesalers pay much less. In fact, a mere 8 percent of firms in the trade sector say that inflation forecasts affect their price setting often, while 80 percent say they never do! The one sliver of good news is that firms with stickier prices are more likely to pay attention to economy-wide inflation forecasts—as should be the case.[16]

Even fewer firms pay attention to forecasts of the overall level of economic activity. When we replaced the inflation rate with the "outlook for the national economy" in the preceding question, about 70 percent of all firms told us they never use such information in price setting, and only 14 percent said they often do. These responses do not flatly contradict economic theory, since the fortunes of an individual firm may correlate poorly with the national business cycle. Still, the sales of some firms must move systematically with the business cycle, else the term "business cycle" would never have been invented![17]

A final relevant question pertains to the elasticity of demand. We asked firms:

A4. If you cut your prices by, say, 10%, by what percent would you expect your unit sales to rise?

This was a difficult question for many firms, who not only do not have an elasticity estimate handy but are unaccustomed to thinking in such terms.[18] Nonetheless, we managed to get (sometimes rough) numerical answers from one hundred and sixty firms, which is 80 percent of the sample. Table 4.13 gives the distribution of responses, expressed as absolute values of price elasticities. While the mean elasticity of 1.1 looks reasonable from the viewpoint of economic theory, the number of zeros is disconcerting. Can it really be true that firms that sell 40 percent of GDP believe that their demand is totally insensitive to price, and that only about one-sixth of GDP is sold under conditions of elastic demand? One possible explanation is that question A4 is ambiguous about whether rival firms are expected to match the price reduction; so some of these firms may have reported their estimated elasticity for the industry rather than for the firm. But, if the numbers in table 4.13 are at all correct, they may offer a simple key to understanding price stickiness because, as even beginning students of economics are taught, only firms with price elasticity of demand greater than unity can increase total revenue by cutting prices.[19]

Table 4.13   Estimated Price Elasticity of Demand (n = 159 Responses)

Elasticity	Percentage of Firms
Zero	40.6%
0.1 to 0.5	28.8
0.51 to 1.0	14.4
1.01 to 2.0	8.8
2.01 to 5.0	5.0
Above 5.0	2.5
Mean = 1.10 Median = .25	

The Nature of Costs

The shape of the cost function, broadly construed, ought to be relevant to the cyclical behavior of prices. For example, chapter 2 mentioned Hall's model, which explains sticky prices by invoking flat marginal cost (MC) curves. So we inquired about several aspects of the firm's cost structure.

A preliminary question, prompted by some responses we had received while the questionnaire was being tested, was:

> A11. How accurately can you estimate how your costs will change when your sales change your level of production by, say, 5–10 percent?

The intent here was to see whether firms believe that they know their marginal costs. About 62 percent of respondents answered "extremely well" or something similar to that. Roughly another quarter said they can estimate MC "moderately well." That left about one-eighth of the sample saying that they can estimate MC "not very well." Since we economists should take encouragement wherever it comes, we think this distribution should be interpreted as good news.

We next asked firms to break down their costs between fixed and variable costs. Our suspicion was that, other things equal, prices would be more flexible in industries with low marginal costs (like airlines) because their profits are more sensitive to their price/ volume decision.[20] In any case, if standard economic theory is even in the right ballpark, the nature of MC must be relevant to pricing decisions.

This question proved difficult for respondents to answer—for several reasons. One was fully anticipated: the answer depends on the time horizon. In the longest run, of course, everything is variable; and in the extremely short run (the next hour, say), nothing is. Rather than try to specify the relevant "run"—which surely differs from firm to firm—a priori, we let each respondent (mentally) select the "run" relevant to his pricing decision by posing the following question:

> A12. Roughly what fraction of your costs do you regard as fixed, that is, the same regardless of your level of production, and what fraction as variable, that is, costs that vary with the level of production?

In a few cases—surprisingly few, actually—the respondent asked us what time horizon we had in mind, in which case we usually answered "the period relevant to price setting" or something like that. But this was rare. In other cases, we got initial responses that seemed implausible—like zero or 100 percent, suggesting that the question had been misinterpreted. In those cases, we normally probed more deeply to see what the respondent really meant.[21] But in a fair number of cases—and this was the big surprise—we found that the "fixed" versus "variable" distinction was just not a natural one for the firm to make. Many interviewees therefore had difficulty answering the question; indeed, 18 executives (9 percent of the sample) never did.

Table 4.14 tabulates the responses given by the remaining 182 firms. The mean response is that 44 percent of costs are fixed in what we will call the short run and 56 percent are variable. (The standard deviation across firms is 25 percent.) The breakdown of costs between fixed and variable does vary across sectors, as might be expected, with fixed costs less important in wholesale and retail trade (with a mean of 33 percent) and in construction and mining (mean = 29 percent), and more important in transportation, communications, and utilities (53 percent) and services (56 percent).[22] While we lack a good metric against which to judge these numbers, fixed costs appear to be more important in the real world than in economic theory.

Another very common assumption of economic theory is that marginal cost is rising. This notion is enshrined in every textbook and employed in most economic models. It is the foundation of the upward-sloping supply curve. However, as we have noted already, Hall has used constant MC as the basis for one family of models of price stickiness. What do business people have to say about their

Table 4.14 Percentage of Costs That Are Fixed (n = 182 Responses)

Percentage Fixed	Percentage of Firms
20 or less	24.7%
20.1 to 40	27.5
40.1 to 60	22.5
60.1 to 80	17.0
Above 80	8.2
Mean = 43.9% (std. dev. = 25.4%)	
Median = 40.0%	

own cost structures? Once again, this proved to be a difficult question because marginal cost is not a natural mental construct for most executives. We translated marginal cost into "variable costs of producing additional units," and posed the following question:

> B7(a). Some companies find that their variable costs per unit are roughly constant when production rises. Others incur either higher or lower variable costs of producing additional units when they raise production.
> How would you characterize the behavior of your own variable costs of producing additional units as production rises?

Ten firms could not answer the question coherently. The other one hundred and ninety answered in their own words, and we grouped the answers into the five categories shown in the five panels of figure 4.1. The options depicted in panels b and d were prompted by answers we received during the pilot study and pretesting stages; they cover cases like a bank that must, at some point, add a new branch office to serve more customers, or a factory which adds a second shift. The overwhelmingly bad news here (for economic theory) is that, apparently, only 11 percent of GDP is produced under conditions of rising marginal cost. Almost half is produced under constant MC (including panel d), which is encouraging for the Hall model. But that leaves a stunning 40 percent of GDP in firms that report declining MC functions, as suggested by Valerie Ramey (1991b). It is, however, possible that some (or even many) of these firms were confusing average cost with marginal cost.

It is natural to wonder whether the distribution of firms across the five MC types depicted in figure 4.1 is at all related to their cyclical sensitivity. If, for example, most of the cyclically sensitive firms have upward-sloping MC curves, then the standard assumption might still be serviceable for business cycle models even though it describes only a minority of all firms. This, however, is not the case. There is hardly any correlation—and certainly no statistically significant relationship—between self-reported cyclical sensitivity (question A6) and the shape of the marginal cost curve (question B7[a]).

These results on the nature of marginal cost, like the findings on inelastic demand reported above, take at least some of the mystery out of price stickiness. After all, one basic reason for expecting prices to rise in booms and fall in slumps is the presumption that demand curves are shifting in and out along upward-sloping sup-

Figure 4.1   Possible Marginal Cost Curves

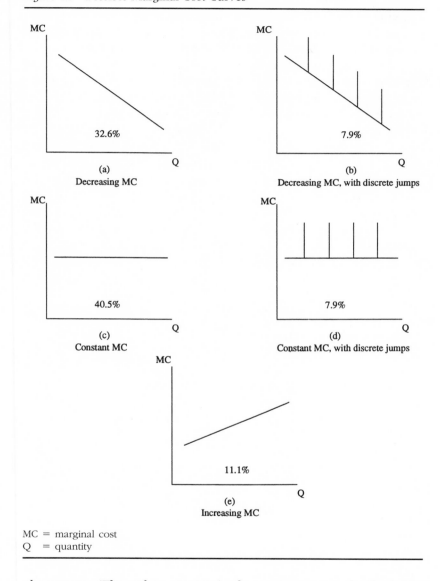

MC = marginal cost
Q = quantity

ply curves. (The other reason is that we expect individual MC curves to shift up and down as economy-wide elements like nominal money wages rise and fall with the cycle.) If the supply curves of cyclically sensitive goods are more commonly downward-sloping, then we would expect their relative prices to move countercyclically instead. Then, if nominal marginal costs rise in booms, nominal prices might not show much cyclicality at all.

Because one of the twelve theories is based on inventories, we next inquired about two other aspects of the firm's technology. First, we asked for the inventory-to-sales ratio (actually, its reciprocal; see question A16).[23] As noted earlier, the mean ratio of inventories to annual sales in the sample is 0.19 and the median is 0.17.[24]

Second, we asked firms what fraction of their output is produced to stock and what fraction is produced to order (question A15).[25] There have been attempts in the past to infer this information from data on finished goods inventories and unfilled orders, but this survey is the first that we know of to obtain direct evidence on this question. The answers are tabulated in table 4.15. For all industries combined, the distribution is close to symmetric around the mean, thin in the middle, and has roughly one-sixth of the firms producing entirely to stock and one-sixth entirely to order. On average, 54 percent of output is produced to stock. But there are substantial differences across industries. Nondurable goods are more commonly produced to stock than are durable goods; this conforms to previous analyses (such as that of Victor Zarnowitz 1973). Wholesale and retail trade firms report that they sell primarily from stock.

Table 4.15 Percentage of Output Produced to Stock

	Percentage of Firms in			
Percentage to Stock	All Industries	Durable Manufacturing	Nondurable Manufacturing	Trade
Zero	15.6%	22.5%	13.0%	5.9%
0.1 to 25	21.1	27.5	21.7	5.9
25.1 to 50	11.0	17.5	8.7	8.8
50.1 to 75	8.3	5.0	4.3	14.7
75.1 to 99.9	26.6	20.0	17.4	41.2
100	17.4	7.5	34.8	23.5
n	109	40	23	34
Mean	54.4%	38.8%	58.4%	77.6%
Std. dev.	40.1	37.8	42.5	29.4
Median	60.0	27.5	80.0	90.0

Chapter Summary

In the study of price stickiness, theories are abundant but facts are scarce. This chapter is an attempt to correct that imbalance, albeit slightly.

Although there is a small "auction-market" sector in the U.S. economy, there certainly appears to be enough price rigidity in most sectors to matter for macroeconomic purposes. According to the survey results, the typical commodity is repriced roughly once a year; and more than 75 percent of GDP is repriced quarterly or less frequently. The mean lag between shifts in supply or demand and the eventual response of prices is about three months; but there is huge variability across firms.

Prices appear to be most sticky in the service sector (which is, of course, the majority of the economy) and least sticky in wholesale and retail trade. Somewhat surprisingly, the survey results give little indication of asymmetry in reaction times between cost and demand shocks or between price increases and price decreases.

Based on the survey responses, we estimate that about 28 percent of private, for-profit, nonfarm GDP is sold under explicit written contracts that fix the nominal price for some period of time. Discounting from these contract prices is apparently much less common than many economists have supposed.

Roughly two-thirds of firms report having implicit contracts in the sense of Okun (1981)—an estimate that makes good sense in view of the survey's finding that some 85 percent of sales are made to regular, rather than "off the street," customers.

Firms report having very high fixed costs—roughly 40 percent of total costs on average. And many more companies state that they have falling, rather than rising, marginal cost curves. While there are reasons to wonder whether respondents interpreted these questions about costs correctly, their answers paint an image of the cost structure of the typical firm that is very different from the one immortalized in textbooks.

Summary of Selected Factual Results

Price Policy	
Median number of price changes in a year	1.4
Mean lag before adjusting price months following	
Demand Increase	2.9
Demand Decrease	2.9
Cost Increase	2.8
Cost Decrease	3.3
Percent of firms which	
Report annual price reviews	45
Change prices all at once	74
Change prices in small steps	16
Have nontrivial costs of adjusting prices of	43
which related primarily to	
the frequency of price changes	69
the size of price changes	14

Sales	
Estimated percent of GDP sold under contracts which fix prices	28
Percent of firms which report implicit contracts	65
Percent of sales which are made to	
Consumers	21
Businesses	70
Other (principally government)	9
Regular customers	85
Percent of firms whose sales are	
Relatively sensitive to the state of the economy	43
Relatively Insensitive to the state of the economy	39

Costs	
Percent of firms which can estimate costs at least moderately well	87
Mean percentage of costs which are fixed	44
Percentage of firms for which marginal costs are	
Increasing	11
Constant	48
Decreasing	41

Chapter 5

Basic Results on the Twelve Theories

When the One Great Scorer comes to write against your name—
He marks—not that you won or lost—but how you played the game.
—GRANTLAND RICE

The main objective of the survey was not to compile the unadorned facts that were examined in chapter 4, fascinating as they may be. Rather, the study was designed to gather the opinions of real-world decision makers on the validity of economists' theories of price stickiness. It is to these central results that we now turn. This chapter focuses on broad-brush findings that cut across the twelve theories. Which theories are most "popular" with actual price setters? Which theories are correlated with which? Are prices more sticky downward than upward?

The following twelve chapters then delve more deeply into the details of each theory, one by one. Numbers, names, and very brief descriptions of each theory are given in table 5.1 for the convenience of the reader. Fuller descriptions were offered in chapter 2; further analysis can be found in chapters 6 through 17.

On the Empirical Validity of the Theories

The most obvious question to ask is how well each of these theories fares in the eyes of our two hundred decision makers. Respondents were asked how important each theory is as a cause of price stickiness in their own firm. Respondents answered in their own

Table 5.1   The Twelve Theories

Theory Number and Name	Brief Description
B1 Nominal contracts	Prices are fixed by contracts.
B2 Implicit contracts	Firms tacitly agree to stabilize prices, perhaps out of "fairness" to customers.
B3 Judging quality by price	Firms fear customers will mistake price cuts for reductions in quality.
B4 Pricing points	Certain prices (like $9.99) have special psychological significance.
B5 Procyclical elasticity	Demand curves become less elastic as they shift in.
B6 Cost-based pricing	Price rises are delayed until costs rise, and these delays cumulate through a multi-stage production process.
B7 Constant MC	MC is flat and markups are constant.
B8 Costly price adjustment	Firms incur costs of changing prices.
B9 Hierarchy	Hierarchical delays slow down decisions.
B10 Coordination failure	Firms hold back on price changes, waiting for other firms to go first.
B11 Inventories	Firms vary inventory stocks instead of prices.
B12 Nonprice competition	Firms vary nonprice elements such as delivery lags, service, or quality.

words, and interviewers coded the responses on the four-point scale, which is reproduced here for convenience:

1 = totally unimportant

2 = of minor importance

3 = moderately important

4 = very important

It is straightforward to compare the average ratings accorded to each of the twelve theories, and we shall do so shortly. But first the reader should be cautioned against identifying the above-mentioned scale with the standard four-point scale used to grade college students. For example, if some theory achieved an average grade of 4.0, that would not connote anything as mundane as a "straight-A" average—something that the best students at every school routinely attain. Rather, it would mean that every single respondent had branded the theory "very important," that is, we had discovered God's truth! Plainly, this is not going to happen. A more plausible standard of excellence would be an average rating of, say, 3.0— which is equivalent to half the firms rating the theory as "of minor importance" and half rating it as "very important." That would be vastly superior to a B average. On the low end, an average score of 1.0 would mean that every single respondent totally rejected the theory—which is closer to brain death than to a D. So it is perhaps more useful to think of the likely range of survey results not as going from 4.0 to 1.0, but rather from a top score of 3.0 for a wonderful theory to, say, 1.5 for a disastrous one.

With this caveat in mind, we turn now to the results of the "beauty contest." Table 5.2 ranks the theories by mean scores (column 4) and also gives the standard deviation across firms (column 5).[1] The other columns require some explanation.

The "*t*-stat" in column 6 is the test statistic for the hypothesis that the theory's mean score significantly exceeds that of the theory ranked just below it. As you can see, a single-rank difference is statistically significant in only a third of the cases. However, seven of the ten two-rank differences (for example, comparing theories B10 and B12) are significant at the 10 percent level, and all nine three-rank differences are significant at the 5 percent level.[2] Thus the rankings shown in table 5.2, while not as sharp as we might like, are certainly not meaningless.

The "accept rate" in column 7 offers an alternative way to rank the theories. Our numerical scale does not really have the cardinal significance that the rankings in column 1 tacitly attribute to it. So, as an alternative, column 7 reports a measure of how many firms "accept" each theory: the fraction of respondents rating the theory as "moderately important" (score 3) or higher. As you can see, the two alternative rankings hardly differ.

We come now to the puzzling column 8, labeled "premise?" Nine of the twelve theories apply only to firms that have some particular characteristic. For example, inventories cannot be an explanation of price stickiness for firms that have no inventories. In each

Table 5.2 Ratings of the Twelve Theories: Full Sample

(1) Rank	(2) Theory	(3) Name	(4) Mean Score	(5) s.d.	(6) t-stat[a]	(7) Accept Rate	(8) Premise?
1	B10	Coordination failure	2.77	1.25	1.0	61.9%	100.0%
2	B6	Cost-based pricing	2.66	1.26	0.6	56.8	100.0
3	B12	Nonprice competition	2.58	1.20	1.6	56.9	77.0
4	B2	Implicit contracts	2.40	1.26	2.1**	51.0	64.5
5	B1	Nominal contracts	2.11	1.25	1.8*	37.2	65.1
6	B8	Costly price adjustment	1.89	1.18	0.4	31.0	64.3
7	B5	Procyclical elasticity	1.85	1.07	0.8	31.3	58.5
8	B4	Pricing points	1.76	1.04	1.8*	25.0	50.8
9	B7	Constant MC	1.57	1.03	0.1	19.7	48.4
10	B11	Inventories	1.56	0.97	1.9*	21.4	86.5[b]
11	B9	Hierarchy	1.41	0.87	1.2	14.1	100.0
12	B3	Judging quality by price	1.33	0.77	—	10.5	21.5

[a] This is the test statistic for the hypothesis that the mean score is significantly greater than that in the row below.

[b] The question was not asked of firms producing services. Thus 86.5 percent is the percentage of these firms that report holding inventories of finished goods.

* denotes significant at the 10 percent level

** denotes significant at the 5 percent level

of these nine cases, we first pose a preliminary factual question (such as, "Does your firm hold inventories?"), and then proceed to inquire about the theory only if the factual question is answered in the affirmative. If not, we skip over the theory and score it as "totally unimportant" by definition. The column marked "premise?" shows the percentage of the sample to which the theory actually applies—that is, for which the factual premise is true. Thus, for example, 64.5 percent of the firms in our sample say they enter into implicit contracts with their customers—as assumed by theory B2. Note that this column shows the percentage for whom the premise actually applies and not the percentage for whom the premise could in principle apply. For example, all firms report that they have at least some repeat customers, so in principle all could have implicit contracts. But only 64.5 percent report that they do in fact have such contracts.

The theories naturally group themselves into three tiers, each with four members. The top group scores well—provided we are not too fussy about grading standards! If these results are believed, economists interested in the microfoundations of sticky prices should be focusing their attention on these four theories. Three of them are part of the modern Keynesian tradition: implicit contracts à la Okun (theory B2), cost-based pricing with lags (B6), and coordination failure (B10). In addition, nominal contracting (theory B1) finishes in fifth place. But the other highly rated theory, nonprice competition (theory B12), has received relatively little attention. It would appear to merit more.

It is worth noting that two of the theories in the top group—implicit contracts and nonprice competition—have especially high "acceptance rates" within their spheres of applicability: 79 percent and 74 percent respectively (that is, .51/.645 = .79). Thus, while there are sectors of the economy to which these theories do not apply, they appear to offer good explanations of price stickiness for a majority of firms, and excellent explanations within their sphere of applicability.

The bottom tier of four theories scores amazingly poorly. Remember, a mean score of 1.5 is equivalent to half the firms rejecting the theory outright and the other half attaching only "minor importance" to it. That two theories—judging quality by price (B3) and hierarchical delays (B9)—actually rate lower than this "minimum" score is remarkable.[3] Unless our results are way off the mark, these theories deserve to be eliminated from further consideration.[4] One of the theories in this bottom tier, hierarchies (B9), was offered by a businessman. Another, that inventory adjustments buffer price changes (B11), is the only theory on the list in which Blinder had a proprietary interest.[5] The remaining two—judging quality by price (B3) and constant marginal cost (B7)—have garnered enormous scholarly attention in recent years.

About half of the private, for-profit economy apparently has the cost structure assumed by Robert Hall in theory B7, in which marginal cost curves are flat within the relevant range. Obviously, the theory does not apply to the other half. But, even within the half of GDP produced under conditions of constant MC, the theory's acceptance rate is only 41 percent. Thus it seems most unlikely that constant marginal cost is a major factor behind aggregate price stickiness.[6] The adverse selection theory (B3) fares much worse. The premise that customers judge quality by price apparently applies to just one-fifth of GDP; and only half of these firms rate it an important cause of price rigidity. Apparently, the adverse selection theory is important in only a corner of the economy.

In the middle comes a group of four theories that earn "average" grades:[7] nominal contracts (B1), costs of price adjustment (B8), procyclical elasticity (B5), and pricing points (B4). These theoretical bottles may be deemed either half full or half empty, depending on tastes. The survey results for these four theories will neither persuade a skeptic nor dissuade a believer. In each case, roughly half of the firms to which the theory applies rate it as "moderately important" or higher. The differences in mean scores stem from the different sizes of the groups which accept the theory's basic premise—ranging from the 51 percent who report the existence of psychological pricing points to the 65.1 percent who have a meaningful volume of nominal contracts.

It is natural to wonder whether the rankings of the twelve theories vary much across industrial sectors. Are some ideas, for example, important in manufacturing but unimportant in services?[8] The answer, as table 5.3 shows, is that the differences across sectors are surprisingly small. The coordination failure theory (B10) ranks first or second in four of the five major sectors, and third in the other. And cost-based pricing (B6) is either first or second in three of the five. Similarly, judging quality by price (B3) and hierarchies

Table 5.3   Ratings of the Twelve Theories, by Industry

Rank	Manufacturing (n = 70)		Services (n = 37)		Trade (n = 54)		Construction and Mining (n = 22)		Transportation, Communications, and Utilities (n = 17)	
1	B12	(2.66)	B10	(3.09)	B10	(2.87)	B6	(3.00)	B6	(3.03)
2	B10	(2.63)	B6	(3.08)	B12	(2.68)	B1	(2.82)	B10	(2.76)
3	B2	(2.61)	B12	(2.51)	B1	(2.38)	B10	(2.45)	B1	(2.71)
4	B6	(2.51)	B2	(2.40)	B2	(2.32)	B12	(2.26)	B12	(2.44)
5	B8	(2.09)	B7	(2.19)	B6	(2.29)	B2	(2.02)	B2	(2.29)
6	B5	(2.01)	B4	(1.93)	B8	(2.13)	B7	(1.73)	B8	(2.03)
7	B1	(1.96)	B5	(1.88)	B4	(1.90)	B5	(1.57)	B9	(1.91)
8	B4	(1.74)	B8	(1.54)	B5	(1.76)	B11	(1.50)	B5	(1.80)
9	B11	(1.56)	B11	(1.48)	B3	(1.61)	B4	(1.39)	B7	(1.76)
10	B9	(1.49)	B1	(1.32)	B9	(1.48)	B3	(1.09)	B4	(1.47)
11	B7	(1.31)	B3	(1.20)	B7	(1.35)	B9	(1.09)	B3	(1.29)
12	B3	(1.27)	B9	(1.12)			B8	(1.09)		

(B9) always rank near the bottom of the list—except that B9 is of middling importance for the transportation, communications, and utilities sector.

Table 5.4 displays the rank correlations among the five columns of table 5.3.[9] They range from a high of 0.87 to a low of 0.54 with an average of 0.70, and all are statistically significant at least at the 10 percent level.

Table 5.4   Rank Correlations of the Rankings in Table 5.3

	Trade	Services	Construction and Mining	Transportation, Communications, and Utilities
Manufacturing	.74	.87	.60	.76
Trade		.56	.66	.54
Services			.67	.78
Construction and mining				.83

Nonetheless, it would be an exaggeration to say that there are no intersectoral differences. Regressions of each of the main theory questions on industry dummy variables yields F statistics that are significant at the 5 percent level for six of the twelve theories.[10] Hence we shall keep industrial sector in mind in the regression analyses that follow in subsequent chapters.

Much macroeconomic interest in price rigidity derives from pondering the following question: Why do not prices respond more vigorously (and hence real output respond less vigorously) to cyclical changes in demand? For this reason, it is of interest to divide the sample by cyclical sensitivity (question A6) and examine how the theories rank within subsamples. If some particular theory is not terribly important across the whole economy, but has high explanatory power in cyclically sensitive industries, then its macroeconomic importance would be greater than is suggested by table 5.2.

However, table 5.5 shows that this is not the case: Differences by cyclical sensitivity are negligible. The rankings in the three columns of the table are substantially identical; only the menu cost theory (B8) is significantly correlated with cyclical sensitivity.[11] Thus firms in cyclically sensitive and cyclically insensitive

Table 5.5   Ratings of the Theories, by Cyclical Sensitivity

Rank	Total Sample (n = 200)		Relatively Insensitive (n = 83)		Relatively Sensitive (n = 88)	
1	B10	(2.77)	B10	(2.75)	B10	(2.80)
2	B6	(2.66)	B6	(2.70)	B6	(2.59)
3	B12	(2.58)	B12	(2.69)	B12	(2.52)
4	B2	(2.40)	B2	(2.46)	B2	(2.35)
5	B1	(2.11)	B8	(2.13)	B1	(2.16)
6	B8	(1.88)	B1	(2.09)	B5	(1.84)
7	B5	(1.85)	B5	(1.95)	B4	(1.81)
8	B4	(1.76)	B4	(1.73)	B8	(1.69)
9	B7	(1.57)	B7	(1.61)	B7	(1.53)
10	B11	(1.56)	B9	(1.46)	B11	(1.52)
11	B9	(1.41)	B11	(1.38)	B3	(1.36)
12	B3	(1.33)	B3	(1.37)	B9	(1.32)

industries do not hold systematically different views on the validity of the theories.

Another interesting question is whether the responses differ according to the degree of price stickiness. After all, firms with highly flexible prices might be expected not to like any of the theories. As noted in chapter 4, there are five different measures of price stickiness: "How often do you change prices?" (question A10) and "How much time elapses before you raise/reduce your prices following a cost/demand shock?" (questions A13[a]–[d]). Because it is useful to have one summary measure, the variable STICKY was created as the first principal component of the five measures of price stickiness.[12] Table 5.6 divides the sample into two groups: above and below the median value of the synthetic variable STICKY. The rankings of the theories do not differ much between firms with relatively high and relatively low values of STICKY. But, as expected, most theories do score higher among firms with relatively sticky prices. The overall mean (averaging across all theories) is 2.11 for firms with relatively sticky prices and 1.90 for firms with relatively flexible prices.

Table 5.6   Ratings of the Theories, by Degree of Price Stickiness

Rank	Total Sample (n = 200)		Relatively Sticky (n = 100)		Relatively Flexible (n = 100)	
1	B10	(2.77)	B12	(2.84)	B10	(2.75)
2	B6	(2.66)	B10	(2.79)	B6	(2.73)
3	B12	(2.58)	B2	(2.61)	B12	(2.32)
4	B2	(2.40)	B6	(2.59)	B2	(2.18)
5	B1	(2.11)	B1	(2.27)	B1	(1.96)
6	B8	(1.88)	B8	(2.10)	B4	(1.75)
7	B5	(1.85)	B5	(1.96)	B5	(1.74)
8	B4	(1.76)	B4	(1.77)	B8	(1.68)
9	B7	(1.57)	B11	(1.63)	B7	(1.59)
10	B11	(1.56)	B9	(1.60)	B11	(1.52)
11	B9	(1.41)	B7	(1.55)	B3	(1.26)
12	B3	(1.33)	B3	(1.41)	B9	(1.22)
Memo						
Overall mean	2.01		2.11		1.90	

Correlations Among the Theories

The twelve theories are not mutually exclusive, nor is one a necessary concommitant of any other. Nonetheless, some theories appear to be closely related while others seem at least somewhat opposed. For example, a firm for which constant marginal cost is an important source of price stickiness probably engages in cost-based pricing. So the scores of theories B6 and B7 should be positively correlated. (They are.) On the other hand, implicit contracts presumably arise only where explicit contracts are absent. Thus B1 and B2 should be negatively correlated. (They are, too.) In general, it is interesting to know which theories are correlated with which.

This question is not as straightforward as it seems because the data are not cardinal; they are categorical but ordered. That is, 4 is larger than 3 and 3 is larger than 2, but the "distance" between these values may not be the same. The standard (Pearson) correlation coefficient is therefore inappropriate, because it assumes cardinality. And the standard χ^2 test of the hypothesis that the distributions of answers to questions B_i and B_j are independent is also inappropriate, because it ignores order and so tells us nothing about the direction of any association. Hence, we report two less-conventional measures of association in table 5.7.

The numbers above the diagonal in table 5.7 are Goodman-Kruskal (1954) gamma coefficients. As this statistic is unfamiliar to most economists, a word on its interpretation seems in order. Suppose firm A rated two theories (4,3) and firm B scored them (1,2). Since firm A rated both theories higher than did firm B, we say that this pairwise comparison is "concordant." If, on the other hand, firm B scored the two theories (3,4), the comparison would be called "discordant." Let C be the fraction of all possible pairwise comparisons that are concordant and D be the fraction that are discordant. The Goodman-Kruskal gamma is defined as $(C - D)/(C + D)$.[13] Like the conventional Pearson correlation coefficient, it ranges from $+1$ to -1; and its asymptotic standard error is known.[14] Values of gamma that are significant at the 10 percent level are presented in boldface in the table.

Table 5.7 Associations Among the Theories[a]

	B1	B2	B3	B4	B5	B6	B7	B8	B9	B10	B11	B12
B1	—	−.24	−.06	−.19	−.05	−.06	−.20	−.06	**.28**	**.14**	−.08	−.14
B2	.01	—	−.10	.00	**.18**	.08	.15	**.19**	.02	−.17	.01	**.19**
B3			—	**.41**	.14	−.19	−.25	.10	**.31**	−.12	−.03	**.33**
B4	.10*		.00	—	−.01	−.05	−.13	.13	.09	**.17**	−.29	.09
B5		.01			—	−.06	.14	−.03	.03	.06	−.03	**.21**
B6						—	**.34**	−.14	.02	.01	−.10	.02
B7					.00		—	.12	−.14	−.08	.12	.06
B8		.02			.08			—	**.33**	.09	**.26**	.07
B9	.01						.01		—	−.03	**.35**	**.18**
B10	.08*	.05	.07*	.05						—	.13	−.13
B11								.03	.02		—	.07
B12	.07*	.01	.00		.01							—

[a] The Goodman-Kruskal gamma is above the diagonal and the *p*-value from ordered probit is below the diagonal. Values of the Goodman-Kruskal gamma with asymptotic *p*-value smaller than .10 are in boldface. Only the ordered probit *p*-values that are smaller than .10 are shown. The nonlinearity of the ordered probit model implies that it matters which variable is the dependent variable. Values marked with * indicate that the alternative ordering gives a probability value greater than .10.

A different measure appears below the diagonal. Since the answers to questions B_i and B_j are categorical but ordered, it is possible to run an ordered probit model that "explains" one by the other.[15] If, say, B_i is the dependent variable and B_j is the independent variable, the significance level of the *t*-statistic of the coefficient of B_j is a natural measure of the strength of the correlation between the two variables. This is reported below the diagonal.[16]

The first thing to notice in table 5.7 is that only about one-third of the entries are in boldface. The importance that a particular firm accords to one theory is sometimes, but not frequently, related to its evaluation of other theories. Second, the two measures of association usually, but do not always, agree.[17] For convenience, we focus on the Goodman-Kruskal gamma statistic in what follows.

Although many pairs of theories are significantly correlated, only a few such correlations are very large in magnitude. According to the gamma statistic, the strongest positive correlations between theories are (with asymptotic standard errors in parentheses):

Theory	Theory	Gamma Statistic
Judging quality by price (B3)	Pricing points (B4)	.41 (.11)
Hierarchy (B9)	Inventories (B11)	.35 (.18)
Cost-based pricing (B6)	Constant MC (B7)	.34 (.10)
Costly price adjustment (B8)	Hierarchy (B9)	.33 (.11)
Judging quality by price (B3)	Nonprice competition (B12)	.33 (.11)
Judging quality by price (B3)	Hierarchy (B9)	.31 (.15).

All of these are significant at the 5 percent level or better. The strongest negative correlations are:

Theory	Theory	Gamma Statistic
Pricing points (B4)	Inventories (B11)	−.29 (.18)
Judging quality by price (B3)	Constant MC (B7)	−.25 (.19)
Nominal contracts (B1)	Implicit contracts (B2)	−.24 (.08)

only the last of which is significant.

At least some of these correlations have intuitive interpretations. The two most natural correlations have already been mentioned:

- We certainly expect the ratings of explicit and implicit contracts (B1, B2) to be negatively correlated, as they are.

- Cost-based pricing with lags (B6) seems to be the natural (though not inevitable) accompaniment to the constant marginal cost theory (B7).

In addition, we find that judging quality by price (theory B3) is apparently a more important source of price stickiness in firms where psychological pricing points (B4) and/or nonprice competition (B12) slow down price responses. The former seems sensible: Consumers with irrational attractions to particular prices may also believe that those prices carry signals of quality. The latter may mean that firms facing sharply kinked demand curves prefer to compete on grounds other than price.

Moreover, the adjustment cost (B8) and hierarchy (B9) theories are positively correlated. This could be because executive decision making time is an important source of adjustment costs, or because high-level executive decisions are required where adjustment costs are large.

However, some of the other correlations defy easy explanation. The reader is invited to check his or her priors against table 5.7.

Are Prices Stickier Downward Than Upward?

That prices are stickier downward than upward is a central tenet of textbook Keynesianism. This assumption is invoked to explain the presumed convexity of the aggregate supply and/or Phillips curve, to explain why recessions last longer and are deeper than periods of production beyond full employment, and so on. In fact, however, econometric support for this common assumption is lacking.[18] The survey results offer further information on this issue. And, to the extent they deliver any verdict at all, it is a surprising one: Our theories do a better job of explaining upward price stickiness than downward price stickiness. This should not come as a surprise to readers of chapter 4, for there we saw that lags in adjusting prices after demand or cost shocks are not systematically longer for negative than for positive shocks.

The evidence on asymmetry is difficult to summarize succinctly for several reasons:

First, the nature of each theory dictated that the asymmetry question, where there was one, was somewhat different in each case.

Second, in three cases, no asymmetry question was asked. Theory B7 is inherently symmetric: If marginal cost functions are flat, prices neither rise in booms nor fall in slumps. Hierarchies (theory B9) also suggests symmetry, though not quite as strongly. Cost-based pricing (theory B6) applies in the downward direction only to firms that regularly experience decreases in costs, which few do.

Third, as mentioned in chapter 3, the asymmetry question for theory B12 (nonprice competition) turned out, inadvertently, to be a loaded question. The main question pertains to price cuts: When demand falls, do you shorten delivery lags, improve service, or improve product quality rather than cut prices? That seems straightforward. But when we reverse the direction, we wind up asking firms if they allow service and/or quality to deteriorate when demand is high. These are things to which few firms want to admit.[19]

And fourth, in one case, the asymmetry question was posed in an infelicitous way that precludes qualitative comparisons. Question B2 was:

B2. . . . The idea is that firms have implicit understandings with their customers—who expect the firms not to take advantage of the situation by raising prices when the market is tight.

How important is [this] in slowing down price adjustments in your company?

Since the question emphasizes periods of peak demand, the asymmetry question asked about slack markets:

B2(b). What about when the demand for your products is weak? Are your customers then willing to let you hold your prices, or do they insist on price reductions?

The answers, shown just below, imply considerable downward rigidity:

1 = usually let us hold prices	51.3%
2 = attitudes are mixed	20.0
3 = usually insist on price reductions	28.7

Unfortunately, there is no way to tell from the answers to B2 and B2(b) whether there is more rigidity in the upward or downward direction.

This leaves seven theories about which clear (and, hopefully, meaningful) asymmetry questions were asked. Of these, four showed evidence of greater stickiness in the upward direction, two suggested approximate symmetry, and only one supported the Keynesian hypothesis that prices are more sticky downward. Since this is an important issue, we proceed now to present the evidence in detail, so each reader can make his or her own judgment. (Readers uninterested in these details and willing to accept our characterization can skip directly to the end of the chapter.)

Nominal Contracts (Theory B1)

The main question applied to price increases. The immediate follow-up question (with answers as indicated) was:

B1(a). Do contracts also prevent prices from decreasing when demand or costs fall? (n = 97)

1 = no, totally inapplicable to price decreases	12.4%
2 = less applicable to price decreases	16.0
3 = yes, just as applicable to price decreases	67.5
4 = yes, even more applicable to price decreases	4.1

Mean response = 2.63

About two-thirds of the responses indicate symmetry. But the asymmetrical responses point overwhelmingly in one direction: toward more rigidity upward than downward. The *t*-test of the hypothesis that the mean response is 3.0 (which connotes symmetry) yields a test statistic of 4.8. The difference between 3.0 and the mean answer of 2.63 is also economically sizable, though not gigantic. Hence, for this theory at least, whatever asymmetry there is in price adjustment seems to be the reverse of what is normally assumed.

Judging Quality by Price (Theory B3)

The overwhelming majority of firms reject this theory for both price increases and price decreases. The question is most naturally posed for price cuts:

B3. Another idea is that firms hesitate to reduce their prices because they fear that customers will interpret a price cut as a signal that the quality of the product has been reduced.

How important is [this] in discouraging or delaying price decreases in your company? (n = 200)

The evaluations of the theory were:

1 = totally unimportant	81.5%
2 = of minor importance	8.0
3 = moderately important	6.3
4 = very important	4.3

Mean response = 1.33

For comparison, the asymmetry question (with answers as shown) was:

B3(c). What about applying this idea to price increases? That is, are you encouraged to raise prices because you think customers will interpret higher prices as an indication of higher quality? (n = 171)

1 = rarely or never	79.1%
2 = sometimes	16.9
3 = most of the time	2.3
4 = always or almost always	1.7
Mean response = 1.27	

Although the questions are not directly parallel, the answers seem comparable. We conclude that there is little, if any, evidence for asymmetry in the reactions to this theory.

Pricing Points (Theory B4)

The asymmetry question in this case was asked only of firms that both reported that threshold pricing points were relevant in their business, and that attached at least some importance to them as a source of price stickiness. The question and answers were as follows:

B4(d). Do thresholds also deter small price decreases when demand or costs fall? (n = 78)

1 = rarely or never	48.7%
2 = sometimes	22.4
3 = always or almost always	28.8
Mean response = 1.80	

When we recall that this question was asked only of firms that reported that psychological thresholds do deter price increases, it is clear that the answers imply considerably more upward than downward rigidity.

Procyclical Elasticity (Theory B5)

A formal statistical test for symmetry can be made in the context of this theory because the asymmetry question is the precise opposite of the main question. Specifically:

B5(c). How important is the effect in the opposite direction? That is, are you hesitant to raise markups when demand rises because you want to attract new customers, and you think these new customers will be quite price conscious? (n = 108)

Answers were given on the same four-point scale used for the main question and, after allowing for missing observations, 103 firms answered both questions.[20] A direct comparison of the responses to the two questions shows clear evidence of more rigidity in the downward direction: forty-eight gave a lower score to B5(c) than to B5, nineteen gave a higher score, and thirty-seven gave the same answer to both. A *t*-test strongly rejects the null hypothesis that the means are equal (t = 4.0, p-value = .0001). Hence this theory gives clear evidence in favor of the Keynesian presumption.

Costs of Price Adjustment (Theory B8)

In this case, we inquired about asymmetry in an indirect way—by asking those firms that did not reject the theory outright the following question:

B8(d). Do you incur these special costs of changing prices when you decrease prices as well? (n = 77)

1 = no	14.3%
2 = yes, but smaller	26.0
3 = yes, about equal	57.1
4 = yes, even larger	2.6
Mean response = 2.48	

It is apparent that many more firms say they have smaller adjustment costs when prices decrease than when they increase, implying more rigidity in the upward direction. A formal test of the null hypothesis that the mean response to question B8(d) is 3.0 yields a *t*-statistic of −5.9, which is significant at any reasonable level.

Coordination Failure (Theory B10)

The asymmetry question for this theory was pretty straightforward:

B10(b). Do you also delay price cuts because you do not want to be among the first firms in the industry to cut prices? (n = 163)

1 = rarely or never	61.3%
2 = sometimes	13.8
3 = usually or always	24.8
Mean response = 1.63	

A direct numerical comparison between these numbers and the distribution of answers to question B10 is not possible. But when we remember that most firms accepted theory B10, it becomes clear that the answers to B10(b) indicate considerably less rigidity in the downward direction. Another way of assessing the evidence is to look at the cross tabulation of B10 and B10(b) among those firms that both agreed with theory B10 (by answering "3" or higher) and answered B10(b). There are 106 such cases. Of these, almost twice as many answered "rarely or never" to B10(b) as answered "usually or always." This is, once again, a strong indication of more upward rigidity.[21]

Inventories (Theory B11)

There is much weaker evidence on the asymmetry question for theory B11 because the relevant question was asked of only twenty-nine firms. Why? First, service companies and transportation, communications, and utilities companies were not asked about theory B11. Second, about one-seventh of the firms in the other sectors do not hold inventories of finished goods. Third, nearly three-quarters of the remaining companies rejected the theory out of hand, and hence were not asked the asymmetry question. For what it is worth, the twenty-nine respondents displayed clear symmetry. The question and distribution of answers were:

> B11(b). Is this idea more important for decreases in demand or for increases in demand? (n = 29)
>
> | | |
> |---|---|
> | 1 = more important for decreases | 34.5% |
> | 2 = about equally important | 27.6 |
> | 3 = more important for increases | 37.9 |
> | Mean response = 2.03 | |

In sum, the scoreboard for the asymmetry issue reads as follows:

More upward rigidity:	Theories B1, B4, B8, B10
Symmetric rigidity:	Theories B3, B7, B9, B11
More downward rigidity:	Theory B5
Downward rigidity irrelevant:	Theory B6
Unknown:	Theories B2, B12

On the basis of this evidence, it seems hard to conclude that firms see prices as stickier downward than upward. Rather, the evidence points modestly toward the opposite conclusion: that there is more upward than downward price stickiness.

Chapter Summary

According to the views of a random sample of two hundred actual price setters, coordination failure (B10), cost-based pricing (B6), and the use of variables other than prices to clear markets (B12) are the most important factors behind sluggish price adjustment. Since implicit contracts of the Okun variety (B2) rank in fourth place and nominal contracting (B1) comes in fifth, four of the top five ideas have a distinctly Keynesian flavor.

Decision makers resoundingly reject the adverse selection theory of price rigidity (that price cuts are deterred because customers judge quality by price—theory B3) and the notion that bureaucratic delays in decision making slow down price changes (theory B9). It also appears that constant marginal costs and markups (theory B7) and the use of inventory adjustments as substitutes for price changes (theory B11) are of limited empirical relevance.

While the rankings of the twelve theories do differ somewhat across broad industrial sectors, the differences are not dramatic. And cyclically sensitive firms give the theories essentially the same ratings as cyclically insensitive firms.

The importance that a particular firm assigns to one theory is often related to its evaluation of the other theories, although the size of such correlations is usually modest. Using the Goodman-Kruskal gamma as a measure of association, the highest positive correlation is 0.41 (between judging quality by price and pricing points) and the largest negative correlation is −.29 (between pricing points and inventories). Positive correlations are more common than negative ones, but most are small.

The survey turned up precious little evidence for the characteristically Keynesian proposition that prices are stickier downward than upward. In fact, only one theory (procyclical elasticity—B5) appears to be asymmetrical in this direction. By contrast, respondents say that four theories (B1, B4, B8, and B10) are more applicable to upward rigidity than to downward rigidity. In conjunction with the survey results on lags presented in chapter 4, and the paucity of econometric evidence in its favor, it appears that the common assumption that prices are stickier downward than upward should be rejected.[22]

Part III
Detailed Findings on Each Theory

Chapter 6

Nominal Contracting

This is the first in a series of twelve short chapters examining the theories one by one. We begin with the simplest imaginable explanation of price stickiness, which posits the existence of nominal contracts that set prices in advance. If such contracts cover any substantial share of GDP and last for nontrivial periods of time, they obviously impart some inertia to the aggregate price level.

Some economists would argue that this idea is not a "theory" at all, for it fails to explain why parties enter into such contracts in the first place. We have no quarrel with this epistemological position which is, after all, only about nomenclature. It has been said that there is both "shallow" contract theory, which assumes the existence and form of contracts and then traces the implications thereof, and "deep" contract theory, which tries to deduce the nature of contracts from first principles. This chapter is concerned only with shallow contract theory.

Nominal Contracting and Price-Level Inertia

The idea that nominal contracting may be central to price stickiness dates all the way back to Keynes's *General Theory*, although Keynes dealt more with nominal wage rigidity than with price rigidity. Simple Keynesian models often assume, either explicitly or tacitly, that the price level, P, is predetermined and that the demand side rules in the short run. A trivial example is:

6.1 $Y_t^d = D(M_t/P_t)$ (aggregate demand)

6.2 $Y_t^s = S(W_t/P_t)$ (aggregate supply)

6.3 $Y_t = \min(Y_t^d, Y_t^s)$ (short-side rule)

6.4 $P_{t+1} - P_t = k(Y_t^d - Y_t^s)$ (price adjustment)

where M is the money supply, W is the nominal wage, P is the price level, and Y is output. Something akin to this model, which is depicted in figure 6.1, is at the heart of most textbook presentations of Keynesian economics. The model is not closed, of course, until we specify the nature of the functions D(.) and S(.) and the determination of money wages. The simplest example of the former is the quantity theory: $D(M/P) = VM/P$; but ordinary IS/LM models yield a demand relationship just like equation 6.1.[1] The function

Figure 6.1   Predetermined Price Level

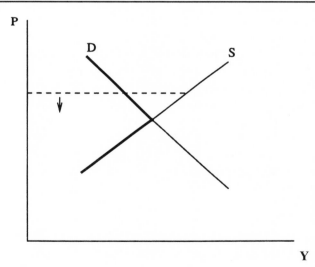

P = price
Y = output
D = demand
S = supply

S(.) is irrelevant (in the short run) when there is excess supply in the goods market—which is the prototypical Keynesian case. But it becomes highly relevant if there is excess demand or equilibrium.

A simple specification, reminiscent of Fischer (1977a),[2] uses the quantity theory for D(.), a log-linear S(.)—which can be derived from a Cobb-Douglas production function, and an assumption that money wages are set one period ahead proportional to expected prices. This last assumption makes aggregate supply depend on unanticipated inflation, as in the so-called Lucas supply function. But if prices are predetermined, one-period-ahead forecasts of inflation are always correct, so Y^s is constant. Thus a log-linear version of this specification is:

6.5 $\quad y_t^d = m_t + v_t - p_t$

6.6 $\quad y_t^s = y_t^* + b(p_t - {}_{t-1}p_t) = y_t^*$

6.7 $\quad y_t = \min(y_t^d, y_t^s)$

6.8 $\quad p_{t+1} - p_t = k(y_t^d - y_t^s).$

The nature of the solution depends on whether there is excess demand or excess supply. In the excess-supply regime ($y = y^d$), it is clear that output depends only on actual money, not on its division into anticipated and unanticipated components, just as in the simplest Keynesian models. In the excess-demand regime, $y = y^s = y^*$ every period. The price level is still inertial; but this stickiness now has no significance for real output because y is no longer given by the quantity theory.

That anticipated money has real effects in the presence of nominal contracts, even under rational expectations, is hardly a deep result. The more interesting—and unanswered—question in this literature is, of course: Why do people write contracts that fix nominal prices in advance?

The existence of contracts per se is not hard to explain. In many circumstances negotiating a new price may require considerable time and effort, and fixing the price contractually for a period of time can economize on these costs. For example, such negotiation costs must be an important reason why labor contracts often fix wages for lengthy periods of time.

However, nominal contracts are far more difficult to rationalize. Presumably, the costs of negotiating and drawing up a contract are roughly the same whether the contract is written in nominal or real terms, so these costs cannot explain the absence of indexed contracts.[3] Similarly, a stable contracted price may be desired by the buyer or seller or both. But, again, wouldn't people want to reduce the uncertainty of the real price?

A partial explanation for the lack of indexation in contracts comes from noting that *complete* indexation would rigidify relative prices, which is not desirable in the face of real shocks. In a world with both real and nominal shocks, partial indexation will usually be optimal.[4] But this analysis cannot explain why zero indexing is overwhelmingly the norm.

There is, of course, another, simpler answer—but one that economists shun—namely, that people suffer from money illusion and rarely think of writing contracts in real terms. It may be that economists will have to admit—albeit reluctantly—the possibility of money illusion. There is, indeed, some provocative survey evidence in favor of this hypothesis.[5]

Nominal Contracts as a Source of Price Stickiness

Two things may be taken for granted. First, some portion of the economy does indeed write binding nominal contracts that fix prices; chapter 4 estimated this portion to be about 25 percent of the private, nonfarm, unregulated, for-profit economy. Second, nominal contracts that last for nontrivial periods of time impart some inertia to the aggregate price level. But how much? How important are nominal contracts as a source of price stickiness? Keynesians have long supposed that such contracts are an important source of price rigidity. New classical economists have disputed this (unproven) contention and argued that the macroeconomy is better modeled as a giant auction hall.

To ascertain the views of actual price setters, we asked our decision makers the following question:

B1. One idea is that many goods are sold under explicit contractual agreements that set prices in advance, so firms are not free to raise prices while contracts remain in force.

How important is this idea in slowing down price adjustments in your company?

The distribution of responses is given in table 6.1.[6] The "rank" shown at the bottom of the table indicates that the mean response of 2.11 places this theory fifth in "popularity" among the twelve theories tested. (For more cross-theory comparisons, see chapter 5.) Since we know that some firms do not have any appreciable volume of nominal contracts, perhaps a more revealing score is obtained by eliminating all the "totally unimportant" responses and computing the mean response among the remaining half of the firms. When this is done, the conditional mean score is 3.19, which is quite high. So our conclusion seems to be something like the following: Nominal contracting is irrelevant to about half the economy but a very important source of price stickiness in the other half.

What does the survey tell us about where in the economy contracts are most important? First, it is (fortunately) true that contracts score higher as a source of price stickiness where firms tell us that contracts are most prevalent (according to question A8)! This is just a consistency check. The "correlation" between the answers to questions B1 and A8 is, of course, positive; the Goodman-Kruskal gamma is .67, which is extremely high for this data set.

Second, the importance of contracts as a source of price rigidity differs systematically by industrial sector, as table 6.2 shows. The χ^2_{24} test of association between question B1 and a set of industry dummies yields a test statistic of 61.7, which is significant well beyond the 0.1 percent level. Contracts do not account for much price stickiness in wholesale and retail trade, but are an important

Table 6.1   B1. How Important Are Nominal Contracts in Slowing Down Price Adjustments? (n=199 Responses)

Code	Response	Percentage of Firms
1	Totally unimportant	49.5%
2	Of minor importance	13.3
3	Moderately important	13.6
4	Very important	23.6

Mean response = 2.11   (mean if > 1 = 3.19)
Rank = 5th

Table 6.2   The Importance of Nominal Contracts in Price Stickiness, by
            Sector (n=199 Responses)

		Percentage of Firms				
Code	Response	Manufacturing	Trade	Services	Construction and Mining	Transportation, Communications, and Utilities
1	Totally unimportant	53.6%	75.7%	43.5%	31.8%	17.6%
2	Of minor importance	14.5	18.9	10.2	4.5	17.6
3	Moderately important	14.5	2.7	11.1	13.6	41.2
4	Very important	17.4	2.7	35.2	50.0	23.5
	Mean response	1.96	1.32	2.38	2.82	2.71
	Rank	7th	10th	3rd	2nd	3rd

source in the transportation, communications, and utilities (TCU)
sector and in construction and mining industries.

What Kinds of Firms Agree with the Theory Most?

Which other attributes of firms might help explain how a specific
company rates the importance of nominal contracts? Before delv-
ing into the results, it is worth discussing which attributes seem to
be the most plausible candidates on a priori grounds—and why.
Note that we use a number of mnemonics in order to refer to the
variables (we have already come across one, STICKY, in an earlier
chapter). We provide a full list of these mnemonics and their definitions in appendix B.

The Costs of Price Stickiness: Generic Attributes

Some characteristics of firms ought to be germane to any theory of
price rigidity. In standard economic theory without inertia or
adjustment costs, a demand or cost shock will always lead a firm to
adjust its price. The profits lost by holding price fixed in the face of
such shocks depend on the magnitude of the shocks and on the cur-

vature of the firm's profit function with respect to price, as detailed in the mathematical appendix to this chapter. Most of the following attributes can be generically interpreted as relating to one of these two factors.

FLATMC (question B7[a]): The profits of firms with flat marginal cost curves will be relatively insensitive to price. For example, if a positive demand shock raises the profit-maximizing price, holding price below the optimal price (that is, producing more) will raise costs more than revenues, since $P < MC$. But the rate of increase of costs is slower if the MC curve is relatively flat. Hence, such firms will lose less by holding price fixed in the face of demand shocks.[7] (This result is demonstrated in the mathematical appendix.) We therefore expect such firms to rate most theories of price rigidity more favorably. FLATMC is defined as a dummy variable that takes on the value 1 if B7(a) equals either 3 (MC is flat) or 4 (MC is flat with discrete jumps).

MCPCT (question A12[b]): Regardless of the slope of the marginal cost schedule, firms with a high level of marginal costs also have profits that are relatively insensitive to price. (See the mathematical appendix.) To understand why, suppose a firm reduces its price in order to raise sales and revenues. In the extreme case of zero marginal cost, the higher revenues translate directly into higher profits; but if marginal cost is higher, the revenues will be offset by higher costs. Question A12 asks what fraction of the firm's costs are fixed and what fraction are variable (MCPCT).[8] Firms with a high proportion of variable costs ought to have stickier prices and rate the theories of price stickiness more favorably.

ELAST (question A4): The profits of firms facing elastic demand curves are relatively sensitive to price, because revenues vary more with price movements. (Again, see the mathematical appendix.) So, other things equal, such firms would be expected to rate theories of price stickiness more favorably. We therefore expect a negative correlation between ELAST and firms' ratings of the theories. Recall, however, that question A4 was not explicit about whether the firm was cutting price on its own or along with its rivals. Thus, ELAST may refer to the firm's elasticity of demand for some firms and to the industry's elasticity of demand for others. As such, ELAST can be viewed as containing significant measurement error, and this ought to weaken any observed correlation.

CYCLICAL (question A6): Firms facing highly cyclical demand conditions will, other things equal, tend to have a relatively variable optimal price, and so would be expected to rate the theories less favorably.

STICKY (questions A10 and A13): As described in chapters 4 and 5, the variable STICKY was created as the first principal component of the five measures of price stickiness. Thus, unless the twelve theories have no value in explaining price rigidity, we should expect a positive correlation between STICKY and the importance of each theory. And, indeed, chapter 5 presented some evidence that this is so. Beyond this trivial arithmetical relationship, firms may have sticky prices for reasons other than the twelve theories examined in this book. If the importance of these "omitted theories" differs systematically between fixed- and flexible-price firms, then STICKY could be correlated with the ratings given to various theories.

The Benefits of Price Stickiness: Specific Attributes

So far, we have discussed only the costs of holding prices sticky in the face of shocks. But what about the benefits of sticky prices? These seem more likely to be theory-specific. Indeed specifying these benefits is, in large measure, what a theory of price stickiness is all about. The following variables seem to be good candidates to help explain which firms will view the nominal contracts theory (B1) most favorably.

IMPLICIT (question B2[a]): Implicit contracts probably are a substitute for explicit contracts. We would therefore expect firms with implicit contracts to rate the nominal contracts theory less favorably.

CONSUMER (question A2[a]): If it is more typical for businesses to purchase items under written contracts than it is for consumers, then firms that sell mostly to consumers might regard the nominal contracts theory less highly than firms that sell mostly to other firms.

STOCK (question A15[a]): Given its demand curve, a firm can fix the price and let the market determine sales (which sounds like nominal contracting), or it can fix the quantity sold and let the market determine price. The latter strategy seems feasible only if production is to stock rather than to order; and it is unlikely to be associated with either nominal contracting or price stickiness. So we expect a negative correlation between the fraction produced to stock (STOCK) and the importance of nominal contracts.[9]

ADJCOSTS (question B8[a]): A firm with explicit costs of changing prices should be more likely to want to hold its price fixed. Such a firm might therefore be more willing to enter into fixed nominal contracts.

REGULARS (question A3): Repeat customers seem much more likely than one-timers to enter into contracts that set prices in advance.

FORESEEN (question B6[d]): Businesses may be more willing to lock into a nominal contract with a predetermined price if cost increases can be foreseen.

The expected and actual correlations of each of these variables with firms' ratings of the importance of nominal contracts is summarized in table 6.3. The variables expected to be correlated with any of the twelve theories are shown in the upper panel, and the variables expected to be correlated with nominal contracting in particular are shown in the middle panel. Because B1 is an ordered categorical variable, three different measures of "correlation" are used in table 6.3, depending on the nature of the variable being considered:

- For *numerical* variables, the table displays the t-statistic for the coefficient in a univariate ordered probit model with B1 as the dependent variable. (Ordered probits will be discussed in detail below.)

- For *categorical but ordered* variables, the table gives the Goodman-Kruskal gamma statistic, with probability values based on asymptotic standard errors. (The Goodman-Kruskal gamma was discussed in chapter 5.)

- Finally, for variables that are *categorical and not ordered* (such as industrial sector), the p-value from a χ^2 test is shown.

Among the five variables that are potentially correlated with any of the twelve theories of price stickiness, only STICKY is statistically significant in explaining the answers to question B1; and it has the expected (positive) sign. ELAST has a negative correlation, as expected, but is not quite statistically significant. MCPCT and CYCLICAL have correlations opposite in sign from what is expected.

Table 6.3   Bivariate Correlates of the Importance of Nominal Contracts

Description	Variable Name	Question	Expected Sign	Correlation	
General correlates of price stickiness					
Industry	INDUSTRY	—	undefined	$\chi_{24}^2 = 61.7$	(p = .00)
Marginal cost	FLATMC	B7(a)	+	t = −0.9	(p = .38)
Fraction of costs that are variable	MCPCT	A12(b)	+	t = −1.8	(p = .08)
Elasticity of demand	ELAST	A4	−	t = −1.4	(p = .15)
Cyclically sensitive	CYCLICAL	A6	−	$\gamma = .05$	(p = .58)
Price stickiness	STICKY	A10, A13	+	t = 2.2	(p = .03)
Predicted correlates of this theory					
Implicit contracts	IMPLICIT	B2(a)	−	$\gamma = -.23$	(p = .04)
Fraction of sales under contract	WRITTEN	A8	+	$\gamma = .67$	(p = .00)
Fraction of sales to consumers	CONSUMER	A2(a)	−	t = −3.6	(p = .00)
Fraction produced to stock	STOCK	A15(a)	−	t = −3.3	(p = .00)
Has costs of price adjustments	ADJCOSTS	B8(a)	+	$\gamma = -.11$	(p = .26)
Fraction sold to regular customers	REGULARS	A3	+	t = 1.4	(p = .18)
Cost increases can be foreseen	FORESEEN	B6(d)	+	$\gamma = .19$	(p = .17)
Other correlates					
Fraction of sales to others (gov't)	GOVT	A2(c)	?	t = 3.4	(p = .00)
Unionization rate in industry	UNION		?	t = 1.7	(p = .09)
Index of coincident indicators	CYCLE		?	t = 2.0	(p = .04)

The variables chosen with the nominal contracting theory specifically in mind fare a bit better. Both CONSUMER and STOCK have negative and highly significant correlations with the importance of nominal contracting; REGULARS and FORESEEN have the correct sign, but are not quite statistically significant.

In addition to the variables that were arguably related to nominal contracting on a priori grounds, three others displayed significant correlations. These are shown in the lower panel of table 6.3. Whereas we saw above that the importance of nominal contracting is negatively associated with the fraction of sales going to consumers, it turns out to be positively associated with the fraction of sales going to government. The theory also is positively correlated with the industry's unionization rate and the cyclical strength of the economy. The reasons are far from clear.

The Ordered Probit Model

The next step is to attempt a multivariate ("regression") analysis of how the importance of nominal contracting as a source of price stickiness varies across firms. What observable attributes of firms help explain the importance they attach to theory B1? As this task involves using the so-called ordered probit model, a model that is used repeatedly in this book, it is worth taking a moment to explain precisely what that model is.

Suppose we have a categorical variable (like the answers to question B1) that can take on one of k discrete values: 1, 2, 3, . . . , k. These responses are ordinal rather than cardinal—for example, 4 is bigger than 3 which is bigger than 2, but there is no sense in which 4 is twice as big as 2. The ordered probit model postulates the existence of a continuous latent variable, call it z, that indicates the firm's evaluation of theory B1. The value of variable z for firm i is assumed to be linearly related to a set of regressors, X_i:

6.9 $z_i = X_i\beta + u_i,$

and the respondent is presumed to give response j (j = 1, . . ., k) if z_i is within a certain range:

6.10 $a_{j-1} < z_i < a_j.$

The model is completed by the assumption that the cumulative distribution function (cdf) of the random error, u, is normal.[10] Thus the probability of observing response j from firm i is the probability that:

6.11 $a_{j-1} - X_i\beta < u_i < a_j - X_i\beta,$

where u is assumed to be normally distributed. In what follows, we will adopt the abbreviated notation OP(B1) = Xβ to denote the ordered probit model explaining B1 by regressors X with coefficients β. The function OP(.) is implicitly defined by 6.9, 6.10, and the assumption of normality.

Estimation is by maximum likelihood, as described in Greene (1993, chapter 21).[11] With k possible responses, the a vector contains k − 1 cutoff points. (One can think of the a vector as having k + 1 elements, but with a_0 and a_k set at negative and positive infinity, respectively.) In addition, any constant term in equation 6.9 would be subsumed into the a vector because, as equation 6.11 makes clear, adding a constant to Xβ and to all the a_j's would leave the model unchanged. Thus, if there are m regressors, there are m + k − 1 parameters to be estimated. In most applications, k can be as large as seven—allowing for intermediate responses like 3.5. The algorithm used to fit the model usually converged rapidly if m was no larger than, say, 10 or 12. But larger numbers of regressors and smaller numbers of observations began to create convergence problems.[12]

Fitting an ordered probit model to the answers to the main questions requires some algorithm, however informal, for choosing among the plethora of potential explanatory variables. The systematic "data mining" procedure we followed started by looking for interviewer effects: We included only the fourteen interviewer dummies as explanatory variables and retained only those that were statistically significant. (Few were.) Next, we added industry dummies, the index of coincident indicators (CYCLE), SIZE (the log of question A1), the four-firm concentration ratio in the firm's four-digit industry (CONC), and the unionization rate in the firm's four-digit industry (UNION),[13] and again dropped variables that were not significant. Having done that, we added other variables from the questionnaire, taking guidance from the bivariate correlations in table 6.3. Variables that were not statistically significant were dropped along the way to conserve degrees of freedom. Finally, as a crude way of minimizing path dependence, we tried at the end to include again some of the variables that were dropped in the earlier stages of the model-fitting process.

Using this rough-and-ready procedure to fit an ordered probit model to the answers to question B1 yields the following regression (with asymptotic standard errors in parentheses):

6.12   OP(B1) = .83 CON + .61 TCU − .011 CONSUMER
    (n=192)   (.27)   (.28)   (.003)

               − .41 IMPLICIT + .13 STICKY
            (.18)   (.05)

    $\log L = -253.5$, $p = .000$, $R_M^2 = .08$, $R_E^2 = .21$

The p-value refers to the χ^2 statistic $2(L_1 - L_0)$ where:

  L_1 = the log likelihood for the estimated model (given by "log L" above);

  L_0 = the log likelihood for a model with only a constant.

It tells us whether the overall relationship is statistically significant. We also show two R^2 statistics. R_M^2 is Daniel McFadden's (1974) pseudo-R^2, defined as $1 - L_1/L_0$. R_E^2 is a variant on McFadden's formula constructed by Arturo Estrella (1995), defined as

$$1 - (L_1/L_0)^{-\frac{2}{n}\log L_0}.$$

Both measures range from 0 to 1 and are rough indicators of how much variance the model explains; but Estrella shows that his formula is analogous to the R^2 in a standard linear regression in ways that McFadden's formula is not.

The regression is highly significant. Of the variables in table 6.3 that showed a meaningful bivariate correlation with the importance of nominal contracting, only CONSUMER, IMPLICIT, and STICKY, plus two industry dummies—CON for construction and mining, and TCU for transportation, communications, and utilities—survived the multivariate analysis. Finally, one interviewer dummy remained significant and was also included, but its coefficient is not shown (and the results are insensitive to its removal).

Regression 6.12 treats the variable STICKY as if it were exogenous, which it clearly is not. If written contracts are the reason that some firms have sticky prices, then the positive correlation reflects reverse causality.[14] Thus, for those who worry that STICKY is an illegitimate regressor, the result of dropping it from regression 6.12 is:

6.13   OP(B1) = .50 CON + .66 TCU − .011 CONSUMER
       (n=191)   (.30)   (.28)   (.003)

              + .0095 GOVT − .33 IMPLICIT
               (.0053)   (.18)

       $\log L = -254.0$, p = .000, $R_M^2 = .08$, $R_E^2 = .20$.

The other coefficients do not change much, although GOVT now enters with a significant coefficient. Similarly, replacing STICKY by the answer to question A13(c) changes the other coefficients only modestly.

The coefficients in the above regressions are the β's in equation 6.9, that is, they represent the marginal effect of each regressor on the latent variable z. Since the units of z are arbitrary, the absolute magnitudes of these coefficients have no ready interpretation.

Other Aspects of Nominal Contracting

About half of our sample reported that nominal contracts play at least some role in slowing down price increases. It is natural to wonder about the symmetric question: Do contracts also slow down price decreases? It is not obvious a priori that they should, because customers would presumably be glad to ignore the contract if the seller were proposing to cut prices.

The answer nonetheless appears to be that contracts do indeed inhibit downward price adjustments as well, though somewhat less than for upward adjustments. Specifically, we asked the 101 firms that did not entirely reject theory B1 the following question:

B1(a). Do contracts also prevent prices from decreasing when demand or costs fall?

Of the ninety-seven respondents, about two-thirds said that contracts impart just as much inertia to price decreases as to price increases. About 4 percent said that contracts cause even more stickiness in the downward direction. But 28 percent told us that contracts are a less important source of stickiness when they want to cut prices. In fact, twelve companies said that contracts account for no stickiness in the downward direction.[15]

Owing perhaps to the enormous influence of George Stigler and James Kindahl's book (1970), many economists suspect that contract prices are "soft" when business is slack. Recall from chapter 4 that most firms told us that discounts from the contract price are uncommon. Here we asked two more pointed questions pertaining to business cycle conditions:

B1(b). Do discounts become more prevalent when sales are weak?

B1(c). Do discounts become deeper when sales are weak?

The answers are tabulated in table 6.4. Each reader may draw his or her own conclusions, but we interpret these numbers as saying that, within the contracting sector, there is relatively little price discounting in recessions. The answers to the two questions are, by the way, very highly correlated.[16]

It is natural to wonder whether the answers to question B1(b) are consistent with those given to question A8(d)—How often are discounts given? Indeed, they are. The Goodman-Kruskal gamma statistic between the two sets of answers is a very high .55, with an asymptotic standard error of .13.

Table 6.4   The Behavior of Discounts When Sales Are Weak

		Percentage of Firms Responding	
Code	Response	More Prevalent? (n=100)	Deeper? (n=100)
1	No	68.5%	73.0%
2	Yes, a little	14.0	13.0
3	Yes, much more	17.5	14.0
	Mean response	1.49	1.41

We asked the 101 firms that told us that contracts make their prices sticky one last question:

B1(d). Do these contracts also prevent the volume of sales and/or production from changing in the short run?

Ninety-seven companies responded. More than 63 percent of them said that contracts rarely or never rigidify quantities. The other 37 percent divided about evenly across the other three possible responses, which were: "in a minority of cases," "in many cases," and "in most or all cases." On average, then, we conclude that contracts impart just a little rigidity to quantity adjustments.

Chapter Summary

Nominal contracts that set prices for finite periods of time are perhaps the most obvious source of price stickiness. Although the theoretical justification for such contracts is thin, we estimated in chapter 4 that they cover about 25 percent of the relevant portion of the GDP. Thus the potential domain of this theory, though limited, is far from trivial.

About 37 percent of firms (weighted by GDP) "accept" this theory in the sense that they give it a rating of 3 or 4. The overall mean response of 2.11 on the four-point scale ranks the idea fifth among the twelve theories tested. Thus the nominal contracting bottle is either half full or half empty, depending on how you wish to look at it.

Apparently, nominal contracts slow down price adjustments considerably more in the construction and mining, TCU, and service sectors than they do in manufacturing and trade. They are a more important source of price stickiness for firms that do most of their business with other firms and for firms that report longer lags in adjusting prices. But they are less important for firms that make use of implicit contracts. Other attributes of firms get us nowhere in explaining the degree of acceptance of the nominal contracting theory. Indeed, our ability to predict who agrees with this theory and who does not is rather modest.

There is some—but not much—evidence of asymmetry in price adjustment; but it goes in the opposite direction from that usually assumed. To the extent that nominal contracts are the cause of sluggish price adjustments, prices are stickier upward than downward. Contrary to what is often suspected, firms tell us that weak sales do not normally provoke discounts off the contract price.[17] Finally, contracts that rigidify prices do not normally rigidify quantities.

Appendix

In a frictionless world, a firm would change its price in response to any change in its environment. Maintaining a fixed price would be costly. This appendix shows how the cost of maintaining a fixed price in the face of a demand shock depends on various characteristics of the firm: the slope of the marginal cost schedule, the level of marginal cost, and the elasticity of demand. Firms that would be expected to have relatively sticky prices based on these characteristics might also be predicted to rate the various theories of price stickiness more favorably.

The typical firm's profit function is:

$$\pi = PQ(P,\delta) - C(Q(P,\delta))$$

where δ is a demand shock and $C(Q)$ is a cost function. The slope of the profit function is given by

$$\partial\pi/\partial P = -Q(\epsilon - 1) + C'\epsilon Q/P.$$

Setting this slope equal to zero yields the familiar formula for the optimal price:

$$P* = C'\epsilon/(\epsilon - 1).$$

The loss from maintaining a fixed price after a demand shock, rather than moving to the new optimum, is given by the difference between profits at the optimal price and profits at the original (no longer optimal) price. Expressing the latter as a second-order Taylor expansion around the optimal price, this loss is:

$$\text{Loss} = \pi(P*) - \left[\pi(P*) + \pi_p(P*)\frac{\partial P*}{\partial\delta} + \frac{1}{2}\pi_{pp}(P*)\left(\frac{\partial P*}{\partial\delta}\right)^2\right]$$

$$= -\frac{1}{2}\frac{\partial^2\pi(P*)}{\partial P^2}\left(\frac{dP*}{d\delta}\right)^2$$

since $\pi_P = 0$ at the optimum.

To simplify the calculations that follow, assume a constant elasticity of demand ($\epsilon \equiv -Q_P P/Q$) and quadratic costs.[18] Given these assumptions, the second derivative of the profit function is:

$$\partial^2 \pi / \partial P^2 = -Q_P(\epsilon - 1) + \epsilon \frac{Q}{P} C'' Q_P + \epsilon \frac{C'}{P}\left(Q_P - \frac{Q}{P}\right)$$

$$= -(\epsilon - 1)\frac{Q}{P} - \epsilon^2 \frac{Q^2}{P^2} C'' \qquad \text{evaluated at P*.}$$

The change in the optimal price is given by

$$\partial P^* / \partial \delta = C'' \epsilon / (\epsilon - 1).$$

(This assumes the normalization $\partial Q / \partial \delta = 1$.) So the loss from maintaining a fixed price is:

$$\text{Loss} = -\frac{1}{2}\left[-(\epsilon - 1)\frac{Q}{P} - \epsilon^2 \frac{Q^2}{P^2} C''\right]\left(C'' \frac{\epsilon}{\epsilon - 1}\right)^2$$

$$= \frac{1}{2}\frac{\epsilon^4}{(\epsilon - 1)^2}\frac{Q^2}{P^2} C''^3 + \frac{1}{2}\frac{\epsilon^2}{\epsilon - 1}\frac{Q}{P} C''^2$$

The questions of interest are how this loss is affected by the slope of the marginal cost function (C''), the level of marginal cost (C'), and the elasticity of demand (ϵ). We take these up in turn.

The Slope of Marginal Cost

The effect of the slope of marginal cost on the loss from holding prices fixed is given by the derivative of the loss with respect to C''. The algebra is simple because P* does not itself depend on C'':

$$\frac{\partial \text{Loss}}{\partial C''} = \frac{3}{2}\frac{\epsilon^4}{(\epsilon - 1)^2}\frac{Q^2}{P^2} C''^2 + \frac{\epsilon^2}{\epsilon - 1}\frac{Q}{P} C'' > 0$$

A flatter marginal cost curve (a smaller C'') reduces the loss from price stickiness in response to a demand shock. Thus, the flatter the marginal cost curve, the stickier we would expect prices to be and the higher we would expect firms to rate the theories.

The Level of Marginal Cost

We next calculate the derivative of the loss from holding prices fixed with respect to the level of marginal cost (holding

C'' constant), noting that P* (and therefore Q) depends on this level:

$$\frac{\partial \text{Loss}}{\partial C'} = \frac{\epsilon^4}{(\epsilon - 1)^2} \frac{QC''^3}{P} \frac{d(Q/P)}{dC'} + \frac{1}{2} \frac{\epsilon^2}{\epsilon - 1} C''^2 \frac{d(Q/P)}{dC'}.$$

Because an increase in marginal cost raises P* and so reduces Q*, this expression is negative. As long as marginal cost is increasing ($C'' > 0$), a larger marginal cost leads to a smaller loss from holding price fixed despite a demand shock. Thus, we would expect prices to be stickier when marginal cost is relatively large. Intuitively, an adverse demand shock reduces Q and revenues; higher marginal cost buffers the impact on profits. However, when marginal cost is constant ($C'' = 0$), the loss from maintaining a fixed price does not depend on the level of marginal costs. This is because a demand shock does not affect P* when marginal cost is constant.

The Elasticity of Demand

We calculate the derivative of the loss from holding prices fixed with respect to the elasticity of demand in the same way, again noting that P* and Q depend on the elasticity. This time the algebra is a bit messier:

$$\frac{\partial \text{Loss}}{\partial \epsilon} = \frac{(\epsilon - 2)\epsilon^3}{(\epsilon - 1)^3} \frac{Q^2}{P^2} C''^3 + \frac{\epsilon^4}{(\epsilon - 1)^2} \frac{QC''^3}{P} \frac{d(Q/P)}{d\epsilon}$$

$$+ \frac{1}{2} \frac{\epsilon(\epsilon - 2)}{(\epsilon - 1)^2} \frac{QC''^2}{P} + \frac{1}{2} \frac{\epsilon^2}{\epsilon - 1} C''^2 \frac{d(Q/P)}{d\epsilon}$$

$$= \frac{\epsilon}{\epsilon - 1} C''^2 \left(\frac{\epsilon^2}{\epsilon - 1} \frac{Q}{P} C'' + \frac{1}{2} \right) \left[\frac{\epsilon - 2}{\epsilon - 1} \frac{Q}{P} + \epsilon \frac{d(Q/P)}{d\epsilon} \right]$$

Calculating that

$$\frac{\partial (Q/P)}{\partial \epsilon} = -(1 + \epsilon) \frac{Q}{P^2} \frac{dP*}{d\epsilon} = \frac{\epsilon + 1}{\epsilon(\epsilon - 1)} \frac{Q}{P}$$

leads to

$$\frac{\partial \text{Loss}}{\partial \epsilon} = \frac{\epsilon(2\epsilon - 1)}{(\epsilon - 1)^2} \frac{Q}{P} C''^2 \left(\frac{\epsilon^2}{\epsilon - 1} \frac{Q}{P} C'' + \frac{1}{2} \right) > 0.$$

A larger elasticity of demand leads to a larger loss from a fixed price, and hence presumably to less sticky prices. Intuitively, a larger elasticity means that any price differential has larger output consequences. In the extreme case of perfectly elastic demand there are enormous consequences from setting P anywhere other than P*. As in the previous case, however, this result depends on increasing marginal cost: When marginal cost is constant ($C'' = 0$), P* does not change with a demand shock. The cost of maintaining a sticky price is then zero, regardless of the elasticity of demand.

Chapter 7

Implicit Contracts

A verbal contract isn't worth the paper it's written on.
—SAMUEL GOLDWYN

Implicit Contracts in Customer Markets: Theory

The implicit contract theory was originated by Costas Azariadis (1975), Martin Baily (1974), and Donald Gordon (1974) to explain wage rigidity. Their idea was that risk-neutral firms provide a form of insurance to their risk-averse workers by stabilizing wages in the face of fluctuations in, say, product demand. This, they argued, leads to an equilibrium (implicit) contract in which employment varies over the cycle while wages remain constant. Because this contract is a risk-sharing arrangement based on optimizing behavior, it must—according to the dictates of neoclassical theory—apply to real rather than to nominal wages.

A few years later, Arthur Okun (1981) applied the idea to prices. This required some adaptation. First, the rationale for implicit contracts in what Okun called "customer markets" was no longer risk sharing. Instead, Okun suggested, firms stabilize prices in order to increase customer loyalty, that is, to decrease the price elasticity of demand. The idea is that customers shop around, but not randomly. Owing to search and other transactions costs, they are more likely to stick with their current supplier than to take their business elsewhere, ceteris paribus. But among the ceteris that might not be held paribus is the price. So stable prices both save customers shopping time and encourage them to look at a longer-run average price rather than the current spot price. In Okun's words (1981, 149):

> [S]ellers . . . can influence the shopping behavior of customers by pledging continuity of an offer. Once sellers commit themselves to maintaining an offer, they promote reliance on intertemporal comparison shopping by buyers. Yesterday's offer has a strong influence on today's demand.
>
> Sellers who have adopted that strategy are inhibited from exploiting increases in demand by raising the price . . . Conversely, when demand is temporarily weak, because sellers cannot pledge continuity of a bargain price, they are less likely to adopt one.

Second, while the implicit contract theory of wages is a theory of constant *real* wages, Okun clearly intended the implicit contract theory of prices to apply to *nominal* prices. Why? Okun's rationale is based on his personal judgments about when customers will consider it fair for a firm to raise its prices. At least some of the steps in his logic are open to dispute, however. Consider the following, for instance:

In Okun's (1981, 153) view, "Price increases that are based on cost increases are 'fair,' while those based on demand increases are often viewed as unfair." This judgment, for which Okun offers only the most casual sorts of evidence, might itself be called into question. But we believe it is probably correct. For one thing, it has received indirect, but nonetheless fairly strong, support from some hypothetical questions posed in a survey conducted by Daniel Kahneman et al. (1986). They found, for example, that most people deem it fair for a grocery store to charge more than the usual price for lettuce if the store had to pay more itself, but unfair to raise the price of a particular type of apple just because it is in short supply (but wholesale costs have not risen). Second, and more to the point, our survey results contain clear direct support for Okun's view, as will be seen later in this chapter.

But how are "costs" to be measured? (Among the many choices are: marginal versus average, long run versus short run, and historic versus replacement.) Okun argues, perhaps not very persuasively, that "the definition and measurement of costs need to be routinized and systematized . . . so that parts of the operation can be delegated to clerical workers . . . " (1981, 156). It is this dictum that leads him to conclude that prices must be based on (supposedly objective) historic costs rather than on forward-looking (and hence subjective) replacement costs. Even ignoring the fact—recognized by Okun— that customers may not know the firm's costs, one might legitimately wonder why pricing decisions need to be delegated in this way.

Yet, even if this point is granted, it is not clear why historical costs must be recorded in nominal terms rather than indexed. Okun discusses at length the reasons for using what he calls FIFO (first in, first out) pricing rather than LIFO (last in, first out) pricing. These boil down to:

- objectivity: Firms know their historic costs.

- stability: Firms want to avoid the costs of changing price tags and to commit to a price advertised to their customers.

But Okun's discussion seems to confound two distinct sources of cost increases. The replacement cost of a widget can rise either because its relative price increases or because there is economy-wide inflation. A reasonable standard of fairness might label the latter as "fair" but the former as "unfair." If so, that would point to an intermediate pricing strategy: indexed FIFO. Why, then, is indexed FIFO pricing not the accepted norm? The answer, we suppose—it is not given by Okun[1]—is that customers suffer from money illusion and so draw no distinction between firms that index their prices to overall inflation and firms that reap real capital gains on inventories.

Thus Okun's "invisible handshake" theory of the product market seems to be built on two central pillars. The first is the notion that both buyers and sellers can gain from organizing a market as a customer market rather than as a spot market. The firm benefits from a less elastic demand curve, and hence higher average profitability; and the customer economizes on transactions costs. But these advantages can be realized only if the relationship endures, which is what leads to the second element: an agreed-upon standard of fairness in pricing. In Okun's hands, this standard embodies both cost-based pricing (which is our theory B6; see chapter 11) and money illusion. Thus it boils down to fixing nominal prices based on historic costs—and then holding them constant for a while.

Testable Implications

As mentioned in chapter 1, the implicit contract theory has proven devilishly difficult to test empirically—whether in labor or product markets. After all, the alleged implicit contracts are tacit agreements that are not written down. And the theory does not predict literal price rigidity, but only that prices are relatively insensitive to fluctuations in demand. In fact, it is hard to know just what the observable implications of the theory are—other than that prices should respond more to costs than to demand. The survey methodology, however, permits a sharper test of the theory.

Most obviously, we can ask firms directly whether they have such tacit agreements with their customers. As chapter 5 reported, the theory gets a fairly high rating in our "popularity poll." More details on this matter are reported in this chapter.

Second, the theory applies only to regular customers with whom the firm expects (or wants) to have repeat business, not to off-the-street customers. Standard data sources do not tell us which firms have mainly one kind of customer and which have mainly the other. So, until this survey, no one knew whether the theory potentially applied to, say, 20 percent of GDP or 80 percent. As reported in chapter 4, we found that roughly 85 percent of GDP is sold to regular customers, and about nine-tenths of all firms do more than half their business with repeat customers. So the potential scope for the theory is vast.

As Okun notes, the theory does not imply that prices should be more rigid downward than upward. On the contrary, it suggests more or less symmetrical stickiness. Unfortunately, as explained in chapter 5, the precise question we posed does not offer a clear measure of the asymmetry, if any exists. The answers do, however, suggest considerable stickiness in both directions.

The central tenet of the theory—that prices should respond much more to cost shocks than to demand shocks—can be assessed directly by asking decision makers, and was.

One key hypothesis, however, was not tested by the questionnaire (except indirectly): the notion that prices are based on historical nominal costs, unadjusted for inflation. The reason for this is simple, and was mentioned in chapter 2: The dichotomy between relative prices and the absolute price level, which is so central and natural to economists, is neither central nor particularly natural to the thinking of ordinary business people. To them, the price means the price—period.

Formal indexation is something that actual price setters rarely encounter or think about much. This was evident from the interviews; the nominal/real distinction just never came up. More concrete and objective evidence is found in the answers to whether economy-wide inflation affects pricing decisions (question A7[b]), which were presented in chapter 4. If a firm has an implicit contract under which the nominal price will be stabilized for some time, the expected rate of inflation should be one of the most important determinants of the price it selects. Yet when asked if forecasts of future economy-wide inflation enter directly into their pricing decisions, roughly half the firms said it never does and only about 28 percent said it often does. (The others said it occasionally does.) From the viewpoint of economic theory, the correct answer should have been "always" for virtually all firms. This is, we think, evidence for money illusion—not just in what people say, but also in what they do.[2]

Survey Results on the Validity of the Theory

What, then, do our decision makers think of the invisible handshake theory of sticky prices? We answer this question by examining the survey responses to a series of questions.

Do Implicit Contracts Exist?

First, a preliminary factual question was asked of all firms—except the eleven companies reporting that virtually all sales are under explicit written contracts:

> B2(a). Another idea has been suggested for cases in which price increases are not prohibited by explicit contracts. The idea is that firms have implicit understandings with their customers—who expect the firms not to take advantage of the situation by raising prices when the market is tight. Is this idea true in your company? (n = 189)

Sixty-nine firms (35 percent of respondents) answered "no," and were asked no further questions about this theory.[3] The other 126 firms (64 percent) answered "yes"; and two firms gave equivocal answers that were neither yes nor no. (Three firms could not answer the question.) Thus, in round numbers, implicit contracts exist in about two-thirds of the economy.

In which sectors are implicit contracts most common? Actually, interindustry differences are quite minor. According to our survey results, implicit contracts are slightly more prevalent than average in manufacturing, and slightly less prevalent in transportation, communications, and utilities. But the differences are modest. The three remaining sectors (trade, services, and construction and mining) cluster tightly around the economy-wide average.

Are Implicit Contracts an Important Source of Price Stickiness?

Although the economy-wide answers to the "popularity poll" question were summarized in chapter 5, the question and its answers are repeated for convenience in table 7.1. Notice that, within the roughly two-thirds of the economy that enters into implicit contracts, these agreements are quite important sources of sticky prices: The average score is a high 3.16.

Like the existence of implicit contracts, the importance of implicit contracts as a source of price rigidity differs only modestly by industrial sector, although they appear to be most important in manufacturing and least important in construction (see table 7.2). A χ^2 test of association between question B2 and a set of industry dummies does not reject independence.[4]

Are Implicit Contracts More Important to Firms with More Repeat Customers?

The theory unequivocally suggests an affirmative answer to this question. How, after all, can a gift shop in an airport develop long-term

Table 7.1   B2. How Important Are Implicit Contracts in Slowing Down Price Adjustments in Your Company? (n = 196 Responses)

Code	Response	Percentage of Firms
1	Totally unimportant[a]	39.3%
2	Of minor importance	9.7
3	Moderately important	22.7
4	Very important	28.3

Mean response = 2.40
Mean if B2(a) = yes: 3.16   (n = 126)
Rank = 4th

[a] This category includes firms that answered "no" to question B2(a).

Table 7.2   The Importance of Implicit Contracts in Price Stickiness, by Sector (n = 196)

		Percentage of Firms				
Code	Response	Manufacturing	Trade	Services	Construction and Mining	Transportation, Communications, and Utilities
1	Totally unimportant[a]	29.7%	36.1%	44.2%	56.8%	47.1%
2	Of minor importance	10.9	19.4	5.8	2.3	5.9
3	Moderately important	28.3	12.5	24.0	22.7	17.7
4	Very important	31.2	31.9	26.0	18.2	29.4
	Mean response	2.61	2.40	2.32	2.02	2.29
	Sample size	69	36	52	22	17
	Mean if B2(a)=yes	3.13	3.06	3.33	2.88	3.44
	Sample size	52	24	29	12	9
	Rank	3rd	4th	4th	5th	5th

[a] This category includes firms that answered "no" to question B2(a).

relationships with its customers? Nonetheless, the data do not support this hypothesis. An ordered probit regression of the answers to question B2(a) (Do you have implicit contracts?) on the fraction of sales made to repeat customers (question A3) yields a t-statistic of merely 0.1. Although the effect is positive, the regression coefficient is not even close to significant. Thus Okun-style implicit contracts are not more common where firms have more regular customers.

Given the absence of correlation between variables B2(a) and A3, it is not surprising that an ordered probit regression of question B2 (the importance of the implicit contract theory) on A3 (repeat customers) yields a coefficient with an insignificant t-statistic of 1.0. As we shall see, this correlation becomes somewhat stronger in a multivariate setting. Nevertheless, the seemingly obvious hypothesis that implicit contracts rigidify prices more where firms sell more of their output to regular customers is—quite surprisingly—only very weakly supported by the data.

Asymmetrical Responses to Cost and Demand Shocks?

We observed in chapter 5 that the questions pertaining to the implicit contract theory do not permit a clean judgment on whether implicit contracts make prices more inertial in the upward or downward direction. The question about weak demand (B2[b]) was worded too differently from the main question about strong demand to make such a comparison:

> B2(b). What about when the demand for your products is weak? Are your customers then willing to let you hold your prices, or do they insist on price reductions? (n = 121)

For convenience, we repeat the responses to this question that were presented in chapter 5:

1 = usually let us hold prices	51.3%
2 = attitudes are mixed	20.0
3 = usually insist on price reductions	28.7

These responses do indicate considerable rigidity in the downward direction. But, again, there is no way to tell whether this rigidity is greater or less than in the upward direction.

What about Okun's more important asymmetry prediction: that prices respond much more to changes in cost than to changes in demand? We tested this hypothesis by posing the following question to those firms that did not reject the theory as totally unimportant:

> B2(c). Does the understanding that prices should remain fixed hold when your costs increase, or do customers see price increases as justified when costs increase? (n = 123)

Twelve companies did not answer, ten of them because their customers do not know what is happening to their costs. The remaining 111 gave the answers tabulated in table 7.3. Keeping in mind that this question is asked only if the firm reports that implicit contracts deter price increases when demand rises, these data constitute a pretty striking confirmation of Okun's hypothesis.[5]

Table 7.3   B2(c). When Costs Increase, Our Customers Normally . . .
             (n = 111 Responses)

Code	Response	Percentage of Firms
1	Still want us to hold our prices	15.3%
2	Attitudes are mixed	13.5
3	Tolerate price increases	71.2
Mean response = 2.56		

We pursued this matter further by asking firms that responded affirmatively to this question (by answering 2 or 3) whether their customers tolerate full pass-through of costs or only partial pass-through.[6] Of the ninety-two usable responses, 59 percent said that their customers tolerate full pass-through while 41 percent said that only partial pass-through would be tolerated. Combining these answers with those in table 7.3, we conclude something like the following. Among firms with implicit contracts of the Okun type, customers reject the notion that cost increases justify price increases in roughly 20 to 25 percent of the cases. About one-third (84.7 percent of 41.3 percent) have customers who accept partial, but not full, pass-through of costs into prices. And just under one-half (84.7 percent of 58.7 percent) have customers who tolerate full pass-through. Once again, this evidence seems broadly consistent with the view of "fair" price increases articulated by Okun.

Are these attitudes symmetric? That is, when costs decline, do customers expect the savings to be passed through to them in the form of lower prices? Or do the implicit contracts allow firms to pocket the profits from cost reductions? Table 7.4 reveals some

Table 7.4   B2(e). When Our Costs Decline, Our Customers Normally . . .
             (n = 88 Responses)

Code	Response	Percentage of Firms
1	Let us keep prices fixed	34.1%
2	Attitudes are mixed	15.3
3	Insist on price decreases	50.6
Mean response = 2.16		

asymmetry here, though perhaps in an unexpected direction: Customers are more likely to expect pass-through of cost increases than cost decreases. According to a conventional *t*-test (using the eighty-seven observations common to both questions), the mean answer to question B2(c) (see table 7.3) is significantly higher than the mean answer to question B2(e).[7] The breakdown between full and partial pass-through of cost decreases hardly differs from what it was in the case of cost increases, however.[8] Out of fifty-five respondents, 62 percent reported that their customers expect full pass-through, while 38 percent reported that partial pass-through is expected.

There is an "objective" check on the asymmetry results for cost versus demand shocks. Recall that we asked firms (in questions A13) how long they usually wait before changing prices after an increase or decrease in demand or costs. If we compare the answers only among the firms that report having implicit contracts (by answering 2 to question B2[a]), we obtain the following comparisons:

There is no notable difference in the delay of price reductions behind decreases in demand or cost. For price increases, there does appear to be a small difference—and in the direction assumed by Okun. But this difference of about ten days is neither large nor statistically significant: Among the seventy-two firms that provided answers to both questions A13(a) and A13(c), we can reject the equality of the means at the 10 percent, but not the 5 percent, significance level. Performing the same calculation for firms that "accept" the theory as an explanation for price stickiness, rather than those that report having implicit contracts, leads to a similar conclusion.

Table 7.5   A13. How Much Time Normally Elapses After a Significant [Increase/Decrease] in [Demand/Cost] Before You [Raise/Reduce] Your Prices?

Question	Type of Shock	Mean Lag (Months)	# of Observations
A13(a)	Demand up	3.2	80
A13(c)	Cost up	2.9	105
A13(b)	Demand down	3.3	80
A13(d)	Cost down	3.4	63

So, among firms with implicit contracts, there does appear to be a slight (and barely significant) tendency for prices to be stickier when demand rises than when costs increase. This is as Okun believed, though the magnitude of the difference is not impressive.

What Kinds of Firms Agree with the Theory Most?

Which attributes of firms help explain how a given firm rates the implicit contract theory? We have already mentioned that the most obvious candidate—the fraction of sales going to regular customers (REGULARS)—does not correlate well with the answers to question B2, and that interindustry differences are modest. But what about other variables? As discussed in chapter 6, several variables (FLATMC, MCPCT, ELAST, CYCLICAL, and STICKY) are expected to be correlated with all of the theories. Beyond those, the following seem to be likely candidates (correlations are summarized in table 7.6).

ELAST (question A4): As discussed in chapter 6, the profits of firms facing highly elastic demand will normally be relatively sensitive to price—implying a relatively large cost to holding prices fixed and therefore a negative correlation with any theory of price stickiness. But there is another reason to expect a correlation with the importance of implicit contracts that may go in the opposite direction.

Recall that Okun based his theory on the idea that firms enter into implicit contracts as a way to make their demand curves less elastic. If so, such contracts should appeal most to the companies with the most elastic demand curves. This appears to be a reason to expect ELAST to be positively correlated with both B2(a) (the existence of implicit contracts) and B2 (the importance of implicit contracts in rigidifying prices). Or is it? Actually, the firms most attracted to implicit contracts should be those most able to reduce their elasticities of demand. The size of the elasticity may be a rough-and-ready proxy for this. But, to the extent that such firms succeed in reducing their price elasticities, the positive correlation may disappear. On balance, the expected sign of the correlation between ELAST and B2 is uncertain—but certainly of interest.

Table 7.6 Bivariate Correlates of the Existence and Importance of Implicit Contracts

Description	Variable Name	Question	Expected Sign	Correlation with	
				Importance (B2)	Existence (B2[a])
General correlates of price stickiness					
Industry	INDUSTRY	—	undefined	$\chi_{24}^2 = 28.1$ (p = .26)	$\chi_8^2 = 10.2$ (p = .26)
Marginal cost	FLATMC	B7(a)	+	t = 0.1 (p = .94)	t = 0.4 (p = .17)
Fraction of costs that are variable	MCPCT	A12(b)	+	t = 0.1 (p = .98)	t = 0.3 (p = .80)
Elasticity of demand	ELAST	A4	?	t = 1.2 (p = .22)	t = 0.8 (p = .45)
Cyclically sensitive	CYCLICAL	A6	−	$\gamma = -.02$ (p = .85)	$\gamma = -.11$ (p = .37)
Price stickiness	STICKY	A10, A13	+	t = 1.8 (p = .07)	t = 1.8 (p = .07)
Predicted correlates of this theory					
Fraction sold to regular customers	REGULARS	A3	+	t = 1.0 (p = .30)	t = 0.1 (p = .91)
Fraction of sales to consumers	CONSUMER	A2(a)	−	t = 0.6 (p = .55)	t = 0.5 (p = .63)
Lose least loyal customers first?	LOYAL	B5(a)	+	$\gamma = .20$ (p = .07)	$\gamma = .39$ (p = .00)
Fraction of sales under contract	WRITTEN	A8	−	$\gamma = -.17$ (p = .04)	$\gamma = -.21$ (p = .05)
Customary interval for price reviews	INTERVAL	A9	+	$\gamma = .16$ (p = .11)	$\gamma = .20$ (p = .12)
Prices based on costs	COSTS	B6	+	$\gamma = .08$ (p = .29)	$\gamma = .17$ (p = .11)
Has costs of price adjustment	ADJCOSTS	B8(a)	+	$\gamma = .21$ (p = .02)	$\gamma = .22$ (p = .06)
Has costs of adjusting output	ADJCOSTQ	B8(j)	−	$\gamma = .14$ (p = .32)	$\gamma = .39$ (p = .03)
Other correlates					
Sales-inventory ratio	S/I	A16	?	t = 1.8 (p = .07)	t = 1.0 (p = .30)
Firms adjust nonprice elements	NONPRICE	B12(a)	?	$\gamma = .24$ (p = .08)	$\gamma = .42$ (p = .00)
Log of firm's annual sales	SIZE	ln(A1)	?	t = −1.5 (p = .15)	t = −2.2 (p = .03)

CONSUMER (question A2[a]): Consumers are presumably less likely than businesses to be involved in the sort of long-term buyer-seller relationships that lend themselves to implicit contracts. Hence we expect a negative correlation between CONSUMER and the answers to B2(a) and B2.

LOYAL (question B5[a]): Question B5(a) asks about elasticity in a different way, namely, by inquiring whether firms have groups of customers who differ in their "loyalty" to the firm, that is, in their sensitivity to price. While the association between the answers to this question and the attractiveness of implicit contracts may not be tight, it does seem plausible that firms that respond positively to question B5(a) would be more likely to enter into such contracts.

WRITTEN (question A8): Naturally, firms that make greater use of explicit written contracts should be less likely to enter into implicit contracts. So a predicted negative correlation is almost a matter of arithmetic.

INTERVAL (question A9): In expounding upon his theory, Okun suggested that "the firm can obtain and provide some benefits to its customers by specifying a period during which it expects to hold prices constant" (1981, 152). Since question A9 asks whether the firm has a regular time interval for price reviews, INTERVAL ought to correlate positively with the answers to B2(a) and perhaps B2— if Okun is right.

COSTS (question B6): Theory B6 pertains to cost-based pricing with lags. Since Okun hypothesized that firms base implicit contract prices on a concept of "fairness" grounded in costs, it seems plausible that firms that base their prices more on costs should be more likely to enter into implicit contracts.

ADJCOSTS (question B8[a]): Since implicit agreements to stabilize prices should be more attractive to firms for which it is costly to change prices, the presence of menu costs should enhance the attractiveness of implicit contracts.

ADJCOSTQ (question B8[j]): The questionnaire asked firms that report adjustment costs for changing prices whether they also have adjustment costs for changing quantities. The thought here was that firms, which report adjustment costs for quantities, would presumably be less likely to enter into contracts that stabilize prices.

B2 and B2(a) are ordered categorical variables, so, as explained in chapter 6, we measure correlation in one of three ways:

- for a continuous variable: the *t*-statistic for the coefficient in an ordered probit regression;

- for an ordered categorical variable: the Goodman-Kruskal gamma statistic (with *p*-value based on the asymptotic standard error);

- for an unordered categorical variable: the *p*-value from a χ^2 test.

In each case, table 7.6 reports the *p*-value of the relevant statistic.

Correlations between most of the thirteen aforementioned variables and the importance of implicit contracts (question B2) have the expected sign, but only four of them—STICKY, LOYAL, WRITTEN, and ADJCOSTS—are statistically significant at the 10 percent level. These same four variables also are the only ones that are significantly correlated with the existence, as opposed to the importance, of implicit contracts (question B2[a]). (ADJCOSTQ is also significantly correlated with B2(a), but the correlation has the wrong sign.) As noted above, it is striking that REGULARS is uncorrelated with either implicit contracts question.

Besides the variables that are suggested by "theory," a few unexplained correlations appear in the data (with signs as indicated) between B2 or B2(a) and the following two variables:

S/I (question A16): Firms that turn over their inventory more frequently (that is, have a higher sales-to-inventory ratio) are more likely to cite the existence and importance of implicit contracts.

NONPRICE (question B12[a]): Firms that vary other nonprice dimensions of their product are more likely to view the implicit contract theory favorably.

SIZE (question A1): Larger firms are less likely to report the existence of implicit contracts.

Which of these bivariate correlations survive in a multivariate setting? Following the orderly search process described in chapter 6 yields the following multivariate ordered probit model for how firms rate the theory (with asymptotic standard errors in parentheses):

7.1   OP(B2) = $-.93$ TCU + .11 STICKY + .013 REGULARS
   (n = 137)   (.63)   (.06)   (.006)

       $-$ .19 WRITTEN + .22 INTERVAL + 2.14 UNION
       (.07)   (.11)   (.93)

       $-.012$ CONC
       (.006)

    log L = -201.8, p = .005, R_M^2 = .05, R_E^2 = .14.

As before, the *p*-value is for the χ^2 test of the overall significance of the regression, R_M^2 is McFadden's pseudo-R^2, and R_E^2 is Estrella's suggested improvement. While the regression is significant, it has relatively little explanatory power.

Other things equal, implicit contracts are a less important source of price stickiness in the transportation, communications, and utilities sector (TCU), where written contracts are more prevalent (WRITTEN), and in more concentrated industries (CONC). They are more important where customers are more likely to represent repeat business (REGULARS), where firms have regular time intervals between price reviews (INTERVAL), where prices are more sticky (STICKY), and in more unionized industries (UNION). Interestingly, the correlation with REGULARS is stronger here than in the bivariate analysis above (but the sample size is very different). No interviewer dummies were significant in the multivariate setting.

There are two potential problems with this regression. First, the variable CONC, which is missing for 56 of the 200 observations, restricts the sample size to 137. Second, as mentioned in the last chapter, some people would argue that STICKY is not a proper regressor. If CONC is dropped from the regression, the sample size rises dramatically, but three of the remaining regressors (TCU, UNION, and REGULARS) nevertheless become insignificant. On the other hand, it turns out that the elimination of CONC makes LOYAL—the dummy variable indicating whether firms have customers with different degrees of loyalty—gain statistical significance. The resulting model is:

7.2   OP(B2) = .10 STICKY + .13 INTERVAL − .15 WRITTEN
   (n = 186)   (.05)   (.09)   (.06)

   + .33 LOYAL
    (.17)

   $\log L = -274.0$, $p = .006$, $R_M^2 = .03$, $R_E^2 = .08$.

If, instead, STICKY is dropped and CONC is retained, we get results that are virtually the same as 7.1. Thus the really robust (partial) correlates of the importance of the implicit contracts theory appear to be WRITTEN and STICKY; INTERVAL, REGULARS, and LOYAL are somewhat less robust. None of these findings are very profound.

Chapter Summary

Arthur Okun (1981) theorized that transactions costs induce firms and customers to enter into implicit agreements that stabilize prices when demand fluctuates. But he believed that such implicit contracts are less likely to rigidify prices when costs rise, because cost increases signal when it is "fair" to raise prices. According to Okun, these implicit contracts display strong money illusion: It is nominal prices, he suggests, not real prices that are stabilized, and nominal, historical costs serve as the standard for "fair" pricing.

Since Okun's book, the distinction between "customer markets" and "auction markets" has become a commonplace in modern Keynesian macroeconomics. But until now economists could only guess how much of the GDP was sold in customer versus auction markets. Responses to this survey suggest that Okun-type implicit contracts cover roughly two-thirds of the private, nonfarm, unregulated, for-profit GDP in the United States. These contracts are slightly more prevalent in the manufacturing sector and slightly less prevalent among utilities. Surprisingly, however, firms with a greater share of "regular" customers are not more likely to enter into implicit contracts.

Across the whole economy, theory B2 is the fourth most popular of our twelve theories. And within the two-thirds of the economy that actually "writes" implicit contracts, these agreements appear to be quite an important source of price stickiness—rating about 3.2 on our four-point scale. Furthermore, the notion that prices should be stabilized seems to apply a bit more to demand shocks than to cost shocks, just as Okun claimed. Customers of firms with implicit contracts usually accept cost increases as valid justifications for price increases; almost half even accept full pass-through of costs into prices.

Chapter 8

Judging Quality by Price

What we obtain too cheap we esteem too lightly.
                                                —THOMAS PAINE

Adverse Selection in the Product Market: Theory

During the 1970s and 1980s, economic theorists increasingly turned their attention to the problems raised by imperfect information in markets and, in particular, to asymmetrically imperfect information—cases in which one party to a transaction is better informed than the other. Literally hundreds of papers were written exploring the implications of two phenomena that potentially bedevil such markets: adverse selection and moral hazard. It is only a slight exaggeration to say that the rulebook of economic theory was substantially rewritten in the process. Joseph Stiglitz (1987), for example, referred to the "repeal" of the law of supply and demand.

Adverse selection was offered by Stiglitz and coauthors (especially Andrew Weiss and Bruce Greenwald) as an explanation for why wages and interest rates do not fall promptly to clear markets. According to Stiglitz and Weiss (1981), a bank unable to distinguish between good credit risks and bad ones will hesitate to raise interest rates in tight markets for fear that only its less creditworthy applicants will continue to apply for loans at the higher rates. According to Weiss (1980), firms that are unable to identify their best workers will hesitate to cut wages in a downturn out of fear that wage reductions will induce the better workers to quit.[1]

The application of this idea to price rigidity is straightforward: Firms may hesitate to cut prices in slack markets out of fear that their customers will infer—incorrectly—that product quality has been reduced. Franklin Allen (1988) modeled a variant of this idea in which the stickiness result turns out to be a good deal more subtle than it appears. Suppose firms in a competitive industry must choose between producing high-quality or low-quality goods. Consumers perceive the quality difference only after they buy the product, so the two types sell for the same price. A firm faces the following trade-off. High-quality goods cost more to produce, and so yield lower current profits. But consumers do not want low-quality goods and will stop patronizing firms that sell them. Hence a firm that opts for low quality today increases its current profits but sacrifices its expected future profit stream.

Thus, Allen models quality as an investment in future profits. Understanding this point is the key to understanding why unobservable quality differences lead to price stickiness in Allen's model, but only if demand shocks are sufficiently serially correlated. With strong positive serial correlation, a favorable demand shock today signals above-average profit opportunities in the future and hence encourages greater investments in quality. But in the absence of serial correlation, Allen shows, prices are actually less sticky than when quality is observable—a surprising result.

Allen's model passes with flying colors the main tests that academic economics imposes on theories these days. It is based on solid and fairly intricate deductive reasoning. It can be expressed elegantly in mathematical language. And it rides (rather than opposes) current waves of fashion. As a result, the notion that price reductions might be inhibited by judging quality by price has come into common currency. Unfortunately, no one knows how well the theory performs on a fourth criterion: empirical veracity. Do firms really believe that their customers judge quality by price? Is that why prices do not fall in slumps? Allen's "empirical evidence" consists of the observation that prices of automobiles and agricultural equipment dropped much less during the Great Depression than did prices of petroleum and agricultural products.[2] We need rather more evidence than that.

In a sense, the adverse selection theory is the quintessential example of why Blinder originally chose such an unorthodox way to study price stickiness. The theory is not just untested, it is virtually untestable by conventional methods. After all, the basic premise is that certain critical dimensions of quality are unobservable—even by the people who buy the product (at least before the fact). How, then, can any objective data tell a poor econometrician whether or not the theory is valid?

Some economists like to take refuge in the Friedmanesque dictum that theories should be judged by their predictions, not their assumptions. But this gets us nowhere in this case because we already know that prices move sluggishly. Price stickiness is precisely what motivated not only this theory but also its competitors. So an econometric finding that prices move "slowly" (by some standard) tells us nothing about the validity of the theory. The interviews which form the basis for this study, of course, were designed precisely to shed light on the reasons *why* prices are sticky.

The Popularity of the Theory

Since Allen's model is only one specific version of the more general idea that customers may judge quality by price, we phrased the question more generally, along the following lines:

> B3(a). Another idea is that firms hesitate to reduce their prices because they fear that customers will interpret a price cut as a signal that the quality of the product has been reduced. Is this idea true in your company?

If this question was answered yes, we next asked:

> B3. How important is it in discouraging or delaying price decreases in your company?

Do actual price setters believe that judging quality by price inhibits price reductions? Not if their own words are to be believed. This theory rates flat last among the twelve theories tested, with a mean score of just 1.33 on the one-to-four scale used in earlier chapters. As mentioned previously, this is an amazingly negative evaluation. The distribution of responses is shown in table 8.1.

The main factor behind this dismal showing is clear in the data. The vast majority of firms—78.5 percent to be precise—deny the premise. They simply do not believe that their customers would "interpret a price cut as a signal that the quality of the product has been reduced." Among the 42 firms that accept the premise, the the-

Table 8.1   B3. How Important Is Judging Quality by Price in Discouraging or
Delaying Price Decreases in Your Company? (n = 200 Responses)

Code	Response	Percentage of Firms
1	Totally unimportant[a]	81.5%[a]
2	Of minor importance	8.0
3	Moderately important	6.3
4	Very important	4.3

Mean response = 1.33
Mean if quality is judged by price: 2.56 (n = 42)
Rank = 12th

[a] This category includes firms that said that their customers do not judge quality by price by answering "no" to question B3(a).

ory attains a respectable average score of 2.56. But there are simply too few such firms to have much of an impact on the aggregate score.

These negative results hold more or less uniformly across all industries. The theory ranks last in the manufacturing and transportation, communications, and utilities (TCU) sectors, second to last (with a mean score of only 1.20!) in trade, and third from last in the other two industrial sectors. It places last among cyclically insensitive industries (with a mean of 1.37) and next to last among cyclically sensitive ones (mean of 1.36). The theory's few boosters seem to be concentrated in the service sector. Of the twenty companies awarding the theory a score of 3 or better, eleven sell services. But this should not be misconstrued as a finding that the adverse selection theory is widely accepted in the service sector; in fact, its mean score there is only 1.61.

However, it may be premature to discard this theory altogether. We can speculate—and it is only a speculation—that the theory might still have relevance for a firm's choice of the *typical* price for a product, even if it does not affect the decision to change a price in response to market conditions. A price that is low because it is "on sale" may not signal low quality in the same way as a price that is typically very low. Our focus is on price stickiness, so we worded question B3 in terms of price changes signaling a reduction in quality. And for our purposes, the theory clearly has no merit. But for other purposes it might.

Other Aspects of the Theory

The theory that judging quality by price inhibits price reductions was developed to explain downward price rigidity, and it seems to apply most naturally in that direction. Hence that is the way the main question (B3) was posed in the questionnaire. However, to test for symmetry or asymmetry, we also posed the question in the opposite direction:[3]

B3(c). What about applying this idea to price increases? That is, are you encouraged to raise prices because you think customers will interpret higher prices as an indication of higher quality? (n = 172)

1 = rarely or never	79.1%
2 = sometimes	16.9
3 = most of the time	2.3
4 = always or almost always	1.7
Mean response = 1.27	

As was noted in chapter 5, the answers to this question indicate approximate symmetry: the theory is rejected by the vast majority of firms for both price increases and decreases.

Let us return now to the main question. As mentioned earlier, 78.5 percent of the sample answered "no" to question B3(a), thereby rejecting the theory out of hand. Another 3 percent of the sample answered "yes," but then rated the theory "totally unimportant" as an explanation of (downward) price rigidity. The remaining thirty-seven firms—which had just told us that the theory has some relevance for them—were then asked under what circumstances the idea applies. Specifically:

B3(b). Does this idea apply only when price cuts are indicated by weak demand, only when price cuts are indicated by lower costs, or in both cases?

The thirty-six responses (one firm did not answer) are tabulated in table 8.2. They indicate that—within the minority of firms to which the theory applies—judging quality by price applies whether price cuts are indicated by demand or cost conditions. But there is a hint here that the theory works better for demand shocks than for cost shocks.

Table 8.2   B3(b). Does Judging Quality by Price Apply When Demand
Declines or When Costs Decline? (n = 36 Responses)

Code	Response	Percentage of Firms
1	Applies only to weak demand	31.9%
2	Applies to both	59.7
3	Applies only to lower costs	8.3

Mean response = 1.76

Correlates of Judging Quality by Price

What attributes of individual firms correlate with their evaluation of
the adverse selection theory? Of the several variables discussed in
chapter 6 (FLATMC, MCPCT, ELAST, CYCLICAL, and STICKY) that
are expected to be correlated with all of the theories, only STICKY is
significantly correlated with the importance of judging quality by price
(table 8.3). Apart from those, the following variables might be thought
to have some intrinsic relationship (if we are not too strict about the
concept) to a firm's ranking of theory B3. But only in the cases of the
first two variables is there a strong a priori case for correlation.

CONSUMER (question A2[a]): On the presumption that businesses are more knowledgeable buyers than are consumers, judging
quality by price should be more important when more sales are
made to consumers (rather than to other businesses). So we expect
a positive correlation. Alternatively, we expect a negative correlation
with the share of sales going to businesses (BUSINESS, question
A2[b]). Both of these expected correlations are borne out in the data.

REGULARS (question A3): Since regular customers should be
able to recognize quality changes better than occasional customers,
judging quality by price should be—and is—less important to firms
that sell more of their output to regular customers.

STOCK (question A15[a]): Goods can be produced either to stock
or to order. Since goods produced to order are at least somewhat
customized, it seems plausible—but not certain—that judging quality by price would be more common when goods are produced to
stock. It turns out to be true.

POINTS (question B4[a]): It is at least plausible—though hardly
a tight deduction—that misperceptions like judging quality by price
are more important where psychological pricing points are more

important. This is strongly confirmed in the data. Indeed, the correlation is one of the strongest in the data set.

FREQ (question A10): If prices are changed frequently in the normal course of business, then consumers are less likely to think that price changes indicate quality changes. So the presumptive correlation is negative. Of course, FREQ is one component of STICKY, which we expect to be positively correlated with any of the theories simply because firms with flexible prices might not like any theory of price stickiness.[4] This correlation is of the expected sign, but is not statistically significant.

LOYAL (question B5[a]): This question, in part, picks out firms whose clientele divides into "loyal" and "casual" constituencies—a division that is similar, but not identical, to "regular" versus "occasional," and so should display the same (negative) correlation as REGULARS. But it does not—the correlation is of the wrong sign.

NONPRICE (question B12[a]): The expected correlation here is unclear. On the one hand, firms that see product quality as an important nonprice determinant of demand may be more concerned about potential adverse consequences from judging quality by price. (Of course, quality competition is only one among several possible reasons to answer "yes" to question B12[a]). On the other hand, firms that actually use changes in quality as a competitive tool must be less concerned. In fact, the correlation is positive but insignificant.

In addition, the rating of theory B3 appears to be positively correlated with whether the firm uses economy-wide output or inflation forecasts in setting its prices (OUTLOOK and INFLATION), and weakly negatively correlated with unionization. We see no obvious reason for these correlations and are inclined to view them as coincidental.

In a multivariate analysis, the production-to-stock variable was dropped because it reduces the sample size substantially. The best ordered probit model for the answers to question B3 was (with asymptotic standard errors in parentheses):

8.1　　$OP(B3) = -.88$ CON $- .0090$ BUSINESS $+ .12$ STICKY
　　$(n = 194)$　　$(.56)$　　　　$(.0034)$　　　　　　$(.07)$

　　　$+ .32$ OUTLOOK $+ .72$ POINTS
　　　$(.14)$　　　　　　$(.27)$

　　$\log L = -116.9$, $p = .000$, $R_M^2 = .13$, $R_E^2 = .17$.

Table 8.3 Bivariate Correlates of the Importance of Judging Quality by Price

Description	Variable Name	Question	Expected Sign	Correlation	
General correlates of price stickiness					
Industry	INDUSTRY	—	undefined	$\chi_{20}^2 = 19.9$	$(p = .47)$
Marginal cost	FLATMC	B7(a)	+	$t = -.7$	$(p = .46)$
Fraction of costs that are variable	MCPCT	A12(b)	+	$t = -1.2$	$(p = .23)$
Elasticity of demand	ELAST	A4	−	$t = -1.0$	$(p = .34)$
Cyclically sensitive	CYCLICAL	A6	−	$\gamma = -.01$	$(p = .94)$
Price stickiness	STICKY	A10, A13	+	$t = 2.1$	$(p = .04)$
Predicted correlates of this theory					
Fraction of sales to consumers	CONSUMER	A2(a)	+	$t = 2.1$	$(p = .04)$
Fraction of sales to businesses	BUSINESS	A2(b)	−	$t = -2.4$	$(p = .02)$
Fraction sold to regular customers	REGULARS	A3	−	$t = -2.5$	$(p = .01)$
Fraction produced to stock	STOCK	A15(a)	+	$t = 1.9$	$(p = .06)$
Pricing points	POINTS	B4(a)	+	$\gamma = .56$	$(p = .00)$
Frequency of price changes	FREQ	A10	−	$t = -1.1$	$(p = .26)$
Lose least loyal customers first?	LOYAL	B5(a)	−	$\gamma = .16$	$(p = .36)$
Firms adjust nonprice elements	NONPRICE	B12(a)	?	$\gamma = .28$	$(p = .18)$
Other correlates					
Economic outlook affects prices	OUTLOOK	A7(a)	?	$\gamma = .26$	$(p = .08)$
Inflation outlook affects prices	INFLATION	A7(b)	?	$\gamma = .30$	$(p = .02)$
Unionization rate in industry	UNION	—	?	$t = -1.7$	$(p = .09)$

As in previous chapters, the *p*-value tests the overall significance of the regression, R_M^2 is McFadden's pseudo-R^2, and R_E^2 is Estrella's suggested measure. In this case, the regression's explanatory power is mediocre. Other things equal, judging quality by price is a less important source of price stickiness in the construction and mining sector (CON) and where a greater fraction of sales are made to other businesses (BUSINESS). The theory is more important among firms with sticky prices (STICKY), firms that use forecasts of the economic outlook in setting their prices (OUTLOOK), and firms that report the existence of threshold prices (POINTS). In addition, one interviewer dummy (not shown) was significant.

Because some readers may worry that STICKY is not a legitimate explanatory variable, we reran the equation without this variable. This change yielded similar results, except that firms that use forecasts of inflation (INFLATION), rather than firms that use forecasts of the economic outlook (OUTLOOK), now show a significantly positive correlation with the theory.

Chapter Summary

The phenomenon of adverse selection has been used to provide a theoretical rationale for price stickiness—namely, that firms hesitate to cut prices in slumps out of fear that consumers will misinterpret price cuts as reductions in quality. Franklin Allen (1988) provided an explicit model of this idea in which stickiness emerges only if serial correlation of demand shocks is sufficiently high. But, to our knowledge, there had been no empirical evidence either for or against the theory—until now. Indeed, such evidence is hard, perhaps impossible, to come by with conventional methods because the quality differences on which the theory is based are unobservable.

One unorthodox way to "test" the theory is simply to ask firms whether they (a) believe their customers judge quality by price and (b) see this phenomenon as a significant source of price stickiness. Apparently, the usual answers to both questions are no. According to our survey, this theory is the least popular among the twelve tested. Only about 20 percent of firms, half of them in the service industries, report that their customers judge quality by price, and only about half of these "agree with" the theory by giving it a score of 3 or higher. To the extent that the adverse selection theory of the product market applies anywhere, however, it seems to apply about equally to price increases and price decreases and regardless of whether they come from cost or demand shocks.

Judging quality by price is a more important source of price stickiness among firms with sticky prices, firms that produce to stock (rather than to order), and firms that believe that important psychological pricing points affect demand in their markets. It is a less important source of price stickiness among firms that sell their output mainly to other businesses, and is less applicable in the construction and mining sector than elsewhere.

Chapter 9

Psychological Pricing Points

The Idea: A Psychologically Kinked Demand Curve?

The next theory tested in the survey did not emerge from the economic literature at all. It has its roots, instead, in the folklore of marketing and seems more closely related to psychologists' concept of "salience" than to economists' models of optimizing behavior.[1] The idea is that certain prices—such as round numbers—have such psychological significance to consumers that they form a kind of barrier against price increases. So prices get "stuck" at numbers like $9.99 or $29.95, rather than move up to, say, $10.32 or $31.43. Such barriers can be breached, of course; but it takes more than the usual stimulus to do so. In that sense, pricing points can be a source of price stickiness.

For example, suppose a particular pair of shoes is selling for $49.99. A firm that perceives a small outward shift of its demand curve or a small upward shift in its marginal cost curve may choose not to raise its price to, say, $51 out of fear that the negative response from its customers will be unusually large. In economists' terms, such a firm believes there is a significant concave kink in its demand curve at the pricing point: Demand there is much more elastic for small price increases than for small price decreases. (See figure 9.1.)

As is well known from the theory of the kinked demand curve, the presence of such a kink tends to rigidify prices under profit maximization because, for example, modest changes in marginal

Figure 9.1   Pricing Points

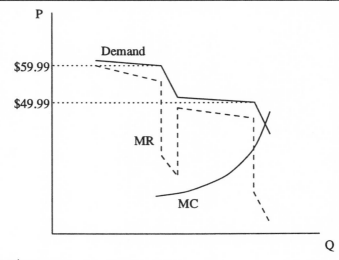

P   = price
Q   = quantity
MR = marginal revenue
MC = marginal cost

cost will elicit no price response. But there is one important difference. Since the psychological barrier presumably relates to nominal
prices, not real prices, this version of the kinked demand curve can
deliver what the standard Hall-Hitch version cannot: an explanation of nominal price stickiness.[2]

As previously noted, the pricing-point idea is based on the folklore of retail merchandising.[3] (Why else would all those prices end
in ninety-nine cents?) It entered the economic literature in an
unusual way. In a detailed study of the prices of three catalogue
companies, Anil Kashyap (1995) noted discrepancies between
actual behavior and the predictions of virtually all the economic
theories he considered. In discussing their pricing policies with practitioners, Kashyap heard the pricing points theory suggested as an
explanation of their strategy.

Upon investigation, however, Kashyap found only limited evidence that these catalogue companies actually price this way. Chapter 2 mentioned that retail food prices end more frequently in forty-
one to fifty cents or seventy-five to one hundred cents than in other

digits, and Kashyap found this to be true in his sample as well. But that can happen if prices always adjust promptly to changes in demand or costs but are simply "rounded off" for convenience. The reasons for such rounding might make an interesting psychological story in itself, but they would not constitute a source of sticky prices. Kashyap did find some limited evidence of stickiness, however. Controlling for cost shocks and for competitors' prices, he found that price changes were less likely to occur when the price was near a (somewhat arbitrarily defined) price point. This finding was statistically significant, however, only for the low-inflation years in his sample. In any case, even if there were strong evidence that three catalogue companies price this way, it would not tell us much about how important pricing points are across the entire economy.

Furthermore, the "theory" is not a full-blown theory at all. It leaves many questions unanswered. What happens, for example, when inertia is overcome and the psychological barrier is breached? Do prices normally jump from one pricing point (say, $49.99) to another (say, $59.99)?[4] And what happens in the downward direction, when demand or costs fall? Do psychological thresholds make firms hesitant to cut prices from, say, $49.99 to $48.50? The survey instrument gives us a chance not only to assess the theory's economy-wide applicability, but also to answer questions such as these. It also enables us to test what appear to be "obvious" implications, such as that pricing points should be most important in retailing and, more generally, to firms that sell mainly to consumers rather than to other businesses.

Survey Results on the Validity of the Theory

Are Kashyap's catalogue firms typical of American industry? We approached this question in two stages. First, we asked each firm if it thinks it has critical threshold prices. Specifically, the question was:

> B4(a). Another idea is that particular threshold prices are more attractive to customers than other prices. For example, a store might think that a shirt sells much better at $19.95 or $20 rather than $20.10.[5] Is this idea true in your company?

The sample split almost exactly down the middle on this question, with half answering "yes" and half answering "no." We then asked the 102 firms that did not answer no to the main question:[6]

B4. How important is it in deterring price increases in your company?

Their answers are tabulated in table 9.1.

The results of the "popularity poll" are pretty clear, and not very supportive of the theory. At the factual level, the pricing-point bottle is half full and half empty in that half the firms recognize the applicability of the idea and half deny it. But, even within the first half, the theory is of only modest importance—receiving a mean score of just 2.49. And since it is, by definition, of no importance to the other half, its economy-wide significance as an explanation of price stickiness is quite minor (mean score = 1.76).

Note, however, that the importance of retail firms in the pricing of final goods is disproportionate to their value added. Car dealers and supermarkets, for example, contribute relatively little of the value added in the items they sell. Yet these are the firms that determine the prices at which automobiles and food are sold. (Of course, the prices they charge are heavily influenced by the costs of their inputs.) Retail sales in 1991 totaled $1,856 billion, or about 74 percent of the goods portion of private, for-profit, unregulated, nonfarm GDP—the part of GDP that is relevant for this survey.[7] By contrast, the value added of the retail sector was only 21.3 percent of the relevant portion of goods GDP.

Table 9.1   B4. How Important Are Threshold Prices in Deterring Price Increases in Your Company? (n = 200 Responses)

Code	Response	Percentage of Firms
1	Totally unimportant[a]	59.5%
2	Of minor importance	15.5
3	Moderately important	15.0
4	Very important	10.0

Mean response = 1.76
Mean among those having threshold prices: 2.49 (n = 102)
Rank = 8th

[a] This category includes firms that said they do not have threshold prices by answering no to question B4(a).

It is natural, therefore, to wonder whether the pricing point idea applies especially well to retailers or, more generally (since we have only seventeen retailers in our sample), to firms that sell directly to consumers. We would expect it to, and the survey answers confirm these expectations in both cases.

Fifteen of our seventeen retailers (88 percent) expressed the belief that their customers do have such psychological pricing points; only 47 percent of other firms did so. This difference is highly significant (t = 3.3). Among the seventeen retail firms, the mean rating of theory B4 was 2.62, which is much higher than its mean score in the rest of the sample (1.67). This difference, too, is highly significant (t = 3.7).

Unfortunately, responses from just seventeen firms are not much to go on. As noted in chapter 4, the overwhelming majority of goods and services represented by our sample are sold to other businesses, not to consumers. In fact, one way to split the sample is to distinguish between those businesses that sell anything to consumers (89 firms) from those that do not (107 firms).[8] When we do this, the presumed implication of the theory is, once again, clearly borne out. The mean score for theory B4 is 2.07 among firms that sell to consumers versus only 1.48 among those that do not. The difference is significant at any conceivable level (t = 4.1). Most of the gap stems from the answers to question B4(a): 71 percent of firms that sell to consumers answered "yes" to this question, versus only 34 percent of firms that do not sell to consumers. Once again, this difference is highly significant (t = 5.5).

Other Aspects of the Theory

One interesting question about the pricing points theory is whether, when one firm breaks the psychological barrier—say, by charging $72 for a pair of shoes rather than $69.95—other firms consider it broken and therefore raise their prices promptly. According to our respondents, the answer is "not necessarily." The precise question, which was posed only to firms that did not totally reject the theory, was:

B4(b). Is the "barrier" broken once one firm raises its price above the critical threshold, so that other firms quickly follow suit? (n = 78)

The answers were:

rarely or never	32.7%
sometimes	26.3
usually or always	41.0

Almost as many firms believe this behavior to be rare as view it to be the norm.

In the marketing literature, pricing points are generally, if not exclusively, invoked in the upward direction: Firms allegedly hesitate before raising prices *above*, say, $69.95. That is why the main theory question (B4) pertained to barriers to price increases, not price decreases. Nonetheless, it is reasonable to wonder whether pricing points also dissuade firms from cutting prices because, say, they do not believe they can sell much more at $68.50 than at $69.95. Apparently, this is not the case; the assumed asymmetry really is present. Table 9.2 shows the asymmetry question we asked and the answers we received. When you recall that this question was asked only of the firms which reported that pricing points deter price increases, at least a little, it is clear that the answers signify a substantial degree of asymmetry. Psychological pricing points apparently apply mainly to price increases.[9]

If particular numbers—such as those ending in ninty-five cents, or nine dollars—have special psychological significance, it would seem plausible that prices would jump from one barrier to another, say from $69.95 to $79.95, when prices rise. Do they? We asked our firms the following question:

B4(c). Once the barrier is broken, do firms in your industry normally raise their prices all the way up to the next critical threshold (e.g., from $19.95 to $20.95), or are smaller increases typical? (n = 72)

The answers were rather surprising:

rarely	50.7%
sometimes	23.6
usually	25.7

Similar answers were obtained when we posed the same question in the downward direction.[10] Only 36 percent of respondents said

Table 9.2 B4(d). Do Thresholds Also Deter Small Price Decreases When Demand or Costs Fall? (n = 78)

1 = rarely or never	48.7%
2 = sometimes	22.4
3 = always or almost always	28.8
Mean response = 1.80	

prices normally fall all the way to the next threshold; 64 percent said they fall less. Apparently threshold prices are walls, not magnets.

Correlates of Pricing Points as a Source of Sticky Prices

What kinds of firms see the pricing point theory as an important source of price stickiness? Following the format of earlier chapters, table 9.3 reports bivariate correlations between various firm characteristics and whether the firm has pricing points (question B4[a]) and the firm's ranking of the theory (question B4).

We have already noted that pricing points are more important if the firm sells more of its output to consumers (CONSUMER), and less important if the firm sells more of its output to businesses (BUSINESS). The presumed reason is that only consumers, not businesses, are susceptible to psychological influences. We also expect to see correlations with the standard set of five variables (FLATMC, MCPCT, ELAST, CYCLICAL, and STICKY) that should in principle be correlated with any of the theories. These expectations do not turn out so well, however. Four of these five variables are uncorrelated with the theory. The elasticity of demand is correlated, but with the opposite sign from that expected. Perhaps firms that believe in—and hence adhere to—pricing points feel that they almost always face quite elastic demand.

In addition, the following variables seem to be likely candidates to help explain which firms view the pricing points theory favorably:

REGULARS (question A3): It seems plausible that regular customers, who are more familiar with the product and purchase it routinely, would be less influenced by pricing points. So the variable REGULARS should correlate negatively with both B4 and B4(a). This expectation is strongly confirmed by the data.

QUALITY (question B3[a]): While the inference is less clear, we may also expect that firms whose customers judge quality by price believe more in the existence and importance of pricing points. After all, each can be viewed (perhaps uncharitably) as a form of psychological illusion afflicting some consumers. In fact, the data show extremely strong positive correlations—among the highest in the entire data set.

WRITTEN (question A8): If the good or service is sold under a contract that specifies the price, the possibility of psychological reactions to price changes would appear to be severely attenuated. Hence we expect—and find—negative correlations with the variable WRITTEN.

The other significant correlations listed in table 9.3 appear mostly to be statistical associations in search of a rationale. However, the positive correlation with whether the firm incurs explicit costs of changing prices (ADJCOSTS) raises the possibility that part of the "adjustment costs" that firms cite may stem from breaching psychological barriers.

Not all of these univariate correlations survive into a multivariate setting, but several do. We conclude this chapter, once again, by presenting ordered probit models explaining how firms rate the pricing points explanation for stickiness. But here we do the job in two stages. First, we develop a statistical model for the answers to question B4(a), the "factual" question of whether the firm has pricing points. The regression is (with asymptotic standard errors in parentheses):

9.1   OP(B4a) = .49 RETSERV + .010 CONSUMER
    (n = 195)   (.24)   (.004)

        − .0094 REGULARS + .62 QUALITY
        (.0056)   (.26)

        − .24 INFLATION + .24 ADJCOSTS
        (.12)   (.12)

    $\log L = -115.7$, $p = .000$, $R_M^2 = .18$, $R_E^2 = .25$,

where, in addition to the variables defined above, RETSERV is a dummy for service and retail firms combined.[11] The fit of the regression is pretty good by the standards of ordered probit models (or

Table 9.3 Bivariate Correlates of the Existence and Importance of Pricing Points

Description	Variable Name	Question	Expected Sign	Correlation with	
				Importance (B4)	Existence (B4[a])
General correlates of price stickiness					
Industry	INDUSTRY	—	undefined	$\chi_{20}^2 = 37.1$ (p = .01)	$\chi_8^2 = 14.5$ (p = .07)
Marginal cost	FLATMC	B7(a)	+	t = 0.0 (p = .97)	t = 0.9 (p = .35)
Fraction of costs that are variable	MCPCT	A12(b)	+	t = −0.2 (p = .83)	t = −1.0 (p = .32)
Elasticity of demand	ELAST	A4	−	t = 2.0 (p = .04)	t = 1.9 (p = .06)
Cyclically sensitive	CYCLICAL	A6	−	$\gamma = .02$ (p = .83)	$\gamma = -.06$ (p = .61)
Price stickiness	STICKY	A10, A13	+	t = 1.0 (p = .34)	t = 0.0 (p = .99)
Predicted correlates of this theory					
Fraction of sales to consumers	CONSUMER	A2(a)	+	t = 4.9 (p = .00)	t = 5.2 (p = .00)
Fraction of sales to businesses	BUSINESS	A2(b)	−	t = −4.0 (p = .00)	t = −4.8 (p = .00)
Fraction sold to regular customers	REGULARS	A3	−	t = −2.5 (p = .01)	t = −3.2 (p = .00)
Quality depends on price	QUALITY	B3(a)	+	$\gamma = .39$ (p = .00)	$\gamma = .53$ (p = .00)
Fraction of sales under contract	WRITTEN	A8	−	$\gamma = -.21$ (p = .02)	$\gamma = -.16$ (p = .10)
Other correlates					
Has costs of price adjustment	ADJCOSTS	B8(a)	?	$\gamma = .25$ (p = .01)	$\gamma = .23$ (p = .04)
Economic outlook affects prices	OUTLOOK	A7(a)	?	$\gamma = -.02$ (p = .85)	$\gamma = -.25$ (p = .06)
Inflation forecasts affect prices	INFLATION	A7(b)	?	$\gamma = -.11$ (p = .31)	$\gamma = -.19$ (p = .08)
Fraction produced to stock	STOCK	A15(a)	?	t = 1.7 (p = .10)	t = 2.2 (p = .03)
Unionization rate in industry	UNION	—	?	t = −2.1 (p = .04)	t = −2.6 (p = .01)
Concentration ratio	CONC	—	?	t = −0.8 (p = .44)	t = −2.7 (p = .01)

models with categorical data, more generally). Generally speaking, the variables that remain significant in the multivariate setting are those with the strongest bivariate correlations. In particular, the share of output sold to consumers and whether customers judge quality by price stand out as the strongest and most robust regressors.

The more interesting question, however, is: Which firms find the pricing points theory an important explanation of price stickiness? Actually, we offer two versions of a "best" regression for this purpose—one that includes two variables with substantial numbers of missing observations (and so shrinks the sample size) and another that excludes these variables:

9.2   OP(B4) = −.42 WHOLECON + .011 CONSUMER
(n = 196)   (.24)   (.003)

   + .40 QUALITY
    (.21)

   $\log L = -217.3$, $p = .000$, $R_M^2 = .07$, $R_E^2 = .16$,

and:

9.3   OP(B4) = −1.09 WHOLECON + .014 CONSUMER
(n = 112)   (.36)   (.004)

   + .0075 ELAST + .45 FORESEEN
    (.0024)   (.22)

   $\log L = -125.3$, $p = .000$, $R_M^2 = .12$, $R_E^2 = .27$,

where WHOLECON is a dummy for the wholesale, and construction and mining industries.[12] Firms in these two sectors tend to view the pricing points theory less favorably than other firms. Interestingly, though, retail trade firms do not stand out as being more likely to view the theory favorably. Retail outlets sell mainly to consumers, of course, and CONSUMER turns out to explain the bivariate correlation of the theory's ranking with retail trade. The most robust regressor is the fraction of sales going to consumers. The dummy variable for judging quality by price (QUALITY) is strongly significant until we include the two variables that shrink the sample size, the elasticity of demand (ELAST) and whether cost increases can be foreseen (FORESEEN). The significance of these two variables is somewhat puzzling. Firms with more elastic demand see pricing points as a more important source of price stickiness, although we hypothesized that firms with more elastic demand would have more flexible prices and think less highly of any theory of price rigidity. The strong correlation of FORESEEN with the importance of pricing points probably is a coincidence.

Chapter Summary

Marketers, especially in retailing, apparently believe that it is important to end prices in certain critical digits—say, 0.95 or 0.99. In economic terms, such psychological pricing points, if they exist, create kinks in demand curves. This "theory" can therefore account for sticky prices in the same way as the standard kinked demand curve theory—but with one important difference: The psychological theory predicts nominal price stickiness whereas the usual economic theory predicts only real price stickiness.

According to the survey results, this theory seems to be valid only in those sectors of the economy that sell to consumers (as opposed to businesses or government)—especially retailing. The vast majority of retailers believe that psychological pricing points exist in consumers' minds. And they give the theory a fairly high average rating of 2.62 as an explanation of price rigidity. But pricing points are viewed as a very poor model of price stickiness by firms that do not sell to consumers (where the average score was only 1.48), which is hardly surprising. Hence its overall rating is only 1.76, one of the lower scores in the survey.

A number of "objective" characteristics of firms correlate significantly with the importance firms attach to the pricing points theory. Chief among these is the share of output sold to consumers, whether customers judge quality by price, and the perceived elasticity of demand. Firms that can foresee their cost increases also tend to rate the theory more highly.

To the extent that certain prices are of peculiar psychological significance, they seem to act more like barriers than magnets. Specifically, thresholds deter price increases much more than price decreases; and, when a barrier is broken, prices typically do not rise or fall all the way to the next barrier. Nor is the barrier necessarily destroyed when a single firm pierces it.

Chapter 10

Procyclical Elasticity of Demand

Are Markups Countercyclical? Why?

According to the most naive view of the cyclical behavior of prices, marginal cost is an increasing function of output and price is equal to marginal cost. Hence prices should be procyclical, as indicated in a supply-demand diagram for a typical industry (see figure 10.1). In a sense, the entire literature on sticky prices revolves around explaining where and why this naive view goes wrong.

One important class of explanations focuses on countercyclical markups of price over marginal cost. The naive view implicitly assumes constant markups; hence procyclical marginal cost (MC) gets translated directly into procyclical price (P). But suppose the markup is countercyclical instead. Then, as marginal cost rises in a boom, the ratio of P to MC falls, leaving open the possibility that prices could be roughly acyclical. Put another way, if marginal cost increases with output, *any* theory of price stickiness must imply that markups are countercyclical.

Two questions naturally arise. The first is factual: Are markups really countercyclical? The second is theoretical: If so, *why* are markups countercyclical?

Some econometric evidence supports the view that markups are countercyclical, that is, that prices fluctuate less than marginal costs. Using data from two-digit manufacturing industries, Mark Bils (1987) finds that price-cost margins tend to decline by about 3.3 percent when employment rises by 10 percent. Using a

Figure 10.1   A Simple View of Procyclical Prices

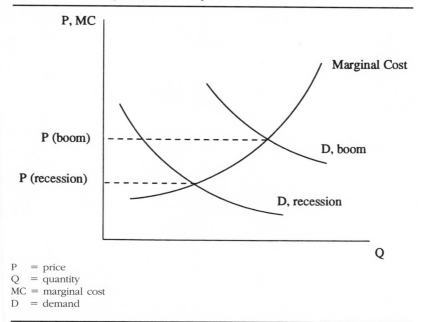

P   = price
Q   = quantity
MC = marginal cost
D   = demand

more flexible functional form, Julio Rotemberg and Michael Woodford (1991) also find strong evidence of countercyclical markups.

The empirical case for countercyclical markups is not airtight, however. Ian Domowitz, Glenn Hubbard, and Bruce Petersen (1988) find procyclical price-cost margins in manufacturing industries on average; only concentrated durable goods industries manifest acyclical or slightly countercyclical markups. This result is further confirmed by the work of Robert Chirinko and Steven Fazzari (1994). In addition, Valerie Ramey (1991b) claims that Rotemberg and Woodford's results are not robust. To identify their model, they must assume an average (steady-state) value for markups. Although the value they assume is in line with Robert Hall's (1988) well-known study of price-cost margins in U.S. industry, it is large relative to the much smaller values that Susanto Basu and John Fernald (1994) find in their work. Ramey argues that a smaller average markup in the Rotemberg-Woodford framework can yield procyclical markups.[1]

Suppose markups are in fact countercyclical. Why might that be? While a number of explanations have been offered (see the papers cited above for a sample), some are uniquely unsuited to an investigation using survey methods.[2] The specific theory of countercyclical markups that we tested is based on the hypothesis that the price elasticity of demand is procyclical. Mechanically the argument is trivial, as we noted in chapter 2. It is well known that marginal revenue (MR) and price are related by:

10.1 $P/MR = \epsilon/(\epsilon - 1)$,

where ϵ denotes the price elasticity of demand (defined so as to have a positive sign). Since a profit-maximizing firm sets marginal revenue equal to marginal cost, the markup is equal to the right-hand side of 10.1, which is a decreasing function of ϵ.[3] Hence a procyclical elasticity of demand yields a countercyclical markup.

Once again, a number of theoretical routes lead to the result that demand elasticities are procyclical. The version we test in the survey is based on the notion that firms have different categories of customers, who vary systematically in their price and income elasticities of demand. These elasticities are smaller for customers who are more "loyal" and larger for customers who are less loyal. Thus, as a firm's demand curve shifts inward during a recession, its customer base becomes more "loyal"—that is, less price-elastic—on average, thereby raising the firm's optimal markup. Conversely, the customer base grows more price-elastic as it expands in booms, resulting in a smaller optimal markup.[4]

This proposition is easy to demonstrate algebraically. Suppose there are two classes of customers: loyal customers with comparatively inelastic (to both price and income) demand and occasional customers with comparatively elastic demand.[5] The firm's overall price elasticity is a weighted average of the price elasticities of the two groups, say:

$$\epsilon = \epsilon_1 w_1 + \epsilon_2 w_2 = \epsilon_1 + (\epsilon_2 - \epsilon_1)w_2,$$

where ϵ_1 and ϵ_2 are the elasticities of loyal and occasional customers respectively (hence $\epsilon_2 > \epsilon_1$) and w_1 and w_2 denote weights. Under the additional assumption that occasional customers have higher short-run *income* elasticities than regular customers, w_2 rises in booms and falls in recessions, thereby making overall elasticity ϵ procyclical even if ϵ_1 and ϵ_2 are constants. Note that the result requires both differential price and income elasticities. Differential price elasticities by themselves are not enough.

We are aware of only one study which tries to estimate how price elasticities change over the business cycle, and it was not terribly successful. The economist Matthew Shapiro (1988) studied eight two-digit manufacturing industries over the years 1949 to 1985. He specified log-linear demand curves of the form:

$$\ln(q_t/Y_t) = a - \epsilon_t \ln P_t + u_t,$$

where q_t is industry output, Y_t is real GNP, P_t is the industry's *relative* price, and the price elasticity ϵ_t is assumed to be a linear function of the state of the business cycle. For econometric reasons, Shapiro's cyclical variable was not GNP, nor the unemployment rate, nor any other standard indicator, but rather the innovation from an estimated random-walk model for GNP. Unfortunately for the theory, his estimates of ϵ_t turn out to be procyclical in only three out of eight industries, and none of these three coefficients is statistically significant. Furthermore, Shapiro identifies the model by *assuming* constant market power over the business cycle; so, even in these three industries, countercyclical market power could conceivably rationalize the results. There thus seems to be little empirical basis for believing that price elasticities are procyclical.

Survey Evidence on the Theory

For purposes of the questionnaire, the idea that price elasticity is procyclical was translated as follows:

> B5(a). It has been suggested that, when business turns down, a company loses its *least* loyal customers first and retains its *most* loyal ones. Since the remaining customers are not very sensitive to price, reducing markups will not stimulate sales very much.
>   Is this idea true in your company?

The sample divided roughly 60 to 40 on this question, with 114 firms answering "yes" and 81 answering "no."[6] The responses display no systematic pattern by industry, but cyclically sensitive firms are somewhat less likely to answer yes than cyclically insensitive firms.[7] We then asked the 114 firms that accepted the theoretical premise as a description what they thought of it as an explanation for sticky prices:

B5. How important is it in explaining the speed of price adjustment in your company?

The answers, which are displayed in table 10.1, fall somewhat short of a ringing endorsement of the theory. Taken at face value, they imply that the notion that cyclical shifts in customer loyalty account for price stickiness has no empirical relevance at all for 56 percent of American industry and substantial relevance for only 31 percent.

When we disaggregate the responses by industry (see table 10.2), manufacturing appears to be the sector of the economy in which this theory has the most validity. But the differences across industries are typically not statistically significant. (However, a t-test of the difference between the mean ratings of the theory for manufacturing firms and construction and mining firms has a p-value of 0.06.) Note, however, that the table conceals an important sectoral difference. If we separate the trade firms into retailers and wholesalers, it turns out that retail firms give the theory a rating of 2.21 on average; the difference between this rating and the mean rating given to the theory by construction and mining firms is statistically significant at the 5 percent level. Because the fraction of firms that accepts the theoretical premise is roughly constant across all sectors,

Table 10.1   B5. How Important Is Procyclical Elasticity in Slowing Down Price Adjustments in Your Company? (n = 195 Responses)

Code	Response	Percentage of Firms
1	Totally unimportant[a]	55.9 %
2	Of minor importance	12.8
3	Moderately important	21.5
4	Very important	9.7

Mean response = 1.85
Mean if B5(a) = "yes"   2.46   (n = 114)
Rank = 7th

[a] This category includes firms that answered "no" to question B5(a).

Table 10.2 The Importance of Procyclical Elasticity in Price Stickiness, by Sector (n = 195 Responses)

		Percentage of Firms				
Code	Response	Manufacturing	Trade	Services	Construction and Mining	Transportation, Communications, and Utilities
1	Totally unimportant[a]	52.2%	50.0%	59.3%	61.9%	66.7%
2	Of minor importance	11.6	15.3	13.9	19.0	0.0
3	Moderately important	19.6	31.9	18.5	19.0	20.0
4	Very important	16.7	2.8	8.3	0.0	13.3
	Mean response	2.01	1.88	1.76	1.57	1.80
	Rank	6th	7th	8th	7th	8th

[a] This category includes firms that answered "no" to question B5(a)

these interindustry differences are entirely the result of the ratings given by firms that accept the basic idea.

Other Aspects of the Theory

There is an ambiguity in the way question B5 is worded—one which might have been avoided but which we deliberately chose to let stand. Specifically, the change in the composition of a firm's customer base when its sales decline might well depend on whether the fall in sales is economy-wide, industry-wide, or specific to the firm. In addition, a single firm's elasticity of demand should depend on how its competitors react when it changes its price. If all prices in an industry rise or fall together, then each firm essentially moves along the industry's demand curve. But if only one firm changes its price while others maintain theirs, the firm should encounter much greater price sensitivity.[8] Rightly or wrongly, we judged these matters too complex—and too wordy—to be embodied in the main question, and so specified none of them. Instead, firms presumably answered under whatever blend of ceteris paribus and mutatis mutandis conditions seemed most relevant to them. But that, of course, means that we cannot know precisely what respondents were assuming when they answered the question.

Does this matter? Probably. A follow-up question asked whether the sales situation for other firms might influence the respondent's reaction to sagging sales. This question was posed immediately to every firm that expressed any belief at all in the procyclical elasticity theory. Specifically:

B5(b). In thinking about that, does it matter whether or not sales at competing firms are falling at the same time? (n = 86)

About 55 percent of the respondents said that their competitors' sales situation "matters a lot," while 23 percent said it "doesn't matter" at all. The remaining 22 percent said it "matters a little."

The final question pertaining to procyclical demand elasticity inquired about symmetry:

B5(c). How important is the effect in the opposite direction? That is, are you hesitant to raise markups when demand rises because you want to attract new customers, and you think these new customers will be quite price conscious? (n = 108)

As observed in chapter 5, the fact that responses were coded on the same four-point scale as used for the main question permits a clean test of symmetry through a comparison of the answers given by individual firms to question B5(c)—which are tabulated in table 10.3—and question B5 (presented in table 10.1). Doing so makes it clear that there is more rigidity in the downward direction; the difference is statistically significant.

Table 10.3   B5(c). How Important Is Procyclical Elasticity in Slowing Down Price Increases? (n = 108 Responses)

Code	Response	Percentage of Firms
1	Totally unimportant	46.8%
2	Of minor importance	16.2
3	Moderately important	23.6
4	Very important	13.4

Mean response = 2.04

What Kinds of Firms Agree with the Theory Most?

Table 10.4 reports bivariate measures of correlation between various firm characteristics and whether the firm agrees with the premise that demand elasticity is procyclical (question B5[a]) and its view of the importance of the theory (question B5).

We noted earlier that cyclically sensitive firms are less likely to accept the premise of the theory; however, cyclical sensitivity does not affect firms' ranking of the theory to any significant extent. Nor is there any apparent association between a firm's view of the theory's relevance and its industry. And none of the remaining "core" variables (FLATMC, MCPCT, ELAST, and STICKY) appear to be correlated with the theory. In the case of ELAST, this nonfinding suggests there is little or no relationship between the *level* of price elasticity and its cyclical sensitivity.

The following additional variables might reasonably be expected to be associated with firms' acceptance of theory B5:

IMPLICIT (question B2[a]): Our version of the countercyclical markup theory bears a strong family resemblance to the implicit contract theory, which is based on the notion that firms have a cadre of loyal customers to whom they pay special attention.[9] In fact, firms that report having implicit contracts with their customers (question B2[a] = 2) give the procyclical elasticity theory (question B5) an average rating of 2.06, while those who deny the existence of such contracts (B2[a] = 1) rate it just 1.51 on average. The difference is statistically significant ($t = 3.9$, $p = .00$). There is a strong and significant statistical association (gamma = 0.40) between the answers to these two questions (B5 and B2[a]). And, the evaluations of the two theories (questions B5 and B2) have a smaller— though still significant—gamma of 0.18.

REGULARS (question A3): We might expect firms with a large number of repeat buyers to be better able to assess customer loyalty; such firms might therefore rate the theory more favorably. This is apparently not the case, however. Perhaps firms with mostly repeat customers may not worry much about customer loyalty.

COSTS (question B6): Firms whose prices depend mainly on costs are perhaps less likely to allow demand conditions to influence their pricing decisions. Although we do indeed see a negative relationship between COSTS and questions B5 and B5(a), it is not statistically significant. Furthermore, there is little relationship between the theory

Table 10.4 Bivariate Correlates of the Existence and Importance of Procyclical Demand Elasticity

Description	Variable Name	Question	Expected Sign	Correlation with	
				B5 (Importance)	B5(a) (Existence)
General correlates of price stickiness					
Industry	INDUSTRY	—	undefined	$\chi^2_{20} = 18.9$ (p = .53)	$\chi^2_4 = 1.2$ (p = .88)
Marginal cost	FLATMC	B7(a)	+	$\gamma = -.04$ (p = .75)	$\gamma = -.05$ (p = .76)
Fraction of costs that are variable	MCPCT	A12(b)	+	$t = -1.4$ (p = .15)	$t = -0.4$ (p = .66)
Elasticity of demand	ELAST	A4	−	$t = 0.0$ (p = 1.0)	$t = -0.1$ (p = .96)
Cyclically sensitive	CYCLICAL	A6	−	$\gamma = -.08$ (p = .39)	$\gamma = -.32$ (p = .00)
Price stickiness	STICKY	A10, A13	+	$t = 1.2$ (p = .25)	$t = 1.4$ (p = .16)
Predicted correlates of this theory					
Implicit contracts	IMPLICIT	B2(a)	+	$\gamma = .40$ (p = .00)	$\gamma = .39$ (p = .00)
Fraction sold to regular customers	REGULARS	A3	+	$t = -0.4$ (p = .70)	$t = -0.0$ (p = .98)
Prices based on costs	COSTS	B6	−	$\gamma = -.06$ (p = .52)	$\gamma = -.13$ (p = .21)
How well can MC be measured	ACCURACY	A11	−	$\gamma = .03$ (p = .72)	$\gamma = -.04$ (p = .76)
Other correlates					
Log of firm's annual sales	SIZE	ln(A1)	?	$t = -1.5$ (p = .13)	$t = -1.9$ (p = .06)
Firms adjust nonprice elements	NONPRICE	B12(a)	?	$\gamma = .36$ (p = .01)	$\gamma = .22$ (p = .17)
Cost increases can be foreseen	FORESEEN	B6(d)	?	$\gamma = -.21$ (p = .10)	$\gamma = -.19$ (p = .29)

and variables MCPCT and ACCURACY (question A11, which asks how well firms think they can judge their marginal costs).

The other correlations (with SIZE, NONPRICE, and FORESEEN) are probably only coincidental, although it is conceivable that a large firm is less able to determine the loyalty of its customer base (hence the negative relationship between a firm's log sales and whether it accepts the theory). Note that NONPRICE and FORE-SEEN tend to affect a firm's assessment of the theory's importance, not its opinion on whether the theory's basic premise is true.

Finally, we consider the results of two ordered probit regressions. It is of interest to know first what kinds of firms believe they can distinguish among customer groups identified by "loyalty," for only such firms can possibly find theory B5 of any importance. Our preferred ordered probit model for question B5(a) is given by the following regression (with asymptotic standard errors in parentheses):

10.2   OP(B5a) = $-$ .10 SIZE $-$ .33 CYCLICAL + .49 IMPLICIT
         (n = 188)   (.04)   (.11)   (.21)

         + .14 COORD $-$ .16 COSTS
           (.08)   (.08)

         $\log L = -115.9$, $p = .0002$, $R_M^2 = .09$, $R_E^2 = .13$.

The regression is significant, but its explanatory power is not impressive.[10] Several variables—SIZE, CYCLICAL, IMPLICIT, and COSTS—carry over from the bivariate analysis, and enter the regression with the predicted signs. In addition, COORD (theory B10) is marginally significant ($p = .09$)—suggesting that firms that are more likely to face coordination failures in their industry are more likely to accept the premise about differential loyalty embedded in question B5.

The best ordered probit model explaining firms' evaluations of the theory itself is:

10.3   OP(B5) = .54 NONPRICE $-$ .008 MCPCT + .48 IMPLICIT
       (n = 173)   (.24)   (.004)   (.20)

       + .18 RATION + .68 RETAIL + .33 MFG
         (.10)   (.31)   (.20)

       $\log L = -207.1$, $p = .0001$, $R_M^2 = .06$, $R_E^2 = .15$.

Again, several bivariate correlations survive into the multivariate context (NONPRICE, MCPCT, and IMPLICIT). In addition, the variable RATION (question A5) enters the regression positively (p = .06), meaning that firms that are more likely to put their customers on allocation give a higher rating to theory B5. Finally, as suggested by the results in section two, retail and manufacturing firms tend to view the theory more favorably, even after controlling for other firm attributes.[11]

Chapter Summary

Since price is the product of marginal cost (MC) times the markup ratio (P/MC), prices can be "sticky" over business cycles even if marginal costs are strongly procyclical—provided that markups are sufficiently countercyclical. Quite a few theoretical models have been built around this simple idea; for example, chapter 2 mentioned a theory due to Rotemberg and Saloner (1986) in which oligopolistic collusion is more likely to break down at business cycle peaks then at troughs.

Our survey tested a particular version of the countercyclical markup idea that could be readily—and tersely—put into plain English for the questionnaire. The idea embodied in theory B5 is that a firm's more "loyal" customers have both lower price elasticities and lower (short-run) income elasticities. As a result, the overall elasticity of demand that firms face rises in booms and falls in slumps.

This theory was not particularly well received by our respondents, however. They gave it an average rating of just 1.85 on our one-to-four scale, which placed it seventh among the twelve theories tested. The theory scored somewhat better within the manufacturing and retailing sectors. In a multivariate ordered probit analysis, theory B5 was deemed to be a more important source of price stickiness by firms that (a) enter into implicit contracts with their customers, (b) consider nonprice competition more important, (c) have lower marginal costs (relative to fixed costs), and (d) ration their customers.

Theory B5 is the only one of the twelve theories for which the survey turned up meaningful evidence of asymmetry in the direction usually assumed. Apparently, differential price elasticities are a stronger source of downward than upward rigidity.

Chapter 11

Cost-Based Pricing:
Lags from the Chain of Production

From little acorns, great oak trees grow.

—ANONYMOUS

The Theoretical Idea

That prices depend on costs hardly qualifies as a new idea. Nor does it, by itself, constitute a theory of price rigidity. It simply says that prices are sticky if costs—presumably marginal costs—are. Since costs primarily depend on other prices (including wages), this statement borders on the tautological: some prices are sticky because others are. Indeed, it has been well known for decades that Keynesian (nominal) rigidity can be rooted in *wage* stickiness, with prices responding rapidly to wages. However, this book is devoted to theories of *price* stickiness, not wage stickiness.

What takes the theory that prices are based on costs beyond the realm of tautology is the fact that goods pass through several stages of production on the way to their final users. For example, raw wood is milled into lumber, sold to a contractor, and becomes part of a house; iron ore is smelted into steel, which is used to make parts for an automobile; and so on.

In his well-known survey of price stickiness, the economist Robert Gordon (1981) took the ancient idea that prices react to costs with a lag and gave it a modern twist. Gordon called attention to "the role of the input-output table in translating prompt price adjustment at the individual level to gradual price adjustment at the aggregate level."[1] The idea is that, if there are many links in the chain of production, short lags between cost changes and price changes at the level of the individual firm could cumulate into long lags between, say, money shocks and the eventual reaction of the aggregate price level.

The idea is reminiscent of John Taylor's (1980) model of staggered wage contracts, and, shortly after Gordon's paper was published, the economist Olivier Blanchard (1983) provided the requisite formalism and equations. Blanchard's model is not actually based on an input-output table, but rather on a simpler linear chain of production. There are n stages of production, indexed 1, . . . n, with stage 0 denoting raw materials and stage n representing final goods. The single input at each stage is the output from the previous stage, and production functions are assumed to be proportional and instantaneous. Hence for each stage i:

11.1 $y_{it} = y_{i-1,t} + c_i$,

where y is log output and c_i is an unimportant scale term.

Prices are fixed for two periods in Blanchard's model. In particular, half of all prices are adjusted in even-numbered periods and half in odd, so the equilibrium pricing relationship for the price of the stage i good is:[2]

11.2 $p_{it} = 0.5 \, p_{i-1,t-1} + 0.5 \, E_t \, [p_{i-1,t+1}]$,

where p is log price and the expectations operator denotes rational expectations.[3] The primary input, which might be thought of as labor, is not produced but is instead supplied as an increasing function of its relative price:

11.3 $y_{0t} = b \, (p_{0t} - p_{nt}) + e_t$ $(b \geq 0)$,

where e_t is a disturbance term. Finally, the nominal demand for final goods is equal to the money supply:

11.4 $y_{nt} = m_t - p_{nt}$.

It is clear from the structure of the model that the macroeconomic lag in the adjustment of final-goods prices to the money supply depends on the microeconomic lag at each firm—which is one "period" in Blanchard's model—and the number of stages of production, n. Specifically, since each lag in the chain of price adjustment takes either zero or two periods, and there are n/2 of each, full adjustment to a money shock takes n periods. But the time pattern of adjustment is complex and depends on the parameters b and n.

The chain-of-production idea surely makes intuitive sense. And no one doubts, first, that prices are based on costs (at least to some extent) and, second, that some time elapses between cost changes and price changes. How could it be otherwise? But it is less obvious that Gordon's cumulation hypothesis takes us very far in explaining aggregate price level stickiness—for at least three reasons.

First, like so many other theories, this one seems designed to explain the prices of *goods*, particularly manufactured goods. But production of goods accounts for only about 40 percent of GDP these days, with manufactured goods comprising less than half of that. Most services involve "production" chains that are quite short—perhaps requiring only one stage beyond raw labor. Law firms and barber shops are good examples. Yet it is widely believed that service prices are more sluggish than goods prices.

Second, the theory's main apparent implication—that the goods that pass through the most stages of production should have the stickiest prices—is notoriously difficult to test. Note that this is not the same as saying that prices of final goods are more sluggish than prices of intermediate goods, as the contrast between tomatoes and computer chips makes clear. Nor is it equivalent to saying that disaggregated prices adjust faster than the prices of more aggregated product groups—compare, say, mobile homes (SIC 2451) with wood products (SIC 24), or printed circuit boards (SIC 3672) with electronic components (SIC 36). In fact, the theory may hold no such implication. Suppose, for example, that aggregate demand shocks first affect the demands for final goods and only later affect the demands for raw materials and intermediate goods. Then if, as in the Blanchard model, the lag is the same at each stage of production, final goods prices should move sooner.

Finally, if the typical lag between cost changes and price changes at the micro level is very short, perhaps just a few days, then many stages of cumulation are needed in order to produce long macroeconomic lags. Blanchard thinks of the adjustment lag as short—no more than a month. His examples, therefore, employ production chains that are ten to one hundred stages long. But a chain composed of, say, three to six stages seems more realistic. This is actually not a fatal blow for the theory; a different assumption about the length of the firm-level adjustment lags is enough to salvage it. The survey evidence reported in chapter 4 suggests that a better estimate of the average length of these lags is three months. So, the aggregate price lag in a chain-of-production model should lie in the nine- to eighteenth-month range—which at least comes closer to the time-series evidence.

On balance, the theory struck us as intuitively appealing, easy to explain to practitioners, and almost certain to have at least some empirical validity. So we included it in the survey as question B6. We now look at how our respondents felt about the idea.

Survey Evidence on the Nature and Validity of the Theory

The specific question we asked regarding cost-based pricing was as follows:[4]

> B6. A different idea holds that prices depend mainly on the *costs* of labor and of materials and supplies that companies buy from other companies. Firms are thought to delay price increases until their costs rise, which may take a while. But then they raise selling prices promptly.
>
> How important is this idea in explaining the speed of price adjustment in your company?

Notice two key features of this question. First, in keeping with the philosophy behind the questionnaire, we asked firms only about their own behavior, not about the cumulation process that allegedly leads to long macroeconomic lags. Second, the question treats the costs of labor and materials symmetrically. We will not be able to distinguish whether firms react differently to wage changes versus changes in materials costs.

The cost-based pricing theory is quite popular, as table 11.1 shows. Its mean score of 2.66 puts it in second place, and is not significantly lower than the mean score of the top-ranked theory (B10, coordination failure, which receives a score of 2.77). However, table 11.2 reveals considerable disparity across industrial sectors in how highly firms rate the theory. Apparently, wholesalers and retailers view cost-based pricing as an excellent theory of price

Table 11.1   B6. How Important Is Cost-Based Pricing with Lags in Slowing Down Price Adjustments in Your Company?
(n = 200 Responses)

Code	Response	Percentage of Firms
1	Totally unimportant	30.0%
2	Of minor importance	13.3
3	Moderately important	18.0
4	Very important	38.8

Mean response   2.66
Mean if B6 > 1   3.36   (n = 140)
Rank = 2nd

stickiness, as do firms in the transportation, communications, and utilities sectors, and those in construction and mining. But the idea is less well-received by service firms—which is not surprising, since the theory was designed to explain the pricing of goods. In addition, there is no apparent association between a firm's cyclical sensitivity and its reception of the theory.[5]

Table 11.2   The Importance of Cost-Based Pricing in Price Stickiness, by Sector (n = 200 Responses)

		Percentage of Firms				
Code	Response	Manufacturing	Trade	Services	Construction and Mining	Transportation, Communications, and Utilities
1	Totally unimportant	35.7%	16.2%	40.7%	18.2%	17.6%
2	Of minor importance	13.6	8.1	14.8	15.9	14.7
3	Moderately important	14.3	27.0	19.4	13.6	14.7
4	Very important	36.4	48.6	25.0	52.3	52.9
	Mean response	2.51	3.08	2.29	3.00	3.03
	Rank	4th	2nd	5th	1st	1st

Table 11.3   Mean Lags in Price Adjustment[a], by Sector (in Months)

Industry	Cost Increases (A13[c])		Cost Decreases (A13[d])	
Manufacturing	3.24	(2.74)	4.06	(3.11)
Trade	0.90	(1.62)	1.36	(2.13)
Retail	0.42	(0.90)	1.25	(2.31)
Wholesale	1.27	(1.96)	1.43	(2.08)
Transportation, communication, utilities	4.23	(3.92)	5.02	(3.85)
Services	3.58	(3.03)	4.79	(5.92)
Construction and mining	1.78	(3.14)	2.00	(3.17)
All industries	2.76	(3.00)	3.27	(3.92)

[a] Standard deviations in parentheses

As presented on the questionnaire, the theory has *two* distinct components: First, firms must delay price increases until costs increase; and second, once costs do increase, price hikes follow quickly.

Chapter 4 presented survey evidence on the second point, some of which we reproduce for convenience in table 11.3. It is evident that the average lag between a cost shock and a price adjustment varies substantially both across and within industrial sectors. Lags are comparatively short for construction and mining firms and trade firms—two of the sectors that rate theory B6 most highly. However, the other sector that finds the theory especially attractive—transportation, communications, and utilities—reports some of the longest adjustment lags. Interpreted literally, Blanchard's model requires that the microeconomic price-adjustment lag be the same for all firms—an hypothesis which is overwhelmingly rejected by the survey data. In fact, the variance across firms is huge—even within an industrial sector. But equal lag lengths is not a critical assumption; it is adopted solely for mathematical convenience.

A more substantive requirement of the theory is that firms delay price increases until their costs actually rise. They are not supposed to raise prices in anticipation of cost increases that they see coming. We quizzed our firms explicitly on this point.[6] First, we asked whether anticipated cost increases are common occurrences or rare events:

B6(d). Are there times when you can clearly foresee price increases for labor or other things you buy? (n = 141)

The answers were definitive. Just over 76 percent answered "yes" (or often) while only seven percent answered "no" (or rarely). The rest gave an answer more or less equivalent to "sometimes." Apparently, anticipated price hikes exist not just in the minds of economic theorists, but also in the real world. We also inquired if, when they see price increases coming, firms try to stockpile inputs in inventory. The sample of 129 respondents divided almost evenly on this question (B6[e]): 48 percent said they do; 52 percent said they do not.

Second, we wanted to know if firms ever raise prices in advance of cost increases, as standard economic theory would seem to imply. So we asked:

B6(f). When you can see cost or wage increases coming, do you raise your own prices in anticipation? (n = 131)[7]

Here the replies were more equivocal. About 55 percent said they rarely or never do so, but about 45 percent said they often do so. This is disturbingly close to an even division of the house. Surprisingly, the answers to question B6(f) are uncorrelated with the ratings given to theory B6. They should be negatively correlated. However, firms answering 1 to question B6 (the idea is "totally unimportant") were not asked question B6(f).

It is not clear whether these responses really represent bad news for the theory. On the one hand, the theory seems to call for firms to wait for actual, not anticipated, cost hikes before raising prices— as the (scant) majority does. Gordon writes:

[T]he typical firm has no idea of the identity of its full set of suppliers when all the indirect links within the input-output table are considered. Because the informational problem of trying to anticipate the effect of a currently perceived nominal demand change on the weighted-average cost of all these suppliers is difficult to formulate and probably impossible to solve. . . the sensible firm just waits by the mailbox for news of cost increases and then, Okun-like, passes them on as price increases.[8]

On the other hand, Blanchard does allow for anticipatory price increases—see equation 11.2. His model generates the desired lags through its ad hoc assumption that nominal prices are fixed for two periods.

Table 11.4   B6(g). Why Do Not Firms Raise Their Prices in the Face of Anticipated Cost Increases?

Reason	Number of Responses
1 It would antagonize or cause difficulty for our customers*	31
2 We lack confidence in our cost forecasts*	10
3 We worry that competing firms won't raise their prices*	32
4 Once costs rise, we can raise our prices promptly*	18
5 People who have to sign off on a price increase might not agree*	3
6 Contracts or regulations prohibit anticipatory price hikes	8
7 It is unethical or unfair to our customers	3
8 Other	16
Total	121

* Represents "stock" answers.

Whenever an executive told us that his company does not raise prices in anticipation of coming cost increases, we asked why not. Since such an answer seems to violate the precepts of standard economic theory, we wanted to know why. There were eighty such cases. Not all respondents offered an explanation, but many gave several; so we received 121 answers in all.

Interviewers encountered a wide variety of free-form answers and needed to classify them in some way. The questionnaire provided a checklist of five "stock" answers (indicated in the table above by an asterisk). But when interviewers heard a reply that was not on the checklist, they were encouraged to write it down in words. The results are tabulated in table 11.4.[9]

The most popular explanations for why prices are not raised in advance (responses 1 and 3 in the table) center around the demand side of the market—adverse customer reactions, and concern about the competitive situation. Fifty-four of the eighty firms gave us one or both of these responses.[10] These two explanations might, in fact, be lumped together; but we view them as slightly different for the following reason. Answer 3 seems to express the kinked demand curve or coordination failure idea, where firms are worried that their price elasticities might be extraordinary if they raise prices before their competitors do. Answer 1 seems to focus more directly on the reactions of customers as opposed to competitors. Some support for this distinction comes from the fact that firms choosing the customer-based explanation rated the implicit contract theory (B2) much more highly and the coordination failure theory (B10) slightly less highly than firms choosing the competition-based explanation.[11]

After these two reasons, the "vote" trails off quickly. Eighteen firms simply said that they have no need for preemptive price changes because they can raise prices promptly once costs rise (response 4 in the table). This, of course, is an incomplete explanation. It says they do not have to raise prices in advance, but it does not explain why they do not want to. Ten firms offered an explanation (number 2) that is more consistent with economic theory: If you lack confidence in your forecasts of future costs, you are less likely to use them in pricing decisions. Three firms chose the hierarchy explanation implicit in theory B9 (response 5 in the table).[12] And eight firms reported contractual or regulatory inhibitions (response 6). Finally, three companies offered some version of a "fairness" explanation (number 7). For example, one retailer told us that the owner of the business considers it unethical to raise prices in advance of costs.

Responses to Different Types of Cost Shocks

Firms were asked several additional questions about how quickly they react to different types of cost shocks: large versus small, specific versus general, and permanent versus transitory.[13] In general, economic theory and the survey results seem to dovetail nicely for each of these issues.

Firms might react faster to large versus small cost shocks for either of two reasons. First, larger shocks might be more readily observable than smaller shocks. Second, adjustment costs might be nonconvex (menu costs are an extreme example). The theoretical expectation, then, is that prices should react faster to large cost shocks than to small ones; and this is precisely what the survey results indicate—overwhelmingly. The question we asked in order to examine this point was:

B6(a). Is the cost pass-through normally faster for *large* cost changes or for *small* cost changes?

We report firms' responses in table 11.5.

Table 11.5   B6(a). Do Firms Change Prices Faster for Large or for Small Cost Changes? (n = 136 Responses)

Code	Response	Percentage of Firms
1	Faster for small cost changes	6.6%
2	About the same	23.2
3	Faster for large cost changes	70.2

Many economic theories emphasize the distinction between general and idiosyncratic cost shocks. Presumably, prices in a competitive market react more vigorously to the former than to the latter. We asked firms the following question:

B6(b). Is the cost pass-through normally faster for cost changes that are believed to be *industry-wide* or for cost changes that are believed to be *unique to your company*?

Although a number of firms found the notion of a firm-specific cost shock difficult to comprehend, this expectation was strikingly borne out by the survey results, which we present in table 11.6.

Finally, we would argue that any dynamic optimizing economic model that includes any intertemporal linkage at all would imply that prices react more to permanent than to temporary cost shocks. The question we asked was:

B6(c). Is the cost pass-through normally faster for cost changes that are believed to be *permanent* or for cost changes that are believed to be *transitory*?

Once again we lost a number of firms because respondents had trouble imputing empirical meaning to the theoretical concept of a "temporary" cost increase. But the firms that answered the ques-

Table 11.6   B6(b). Do Firms Change Prices Faster for Idiosyncratic or Industry-Wide Cost Changes? (n = 128 Responses)

Code	Response	Percentage of Firms
1	Faster for idiosyncratic cost changes	7.8%
2	About the same	15.6
3	Faster for industry-wide cost changes	76.6

tion agreed overwhelmingly with this prediction of economic theory, as the responses in table 11.7 indicate.

In sum, we find strong evidence that firms react more quickly to cost shocks that are large, and/or industry-wide, and/or permanent.

Correlates of Agreement with the Theory

What characteristics are correlated with the importance that firms attach to cost-based pricing with lags as a source of price stickiness? Table 11.8 reports bivariate measures of association between firms' assessment of theory B6 and various firm attributes.

There are few noteworthy correlations.[14] Moreover, only one of the "core" variables is significantly correlated with the theory (MCPCT, the fraction of total costs that are variable).[15]

Three correlations would be expected on a priori grounds. First, firms that enter into implicit contracts with their customers (IMPLICIT, question B2[a]) tend to be more favorably disposed to the theory. This finding is consistent with Okun's (1981) view of "fairness": customers with implicit contracts find price increases to be permissible when they result from cost increases. Second, a positive relationship between the importance of the theory and the fraction of output firms sell to government (GOVT, question A2[c]) is consistent with the perceived fact that cost-plus pricing is more prevalent in sales to government units than in sales to private customers.[16] Finally, as cost-based pricing requires firms to be aware of (and react to) changes in their costs, we might expect that firms that engage in cost-based pricing should be able to more accurately assess their marginal costs (ACCURACY, question A11). In fact, however, ACCURACY is negatively correlated with the theory—though the correlation is not statistically significant. The remaining correlations, which

Table 11.7 B6(c). Do Firms Change Prices Faster for Permanent or Transitory Cost Changes? (n = 120 Responses)

Code	Response	Percentage of Firms
1	Faster for transitory cost changes	5.8%
2	About the same	28.3
3	Faster for permanent cost changes	65.8

Table 11.8 Bivariate Correlates of the Importance of Cost-Based Pricing

Description	Variable Name	Question	Expected Sign	Correlation with B6
General correlates of price stickiness				
Industry	INDUSTRY	—	undefined	$\chi^2_{20} = 24.4$ (p = .23)
Marginal cost	FLATMC	B7(a)	+	$\gamma = -.06$ (p = .59)
Fraction of costs that are variable	MCPCT	A12(b)	+	$t = 2.7$ (p = .01)
Elasticity of demand	ELAST	A4	−	$t = 1.4$ (p = .17)
Cyclically sensitive	CYCLICAL	A6	−	$\gamma = -.01$ (p = .88)
Price stickiness	STICKY	A10, A13	+	$t = -0.7$ (p = .47)
Predicted correlates of this theory				
Implicit contracts	IMPLICIT	B2(a)	+	$\gamma = .17$ (p = .11)
Fraction of sales to others (gov't)	GOVT	A2(c)	+	$t = 2.6$ (p = .01)
How well can MC be measured	ACCURACY	A11	+	$\gamma = -.11$ (p = .22)
Other correlates				
Customers are put on allocation	RATION	A5	?	$\gamma = -.14$ (p = .12)
Quality depends on price	QUALITY	B3(a)	?	$\gamma = -.29$ (p = .01)
Frequency of price changes	FREQ	A10	?	$t = -1.6$ (p = .11)
Sales-to-inventory ratio	S/I	A16	?	$t = -2.0$ (p = .04)
Concentration ratio	CONC	—	?	$t = -2.0$ (p = .05)
Log of firm's annual sales	SIZE	ln(A1)	?	$t = -3.3$ (p = .00)

are quite strong in several cases, seem to have little theoretical justification.

For what it is worth, we next construct an ordered probit model for firms' rating of the theory. Since two of the bivariate correlations involve variables that tend to curtail the sample size severely (S/I and CONC), we report two specifications of the model—one that excludes these variables in order to preserve sample size, and one which attempts to include them.[17] Our preferred "full sample" model is given by the following:[18]

11.5 OP(B6) = −.53 SERV − .38 MFG − .11 SIZE + .009 GOVT
(n = 190)   (.22)   (.20)   (.04)   (.005)

+ .33 IMPLICIT − .43 QUALITY + .007 REGULARS
(.18)   (.21)   (.004)

log L = −265.3, p = .00, R_M^2 = .07, R_E^2 = .20.

The regression is significant, though its fit is modest at best. Service and manufacturing firms are less likely to view the theory as an important explanation of price stickiness, as suggested by the results reported in table 11.2. Four bivariate correlations—SIZE, GOVT, IMPLICIT, and QUALITY (question B3[a])—appear in the multivariate regression; two of these (GOVT and IMPLICIT) were on the list of a priori reasonable correlations. In addition, REGULARS (question A3, the fraction of sales to repeat customers) enters the regression with a positive coefficient (p = .08).

The best subsample regression using the inventory variables is given by:[19]

11.6 OP(B6) = −.005 S/I − .18 SIZE + .015 REGULARS
(n = 95)   (.002)   (.05)   (.008)

+ .78 POINTS − 1.33 QUALITY − .35 ACCURACY
(.26)   (.37)   (.18)

log L = −119.0, p = .00, R_M^2 = .18, R_E^2 = .46.

The concentration ratio fails to enter the regression once we control for other variables. The only inventory variable that enters is S/I (the sales-to-inventory ratio), which maintains its negative correlation with the importance firms attach to the theory.[20] Several variables—SIZE, REGULARS, and QUALITY—are common to both the full-sample and inventory-subsample specifications; ACCU-RACY, which was on the list of a priori reasonable correlations, also enters the subsample regression. The partial correlation with POINTS (question B4[a], regarding the presence of psychological pricing points), is very likely coincidental.

Chapter Summary

Because most goods pass through several stages of production on the way to their final users, the elementary notion that prices react with a lag to costs becomes a potential theory of *macroeconomic* price stickiness as short microeconomic lags cumulate into long macroeconomic lags. A crude calculation suggests that the numbers work out about right: If the lag between cost increases and price increases at a single firm is about three months, as the survey results suggest, then a three- to six-stage production chain will yield a lag of nine to eighteen months before a nominal shock is fully reflected in prices.

Firms in our sample reacted quite favorably to the notion that prices respond with a lag to costs. We did not ask them to evaluate the cumulation hypothesis per se, however, because that was likely beyond their ken. Firms in the trade, construction and mining, and transportation, communication, and utilities sectors found the theory particularly attractive. But firms' characteristics do little to help us explain their assessment of the theory. As economic theory suggests, firms delay price adjustments longer if cost shocks are small, transitory, or firm-specific. They react more promptly to large, permanent, and industry-wide cost increases.

The theory of cost-based pricing seems to proscribe anticipatory price increases: Firms are supposed to wait for their costs to rise before raising prices.[21] Is this true in the real world? Our firms tell us that they frequently do see cost increases coming, but that they raise prices in advance in less than half of such cases. Why not? The main reasons firms give for such patience have to do with fear of adverse customer reactions and loss of market share if their prices are raised ahead of their competitors'.

Chapter 12

Constant Marginal Cost

It is rare for anyone but an economist to suppose that price is
predominantly governed by marginal cost.

—J. M. KEYNES

The Theory

One simple theory of price rigidity begins by expressing the price of
some representative firm in the following cumbersome way:

$$12.1 \quad P = \left(\frac{P}{MR}\right)\left(\frac{MR}{MC}\right) MC$$

As we have remarked before, it is well known that the ratio of price
to marginal revenue is a decreasing function of the elasticity of
demand, as in the following equation:

$$12.2 \quad \frac{P}{MR} = \frac{\epsilon}{\epsilon - 1} = f(\epsilon),$$

and that profit maximization sets the middle term in 12.1 equal to
unity. Hence:

$$12.3 \quad P = f(\epsilon)MC.$$

So, if marginal cost and the elasticity of demand are both approximately constant over the business cycle, then P will be
constant, too.

Notice several things about this apparently trivial result. First,
since equations 12.1 to 12.3 are all homogeneous of degree one in

the nominal variables, the analysis implicitly applies to *relative* prices and *real* marginal costs. It really says that *markups* are constant over the business cycle. Nominal prices are sticky only if nominal marginal costs are.

Second, constancy of ϵ over the business cycle is really two separate requirements, neither of which has a persuasive theoretical rationale:

One, that the demand curve must have constant elasticity, so that movements along an individual firm's demand curve do not change ϵ. Isoelastic demand curves are, of course, nothing but a mathematically convenient fiction. However, there is no strong theoretical presumption that ϵ should either rise or fall with output.[1]

And two, that upward and downward shifts of the demand curve over the business cycle must not change the elasticity directly. Theory B5, for example, is based on the contrary notion that the elasticity of demand is procyclical—and, therefore, that markups are countercyclical—because booms bring in customers with more elastic demand.

Although price stickiness was not its focus, the economist Robert Hall's (1986) fascinating work revived interest in the very old idea that prices might vary little over the cycle because marginal cost is constant. Hall's main objective was to explain the observed procyclical behavior of total factor productivity—the so-called Solow residual. So his focus was on the cyclical behavior of quantities, not prices. Nonetheless, the two issues are related, at least in Hall's formulation. To see how, we must make a quick detour through his analysis.

Start with a standard production function, $Q = AF(L,K)$, where A stands for technology. Letting lower-case letters denote growth rates yields the familiar growth-accounting equation:

$$12.4 \quad q_t = a_t + \frac{LF_L}{F} l_t + \frac{KF_K}{F} k_t$$

Marginal cost is the wage divided by the marginal product of labor. We can therefore define the markup m as:

$$m \equiv P/MC = PAF_L/W,$$

which can be rewritten:

12.5 $F_L = mW/AP$.

It follows immediately that:

12.6a $\dfrac{LF_L}{F} = m\,\dfrac{WL}{PQ} = ms$

where s is labor's share. By identical reasoning, under constant returns to scale:

12.6b $\dfrac{KF_K}{F} = m(1 - s)$,

where $1 - s$ is capital's share. Substituting the two versions of 12.6 into 12.4 gives Hall's central equation:

12.7 $q_t = a_t + m\,[sl_t + (1 - s)k_t]$.

Hall uses this equation to estimate m under two critical assumptions. The first is that a_t is equal to a constant plus a random error term that is uncorrelated with output. This rules out real business cycles. The second is that the markup is a constant. Under these two assumptions, Hall estimates m to be substantially greater than one in many U.S. industries, which points to considerable market power. (Under perfect competition, of course, m = 1.)

Since the Solow residual is:

$$a + (m - 1)\,[sl_t + (1 - s)k_t] + u_t,$$

Hall's explanation for procyclical productivity is that m is greater than one; that is, there is market power. Under this hypothesis, the Solow residual would be procyclical because inputs grow faster in booms than in slumps.

Now what does all this have to do with price stickiness, or even with constant marginal cost? After all, Hall's expression for nominal marginal cost, W/AF_L, is procyclical if the production function has the usual concave shape. Hall answers this question by pointing out and quickly resolving a paradox: The high degree of market power that he estimates with U.S. data is hard to reconcile with the comparatively low level of business profits.

Hall's explanation is that fixed costs are substantial (which suggests that there is a great deal of "excess capacity"). Thus he envisions a world in which the typical marginal cost curve is flat up to capacity and then approximately vertical, as depicted in figure 12.1. When a competitive firm with P = MC is producing on the flat portion of its MC curve, it is making no contribution to its fixed costs. To cover fixed costs in the long run, it must therefore spend a reasonable amount of time on the vertical portion of its MC curve—charging high prices in periods of peak demand. But a firm with substantial market power need do no such thing. Since it maintains its price above marginal cost at all times, it is constantly earning a contribution toward its fixed costs. That is why, in Hall's (1986, 315) words, "a finding of market power points in the direction of constant marginal cost."

Figure 12.1   Hall's Presumed Marginal Cost Curve

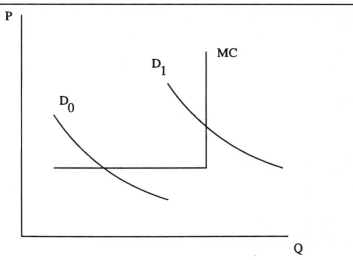

P   = price
Q   = quantity
D   = demand
MC = marginal cost

Notice the modest phrasing: "points in the direction of." Hall frankly admits that there are other explanations of how market power might coexist with low profit rates. He claims only that their conjunction lends credence to what is otherwise a plausible hypothesis: that marginal cost is constant up to capacity. The last link in the argument—from constant MC to sticky prices—is trivial, and was made in the first paragraph of this chapter.

Several empirical questions immediately spring to mind such as:

1. Do firms really base prices on marginal cost, rather than, say, on average cost?

2. Do real-world marginal cost curves look like figure 12.1?

3. Is the optimal markup constant over the business cycle?

Each of these has been subject to empirical and theoretical dispute.

Regarding the first point, there is a long literature—dating at least from Hall and Hitch (1939; see chapter 2)—suggesting that average costs are more important in pricing than marginal costs, despite the teachings of economists. Recently, for example, Anil Kashyap (1995, 259) observed that the prices of nearly identical goods sold by different mail-order retailers rise and fall at different times. If all retailers experience changes in marginal costs at the same time, as they should, markups cannot be fixed. Stephen Cecchetti's (1986) finding that magazine prices remain constant in nominal dollars for long periods of time also makes it hard to believe that constant MC and a fixed markup can describe this industry.

That MC is constant in the short run contradicts a standard assumption of classical production theory if there is any fixed factor of production.[2] Indeed, as Keynes once wrote to Ohlin, "I have always regarded decreasing physical returns in the short period as one of the very few incontrovertible propositions of our miserable subject!"[3] Specifically, suppose $Q = AF(K,L)$ with labor variable and capital fixed. Then $MC = W/AF_L$, and F_L declines as output increases because $F_{LL} > 0$. That, of course, is why textbook MC curves are always drawn upward sloping (or, perhaps, U-shaped). In sharp contrast to the textbook view, Valerie Ramey (1991a) has offered evidence that MC actually declines with output in several industries. The issue is far from settled.

As discussed in chapter 10, there also is a fair bit of evidence that markups are not constant, but rather are countercyclical—although the issue remains open. Indeed, countercyclical markups are often offered as a reason why prices remain approximately constant even with upward-sloping marginal cost curves. That is the essence of theory B5 (see chapter 10). When combined with a flat marginal cost schedule, countercyclical markups would imply countercyclical prices.

But perhaps the most fundamental point is the one raised at the outset: even with constant MC and constant markups, prices are sticky in nominal terms only if marginal costs are. Hence (nominal) price stickiness does not follow from constant (real) marginal costs alone.

On the Empirical Validity of the Theory

To believe in constant marginal cost as a theory of price rigidity (theory B7 on the questionnaire), you must accept two premises: first, that marginal costs are constant, and second, that this constancy is an important source of sticky prices. Hence, we evaluated theory B7 in two stages.

We began by asking about the shape of the firm's marginal cost curve. This turned out to be quite tricky because the term "marginal cost" is not in the lexicon of most business people; the concept itself may not even be a natural one.[4] For purposes of the survey, we translated "marginal cost" into "variable costs of producing additional units," and posed the following question:

B7(a). Some companies find that their *variable costs per unit* are roughly *constant* when production rises. Others incur either *higher* or *lower* variable costs of producing additional units when they raise production. How would you characterize the behavior of your own variable costs of producing additional units as production rises?

This proved to be a difficult question for our respondents to answer. It often had to be repeated, rephrased, or explained. Even so, ten of our two hundred firms were unable to answer the question. Each of the other one hundred and ninety executives answered in his own words, sometimes at great length, and inter-viewers had to classify the responses into one of five categories offered on the questionnaire.[5] The simplest way to summarize the answers is graphically, as was done in figure 4.1. Figure 12.2 repeats this information; it depicts five possible shapes for the MC curve

Figure 12.2   Possible Marginal Cost Curves

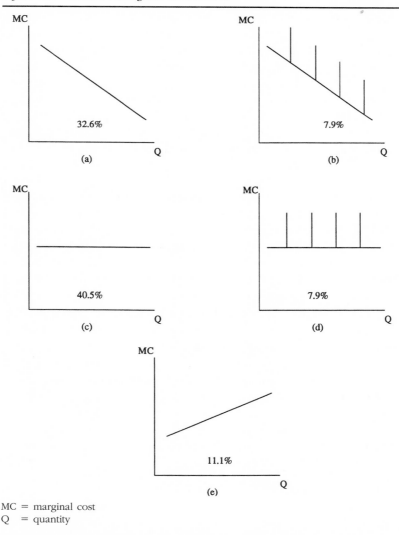

MC = marginal cost
Q = quantity

and the fraction of firms selecting each. The spikes in panels (b) and (d) indicate cases in which costs jump discretely when output crosses certain critical thresholds—as when a bank opens a new branch office or a railroad adds an additional car.

The answers are fascinating, especially when juxtaposed against the standard neoclassical assumption that panel (e) is the rule. Only 11 percent of firms report that their MC curves are rising (panel [e]). By contrast, about 40 percent claim that their MC curves are falling, presumably globally (panels [a] and [b]). The good news for the constant marginal cost theory is that approximate constancy of MC (panels [c] and [d]) is the modal case—encompassing 48.4 percent of GDP. The bad news is that this group accounts for less than half of GDP and that almost as many firms (40.5 percent) say they have falling MC (panels [a] and [b]). If anything, it appears that Hall did not go far enough in arguing against the standard neoclassical view that the MC curve is upward-sloping. Taken at face value, the results are somewhere between Valerie Ramey (1991a) and Robert Hall (1986).

The experiences of the interviewers lead us to discount these results somewhat because many executives had difficulty understanding the question, and some may have confused marginal with average cost.[6] It is surely not surprising that many firms have falling AC—even globally. Nonetheless, the subjective discount applied to these responses would have to be severe before we read figure 12.2 as indicating that rising MC is the norm.

In any case, if a firm denied having constant MC, we certainly could not ask whether constant MC is an important source of sticky prices. So the main question for theory B7 was posed only to firms that classified themselves in panel (c) or panel (d) of figure 12.2— ninety-two companies in all. The others were automatically coded as answering "totally unimportant" to the following question:

B7. It has been suggested that many firms base prices on costs. Hence firms with constant variable costs per unit have no reason to change prices when production changes.

How important is this idea in explaining the speed of price adjustment in your company? (n = 90)

Table 12.1 summarizes the answers. They give the theory a pretty poor rating. Firms representing almost three-quarters of GDP

Table 12.1   B7. How Important Is Constant Marginal Cost in Explaining
the Speed of Price Adjustment in Your Company? (n = 190)

Code	Response	All Firms	Percentage of Firms with Flat MC
1	Totally unimportant	73.1%[a]	43.9%
2	Of minor importance	7.2	15.0
3	Moderately important	9.0	18.9
4	Very important	10.6	22.2
	Mean response	1.57	2.19
	Number of responses	190	90
	Rank	9th	

[a] This category includes firms that said MC was not constant by choosing responses 1, 2, or 5 to question B7(a).

reject the theory outright, either because their MC curves are not flat (52 percent) or because they do not see constant MC as an important cause of price rigidity (21 percent). Only about 20 percent of respondents "accept" the theory in the sense that they give it a rating of 3 or higher. The theory gets an average score of only 1.57 on the now-familiar four-point scale, which is low in an absolute sense and places the theory ninth of the twelve evaluated in the survey. Theory B7 ranks a dismal eleventh among manufacturers and dead last among service companies. (Naturally, it fares better in the other sectors.) Even within the population of firms that report constant MC curves, the average rating of theory B7 is only 2.19, which, had it been obtained over the whole sample, would have ranked the theory fifth overall. In brief, it seems most unlikely that constant marginal cost is an important factor behind macroeconomic price rigidity.

As hinted in the previous paragraph, there are some important differences across industrial sectors, however. These are shown in table 12.2. Firms in wholesale and retail trade are the theory's biggest supporters. Their average rating of 2.19 is significantly greater than that given by firms in the other sectors (t = 4.1). Similarly, the low scores in the manufacturing and service sectors are significantly below those in the other sectors (with *t*-ratios of 2.6 and 1.8 respectively).

Table 12.2   The Importance of Constant MC for Price Stickiness, by Sector

		Percentage of Firms				
Code	Response	Manufacturing	Trade	Services	Construction and Mining	Transportation, Communications, and Utilities
1	Totally unimportant[a]	82.3%	51.4%	81.6%	68.2%	64.7%
2	Of minor importance	8.5	5.7	6.1	4.5	11.8
3	Moderately important	5.4	15.7	8.2	13.6	5.9
4	Very important	3.8	27.1	4.1	13.6	17.6
	Mean response	1.31	2.19	1.35	1.73	1.76
	Sample size	65	35	49	22	17
	Mean if B7(a) = 3 or 4	1.67	3.18	1.74	2.78	2.44
	Sample size	30	19	23	9	9
	Rank	11th	5th	11th	6th	9th

[a] This category includes firms that said MC was not constant by choosing responses 1, 2, or 5 to question B7(a).

Interestingly, the differences of opinion displayed in table 12.2 do not stem from different distributions of cost structures across industries. In fact, the answers to question B7(a) are nearly the same across sectors. Rather, the differences reflect disparate evaluations of the importance of constant MC in price stickiness among firms reporting constant MC.

Correlates of the Theory

To shed some light on the characteristics of firms that help explain both the existence and the importance of flat marginal cost curves, we begin by creating two alternative versions of question B7(a), which asks firms about the shape of their marginal cost curves. First, we construct a dummy variable called FLATMC, which takes on a value of one for firms that report having flat marginal cost, either with or without jumps at discrete points, and is zero otherwise:

FLATMC = 1 if B7(a) = 3 or 4 (constant MC)
          = 0 otherwise (rising or declining MC)

Second, we construct a three-way indicator variable, called SLOPE, that distinguishes among cases of rising, flat, and declining marginal cost:

SLOPE = 0 if B7(a) = 5 (rising MC)
          = 1 if B7(a) = 3 or 4 (constant MC)
          = 2 if B7(a) = 1 or 2 (declining MC)

We constructed this variable in order to investigate the determinants of the shape of firms' marginal cost curves. Note that SLOPE is ordered, and so is amenable to explanation using an ordered probit model.

The shape of the marginal cost curve is an aspect of the firm's technology, and our survey results tell us little about the technologies of our respondents' businesses. One thing we do know— or rather estimate—is the fraction of costs that are variable (MCPCT, question A12[b]). Hall's prototypical firm with flat marginal cost has substantial fixed costs and chronic excess capacity. Therefore, if Hall is right, we should be more likely to find flat marginal costs in firms with a small share of variable costs. Thus, we might expect a negative correlation between the slope of the marginal cost schedule (SLOPE or FLATMC) and the level of marginal costs (MCPCT).

Recall that MCPCT is one of the variables discussed in chapter 6 that we argued might be positively correlated with price stickiness, and therefore with any theory of price rigidity. However, as shown in the appendix to chapter 6, this positive correlation is expected to hold only when marginal cost is increasing, not when marginal cost is flat.[7] Therefore, we maintain the prediction of negative correlations between MCPCT and both the existence of flat marginal cost and its importance in explaining price stickiness. As shown in table 12.3, however, MCPCT turns out to be uncorrelated with either of these variables. One explanation for the lack of correlation may be

Table 12.3 Bivariate Correlates of the Importance of Flat Marginal Cost

Description	Variable Name	Question	Expected Sign	Correlation with		
				B7	FLATMC	SLOPE
General correlates of price stickiness						
Industry	INDUSTRY	—	undefined	$\chi^2_{20} = 26.5$ (p = .15)	$\chi^2_4 = 1.2$ (p = .88)	$\chi^2_8 = 8.5$ (p = .38)
Elasticity of demand	ELAST	A4	?	t = −0.8 (p = .43)	t = −1.4 (p = .17)	t = 1.4 (p = .16)
Cyclically sensitive	CYCLICAL	A6	−	$\gamma = -.03$ (p = .81)	$\gamma = -.07$ (p = .55)	$\gamma = -.07$ (p = .46)
Price stickiness	STICKY	A10, A13	+	t = −0.6 (p = .53)	t = −0.7 (p = .46)	t = 0.4 (p = .72)
Predicted correlates of this theory						
Fraction of costs that are variable	MCPCT	A12(b)	−	t = 0.5 (p = .61)	t = −1.4 (p = .17)	t = −0.9 (p = .36)
Prices based on costs	COSTS	B6	+	$\gamma = .34$ (p = .00)	$\gamma = -.06$ (p = .59)	$\gamma = .01$ (p = .88)
Other correlates						
Log of firm's annual sales	SIZE	ln(A1)	?	t = −2.6 (p = .01)	t = −0.3 (p = .76)	t = 0.1 (p = .93)
Some prices regulated	REGULATE	A14	?	$\gamma = -.29$ (p = .10)	$\gamma = -.05$ (p = .78)	$\gamma = -.09$ (p = .54)
Implicit contracts	IMPLICIT	B2(a)	?	$\gamma = .27$ (p = .09)	$\gamma = .06$ (p = .70)	$\gamma = .03$ (p = .84)
Holds inventories	INVENTORY	B11(a)	?	$\gamma = .54$ (p = .00)	$\gamma = .13$ (p = .47)	$\gamma = -.19$ (p = .27)
Pricing points	POINTS	B4(a)	?	$\gamma = -.09$ (p = .55)	$\gamma = .10$ (p = .50)	$\gamma = -.29$ (p = .02)
Has costs of price adjustment	ADJCOSTS	B8(a)	?	$\gamma = -.07$ (p = .58)	$\gamma = .01$ (p = .93)	$\gamma = .20$ (p = .05)

measurement error. Recall that respondents had trouble describing the slope of their marginal cost schedules, and they even had trouble with the concept of splitting their costs into fixed and variable components. Another explanation, of course, is that the Hall analysis is barking up the wrong tree.

We learned back in chapter 5 that there is a strong positive correlation between the importance firms attach to the flat marginal cost theory and the importance they attach to the cost-based pricing theory (COSTS, question B6). This correlation is repeated for convenience in table 12.3. It makes good sense, because cost-based pricing seems an important part of Hall's model of flat marginal cost.

Table 12.3 next displays four variables that turned out to be significantly correlated with the importance of the flat marginal cost theory, even though there seems to be no clear theoretical reason to expect so on a priori grounds. Firms that have larger annual sales (SIZE), firms that have implicit contracts not to raise prices when the market is tight (IMPLICIT), and firms that hold inventories (INVENTORY) are all more likely to react favorably to the flat marginal cost theory. Firms that report some regulatory restrictions on their freedom to adjust prices (REGULATE) are somewhat less likely to find theory B7 important.

By contrast, none of the variables in the data set were correlated with the existence (as opposed to importance) of flat marginal costs, as measured by FLATMC. However, two variables were correlated with the three-way measure of the shape of firms' marginal cost schedule—the variable SLOPE. Firms that have pricing points (POINTS) are more likely to have rising marginal costs; and firms that have explicit costs of price adjustment (ADJCOSTS) are more likely to have declining marginal costs. These correlations have no ready explanations.

Even in a multivariate setting, we still could not find any strong correlations between firm characteristics and the existence of flat marginal cost (FLATMC), although a few variables have weak (partial) correlations that are very sensitive to which other variables are included in the probit model.[8] We did find some stable correlates with the variable SLOPE describing the shape of firms' marginal cost schedules, however, although the overall fit of the model was not very high. Following our standard search procedure yields the following multivariate ordered probit model:

12.8   OP(SLOPE) = .36 MFG − .41 POINTS + .20 ADJCOSTS
       (n = 154)   (.21)   (.19)   (.11)

       + .0076 ELAST
       (.0045)

    $\log L = -140.2$, $p = .001$, $R_M^2 = .07$, $R_M^2 = .13$.

As can be seen, the bivariate correlations with POINTS and ADJ-
COSTS remain significant in a multivariate setting. In addition,
manufacturing firms are more likely to report declining marginal
cost, as are firms with a high elasticity of demand. (The equation
also includes one interviewer dummy; as usual, its removal does
not change the results very much.)

    We were far more successful at finding correlates with the im-
portance of theory B7. Our best ordered probit model for this variable was:

12.9   OP(B7) = −3.88 MFG − 2.62 TRADE + .98 IMPLICIT
       (n = 92)   (.99)   (.93)   (.39)

       + .62 COSTS + .93 INVENTORY + .019 CONC
       (.18)   (.36)   (.008)

    $\log L = -72.0$, $p = .000$, $R_M^2 = .24$, $R_E^2 = .43$.

As we saw in table 12.2, the flat marginal cost theory performed
worst among manufacturing firms, and this correlation is maintained in the multivariate setting. Surprisingly, though, wholesale
and retail trade (TRADE) firms rate the theory less favorably in a
multivariate setting than do firms in the omitted industries—even
though table 12.2 showed that the theory performed best in trade.
In addition, three of the four variables that have significant bivariate correlations with the importance of theory B7—IMPLICIT,
COSTS, and INVENTORY—retain these correlations in the ordered
probit model 12.9. Finally, firms that are in concentrated industries
(CONC) tend to rate theory B7 more favorably.[9]

    The inclusion of INVENTORY and CONC reduces the sample size
of equation 12.9 considerably. We therefore also present equation
12.10, the best ordered probit model that omits those variables.
Only two variables remain significant, and now the puzzling nega-

tive coefficient for wholesale and retail trade firms becomes positive again. Clearly, the correlation between question B7 and TRADE
is not very robust. The overall fit of the equation is a good deal
worse than that of equation 12.9.

12.10   OP(B7) = .72 TRADE + .27 COSTS
      (n = 188)   (.23)   (.08)

   $\log L = -162.4$, p $= .000$, $R_M^2 = .07$, $R_E^2 = .13$.

Chapter Summary

Firms with constant marginal cost have no need to adjust their (relative) price in response to a demand shock. This idea—which is
admittedly incomplete because it presumes that the level of nominal marginal cost does not change with the demand shock—provides a simple and clear theory of price stickiness.

This simple theory presumes, first of all, that firms' marginal cost
schedules are, in fact, flat. This presumption receives some support
from our survey, although the results must be qualified by noting
that many respondents had trouble understanding the question and
may have confused marginal with average cost. Almost half of our
sample reports that their "variable costs of producing additional
units" are constant. Unfortunately for neoclassical economic theory,
however, most of the rest report *declining* marginal cost. Only 11
percent claim to have the upward-sloping marginal cost schedules
that populate economics textbooks.

As an explanation of price stickiness, however, the flat marginal
cost theory does not fare very well. Even the ninety firms that
report having constant marginal cost rate the theory only "of minor
importance," on average. In the full sample, the theory ranks ninth
out of the twelve theories examined in this book. The flat marginal
cost theory fares particularly poorly among manufacturing firms,
but is viewed somewhat more favorably by firms that attach importance to the cost-based pricing theory. Firms that hold inventories,
that have implicit contracts with their customers, and that are in
concentrated industries also rate the theory relatively favorably.

Chapter 13

Costs of Adjusting Prices

The Theory of Adjustment Costs: Two Variants

Among the simpler reasons why prices might be sticky is the idea that it is costly for firms to change their prices. Clearly, a profit-maximizing firm facing such adjustment costs will change its prices less often than an otherwise identical firm without such costs.

Adjustment costs for prices are typically modeled in one of two ways. In the first variant, adjustment costs are convex and, where explicit solutions are needed, quadratic. The best-known example is by the economist Julio Rotemberg (1982). In his model, firms minimize the expected discounted present value of:

13.1 $\quad (p_t - p_t^*) + c(p_t - p_{t-1})^2$

Here p_t^* is the price that equates marginal revenue with marginal *production* costs, and is thus the price the firm would select in the absence of adjustment costs. The second term in 13.1 is the cost a firm incurs when changing its price. Rotemberg shows that the time path of prices takes the form:

13.2 $\quad p_t = ap_{t-1} + \left(\dfrac{a}{c}\right)\displaystyle\sum_{j=0}^{\infty} \left(\dfrac{a}{1+r}\right)^j {}_tp_{t+j}^*,$

where ${}_tp_{t+j}^*$ is the (rational) expectation, formulated at time t, of what p^* will be at time $t + j$. In this expression, r denotes the firm's discount rate and a is the stable root of the following quadratic equation, which arises frequently in rational expectations models:

$$13.3 \quad z^2 - \left[\frac{(1 + r)}{c} + (2 + r)\right] z + (1 + r) = 0.$$

The implication of equation 13.2 is that actual prices adjust sluggishly—specifically, with a geometric distributed lag—toward their long-run level.

Rotemberg combines this microeconomic model of gradual price adjustment with a simple macroeconomic model in which the money supply drives aggregate demand, draws some implications, and tests the hypothesis of instantaneous price adjustment. While he rejects that hypothesis, there are problems with some of the other estimated parameters of his model.

The quadratic cost assumption appears to have been borrowed uncritically from the literature on the costs of adjusting physical inputs.[1] But the analogy between physical adjustments and price adjustments is strained. Adjustment costs for physical inputs (for example, capital stock) are alleged to arise from such things as installation costs and disruptions in the production process. It seems reasonable to suppose that such costs are an increasing function of the size of the input change. The assumption that adjustment costs rise at an increasing rate is more dubious, but at least it is not totally implausible. However, changing a price does not disrupt activities on the factory floor. And it is hard to see why the cost of "installing" a price increase should be quadratic in the size of the price hike. Is it really four times as costly to change a price by twice as much?

An alternative way to model adjustment costs is as a lump sum that must be paid any time the firm changes its price, namely:

$$13.4 \quad \text{Adjustment costs} = \text{f (a constant)} \quad \text{if } \Delta p \neq 0$$
$$= 0 \qquad\qquad\quad \text{if } \Delta p = 0.$$

Thus, changing a price by a dollar costs the same as changing it by a nickel. Such adjustment costs have come to be called "menu costs" because the expense of printing new menus is the clearest example. The presence of menu costs can give rise to an optimal pricing strategy known as an (S,s) rule.[2] Say a firm faces positive (though uncertain) aggregate inflation. If the firm keeps its own price constant, its real price will tend to fall over time at a stochastic rate. A firm pursuing an (S,s) rule waits until its real price reaches some lower threshold s, whereupon it instantaneously adjusts its nominal price so that its real price returns to the upper bound S.[3]

Until the work of economist Gregory Mankiw (1985), menu costs were thought to be too small to rationalize any substantial degree of price rigidity. But Mankiw pointed out that, because profit functions are flat near their optimum, even small menu costs can lead to large deviations between actual and (first-best) equilibrium prices.[4]

In Mankiw's model, a monopoly firm has constant marginal production costs in real terms and faces a downward-sloping demand curve. The standard solution equates real marginal cost to real marginal revenue, leading to an equilibrium *real* price p*. Nominal variables are proportional to real variables; think of the constant of proportionality as being nominal GDP, Y.

The wrinkle in Mankiw's model is its assumption of nominal price rigidity: The firm must set its nominal price, P, one period ahead, based on its expectation of Y. Hence it picks $P = Y^e p^*$. If Y turns out to be different from Y^e, the firm would prefer to set a different nominal price. But it can change its price only if it pays a fixed cost f. Prices are therefore rigid (for one period) if f exceeds the profit gained from changing the real price from $(Y^e/Y)p^*$ to p*. Mankiw demonstrates that this profit gain is of second order, while the social gain from changing the price—the increase in consumer plus producer surplus—is of first order. Hence even a relatively small fixed cost might induce rigid prices and stand in the way of large social gains.

Quadratic and fixed adjustment costs have starkly different implications for the behavior of prices at the level of the firm. If adjustment costs are convex, a firm wishing to raise its price from p_0 to p_1 will do so gradually, in a series of small steps, rather than all at once. So we should observe frequent but small price changes, as shown in panel (a) of figure 13.1. On the other hand, if the costs of price adjustment are independent of the size of the change, an (S,s) pricing rule should produce price stickiness of a very particular kind: Prices should remain constant for periods of time and then

Figure 13.1 Price Adjustment with Convex Costs and Menu Costs

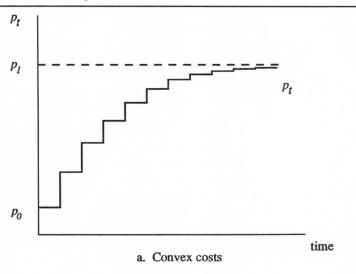

a. Convex costs

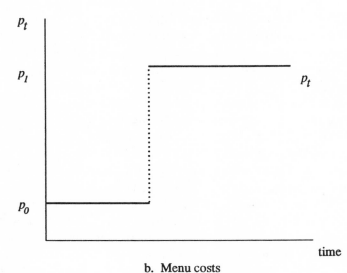

b. Menu costs

p = price

jump abruptly, as illustrated in panel (b) of the figure. So we should observe infrequent price changes of sizable magnitude.

Unfortunately, the predictions of the two classes of models at the aggregate level are not as clear-cut. First consider the quadratic cost version of the theory. Equation 13.2 indicates that the quadratic-cost version of the theory leads to a partial adjustment model of prices—that is, lagged prices should enter the price equation. As an empirical matter, they do, of course; price level inertia is a well-documented fact.[5] But this is hardly a powerful test of the Rotemberg model. For one thing, we noted in chapter 1 that any model of sticky prices will imply that price adjustment is sluggish. So finding that lagged price enters the price equation does not help us discriminate among alternative models of price stickiness. Furthermore, the economist Thomas Sargent (1971) pointed out years ago that rational expectations will cause lagged inflation to enter any equation for inflation—even one based on forward-looking, market-clearing behavior—so long as past inflation helps forecast future inflation. We therefore think it fair to say that macroeconomic time-series models of price adjustment shed little light on the validity of the convex adjustment costs theory.

The aggregate implications of the menu cost model are even harder to pin down. Blinder's (1981) analysis of (S,s) inventory models suggested that aggregation of (S,s) models of pricing behavior should result in something resembling the stock-adjustment model at the macro level. But two related papers by the theorists Andrew Caplin and Daniel Spulber (1987) and Andrew Caplin and John Leahy (1991) demonstrated that such models can generate diametrically different predictions: The aggregate price level can be either extremely flexible or extremely rigid.

The economists Ricardo Caballero and Eduardo Engel (1991) present a general framework for thinking about these results. An intuitive explanation runs as follows. Imagine an economy composed of a large number of firms using the identical (S,s) rule. Assume first that the real prices of these firms tend to be bunched close together, as might be the case if firm-specific shocks to real prices were relatively unimportant compared to aggregate shocks. In such a situation, which is reminiscent of Caplin and Leahy's model, the aggregate price level can be quite rigid. The economy behaves like a single firm pursuing an (S,s) rule writ large.

Now consider the polar opposite case, where firm-specific shocks are quite important and firms' real prices are therefore evenly spread between the (S,s) bounds. In this case, inflation pushes each firm's real price down, causing at least some firms' real prices to fall to the critical lower bound, s, and thus inducing them to raise their prices. At the end of the adjustment process, the distribution of real prices is the same as it was before the shock; most real prices have moved down, and the gap near the upper bound S has been filled by the firms who raised their prices. The aggregate price level therefore manifests no inertia. This is the result that Caplin and Spulber obtain.

Aggregate predictions of the menu cost model notwithstanding, the model's principal implication remains unambiguous at the level of the individual firm, namely that firms should avoid small and frequent price changes. That both Dennis Carlton (1986) and Anil Kashyap (1995) found what appear to be very small price changes in actual transactions data appears to be bad news for the menu cost theory. However, Daniel Levy et al. (1996) report data on both price changes and the costs involved in changing prices for supermarkets that seem to confirm the menu cost theory quite strongly.

Survey Evidence on Adjustment Costs

Our survey offers a more direct way to discriminate between the two versions of the adjustment cost theory. First, we asked firms if they really have adjustment costs of changing prices:

> B8(a). Another idea is that the act of changing prices entails special costs in itself, so firms hesitate to change prices too frequently or by too much. The costs we have in mind are *not* production costs, but costs like printing new catalogs, price lists, etc. or hidden costs like loss of future sales by antagonizing customers, decision making time of executives, problems with salespeople, and so on.
>
> Does your firm incur such costs when it changes prices?

Notice that there is at least one item on this list that economic theorists would not normally classify as an adjustment cost: the notion that today's change in price might affect tomorrow's demand curve ("loss of future sales by antagonizing customers"). There is certainly a danger that respondents might have confused the idea that q_{t+1} depends on Δp_t—which would constitute a genuine adjustment cost—with the simpler idea that a price hike today probably means that tomorrow's price is higher. Unfortunately, there is no way around this problem. When real business people talk about the costs of changing prices, one of the first things they mention is antagonizing customers (see table 13.3 below). So we could not very well omit it from the list. But it may be unrealistic to expect respondents to distinguish carefully between a demand function of the form $q_t = D(p_t)$ and one of the form $q_t = D(p_t, \Delta p_{t-1})$ in the context of an interview.

With this caveat in mind, we proceed to the answers to question B8(a), which are shown in table 13.1. What you make of these results depends on how you interpret the intermediate response "yes, but trivial." If it is viewed as affirming the existence of adjustment costs, then firms representing almost two-thirds of GDP report having such costs—a sizable amount. If, on the other hand, we treat trivial adjustment costs as, well, trivial, then the adjustment cost theory applies to only 43 percent of the economy.

In thinking about these results, it is important to remember that the choices listed in the table were not presented to respondents in multiple-choice format. Rather, respondents answered in their own words; interviewers then coded the answers on the scale indicated in table 13.1. Thus a response was coded 2 only if the interviewee explicitly mentioned—without prompting—that adjustment costs were very small. This inclines us toward the second interpretation: that less than half of GDP is produced by firms with meaningful adjustment costs.

Table 13.1   B8(a). Does Your Company Have Explicit Costs of Price Adjustment? (n = 200 Responses)

Code	Response	Percentage of Firms
1	No	35.8%
2	Yes, but trivial	21.3
3	Yes	43.0

Mean response = 2.07

Differences in the answers to question B8(a) across industries are considerable, as an examination of table 13.2 reveals. Explicit costs of price adjustment are most commonly faced by manufacturing firms and by firms in the transportation, communications, and utilities sectors; they are rarely faced by construction and mining companies. Somewhat surprisingly—if you are thinking about literal menu costs—wholesalers and retailers ("trade" firms) are less likely than average to report adjustment costs. These cross-industry differences are statistically significant.[6]

What is the source of these adjustment costs? We posed this question to any firm that said both that it had adjustment costs, and did not dismiss the adjustment cost theory as "totally unimportant."[7] There were eighty-one such companies which, in total, offered 179 answers; we tabulate them in table 13.3.

The first response includes literal menu costs; responses 2 and 4 are also naturally interpreted as types of menu costs. The loss of future sales that results from antagonizing customers (response 5) is a kind of adjustment cost that seems more likely to be convex in the size of the price change than lump sum. (The cost of securing the cooperation of the sales force could conceivably be either lump sum or convex.) Of the eighty-one firms that answered this question, sixty-one cited at least one of the menu-type costs listed above; thirty-seven firms cited two of them; and twelve cited all

Table 13.2   Presence of Explicit Costs of Price Adjustment, by Sector (n = 200 Responses)

		Percentage of Firms				
Code	Response	Manufacturing	Trade	Services	Construction and Mining	Transportation, Communications, and Utilities
1	No	18.6%	48.6%	32.4%	86.4%	23.5%
2	Yes, but trivial	26.4	23.0	21.3	4.5	17.7
3	Yes	55.0	28.4	46.3	9.1	58.8
	Mean response	2.36	1.80	2.14	1.23	2.35
	Sample size	70	37	54	22	17

Table 13.3   B8(b). What Is the Nature of Adjustment Costs for Changing
             Prices in Your Company?

	Type of Cost	Number of Responses
1	Printing new catalogs, new price lists, new packaging, etc.	51
2	Informing salespeople and customers	43
3	Getting the sales force to cooperate	8
4	Decision making time of executives	28
5	Loss of future sales by antagonizing customers	49
	Total	179

three. Thus, these responses provide strong (though not over-whelming) evidence that adjustment costs for prices are lump sum in nature (like equation 13.4) rather than convex in the size of the change (like equation 13.1).

The impression that menu costs are dominant is strongly cor-roborated by table 13.4. Since menu costs deter frequent price changes while convex costs deter large price changes, we asked the eighty-one firms that attributed at least some importance to the adjustment cost theory whether the costs of changing prices comes mainly from changing prices often or by large amounts. By a mar-gin of more than five to one, respondents gave the answer we would expect if costs were lump sum, rather than convex.

A related question was asked of *all* firms in part A of the ques-tionnaire (table 13.5). Once again, the responses show that an overwhelming majority of firms do *not* approach their target price in a series of small steps, as the quadratic cost model would pre-

Table 13.4   B8(c). Do These Costs of Changing Prices Come Mainly from
             Changing Prices Often or Mainly from Changing Them by
             Large Amounts? (n = 81 Responses)

Code	Response	Percentage of Firms
1	Mainly from often	69.1%
2	Mainly from large amounts	13.6
3	Both	17.3

Table 13.5   A10(b). When You Do Raise or Lower Prices, Do You
Normally Do It All at Once or in a Series of Smaller Changes?
(n = 198 Responses)

Code	Response	Percentage of Firms
1	Normally all at once	74.0%
2	It varies	9.6
3	Normally in small steps	16.4

dict, but prefer to jump there all at once, which is consistent with firms' following an (S,s) rule. (Again see figure 13.1.) Note that we say "consistent with" an (S,s) rule; this choice of wording is deliberate. A firm that follows a strategy whereby prices are reviewed at fixed intervals and compared with some target (real) price might also change its prices all at once, rather than incrementally. (If adjustment costs are lump sum, however, some variant of the (S,s) pricing rule will probably be the optimal rule to follow.)

Taken as a whole, the survey evidence makes a rather convincing case that lump sum adjustment costs are much more important in practice than are convex costs.[8] We note in passing that this conclusion in no way contradicts the evidence presented by Carlton (1986) and Kashyap (1995). Tables 13.4 and 13.5 suggest that convex adjustment costs apply to around 20 percent of GDP. Thus it should not be difficult to find examples of very small price changes. Carlton, for example, finds that the percentage of price changes smaller than 1 percent in absolute value ranged from zero (for household appliances) to as high as 32 percent (for cement) in annual data.[9] But small price changes are the exception, not the rule.[10]

It is natural to wonder whether convex or lump sum adjustment costs are found in particular industrial sectors. Could it be, say, that construction firms typically have convex costs while retailers mainly have menu costs? The answer is no. The responses to questions B8(c) and A10(b) display no clear pattern by industry (a chi-square test fails to reject independence in both cases).

We now turn to the main question concerning the importance of adjustment costs in explaining price stickiness. Immediately after asking all firms whether they faced adjustment costs in changing prices (question B8[a]), we asked those firms that did not answer "no" the following question:

B8. How important are these costs in slowing down price adjustments in your company?

We tabulate firms' responses in table 13.6. The theory scores very well among the eighty-five firms that report nontrivial adjustment costs, receiving an average rating of 2.97. But because so many companies have either trivial or no adjustment costs, its overall rating is quite low. The average score of 1.89 (a bit below "of minor importance") places it sixth among the twelve theories tested.

Table 13.7 presents firms' responses to question B8 disaggregated by industry. Largely because they report having no adjustment costs of any kind, construction and mining firms view adjustment costs as an unimportant source of price stickiness. Likewise, retailers and wholesalers give the theory a relatively low ranking.[11]

Other Aspects of the Theory

The usual theoretical presentations of the adjustment cost theory of price stickiness assume that the costs of price increases and decreases are equal. This is obvious if the costs of price adjustment are quadratic. Similarly, the menu cost variant holds that a lump-sum "toll" must be paid to change a price in either direction.

Table 13.6   B8. How Important Are Costs of Changing Prices in Slowing Down Price Adjustments in Your Company? (n = 200 Responses)

Code	Response	Percentage of Firms
1	Totally unimportant[a]	59.3%
2	Of minor importance	9.8
3	Moderately important	14.3
4	Very important	16.8

Mean response = 1.89
Mean if B8(a) = "yes" 2.97   (n = 85)
Rank = 6th

[a] This category includes seventy-one firms that answered "no" to question B8(a).

Table 13.7   The Importance of Adjustment Costs in Price Stickiness, by Sector (n = 200 Responses)

		Percentage of Firms				
					Construction and Mining	Transportation, Communications, and Utilities
Code	Response	Manufacturing	Trade	Services		
1	Totally unimportant[a]	47.9%	70.3%	53.7%	95.5%	52.9%
2	Of minor importance	13.6	13.5	7.4	0.0	5.9
3	Moderately important	20.0	8.1	11.1	4.5	26.5
4	Very important	18.6	8.1	27.8	0.0	14.7
	Mean response	2.09	1.54	2.13	1.09	2.03
	Rank	5th	8th	6th	12th	6th

[a] This category includes firms that answered "no" to question B8(a).

However, if adjustment costs arise mainly from "antagonizing customers," meaning that this period's demand is a decreasing function of Δp_{t-1}, we might expect asymmetry: Customers may well be antagonized more by a price increase than they are gratified by a price decrease. Prompted by an earlier report on our survey results, the theorist Hugh Sibly (1995) developed a model with precisely this property. In Sibly's model, demand is viewed as a decreasing function of both price and "customer disenchantment." The latter grows when prices rise and shrinks when prices fall; but, owing to the presence of "loss aversion," a rise in disenchantment from a price increase is less than fully offset by an equal price reduction.[12] Sibly shows that this sort of demand specification induces a region within which prices are rigid, that is, are insensitive to small changes in costs or demand.

The survey responses are broadly consistent with these expectations, though they perhaps display more asymmetry than we might have supposed a priori. In table 13.8, we give the precise wording

Table 13.8   B8(d). Do You Incur These Special Costs of Changing Prices
When You Decrease Prices as Well? (n = 77 Responses)

Code	Response	Percentage of Firms
1	No	14.3%
2	Yes, but smaller	26.0
3	Yes (about equal)	57.1
4	Yes, even larger	2.6

Mean response = 2.48

of the question we used in order to test for symmetry, along with a tabulation of firms' responses.

While a majority of firms (57 percent) report that their adjustment costs are symmetric, the remaining 43 percent offer a lopsided appraisal of the asymmetry—more than 40 percent say that adjustment costs are smaller (or nonexistent) for price cuts, while less than 3 percent (only two firms) say that they are larger. These responses have a certain integrity because firms stating that their adjustment costs are of the menu cost variety (that is, that they entail printing price lists, informing salespeople, or decision making time of executives) are significantly more likely to say that these costs are symmetric. In contrast, firms whose adjustment costs result from "antagonizing customers" are significantly more likely to say that the costs are smaller for price cuts.[13]

Even if adjustment costs are symmetric, however, it need not follow that prices are equally sticky in either direction. As Laurence Ball and Gregory Mankiw (1994) note, menu costs imply that prices will be stickier downward than upward if inflation is positive. Because economy-wide inflation tends to reduce a firm's relative price automatically, it takes a larger negative shock (in absolute value) to induce an active price reduction than a positive shock to induce a price increase. Our questionnaire asked only whether adjustment costs are symmetric—not whether the theory itself is as important for price decreases as for price increases. It may well be that this distinction would have been too subtle for our respondents in any case.

The survey was also able to address a fundamental question that often confronts proponents of the adjustment cost theory of price rigidity. It may well be, the argument runs, that there are adjustment costs for changing prices. But surely there are also adjustment costs for changing quantities. Since the feeling of some (perhaps most) economists is that adjustment costs for quantity changes must be larger than those for price changes, adjustment costs are sometimes dismissed out of hand as an implausible explanation for sticky prices.[14]

To repeat a time-worn (but oft-ignored) precept, the relative sizes of the two types of adjustment costs should be decided empirically. This is, of course, impossible to do with standard data, as no direct measurements of adjustment costs exist. The survey offered a unique way to approach this question, and we did so with a series of questions (B8[f] through B8[k] on the questionnaire). First, we asked firms whether they prefer to adjust their price or their output when demand changes. The majority preferred to change output, so we then asked an open-ended question: Why? Finally, we asked directly whether the firm also faces explicit costs of changing output. We proceed now to the details.

Two questions inquired about reactions to changes in demand: Do firms prefer to adjust prices or quantities when demand rises (or falls)? Before looking at the answers, consider what the most naive economic theory says about what the answers should be. For the sake of illustration, suppose the firm has quadratic total costs $C(q)$ (so its marginal cost curve is linear) and a linear demand curve for its output:

$$C(q) = Aq + (a/2)q^2$$
$$q = -bp + e$$

where e denotes shifts of the demand curve. It is straightforward to show that the optimal responses of price and quantity to a demand shock are:

$$dp/de = (1 + ab)/b(2 + ab)$$
$$dq/de = 1/(2 + ab)$$

Economic theory commonly assumes that marginal cost rises with output ($a > 0$), in which case both responses are positive and $dq/de < 1/2$. The implication is that price increases will absorb more than half of any demand shock.[15] It is the belief that price reactions are typically more muted than this that gives rise to concerns about "price stickiness."

Increasing marginal cost is not the only possible case, however. Indeed, we learned in chapter 12 that only 11 percent of firms categorize themselves this way. If marginal cost is constant ($a = 0$), then the fraction of a demand shock that is absorbed by price increases is exactly one-half. With declining marginal cost ($a < 0$), it is less than one-half. Declining marginal cost will not violate the second-order condition for a maximum so long as $2 + ab > 0$. Thus, if $a < 0$ but

$$1 + ab < 0 < 2 + ab,$$

then prices will fall when demand increases and rise when demand decreases. We learned in chapter 12 that almost one-third of the firms in our sample claim to have declining marginal cost. Hence, we should not be too surprised to find that many firms deny, say, that increases in demand lead to price hikes. This is in fact what we do find, as table 13.9 shows. Firms prefer quantity adjustments to price adjustments whether demand is increasing or decreasing. But the margin is overwhelming for increases, slender for decreases.

By now, we are familiar with what might be called the anti-Keynesian asymmetry in price adjustment exhibited in this table: prices

Table 13.9 Firms' Reactions to Changes in Demand

B8(f). When Your Demand Rises, Do You Normally Prefer to Raise Your Production, Increase Your Prices, or Both? (n = 78)

Code	Response	Percentage of Firms
1	Prefer to raise production	61.5%
2	Prefer to raise prices	4.5
3	Prefer to raise both	34.0

B8(h). When Your Demand Falls, Do You Normally Prefer to Decrease Your Production, Cut Your Prices, or Both? (n = 76)

Code	Response	Percentage of Firms
1	Prefer to decrease production	36.8%
2	Prefer to decrease prices	27.0
3	Prefer to decrease both	36.2

appear to be more flexible downward than upward. Another way to see this asymmetry is as follows. Of the seventy-six firms that answered both of the questions in table 13.9, thirty-five gave the same answer for increases in demand as they did for decreases. Of the forty-one firms that gave different answers, thirty-three are more likely to change prices when demand falls and only eight are more likely to change prices when demand rises. That is a sizable degree of asymmetry.

We followed each of the questions shown in table 13.9 with a simple query: "Why is that?" Since the question was open-ended, the answers are not easy to summarize. Consider first the follow-up to question B8(f), about increases in demand. Forty-eight of the seventy-eight firms prefer boosting output to raising price. In total, they offered fifty-eight reasons for this preference (table 13.10).

The first and most popular answer is essentially the one that we have just discussed: costs may be declining, so the rational reaction is not to raise prices. (Remember, however, that real-world business executives rarely distinguish carefully between declining average cost and declining marginal cost.) The second response suggests a concern with market share that is not part of the standard neoclassical model, though we could also read this as saying that the

Table 13.10   Why Do Firms Prefer to Raise Output Rather Than Price When Demand Rises?

	Reason	Number of Responses
1	Some aspect of the cost structure (for example, declining costs)	12
2	Desire to maintain or increase market share	9
3	Competitive pressures make price hikes difficult or impossible	9
4	Don't want to antagonize customers, or want to build future sales	7
5	Menu costs of changing prices	5
6	Implicit contracts	3
7	Fairness	3
8	Other	10
	Total	58

price elasticity of demand is quite high. The third answer indicates that the market is too competitive to give the firm much latitude in pricing. The next two explanations are examples of the adjustment costs that underlie theory B8; indeed, with some liberty, the last two might also be placed under the heading of "not antagonizing customers."

We now briefly consider the follow-up question to question B8(h), which asks about firms' responses to declines in demand. Only twenty-eight firms (out of seventy-six) prefer reducing their output to cutting their price. When we asked why, they offered a total of twenty-nine reasons, listed in table 13.11.

Only one firm explicitly mentioned menu costs of changing prices.

In sum, then, differential adjustment costs do not appear to be the predominant reason why firms prefer to change quantity rather than price—even among the minority of firms that report meaningful adjustment costs.

Our next question inquired directly about adjustment costs for changing quantities. It is the alleged show-stopper question that many economic theorists use to dismiss adjustment-cost theories of price stickiness.

> B8(j). Do you incur special costs from the act of changing your production—analogous to the special costs you incur when you change prices? We have in mind things like temporary halts in production, expenses in recruiting new workers, etc.

We report firms' responses in table 13.12.

We think it surprising that about a third of the firms deny having any adjustment costs for changing production. While the sample distributes itself almost evenly across the three categories, one

Table 13.11 Why Do Firms Prefer to Reduce Output Rather Than Price When Demand Declines?

	Reason	Number of Responses
1	Demand is relatively inelastic	10
2	Some aspect of the cost structure	4
3	Implicit contracts	3
4	Other	12
	Total	29

Table 13.12   B8(j). Does Your Company Have Explicit Costs of Output Adjustment? (n = 77 Responses)

Code	Response	Percentage of Firms
1	No	34.4%
2	Yes, but minor	26.6
3	Yes	39.0

should remember that this question was asked only of firms that report meaningful costs of adjusting prices—which biases the results against the relative importance of adjustment costs for output.[16] Nonetheless, we read the responses as saying that adjustment costs for quantities are typically smaller than adjustment costs for prices—a surprising finding. Furthermore, the most likely respondent error in answering this question—mistaking adjustment costs for production costs—would create a bias against this finding (that is, produce an excessive number of 3s).

We inquired about this finding somewhat more directly via the following question:

B8(k). Then why do you change production rather than change prices?

Forty firms answered this question; all of them had told us they face adjustment costs for prices, and all but one had reported adjustment costs for quantities as well. In total, we received forty-four coherent answers (some firms answered more than once). They break down as follows in table 13.13.

Table 13.13   Why Do Firms with Adjustment Costs for Output Change Production Instead of Prices?

	Reason	Number of Responses
1	It is less costly to adjust output than it is to adjust price[17]	18
2	Competition or concern with market share	9
3	Some aspect of the cost structure	4
4	Demand is inelastic	2
5	Implicit contracts	4
6	Other	7
	Total	44

These responses reinforce the impression left by table 13.12. Firms apparently perceive larger adjustment costs in changing prices than in changing levels of production.

Correlates of Adjustment Costs

Table 13.14 reports bivariate correlations between various firm characteristics and whether the firm faces adjustment costs for prices (question B8[a]) and the importance of adjustment costs as a source of price rigidity (question B8). Unlike many of the other theories we tested, questions B8 and B8(a) display significant correlations with quite a few variables.

Five of the "core" variables (INDUSTRY, FLATMC, MCPCT, CYCLICAL, and STICKY) are strongly correlated with firms' assessments of the theory, although for one variable (MCPCT) the correlation has the opposite sign of that predicted by theory. In all but one case, these variables are correlated with both the presence and the importance of adjustment costs. The exception is FLATMC, an indicator variable for whether the firm's marginal cost curve is flat. It is correlated only with firms' rating of the theory, not with the presence or absence of adjustment costs.

A number of other correlations are reasonable on a priori grounds, particularly if we take an expansive view of what might constitute an adjustment cost:

OUTLOOK and INFLATION (questions A7[a] and A7[b]): Economic theory views all firms as forward-looking. But firms with adjustment costs for prices have especially strong incentives to look ahead. In the case of convex adjustment costs, the optimal path for prices explicitly incorporates a rational expectation of future prices.[18] Similarly, firms with lump sum costs of price adjustment that follow (S,s) pricing rules need to know the rate of inflation in order to choose optimal values for their (S,s) bounds.[19] In fact, both variables are associated with the presence of adjustment costs; INFLATION is also associated with firms' ranking of the theory.

POINTS (question B4[a]): Breaking through psychological pricing points represents a kind of adjustment cost. Firms that report such pricing points do indeed tend to report that adjustment costs are present and of some importance.

STOCK (question A15[a]): Price lists are probably more common for items produced to stock, as opposed to items produced to order. We would therefore expect to see a positive association between the adjustment-cost theory and the fraction of a firm's output produced to stock; in fact we do.

HIERARCHY (question B9): Getting management to sign off on a price increase is a clear form of menu cost. There is a substantial positive correlation between the answer to question B9 and the theory of costly price adjustment.

BUFFERS and INVENTORY (questions B11 and B11[a]): As noted in Chapter 2 (and again in chapter 16), inventories can be used to buffer both prices and output from fluctuations in sales. Firms that find it costly to adjust prices (relative to adjusting sales and inventories) should avail themselves of this opportunity more. Correspondingly in our sample, firms that hold inventories and use them to buffer prices tend to attach more importance to the adjustment cost theory of price stickiness.

INTERVAL (question A9): Deviating from a set time interval for reviewing prices might well give rise to an adjustment cost. In fact, firms that report having such a fixed period are much more likely to have adjustment costs and to view them as important.

IMPLICIT (question B2[a], recoded): Firms that have implicit contracts with their customers are probably more likely to view antagonizing customers through price changes as a relevant cost. There is in fact a positive correlation between the adjustment cost theory and the presence of implicit contracts.

REGULATE (question A14): Dealing with regulatory authorities is a type of menu cost; firms are more likely to report that adjustment costs are present if they must cope with some sort of regulation in order to change prices.

Several of the other significant correlations displayed in table 13.14 may be more than mere coincidences. Here are some conceivable explanations:

CONSUMER and GOVT (questions A2[a] and A2[c]): Dealing with fewer customers might lower menu costs, hence the negative correlation with the fraction of output sold to government and the positive correlation with the fraction sold to consumers.

Table 13.14 Bivariate Correlates of the Existence and Importance of Adjustment Costs

Description	Variable Name	Question	Expected Sign	Correlation with	
				B8 (Importance)	B8(a) (Existence)
General correlates of price stickiness					
Industry	INDUSTRY	—	undefined	$\chi^2_{24} = 36.1$ (p = .05)	$\chi^2_{16} = 44.4$ (p = .00)
Marginal cost	FLATMC	B7(a)	+	$\gamma = .33$ (p = .00)	$\gamma = .01$ (p = .93)
Fraction of costs that are variable	MCPCT	A12(b)	+	t = −1.4 (p = .16)	t = −2.2 (p = .03)
Elasticity of demand	ELAST	A4	–	t = −0.1 (p = .91)	t = −0.5 (p = .62)
Cyclically sensitive	CYCLICAL	A6	–	$\gamma = -.27$ (p = .00)	$\gamma = -.17$ (p = .06)
Price stickiness	STICKY	A10, A13	+	t = 2.1 (p = .03)	t = 2.9 (p = .00)
Predicted correlates of this theory					
Economic outlook affects prices	OUTLOOK	A7(a)	+	$\gamma = .12$ (p = .28)	$\gamma = .25$ (p = .02)
Inflation outlook affects prices	INFLATION	A7(b)	+	$\gamma = .21$ (p = .02)	$\gamma = .31$ (p = .00)
Psychological pricing points	POINTS	B4(a)	+	$\gamma = .22$ (p = .05)	$\gamma = .23$ (p = .04)
Fraction produced to stock	STOCK	A15(a)	+	t = 1.5 (p = .13)	t = 1.9 (p = .06)
Hierarchy slows pricing decisions	HIERARCHY	B9	+	$\gamma = .33$ (p = .00)	$\gamma = .29$ (p = .02)
Inventories slow price changes	BUFFERS	B11	+	$\gamma = .26$ (p = .09)	$\gamma = .08$ (p = .62)

Firm holds inventories	INVENTORY	B11(a)	+	$\gamma = .28$	(p = .06)	$\gamma = .19$	(p = .20)
Customary interval for price reviews	INTERVAL	A9	+	$\gamma = .30$	(p = .01)	$\gamma = .37$	(p = .00)
Implicit contracts	IMPLICIT	B2(a)	+	$\gamma = .22$	(p = .07)	$\gamma = .22$	(p = .06)
Some prices regulated	REGULATE	A14	+	$\gamma = .21$	(p = .11)	$\gamma = .31$	(p = .01)
Fraction of sales to consumers	CONSUMER	A2(a)	+	$t = 1.4$	(p = .16)	$t = 1.7$	(p = .09)
Fraction of sales to others (gov't)	GOVT	A2(c)	−	$t = -1.7$	(p = .08)	$t = -1.8$	(p = .07)
Log of firm's annual sales	SIZE	ln(A1)	+	$t = 2.9$	(p = .00)	$t = 2.5$	(p = .01)
Other correlates							
Frequency of price changes	FREQ	A10	?	$t = -2.6$	(p = .01)	$t = -2.3$	(p = .02)
Has costs of adjusting output	ADJCOSTQ	B8(j)	?	$\gamma = .32$	(p = .01)	$\gamma = .48$	(p = .06)
Index of coincid. indicators	CYCLE	—	?	$t = 2.3$	(p = .02)	$t = 2.5$	(p = .01)
Customers are put on allocation	RATION	A5	?	$\gamma = .16$	(p = .07)	$\gamma = .13$	(p = .19)
Lose least loyal customers first	LOYAL	B5(a)	?	$\gamma = -.20$	(p = .09)	$\gamma = -.09$	(p = .48)
Prices based on costs	COSTS	B6	?	$\gamma = -.14$	(p = .11)	$\gamma = .02$	(p = .81)
Cost increases can be foreseen	FORESEEN	B6(d)	?	$\gamma = .29$	(p = .07)	$\gamma = .37$	(p = .00)

SIZE (log of annual sales, question A1): Large firms are much more likely to report adjustment costs and view them as a source of price rigidity. This might be because it is more difficult for large firms to coordinate price increases (this is a variant of the hierarchy argument).

The strong negative correlation between FREQ (question A10) and the theory is unsurprising, and not terribly interesting, in light of the theory's significant correlation with STICKY (of which FREQ is a component). The strong positive association between adjustment costs for prices (both their presence and their importance) and adjustment costs for quantities (ADJCOSTQ) may be surprising on a priori grounds, but complements a point made earlier: firms that face adjustment costs for prices are more likely to face adjustment costs for quantities as well.[20] One mildly disturbing correlation involves the state of the business cycle as of the date of the interview (CYCLE); fortunately, it does not survive into a multivariate context. We can think of no reasonable explanations for the remaining correlations (with RATION, LOYAL, COSTS, and FORESEEN).

A number of these correlations also survive in a multivariate context. We first ask what sort of firms report nontrivial adjustment costs for prices. Our preferred ordered probit model for question B8(a) is as follows (with asymptotic standard errors in parentheses):[21]

13.5 $OP(B8a) = .54$ MFG $- 1.33$ CON $- .65$ RETAIL
 (n = 195)   (.21)   (.36)   (.36)

   $+ .011$ CONSUMER $+ .36$ INFLATION $- .22$ CYCLICAL
    (.003)   (.11)   (.10)

   $+ .20$ INTERVAL
    (.10)

   $\log L = -185.1$, $p = .000$, $R_M^2 = .16$, $R_E^2 = .33$.

The regression fits the data quite well. Out of the dozen or so variables that manifested significant bivariate correlations with question B8(a), four (CONSUMER, INFLATION, CYCLICAL, and INTERVAL) enter the regression model. In addition, manufacturing firms are more likely to face adjustment costs for prices, and construction and mining firms are less likely (perhaps because most construction output is made to order, and much mining output is sold in flexible-price markets). The surprising negative relationship between the presence of adjustment costs and whether a firm is a retailer (noted earlier) is also present.

The best ordered probit model explaining firms' assessments of the importance of adjustment costs as a source of price stickiness is:[22]

13.6 $\text{OP(B8)} = -1.84\ \text{CON} - 1.46\ \text{RETAIL} - .57\ \text{WHOLESALE}$
(n = 175)   (.53)   (.43)   (.32)

$+ .46\ \text{FLATMC} - .35\ \text{CYCLICAL} + .008\ \text{CONSUMER}$
(.19)   (.11)   (.003)

$- .15\ \text{WRITTEN} - .48\ \text{LOYAL}$
(.07)   (.20)

$\log L = -196.8,\ p = .000,\ R_M^2 = .13,\ R_E^2 = .30.$

Construction and mining and trade firms are again less likely to view adjustment costs as an important source of price stickiness. Several bivariate correlations carry over to the multivariate regression, though none are from the list of correlates that seemed reasonable on a priori grounds. In addition, WRITTEN enters the regression; firms with a higher fraction of sales under written contracts are less likely to perceive adjustment costs as an important source of price rigidity. This is not unreasonable.

The bivariate correlations in table 13.14 suggest that several variables related to inventories might enter these regressions. Including these variables, however, reduces the sample size significantly. We therefore report two additional ordered probit models which include any significant inventory variables. For question B8(a), the best "inventory subsample" model is given by:

13.7 $\text{OP(B8a)} = 1.25\ \text{MFG} + .60\ \text{INFLATION} + .009\ \text{STOCK}$
(n = 109)   (.31)   (.16)   (.003)

$- 2.12\ \text{UNION} - .89\ \text{QUALITY} + .83\ \text{POINTS}$
(1.02)   (.37)   (.26)

$+ .36\ \text{HIERARCHY}$
(.17)

$\log L = -99.4,\ p = .000,\ R_M^2 = .21,\ R_E^2 = .41.$

STOCK, the inventory variable that was most strongly correlated with the presence of adjustment costs, also enters the multivariate regression. Only the manufacturing dummy (MFG) and INFLATION, which asks whether firms use forecasts of aggregate inflation in setting their prices, are common to both variants of the B8(a) regression. While HIERARCHY and POINTS did at least manifest strong bivariate correlations with question B8(a), the other variables in the regression (UNION and QUALITY) did not.[23]

Slightly better results obtain for the regression explaining firms' rating of the theory. The best inventory subsample model for B8 is:

13.8   OP(B8) = −.88 TRADE + .63 FLATMC − .37 CYCLICAL
(n = 100)   (.37)   (.27)   (.16)

       − .64 LOYAL + .009 STOCK − 1.92 UNION
       (.27)   (.004)   (1.17)

       + .53 INFLATION + .56 IMPLICIT
       (.17)   (.30)

       $\log L = -102.9$, $p = .000$, $R_M^2 = .18$, $R_E^2 = .39$.

Again STOCK enters the model, as do a number of variables from the bivariate analysis, and UNION.[24]

If we are willing to restrict the sample even further, we can include ELAST, the firm's price elasticity of demand:

13.9   OP(B8) = −1.32 TRADE + 1.00 FLATMC − .32 CYCLICAL
(n = 83)   (.43)   (.32)   (.18)

       − 1.20 LOYAL + .012 STOCK + .55 INFLATION
       (.33)   (.004)   (.20)

       + 1.03 IMPLICIT + .04 ELAST
       (.40)   (.01)

       $\log L = -78.0$, $p = .000$, $R_M^2 = .26$, $R_E^2 = .54$.

Note that ELAST enters the regression with a positive sign; theory predicts that its sign should be negative. All variables except UNION are common to both specifications.

Although these results are probably largely driven by our truncating the sample so severely, they do appear to confirm that the bivariate correlation between the fraction produced to stock and firms' assessment of the adjustment cost theory is robust to conditioning on other variables.

Chapter Summary

The idea that firms might face adjustment costs of changing prices has been used by a number of authors to explain aggregate price rigidity. The survey allowed us to assess how common these costs actually are; we estimate that less than half of all firms face nontrivial adjustment costs. We were also able to test two competing versions of the adjustment cost model—one in which the cost of changing prices is increasing in the size of the change (convex costs), and one in which firms face a lump sum cost any time they adjust their price (menu costs). We found that adjustment costs appear to be better characterized as lump sum. However, convex costs are faced by a significant minority of firms; so the very small price changes that are observed for some goods should not be construed as a rejection of the menu cost theory in the aggregate.

Although menu costs are often modeled as symmetric, the lump sum costs that firms actually face appear to be extremely asymmetric. Firms told us that adjustment costs are larger for price increases than for price cuts. Apparently, these adjustment costs involve things other than printing new price lists, putting new price tags on goods, and so on. The notion that price increases "antagonize consumers," while price decreases do not, may be the most plausible explanation.

We also found that firms in the trade sector (retailers and wholesalers) are less likely to rate adjustment costs as an important source of price rigidity. Since the classic examples of menu costs are based on the way that these types of firms set their prices, this finding came as a bit of a surprise—and again argues against the literal interpretation of "menu" costs.

We were also able to use the survey in order to judge the merits of a popular argument against the adjustment cost story. Some have claimed (without offering empirical evidence) that adjustment costs for prices cannot possibly be greater than adjust-costs for quantities, and so are an implausible explanation of price rigidity. Surprisingly, the survey evidence suggests that this argument is wrong—although our results may be biased by the fact that we asked about adjustment costs for output only if the firm reported adjustment costs for prices. Many firms with adjustment costs for prices report no adjustment costs for changing production. Moreover, of the firms that reported adjustment costs for prices and quantities, a significant fraction said that adjusting output was less costly.

Chapter 14

Hierarchy

> The big firm is always in danger of becoming . . . an elaborate
> hierarchy, in which every decision requires the consulting of this
> man, the referring to that man, the permission of a third, the agree-
> ment of a fourth, so that decisions become endlessly delayed.
> —E. A. G. ROBINSON

The Hierarchical Structure of Large Firms

The hierarchy theory attributes price stickiness to delays in getting
a large, hierarchical organization to act. If many people are required
to "sign off" on a price change, prices may be incapable of changing rapidly in response to changes in the firm's environment.

This theory is the only one of the twelve examined in this book
that was not culled from the economic literature. Rather, it was suggested by a businessman. As noted in chapter 3, six executives volunteered to help us pretest the questionnaire. At the end of each of
these six interviews, we asked whether we had omitted any factor
that was important in slowing down price adjustments. One respondent, who was responsible for pricing in a large manufacturing
company, suggested hierarchical delays. It struck us as precisely the
sort of phenomenon that might be empirically important in big
companies, and yet totally ignored by economic theory.

There certainly is plenty of anecdotal evidence that large companies sometimes move ponderously. Indeed, one standard explanation of the limits on economies of scale invokes organizational
sluggishness and the difficulty of managing larger and larger firms.[1]
Large corporations devote considerable attention to—and management consultants reap considerable income from—devising organizational strategies to keep decision making flexible and responsive.
So the notion that hierarchies may slow down price changes does
have the ring of plausibility.

Hierarchy could be considered a theory of either nominal or real price rigidity. On the one hand, even raising prices to stay in line with overall inflation requires an affirmative decision on the part of the firm. On the other hand, the firm could decide to index its price automatically, in which case an affirmative decision would be necessary only if the firm wanted to change its real (relative) price. Of these two scenarios, nominal rigidity seems more likely, as explicit indexing in the real business world is quite rare.

Survey Results on the Validity of the Theory

The precise question asked of firms was:

> B9. Some people think that price changes are slowed down by the difficulty of getting a large, hierarchical organization to take action.
>   How important is this idea in explaining the speed of price adjustment in your company?

Responses to this question were summarized in chapter 5 and are repeated for convenience in table 14.1. Briefly, the theory performed extremely poorly. Of the twelve theories, hierarchy ranked next to last. While it is possible that many executives are reluctant to admit that their firms are plagued by hierarchical delays, we were generally impressed by the respondents' high level of candor.

The importance of hierarchy in explaining price stickiness is low in every industrial sector, although it ranks considerably higher in the transportation, communications, and utilities (TCU) sector than elsewhere (see table 14.2). The mean score in TCU is significantly higher (at the 10 percent level) than the mean score in either trade

Table 14.1   B9. How Important Is Hierarchy in Slowing Down Price Adjustments in Your Company? (n = 199 Responses)

Code	Response	Percentage of Firms
1	Totally unimportant	78.9%
2	Of minor importance	7.0
3	Moderately important	8.3
4	Very important	5.8

Mean response = 1.41
Rank = 11th

Table 14.2   The Importance of Hierarchy in Slowing Down Price
Adustment, by Sector (n = 199)

		Percentage of Firms				
Code	Response	Manufacturing	Trade	Services	Construction and Mining	Transportation, Communications, and Utilities
1	Totally unimportant	77.1%	89.2%	75.5%	95.5%	52.9%
2	Of minor importance	4.3	9.5	7.5	0.0	20.6
3	Moderately important	11.4	1.4	10.4	4.5	8.8
4	Very important	7.1	0.0	6.6	0.0	17.6
	Mean response	1.49	1.12	1.48	1.09	1.91
	Sample size	70	37	53	22	17
	Rank	10th	12th	10th	11th	7th

or construction and mining, the two industries in which the theory scored the lowest. Even within the TCU sector, however, more than half of the firms rated the hierarchy theory as "totally unimportant."

The hierarchy theory is intended to apply to large firms only. And, as table 14.3 shows, the theory does fare quite a bit better among the twelve firms in the sample that had more than ten billion dollars in sales. For that small group of firms (but large share of sales), the theory ranked sixth among the twelve theories. Still, half of even those very large firms rated the theory as "totally unimportant."

We asked the forty-two firms that gave the theory a score of 2 or higher to explain—in their own words—what causes the price delays. Fifty-three responses were offered and our attempt to summarize them is reported in table 14.4. The most important reason given was also the most straightforward: that many people have to sign off on a price change. A few firms also noted that hierarchical organizations are very cautious about changing prices.

Table 14.3   The Importance of Hierarchy in Slowing Down Price
Adjustment, by Firm Size

		Annual Sales		
Code	Response	Less than $1 billion	$1–10 billion	More than $10 billion
1	Totally unimportant	83.7%	74.6%	50.0%
2	Of minor importance	4.5	11.9	8.3
3	Moderately important	8.1	7.1	16.7
4	Very important	3.7	6.4	25.0
	Mean response	1.32	1.45	2.17
	Sample size	123	63	12
	Rank	12th	10th	6th

What Kinds of Firms Agree with the Theory Most?

Among the characteristics of firms, size (measured here by the log of sales) is the one that would be expected to be most important for explaining hierarchy. And we have already seen that large firms and firms in the transportation, communications, and utilities sector tend to rate the hierarchy theory more favorably than other firms—though still not very highly. Which other attributes of firms help explain how a given firm rates the hierarchy theory? Other than the usual five variables (FLATMC, MCPCT, ELAST, CYCLICAL, and STICKY) that might be thought on a priori grounds to be correlated with any theory of price stickiness, no other variables come to mind as logical candidates. Empirically, however, several other variables turn out to be correlated with the rating assigned to the hierarchy theory.

Table 14.4   B9(a). What Do You Think Causes These Delays?

Reason	Number of Responses
Several/many people have to sign off on a price change	27
Hierarchical organizations tend to be cautious	8
People worry about the public-relations aspects of price increases	6
Other	12
Total	53

Table 14.5 repeats the finding that large firms (measured by the log of sales) rate the hierarchy theory more favorably. A dummy variable for firms with more than ten billion dollars in sales (SIZE10B) seems to capture this effect nearly as well as does a log-linear relationship. Firms with stickier prices (STICKY) also rate the theory more favorably.

A miscellany of other variables, shown in the lower panel of table 14.5, also turn out to be correlated with the importance of hierarchy. Firms with the following characteristics are all more likely to view the hierarchy theory more favorably: those that make use of output or inflation forecasts in setting prices (OUTLOOK and INFLATION), those that use written contracts (WRITTEN), firms that have some regulatory price restrictions (REGULATE), and firms that have menu costs of either price or output changes (ADJCOSTS and ADJCOSTQ). Note that all or most of these are attributes of more formal management processes—describing just the sort of firm that might be subject to hierarchical delays. In addition, firms that were interviewed when the economy was in a stronger cyclical position (CYCLE) tended to rate the theory more favorably.

Given that there is no intrinsic reason for these univariate correlations, it would not be surprising if most of them were to disappear once we control for firm size. This is, in fact, the case. The search process described in chapter 6 yields the following multivariate ordered probit models (with asymptotic standard errors in parentheses):

14.1　　OP(B9) = 1.05 SIZE10B + .24 STICKY − .30 ACCURACY
　　　(n = 190)　　(.44)　　　　　　(.07)　　　　　　(.15)

　　　+ .53 LOYAL
　　　(.23)

　　　log L = −127.5, p = .000, R_M^2 = .17, R_E^2 = .25.

14.2　　OP(B9) = .11 SIZE + .23 STICKY − .32 ACCURACY
　　　(n = 190)　(.05)　　　(.07)　　　　　　(.16)

　　　+ .51 LOYAL
　　　(.23)

　　　log L = −127.7, p = .000, R_M^2 = .16, R_E^2 = .25.

Table 14.5 Bivariate Correlates of the Importance of Hierarchy

Description	Variable Name	Question	Expected Sign	Correlation with B9	
General correlates of price stickiness					
Industry	INDUSTRY	—	undefined	$\chi_{20}^2 = 30.4$	(p = .06)
Marginal cost	FLATMC	B7(a)	+	t = −0.9	(p = .36)
Fraction of costs that are variable	MCPCT	A12(b)	+	t = −1.1	(p = .27)
Elasticity of demand	ELAST	A4	−	t = −0.5	(p = .65)
Cyclically sensitive	CYCLICAL	A6	−	$\gamma = -.14$	(p = .25)
Price stickiness	STICKY	A10, A13	+	t = 4.0	(p = .00)
Predicted correlates of this theory					
Log of firm's annual sales	SIZE	ln(A1)	+	t = 2.9	(p = .00)
Sales at least $10 billion	SIZE10B	A1	+	$\gamma = .59$	(p = .00)
Other correlates					
Economic outlook affects prices	OUTLOOK	A7(a)	?	$\gamma = .28$	(p = .03)
Inflation forecasts affect prices	INFLATION	A7(b)	?	$\gamma = .34$	(p = .00)
Fraction of sales under contract	WRITTEN	A8	?	$\gamma = .27$	(p = .01)
Some prices regulated	REGULATE	A14	?	t = 3.2	(p = .00)
Index of coincident indicators	CYCLE	—	?	t = 2.0	(p = .04)
Quality depends on price	QUALITY	B3(a)	?	$\gamma = .29$	(p = .07)
Has costs of price adjustment	ADJCOSTS	B8(a)	?	$\gamma = .29$	(p = .02)
Has costs of adjusting output	ADJCOSTQ	B8(j)	?	$\gamma = .42$	(p = .01)

Other than size, only three variables survive into the multivariate setting.[2] Firms with stickier prices (STICKY) and firms that have customers with different degrees of loyalty (LOYAL) tend to rate the theory more favorably; firms that can estimate their marginal cost reasonably accurately (ACCURACY) tend to rate the theory less favorably. Neither LOYAL nor ACCURACY were significant in the bivariate analysis, and there is no clear interpretation of their significant (partial) correlations here. Regarding size, the dummy for firms with more than ten billion dollars in sales (SIZE10B) seems to explain the theory slightly better than does including the log of sales (SIZE) in a simple linear fashion. (When both variables are included as explanatory variables, SIZE10B gets a slightly higher t-ratio than SIZE.) But, in either case, the fit of the regression is pretty good.

Because STICKY may not be an appropriate explanatory variable (see the discussion in chapter 6), we then omitted this variable from the analysis. In this case, two additional variables (INFLATION and WRITTEN) become significant, although the overall fit of the equation declines a little:

14.3   OP(B9) = .98 SIZE10B − .41 ACCURACY + .49 LOYAL
    (n = 185)   (.42)   (.16)   (.23)

       + .32 INFLATION + .14 WRITTEN
      (.13)   (.07)

     $\log L = -128.9$, $p = .000$, $R_M^2 = .15$, $R_E^2 = .23$.

Chapter Summary

The hierarchy theory attributes price stickiness to delays in getting a large hierarchical organization to move. Results of the survey were not encouraging to believers in this theory, however. For very large firms (over ten billion dollars in sales), the theory performed moderately well. For smaller firms, however, it performed abysmally. Overall, the hierarchy theory ranked eleventh out of the twelve theories tested. Among firms rating the theory of at least minor importance, most cited the necessity for many people to sign off on a price change as the source of the hierarchical delays.

Chapter 15

Coordination Failure

Coordination Failure: Theory

According to the coordination failure theory, price setting involves an important element of "following the crowd." Suppose demand in a particular industry rises, warranting an increase in relative price. An individual firm in that industry will certainly want to raise its price if it thinks that other firms are going to raise theirs. And other firms might feel the same way. But each firm worries that its competitors might not raise their prices; so each waits for the others to move first. Absent an effective coordinating mechanism that would enable all the firms in the industry to move in concert, the result may be that the price remains fixed. Similar coordination failures can arise when prices need to fall, or in the case of changes in costs rather than in demand.

One obvious solution to this coordination problem is to have a price leader. However, it is far from certain that any single firm would have the ability or desire to remain the price leader for a long period of time. Another solution is to engage in collusive behavior. But, even aside from its illegality, such collusion can be very difficult to sustain, particularly in a monopolistically competitive industry. So coordinated price movements may be hard to achieve and even harder to maintain.

Coordination failure is a very old idea. In the older Keynesian literature, for example, the economists Robert Clower (1965) and Axel Leijonhufvud (1968) argued that there may be multiple equilibria associated with different levels of product demand and labor demand. They argued that, if all firms hired more workers, the additional labor income would boost product demand and validate the additional hiring; but no firm has a strong incentive to increase hiring unilaterally if product demand is weak. More recently, Russell Cooper and Andrew John (1988) showed that a necessary condition for the existence of such multiple equilibria is what they call "strategic complementarity"—a situation in which one agent's desired action depends positively on the actions of other agents.

Laurence Ball and David Romer (1991) applied this notion of strategic complementarity to pricing decisions under imperfect competition. Since a firm gains market share if other firms raise their prices, there is a strategic complementarity: One firm's optimal price increase depends positively on other firms' price increases. In addition, the Ball-Romer model includes small menu costs of price adjustment that keep prices from adjusting instantaneously to small changes in monetary policy. In their model, sufficiently large monetary shocks—say, bigger than x_N—will induce all firms to adjust prices. But menu costs will prevent any firm from adjusting its price if monetary shocks are small enough—say, smaller than x_A. For the intermediate range of monetary policy actions between x_A and x_N, there are two possible equilibria: price stickiness and complete price adjustment. Each firm will raise its price only if it expects the other firms to do the same.

Up to now, there has been no direct evidence bearing on the importance of coordination failures for explaining price rigidity. Ball and Romer note that price stickiness appears to vary across countries in ways that are hard to explain, and this could be consistent with a multiple equilibrium model. But it could also mean many other things, including that economists do not have a good understanding of the causes of price stickiness! Julio Rotemberg and Michael Woodford (1991) suggest that countercyclical markups are evidence for the sort of tacit collusion that would eliminate such coordination problems. But, as noted in chapter 10, collusion is far from the only possible explanation of countercyclical markups.

Survey Results on the Validity of the Theory

What do our decision makers think of the coordination failure theory of sticky prices? The precise question we asked was:

> B10. The next idea is that firms would often like to raise their prices, but are afraid to get out of line with what they expect competitors to charge. They do not want to be the first ones to raise prices. But, when competing goods rise in price, firms raise their own prices promptly.
>
> How important is this idea in explaining the speed of price adjustment in your company?

Responses to this question were summarized in chapter 5, and are repeated for convenience in table 15.1. Among the twelve theories, coordination failure ranked first, with a mean response of 2.77.

Coordination failure is an important source of price rigidity in every industrial sector, never ranking lower than third. (See table 15.2.) But it appears to be especially important in trade, where the average score is 3.09. The mean score in trade is significantly higher (at the 10 percent level) than the mean score in either construction and mining or manufacturing, the two industries in which the theory scored the lowest.

For firms that rated the theory at least of minor importance, we next asked why they do not want to get out of line with what

Table 15.1   B10. How Important Is Coordination Failure in Slowing Down Price Adjustments in Your Company? (n = 198 Responses)

Code	Response	Percentage of Firms
1	Totally unimportant	27.5%
2	Of minor importance	10.6
3	Moderately important	19.4
4	Very important	42.4

Mean response = 2.77
Rank = 1st

Table 15.2   The Importance of Coordination Failure in Explaining Price
             Stickiness, by Sector (n = 196)

		Percentage of Firms				
Code	Response	Manufacturing	Trade	Services	Construction and Mining	Transportation, Communications, and Utilities
1	Totally unimportant	32.1%	20.0%	25.0%	38.6%	17.7%
2	Of minor importance	14.3	8.6	3.7	9.1	23.5
3	Moderately important	12.1	14.3	30.6	20.5	23.5
4	Very important	41.4	57.1	40.7	31.8	35.3
	Mean response	2.63	3.09	2.87	2.45	2.76
	Sample size	70	35	54	22	17
	Rank	2nd	1st	1st	3rd	2nd

they expect competitors to charge. The 142 firms offered 188
responses (table 15.3). As would be expected, the large majority
gave responses indicating that they do not want to lose market
share to their competitors. A sizable minority also mentioned that
customers would be antagonized if the firm moved out of line
with its competitors.

Table 15.3   B10(a). Why Not Raise Prices Ahead of Competitors?

Reason	Number of Responses
If we raised our prices first, we would lose too much business to low-price competitors	106
When other companies raise prices, we can raise ours without antagonizing our customers	36
We cannot sell anything at prices above those of our competitors	31
Other	15
Total	188

Asymmetrical Responses?

As observed in chapter 5, the coordination failure theory seems to hold much more strongly in the upward direction than in the downward direction. The asymmetry question was:

> B10(b). Do you also delay price cuts because you do not want to be among the first firms in the industry to cut prices? (n = 163)[1]

Responses are shown in table 15.4. Whereas most firms rated theory B10 of at least moderate importance for slowing down price increases, we see that most firms "rarely or never" delay price cuts for fear of coordination failure. Focusing on those firms that agreed with theory B10 (by answering 3 or higher), we see that almost twice as many answered "rarely or never" as answered "usually or always."

This strong degree of asymmetry may not be surprising. Most firms cited fear of losing market share as the reason they do not want to raise prices ahead of their competitors. But this concern does not arise for a price cut, which would lead to an increase in market share.

It is interesting to contrast these results to what one would expect if firms behaved according to the kinked demand curve theory. (Remember, we did not include the kinked demand curve theory in our survey because we were afraid it came a bit too close to explicit collusion.) That theory holds that firms hesitate to cut prices precisely because they do expect rivals to match price cuts (but not

Table 15.4   B10(b). Do You Also Delay Price Cuts Because You Do Not Want to Be Among the First Firms in the Industry to Cut Prices?

Code	Response	Percentage of	
		All Firms	Firms with B10 > 3
1	Rarely or never	61.3%	53.8%
2	Sometimes	13.8	16.5
3	Usually or always	24.8	29.7
Mean response		1.63	1.76
Number of responses		163	106

price increases)—the opposite of the query in question B10(b). Thus, the negative response to question B10(b) might be taken to support the kinked demand curve theory. On the other hand, the responses to that question might instead be interpreted as saying that price cuts are not delayed for any reason, which is not the prediction of the kinked demand curve theory.

For the seventy-three firms that reported anything higher than "rarely or never" to question B10(b), we again asked why they do not want to get out of line with what they expect competitors to charge. We received seventy-two responses from sixty-four firms. Most respondents said that lower prices would hurt profits, which is not a terribly informative answer. Several of these respondents clarified that cutting prices would hurt profits because it would start a price war.

What Kinds of Firms Agree with the Theory Most?

Which attributes of firms help explain how a given firm rates the coordination failure theory? In addition to the usual suspects (FLATMC, MCPCT, ELAST, CYCLICAL, and STICKY), a few other variables suggest themselves as possible candidates. We list them here and summarize the correlations in table 15.5:

ELAST (question A4): In addition to the usual reason to expect a negative correlation between the elasticity of demand and any theory of price stickiness, ELAST seems to relate specifically to the coordination failure theory. Firms might face inelastic demand because they are in oligopolistic markets—just the setting in which

Table 15.5 B10(c). Why Not Cut Prices Ahead of Competitors?

Reason	Number of Responses
Lower prices would hurt our profits	47
We worry that the need for a price cut is temporary	6
If we cut prices first, we would get more business than we want or can handle	3
Other	16
Total	72

coordination problems would appear to be the most relevant.[2] Thus, we have a second reason to expect a negative correlation between ELAST and the importance of coordination failure. This prediction is confirmed in the data.

CONC: Similarly, the four-firm concentration ratio in the firm's four-digit industry (CONC) is an indirect measure of the degree of competition in the industry. Because the theory appears to relate to an environment in which firms have at least some market power, we would expect a positive correlation between CONC and the importance of coordination failures. The data display no such correlation, however.

REGULARS (question A3): Firms that report the existence of regular customers might be less worried about losing these customers if their price is temporarily out of line with those of their rivals. Thus, we might expect a negative correlation between REGULARS and the importance of coordination failures. It turns out, however, that the data show a significant positive correlation.

IMPLICIT (question B2[a], recoded): Similarly, firms that have implicit agreements with their customers not to change prices ought to be less concerned with having prices that differ from those of their rivals. Thus, we expect a negative correlation between IMPLICIT and the importance of coordination failures. This expected correlation is borne out, although it is not quite statistically significant.

WRITTEN (question A8): Firms with prices fixed by written contracts have less scope for timing their pricing decisions to match those of their rivals. We therefore might expect such firms to rate the coordination failure theory less favorably. There is no such correlation in our data, however.

ADJCOSTS (question B8[a]): In the Ball-Romer model, strategic complementarity alone cannot generate coordination failures. It must be combined with some source of nominal rigidity (such as menu costs). So, we expect the theory to fare better among firms that report having explicit costs of price adjustment. The data show no such correlation, however.

INTERVAL (question A9): Firms that are most concerned with matching competitors' prices would seem least likely to adopt a fixed time interval between price reviews. So the expected correlation is negative. This expectation is strongly borne out by the data.

NONPRICE (question B12[a]): If prices are just one element of a vector of characteristics that matter to consumers, firms may compete on the nonprice dimensions, and it therefore becomes less important for prices per se to be in line with those of one's rivals. We therefore expect a negative correlation between NONPRICE and the importance of coordination failures. These two variables turn out to be uncorrelated, however.

A few other variables are correlated with the importance of coordination failure. These are shown in the bottom panel of table 15.5. Firms with some regulatory price restrictions (REGULATE) tend to view the coordination failure theory more favorably, which seems odd.[3] Firms that make use of inflation forecasts in setting prices (INFLATION) and firms that can estimate their marginal cost accurately (ACCURACY) tend to view the coordination failure theory less favorably. (Firms that make use of output forecasts, rather than inflation forecasts, also tend to view the theory less favorably; but this correlation is not statistically significant.) These correlations defy easy explanation.

Which of these correlations survive in a multivariate setting? The orderly search process described in chapter 6 yields the following multivariate ordered probit model (with asymptotic standard errors in parentheses):

15.1   OP(B10) = .35 FLATMC − .011 ELAST − .32 INFLATION
        (n = 153)   (.19)   (.005)   (.11)

        + .72 REGULATE
        (.23)

        $\log L = -214.8$, $p = .000$, $R_M^2 = .05$, $R_E^2 = .15$.

But if the variable ELAST is dropped from the equation in order to increase the sample size, a variety of other variables become significant as well:

15.2   OP(B10) = .31 FLATMC − .33 INFLATION + .57 REGULATE
        (n = 182)   (.17)   (.10)   (.22)

        + .0069 REGULARS − .29 ACCURACY − 1.02 UNION
        (.0042)   (.13)   (.57)

        $\log L = -248.0$, $p = .000$, $R_M^2 = .06$, $R_E^2 = .17$.

Table 15.6 Bivariate Correlates of the Importance of Coordination Failure

Description	Variable Name	Question	Expected Sign	Correlation with B10	
General correlates of price stickiness					
Industry	INDUSTRY	—	undefined	$\chi_{24}^2 = 33.4$	(p = .10)
Marginal cost	FLATMC	B7(a)	+	t = 1.7	(p = .08)
Fraction of costs that are variable	MCPCT	A12(b)	+	t = 0.8	(p = .45)
Elasticity of demand	ELAST	A4	−	t = −1.7	(p = .08)
Cyclically sensitive	CYCLICAL	A6	−	$\gamma = .03$	(p = .72)
Price stickiness	STICKY	A10, A13	+	t = 0.2	(p = .82)
Predicted correlates of this theory					
Concentration ratio	CONC	—	+	t = −0.5	(p = .62)
Fraction sold to regular customers	REGULARS	A3	−	t = 1.8	(p = .07)
Implicit contracts	IMPLICIT	B2(a)	−	$\gamma = -.16$	(p = .15)
Fraction of sales under contract	WRITTEN	A8	−	$\gamma = .09$	(p = .25)
Has costs of adjustment price	ADJCOSTS	B8(a)	+	$\gamma = -.05$	(p = .63)
Customary interval between price reviews	INTERVAL	A9	−	$\gamma = -.24$	(p = .02)
Firms adjust nonprice elements	NONPRICE	B12(a)	−	$\gamma = -.03$	(p = .85)
Other correlates					
Inflation forecasts affect prices	INFLATION	A7(b)	?	$\gamma = -.30$	(p = .00)
Know MC well	ACCURACY	A11	?	$\gamma = -.20$	(p = .03)
Some prices regulated	REGULATE	A14	?	t = 2.1	(p = .03)

Other things equal, coordination failure is a more important source of price stickiness among firms with flat marginal cost curves (FLATMC) and firms that face some legal restrictions on changing prices (REGULATE), and are less important where firms make use of inflation forecasts in setting prices (INFLATION). A less robust positive correlation also is found for firms with a large fraction of sales going to regular customers (REGULARS), and less robust negative correlations are found where firms face more elastic demand curves (ELAST), where firms can estimate their marginal cost curves accurately (ACCURACY), and in industries that are highly unionized (UNION). Of these eight variables, two were anticipated on a priori grounds (FLATMC and ELAST). The others have no clear interpretation.

Chapter Summary

Coordination failure can lead to price rigidity if each firm would adjust its price if it expected other firms to do so, but also would hold prices fixed if it expected other firms not to change their prices. Firms rate the coordination failure theory first among all the theories tested in this book. More than 60 percent of the firms surveyed, and more than 70 percent of wholesale and retail trade firms, rate the theory at least moderately important as an explanation of the speed of price adjustment.

Coordination failure is more important for explaining stickiness in price increases than it is for explaining stickiness in price declines. Most firms report that they "rarely or never" delay price cuts because they do not want to be among the first firms in the industry to lower their prices.

The importance of the coordination failure theory is correlated with the following firm characteristics (with the sign of the correlation as indicated):

- Has a flat MC curve (+)

- faces some legal restrictions on changing prices (+)

- makes use of aggregate inflation forecasts (−)

- sells more to regular customers ($+$)
- faces more elastic demand curves ($-$)
- can estimate MC accurately ($-$)
- unionization of the firm's industry ($+$).

The last four of these correlations are somewhat fragile, however.

Appendix

Perfect Competition in the Ball-Romer Model

In the Ball and Romer (1991) model, a coordination failure leads to sticky prices. When the economy experiences a monetary shock x greater than some upper bound, x_N, all firms find it optimal to pay a menu cost and raise their prices. When the shock is less than some lower bound, x_A, no firm raises its price. In the intermediate range $x_A < x < x_N$, firms adjust only if other firms adjust. There are therefore two equilibria, one with sticky prices and one with flexible prices.

Ball and Romer use the the ratio x_N/x_A to measure the range of multiple equilibria. They note (in their footnote 11) that as the goods market approaches perfect competition, both x_N and x_A approach zero, but the ratio x_N/x_A approaches infinity. (See the upper panel of figure 15.1.) So they argue that the range of multiple equilibria becomes very large under perfect competition. This claim seems peculiar, however, because when x_N is close to zero almost any monetary shock will be greater than x_N and so large enough to induce virtually all firms to adjust. It seems more reasonable to measure the range of multiple equilibria by the difference between x_N and x_A. In the remainder of this appendix, we demonstrate that, using this metric, the range of multiple equilibria is largest not when the product market is perfectly competitive, but when there is substantial market power.

The Ball and Romer model is based on Oliver Blanchard and Nobuhiro Kiyotaki (1987). Firms produce differentiated goods and purchase the products of other firms in imperfectly competitive markets. Money is required for transactions. When faced with a demand shock, a firm adjusts its price if the benefit of doing so is larger than

Figure 15.1 Range of Multiple Equilibria in the Ball-Romer Model

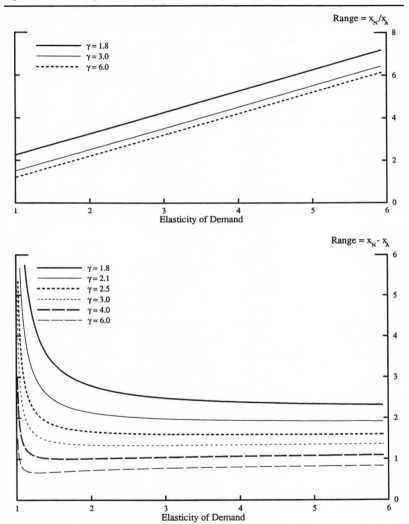

some nominal menu cost, z. Given these assumptions, Ball and Romer derive the following expression for the utility of producer i as a function of real balances (M/P) and the ratio of the firm's price (P) to its optimal price in the absence of menu costs (P*):

$$15.3 \quad V\left(\frac{M}{P}, \frac{P_i}{P_i^*}\right) = \left(\frac{M}{P}\ \gamma(1 - \epsilon + \epsilon\phi)\right)\left[\left(\frac{P_i}{P_i^*}\right)^{1-\epsilon} - \frac{\epsilon - 1}{\gamma\epsilon}\left(\frac{P_i}{P_i^*}\right)^{-\gamma\epsilon}\right]$$

Here ϵ (>1) is the elasticity of demand, γ (>1) is the degree of increasing marginal disutility of labor, and ϕ equals $1 - (\gamma - 1)/(\gamma\epsilon - \epsilon + 1) < 1$. From this, Ball and Romer derive the equilibrium values of x_A and x_N:

$$15.4 \quad x_A = \left(\frac{2z}{-V_{22}}\right)^{1/2}$$

$$15.5 \quad x_N = \frac{1}{1 - \phi}\ x_A$$

They note that the ratio of x_N to x_A shown in equation 15.5 approaches infinity as the elasticity of demand (ϵ) approaches infinity, even though both x_N and x_A approach zero.

We wish to investigate how the range x_N minus x_A depends on the elasticity of demand. This is given as follows:

$$15.6 \quad \text{Range} \equiv R = x_N - x_A = \frac{\phi}{1 - \phi}\left(\frac{2z}{-V_{22}}\right)^{1/2}$$

$$15.7 \quad \frac{\partial R}{\partial \epsilon} = \left(\frac{2z}{-V_{22}}\right)^{1/2}\left[1 - \frac{(\epsilon - 1)(\gamma - 1) + 1}{\gamma - 1}\ \frac{1}{-2V_{22}}\ \frac{\partial(-V_{22})}{\partial \epsilon}\right].$$

Some tedious calculations show that:

$$15.8 \quad -V_{22} = -(\epsilon - 1)\left(\frac{M}{P}\right)^{\gamma(1-\epsilon+\epsilon\phi)}\left[\epsilon\left(\frac{P_i}{P_i^*}\right)^{-\epsilon-1} - (\gamma\epsilon + 1)\left(\frac{P_i}{P_i^*}\right)^{-\gamma\epsilon-2}\right]$$

$$= (\epsilon - 1)(1 + \epsilon(\gamma - 1)) \text{ when evaluated at the equilibrium } \frac{M}{P} = \frac{P_i}{P_i^*} = 1, \text{ and that}$$

15.9 $\dfrac{\partial(-V_{22})}{\partial\epsilon} = (2\epsilon - 1)(\gamma - 1) + 1.$

Plugging these into equation 15.7, we obtain:

15.10 $\dfrac{\partial R}{\partial\epsilon} = \left(\dfrac{2z}{-V_{22}}\right)^{1/2}\left[1 - \dfrac{(\epsilon - 1)(\gamma - 1) + 1}{\gamma - 1}\right.$

$\left. \cdot\ \dfrac{((2\epsilon - 1)(\gamma - 1) + 1)}{2(\epsilon - 1)(\gamma - 1)(1 + \epsilon(\gamma - 1))}\right]$

$= \left(\dfrac{2z}{-V_{22}}\right)^{1/2}\left[\dfrac{(\epsilon - 1)(\gamma - 1)^2 - \epsilon(\gamma - 1) - 1}{2(\epsilon - 1)(\gamma - 1)(1 + \epsilon(\gamma - 1))}\right]$

The sign of this derivative turns out to depend on the magnitude of γ, the indicator of how rapidly the marginal disutility of labor rises. When $1 < \gamma \le 2$, it is negative. Thus, as the product market becomes more competitive, the range of multiple equilibria becomes smaller—not larger, as does Ball and Romer's ratio. When $\gamma > 2$, this derivative is not monotonically negative. Nevertheless, some numerical results suggest that as long as γ is not too large— say, less than 4—the range increases very slowly whenever it is increasing in ϵ. Some simulation results are shown in the lower panel of figure 15.1. (The units of the range are arbitrary; the qualitative shape is what matters.) Roughly speaking, then, the range of multiple equilibria declines with ϵ and then levels out. We are most likely to have multiple equilibria when firms have substantial market power, not when they have no market power.

Chapter 16

Inventories

Inventories and Sticky Prices: Theory

Many sellers of goods—but not of services—hold finished goods in inventory. Economists have long viewed such inventories as buffer stocks which firms can and do use to smooth fluctuations in production relative to those in sales. The presumed reason is that cost curves are convex—which implies that it is costly to vary output. So, although the term is rarely used in this context, inventories make output "stickier" than underlying demand.

In the early 1980s, several authors—notably Patricia Reagan (1982) and Alan Blinder (1982)—observed that a similar argument can be made about prices. The basic idea is simple. If a surge in demand is met—at least partially—by drawing down inventories, then price will increase less than it would if inventories were not changed. In essence, the short-run supply curve is made more elastic by the firm's ability to vary inventories.

Our intuition can be honed with the aid of figure 16.1, which is adapted from Blinder (1982). It shows an upward-sloping marginal cost curve, $MC = C'(y)$, and a downward-sloping marginal revenue curve, $MR = R'(x)$, which is buffeted by a demand shock, e. Without inventories, the equilibrium point, E, would bounce up and down along the MC curve, causing fluctuations in both output and price.

But a profit-maximizing firm that can store goods in inventory operates on two margins simultaneously. In deciding how much

Figure 16.1 The Inventory Theory

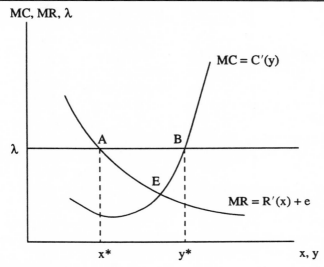

MC = marginal cost
MR = marginal revenue

input to turn into finished-goods inventories, it compares marginal production costs (MC) with the shadow value of inventories—indicated by λ on the diagram (see point B). But in deciding how many goods to take out of inventory and sell, it compares the shadow value of inventories with marginal revenue (MR)—see point A. In the example shown in the diagram, λ sits above the crossing point of MC and MR; so the firm produces (y*) more than it sells (x*), and thus adds to its inventory. But it is optimizing on both margins.

The diagram highlights the key parameter that governs the degree of price stickiness: the responsiveness of the shadow value of inventories, λ, to the demand shock, e. If dλ/de is close to unity, then λ moves approximately as much as the MR curve. In that case, demand shocks lead to large changes in output (y) but small changes in sales (x). But in order to keep sales relatively constant as the demand curve shifts about, price must vary quite a lot. So prices are not "sticky" in this case.

But now suppose that dλ/de is close to zero, meaning that λ hardly budges when the demand curve shifts. Then the diagram shows that x will move around quite a lot as e fluctuates, while y will change little. In this case, prices are relatively rigid.

Blinder (1982) proves that the responsiveness of λ to fluctuations in e, $d\lambda/de$, depends principally on two things: the persistence of demand shocks, and the shapes of the two cost functions—for producing output and for storing inventory. Specifically, prices are stickier when demand shocks are more transitory, and when the costs of varying inventory stocks are lower.

There is not a great deal of evidence on the validity of this theory, one way or the other. Much ink has been spilled on the production side of this story—whether, as predicted by this simple theory, inventories lead to smoother production.[1] But we know of no direct evidence as to whether inventories help smooth prices.

Furthermore, as pointed out in chapter 2, the central implication of this theory is actually rather delicate. It is not that firms with higher stocks of finished-goods inventories—relative, say, to sales—should have stickier prices. Rather it is that, among firms with equally variable demand shocks, those that can vary their inventory stocks more cheaply should have stickier prices. Needless to say, this is not an easy implication to test by conventional econometric methods. The survey method may be somewhat more promising.

Survey Results on the Validity of the Theory

Because services cannot be held in inventory, inventories cannot be a source of price rigidity for firms in the service sector; the inventory theory is simply irrelevant to them. Therefore, with a few exceptions, we only asked this question of firms in the manufacturing, trade, and mining sectors.[2] We began by asking this subsample of 111 firms whether they in fact hold inventories:

B11(a). Still another idea has been suggested for firms that hold inventories of the goods they sell.
Does your firm hold such inventories?

No	13.5%
A little	15.8
Yes	70.7

We then asked the following main theory question only of the 96 firms that answered "yes" or "a little":

> B11. According to this idea, a firm's initial response to fluctuations in demand is to let inventory stocks, rather than prices, vary. That is, when demand rises, they first let inventories fall rather than raise prices. And when demand falls, they first let inventories build up rather than reduce prices.
>
> How important is this idea in explaining the speed of price adjustment in your company?

As shown in table 16.1, the inventory theory fares exceptionally poorly, earning a mean score of only 1.56. Note that this score includes fourteen firms that do not hold inventories—although in principle they could—and so automatically rate the theory "totally unimportant."[3] But even among the ninety-six firms that report holding inventories, two-thirds rate the theory "totally unimportant," and the mean score is a dismal 1.65. This result does not differ much between the manufacturing and trade sectors; both types of firms rate the theory poorly.

Section A of the questionnaire posed two questions that pertain to inventory use. Question A15(a) asked for the percent of output that is produced to stock (rather than to order), and question A16 asked how many times per year the firm's inventory stock turns over. (These questions were asked of the same set of firms that were

Table 16.1 B11. How Important Are Inventories in Deterring Price Increases in Your Company? (n = 110 Responses)

Code	Response	Percentage of Firms
1	Totally unimportant[a]	71.8%
2	Of minor importance	6.8
3	Moderately important	14.5
4	Very important	6.8

Mean response = 1.56
Mean among those holding inventories: 1.65   (n = 96)
Rank = 10th

[a] This category includes fourteen firms that said they do not hold inventories by answering "no" to question B11(a).

asked question B11.) As expected, the responses to these two questions are strongly correlated with whether firms report holding inventories (question B11[a]); this is really a consistency check. However, their correlations with the importance that firms attach to the inventory theory (question B11) are not very strong. Firms that produce a larger share of output to stock, and firms that have a large inventory-to-sales ratio, do rate the theory a bit more favorably. But these correlations are not statistically significant.

Further questions pertaining to the inventory theory were asked only of the thirty-one firms that rate inventories at least "of minor importance" in explaining price stickiness. We proceed to those questions, mindful that, with so few responses, results must be taken with several grains of salt.

Theory suggests that the degree to which firms use inventories to shield prices from demand shocks ought to depend on whether demand shocks are perceived as transitory or permanent. A transitory increase in demand can—and in theory probably should—be met out of inventories, which are then replenished gradually. But with a permanent increase in demand, there is no reason to delay the inevitable price adjustment. We posed the question as follows:

B11(c). Suppose you thought a change in demand was transitory rather than permanent. Would that make you more likely to change prices or more likely to change inventories? (n = 29)

More likely to change inventories	79.3%
About the same	3.5
More likely to change prices	17.2

Firms respond to this question as theory would predict. Transitory shocks are much more likely to elicit inventory adjustments than price adjustments.

We next asked why firms often or sometimes prefer adjusting inventories to changing prices. Thirty-two responses were offered (without any prompting) by twenty-eight firms; and they are shown in table 16.2. Ten respondents said that it costs less to let inventories vary than to change prices—which is, more or less, the answer suggested by the theory—and only five mentioned waiting to adjust their prices until they could judge whether the change in sales is permanent.

Table 16.2 B11(d). Why Change Inventory Rather than Prices?

Reason	Number of Responses
It costs less to let inventories vary than to change prices.	10
It does not antagonize customers.	7
We like to delay price changes until we are confident that the increase or decrease in sales is permanent.	5
Market forces may make it hard to make a price increase stick.	3
Other	7
Total	32

Asymmetrical Responses?

As observed in chapter 5, the inventory theory seems to apply about equally in the upward and downward directions—at least in principle. Interestingly, however, most firms view the theory as more applicable in one direction than the other. But the number of respondents who feel that the idea is more important for increases in demand is about equal to the number who feel that the idea is more important for decreases in demand:

B11(b). Is this idea more important for decreases in demand or for increases in demand? (n = 29)

More important for decreases	34.5%
About equally important	27.6
More important for increases	37.9

On balance, these results suggest pretty symmetric price stickiness. Again, however, one should not lean too hard on results derived from only twenty-nine responses.

What Kinds of Firms Agree with the Theory Most?

As discussed above, theory suggests that firms that can vary their inventories most cheaply should use inventories to dampen price fluctuations most—and therefore should find the theory most attractive. Unfortunately, none of the survey questions relate precisely to this aspect of firms—which would have been very hard to do. One related characteristic is whether the firm can see cost increases coming (FORESEEN, question B6[d]). Such firms have an incentive , for instance, to purchase temporarily inexpensive inputs and (possibly) produce for inventory before the cost increase occurs. Conversely, they have an incentive to limit their purchases of temporarily expensive inputs, and run down their inventories, when they anticipate a cost reduction. The data strongly support this predicted correlation. Firms that can foresee cost increases (FORESEEN) are much more likely to rate the inventory theory favorably—indeed, the Goodman-Kruskal gamma of 0.40 is one of the highest in the data set.

A second plausible correlate of the importance of the inventory theory is whether the firm sometimes finds it necessary to put customers on allocation, thereby limiting the amount they can buy (RATION, question A5). Firms that think they may need to do this often may have an incentive to hold enough inventories to meet spikes in demand—supposing that rationing is costly. Indeed there is a positive and significant correlation between RATION and the importance firms attach to the inventory theory.

In addition, we have already discussed two variables that pertain specifically to inventories: the share of output produced to stock rather than to order (STOCK, question A15[a]), and the sales-to-inventory ratio (S/I, question A16). These two variables display the expected correlations with the importance of the inventory theory, but they are not statistically significant. Finally, we tested the usual five variables (FLATMC, MCPCT, ELAST, CYCLICAL, and STICKY) that might be expected to be correlated with any of the theories. Only MCPCT comes close to being statistically significant.

One other variable, given in the last line of table 16.3, also turns out to be correlated with the importance of the inventory theory. Firms that use pricing points (POINTS) tend to view the theory less favorably. This correlation has no apparent explanation.

To see which of these correlations survive in a multivariate context, we followed the usual search process to obtain the following ordered probit model (with asymptotic standard errors in parentheses):

16.1   OP(B11) = .72 FORESEEN + .36 RATION − .74 POINTS
        (n = 97)   (.35)   (.17)   (.33)

        − .52 ACCURACY
          (.24)

        $\log L = -64.2$, p = .000, R_M^2 = .14, R_E^2 = .24.

Table 16.3 Bivariate Correlates of the Importance of Inventories

Description	Variable Name	Question	Expected Sign	Correlation with B11
General correlates of price stickiness				
Industry	INDUSTRY	–	undefined	$\chi_{20}^2 = 15.6$ (p = .74)
Marginal cost	FLATMC	B7(a)	+	t = 1.1 (p = .27)
Fraction of costs that are variable	MCPCT	A12(b)	+	t = 1.6 (p = .11)
Elasticity of demand	ELAST	A4	–	t = −0.6 (p = .55)
Cyclically sensitive	CYCLICAL	A6	–	γ = .11 (p = .45)
Price stickiness	STICKY	A10, A13	+	t = 1.1 (p = .27)
Predicted correlates of this theory				
Cost increases can be foreseen	FORESEEN	B6(d)	+	γ = .40 (p = .10)
Customers are put on allocation	RATION	A5	+	γ = .25 (p = .07)
Fraction produced to stock	STOCK	A15(a)	+	t = 1.4 (p = .17)
Sales-to-inventory ratio	S/I	A16	–	t = −0.4 (p = .72)
Other correlates				
Pricing points	POINTS	B4(a)	?	γ = −.32 (p = .06)

Other things equal, inventories are a more important source of price stickiness among firms that can foresee cost changes (FORE-SEEN) and firms that sometimes allocate goods to customers (RATION). They are less important where firms use pricing points (POINTS) and know their marginal cost curves reasonably accurately (ACCURACY). As discussed above, the correlations with FORESEEN and RATION might have been predicted a priori, but the correlations with the latter two variables are not easily explained. In addition, one interviewer dummy was significant; but, as usual, its removal does not affect the results.

Chapter Summary

If they are used to buffer demand shocks, inventories of finished goods can be a source of price stickiness. When asked about this theory, however, firms reject it resoundingly. In many ways, this strong negative finding illustrates the payoff to the unorthodox survey methodology. The inventory theory of price stickiness passes most of the tests that economists conventionally use to appraise theories: It can be derived rigorously from first principles; it is consistent with a wide body of existing economic theory; and it makes intuitive sense (and thus meets the "armchair empiricism" test). Unfortunately, real business people deny that they act as the theory says.

The inventory theory gets low marks in all industrial sectors, even among firms that hold significant amounts of inventory. (It is, of course, irrelevant to firms that cannot or do not hold stocks of finished goods.) Firms that can see cost increases coming in advance, and thus may want to vary inventories as a cost-minimization strategy, and firms that worry about having to ration their customers are more likely to agree with the theory than are other firms.

Although the inferences are based on small samples, and are therefore tenuous, at least two implications of the inventory theory are confirmed by the survey results. The stickiness in price adjustment induced by inventories appears to be roughly symmetric—as would be implied by the quadratic cost functions in, for example, Blinder (1982). And firms are more likely to use inventories to buffer demand shocks if they perceive those shocks to be transitory rather than permanent.

Chapter 17

Nonprice Competition

An economist is someone who knows the price of everything,
but the value of nothing.

—A MISQUOTATION OF OSCAR WILDE

Markets That Do Not Clear by Price: Theory

It is no accident that this book focuses exclusively on price behavior. Economists generally look upon prices as the principal vehicle used to clear markets and to allocate resources. In many conceptually simple—though perhaps technically dense—expositions of the theoretical virtues of the market mechanism, it is said that the market price embodies everything that buyers and sellers need to know about the commodity in question. That is quite a sweeping claim, once you stop to think about it.

But several authors, most notably Dennis Carlton (1989), have argued that markets may clear along dimensions other than price. A few prominent examples are delivery lags, product quality, selling effort, and level of service. In an important sense, the elements of this vector of alternative ways to clear the market may be substitutes. Neoclassical economic theory typically assumes that a firm will respond to excess demand by raising its price. But the firm may have other options it considers more attractive. It might prefer to lengthen its delivery lag, as emphasized earlier by Louis Maccini (1973) and Dennis Carlton (1984). Or it might prefer to reduce its selling efforts, to allow its service to customers to deteriorate, or even to reduce the quality of its product—all of which will reduce its production costs.

The optimal mix of clearing mechanisms will depend on the usual considerations—principally, the nature of cost and demand functions. As Carlton (1989) persuasively argued, there is no reason to think that all of the burden of clearing markets always falls on price. As he puts it (p. 936), "It is costly to create a market that clears by price alone," and most markets are not organized this way. Indeed, there is a general presumption in neoclassical economics that an optimizing firm will normally use every instrument at its disposal—at least a little bit. So, on standard neoclassical grounds, we should expect nonprice methods of clearing markets to be the norm, not the exception.

Apart from the work of Maccini and Carlton on changes in delivery lags as an alternative to price movements, there does not appear to be much empirical work on this question. The survey evidence reported in this chapter therefore fills a gap in our knowledge of an important phenomenon that has heretofore been treated only theoretically.

Survey Results on the Validity of the Theory

As usual, we first asked whether the premise holds:

> B12(a). According to the last idea we want to investigate, firms don't cut prices much when demand falls because price is just one of several elements that matter to buyers. More frequently, they shorten delivery lags, make greater selling efforts, improve service, or improve product quality.
>   Is this true of your company?
>
> | | |
> |---|---|
> | No | 23.0% |
> | Yes | 77.0 |

For those respondents who answered "yes," we then asked the following main theory question:

> B12. How important is this idea in slowing down price adjustments in your company/division?

As shown in table 17.1, the nonprice competition theory scores quite well. More than half of the firms rate the theory as at least moderately important in explaining price stickiness. The theory ranks third overall.

Table 17.1 B12. How Important Is Nonprice Competition in Slowing Down Price Adjustments? (n = 197 Responses)

Code	Response	Percentage of Firms
1	Totally unimportant[a]	30.2%
2	Of minor importance	12.9
3	Moderately important	25.9
4	Very important	31.0

Mean response = 2.58
Mean among those with B12(a) = yes: 3.08   (n = 151)
Rank = 3rd

[a] This category includes forty-six firms that said they do not use nonprice competition by answering "no" to question B12(a).

Table 17.2 shows that the theory scores well in all industries. It ranks highest among manufacturing and service firms, with more than 30 percent of these firms rating the theory "very important." The theory does least well among firms in the construction and mining and TCU sectors. But, even in those industries, the theory ranks fourth. In fact, a t-test cannot reject the hypothesis that the mean score in services is equal to the mean in construction and mining. So perhaps we should not make too much of intersectoral differences.

For firms that rated the theory at least of minor importance, we asked for more details about which nonprice elements are important. The 139 firms that responded offered 278 responses, which are tabulated in table 17.3.

Four aspects of nonprice competition are mentioned most frequently (and about equally often): service, quality, delivery lags, and sales effort. About a quarter of the firms also mentioned offering ancillary items at low or zero cost. Note, however, that the wording of question B12 may have prompted some of these responses.

As with inventories, theory suggests that firms' use of, say, delivery lags to buffer the effects of a demand shock on prices ought to depend on whether the demand shock is perceived as being transitory or permanent. Following exactly the same logic as with inventories, a transitory reduction in demand can be met by temporarily shortening delivery lags. But with a permanent change in demand,

Table 17.2 The Importance of Nonprice Competition in Price Stickiness, by Sector (n = 197)

		Percentage of Firms				
Code	Response	Manufacturing	Trade	Services	Construction and Mining	Transportation, Commu- nications, and Utilities
1	Totally unimportant[a]	27.9%	31.4%	27.8%	38.1%	35.3%
2	Of minor importance	10.7	14.3	13.9	16.7	11.8
3	Moderately important	29.3	25.7	21.3	26.2	26.5
4	Very important	32.1	28.6	37.0	19.0	26.5
	Mean response	2.66	2.51	2.68	2.26	2.44
	Sample size	70	35	54	21	17
	Mean if B12(a) = yes	3.00	3.04	3.15	3.04	3.04
	Sample size	58	26	42	13	12
	Rank	1st	3rd	2nd	4th	4th

[a] This category includes firms that answered "no" to question B12(a).

Table 17.3 B12(b). What Nonprice Elements Are Important in Your Case?

Answer	Number of Responses
Improving service	59
Improving product quality	57
Shortening delivery lags	56
Greater selling efforts	55
Offering some ancillary good or service at a low or zero price	39
Increasing variety	5
Other	7
Total	278

there is no reason to delay the inevitable price adjustment. The same might be true for improving sales effort and other nonprice aspects of service—although, unlike inventories and delivery lags, one can more easily imagine a firm making permanent changes on these margins.

We posed the question as follows:

B12(d). Suppose you thought a change in demand was transitory rather than permanent. Would that make you more likely to change prices or more likely to change service? (n = 116)

More likely to change service	60.3%
About the same	10.3
More likely to change prices	29.3

Notice that we phrased the question in terms of service, intending this word to be a generic term. By coincidence (or was it?), service turns out to be the most popular choice in table 17.3. Nonetheless, only about 42 percent of the respondents explicitly cited service as an important dimension of nonprice competition. In general, firms respond to question B12(d) more or less as theory would predict, just as they did with inventories. Transitory shocks are much more likely to elicit changes in service than changes in price.

We then asked why firms sometimes prefer changing conditions of service to changing prices. We received a plethora of answers: 161 responses from 120 firms. (See table 17.4.) The most common response was reminiscent of the implicit contracts theory: that customers are antagonized less by changing conditions of service than by changing prices.[1] Many firms gave a rather uninformative—though theoretically correct—response, suggesting simply that it costs less to let service vary than to change prices. (Recall that respondents answered in their own words.) Several firms also suggested that demand is more elastic with respect to service than with respect to price. And twenty-five firms made explicit or implicit reference to the transitory/permanent distinction.

Asymmetrical Responses?

As discussed in chapter 5, the nonprice competition theory may be a loaded question when it is used to explain why prices are sticky

Table 17.4   B12(e). Why Change Conditions of Service Rather
Than Prices?

Reason	Number of Responses
It does not antagonize customers as much	55
It costs less to vary service than to vary prices	44
Demand is more elastic with respect to service than with respect to price	13
We like to delay price changes until we are confident that the increase or decrease in sales is permanent	13
Changes in service are easier to reverse, should that prove necessary	12
Other	24
Total	161

following an increase in demand. Few firms will want to admit to
allowing service to deteriorate rather than to raising prices. Perhaps
for this reason, more than 70 percent of respondents view the theory as more applicable to the case of a decrease in demand. Still, a
minority of about one-fourth of respondents view the theory as
equally applicable to increases in demand as to decreases in
demand:

> B12(c). Is the same idea applicable to increases in demand. That is,
> do you economize on some aspect of service rather than raise prices?
> (n = 138)

> | | |
> |---|---|
> | More applicable to increases in demand | 2.2% |
> | About equally applicable | 26.8 |
> | More applicable to decreases in demand | 71.0 |

What Kinds of Firms Agree with the Theory Most?

The nonprice competition theory, as described above, is really
quite general in that nearly all firms can alter some aspects of their
product other than price in response to a change in their environment. At its most basic level, then, the theory might be
expected to apply to all firms. Nevertheless, there are a few specific attributes of some firms that might make varying delivery
lags, product quality, or service attractive to them as alternatives

to price hikes. These attributes are discussed here, and the correlations are shown in table 17.5.

QUALITY (question B3[a]): Some firms believe that their customers use price as a signal of product quality. The implication is that the product's quality is not perfectly known—for why else would customers need to infer it from the price? Such a situation appears tailor-made for a firm to try to skimp on quality when demand is strong. Therefore, we might expect to see a positive correlation between QUALITY and firms' ratings of the importance of theory B12. As seen in table 17.5, this is just what we find—and very strongly.

REGULARS (question A3): The above line of reasoning suggests that firms with many regular customers ought to hesitate before allowing quality to deteriorate. If regular customers eventually detect the quality deterioration, they may cease to be regular customers. For this reason, we expect a negative correlation between REGULARS and the importance of the theory. And, as shown in the table, the data support this anticipated negative correlation.

RATION (question A5): Some firms report that they sometimes put customers on allocation and limit the amount the customers can buy. By definition, such firms do not use prices to clear the market instantaneously, and ought to be expected to rank the nonprice competition theory more favorably. As shown in the table, however, RATION is not strongly correlated with the evaluation of theory B12—and the sign is wrong.

The bottom of table 17.5 shows some other characteristics of firms that turn out to be correlated with the importance they attach to the nonprice competition theory. We noted above that, when asked why they prefer to adjust service rather than to adjust price, many firms responded with an answer reminiscent of the implicit contracts theory: that raising prices would antagonize their customers. It is therefore not surprising that IMPLICIT is strongly correlated with the importance of the nonprice competition theory, even though that correlation might not have been expected on a priori grounds. Two other attributes are also correlated with the importance of the theory—firms that make use of inflation forecasts in setting prices (INFLATION) tend to rate the theory more favorably, and firms in highly unionized industries tend to rate the theory less favorably. These are correlations in search of an explana-

Table 17.5 Bivariate Correlates of the Importance of Nonprice Competition

Description	Variable Name	Question	Expected Sign	Correlation with B12	
General correlates of price stickiness					
Industry	INDUSTRY	–	undefined	$\chi_{24}^2 = 16.8$	(p = .86)
Marginal cost	FLATMC	B7(a)	+	t = 0.1	(p = .91)
Fraction of costs that are variable	MCPCT	A12(b)	+	t = −1.1	(p = .29)
Elasticity of demand	ELAST	A4	−	t = −0.2	(p = .84)
Cyclically sensitive	CYCLICAL	A6	−	γ = −.06	(p = .47)
Price stickiness	STICKY	A10, A13	+	t = 2.5	(p = .01)
Predicted correlates of this theory					
Quality depends on price	QUALITY	B3(a)	+	γ = .30	(p = .00)
Fraction sold to regular customers	REGULARS	A3	−	t = −1.8	(p = .07)
Customers are put on allocation	RATION	A5	+	γ = −.11	(p = .19)
Other correlates					
Inflation outlook affects prices	INFLATION	A7(b)	?	γ = .15	(p = .07)
Implicit contracts	IMPLICIT	B2(a)	?	γ = .35	(p = .00)
Unionization rate in industry	UNION	–	?	t = −1.9	(p = .05)

tion. Finally, of the five variables that might be expected to be correlated with any of the theories (FLATMC, MCPCT, ELAST, CYCLICAL, and STICKY), only the last is significantly correlated with the rating of theory B12.

Which of these univariate correlations survive in a multivariate setting? Following our standard search process yields the following multivariate ordered probit model (with asymptotic standard errors in parentheses):

17.1 OP(B12) = −.0087 REGULARS + .64 IMPLICIT
(n = 191)   (.0039)   (.17)

+ .46 QUALITY + .058 CYCLE
(.20)   (.023)

$\log L = -306.5$, $p = .000$, $R_M^2 = .04$, $R_E^2 = .14$.

Other things equal, nonprice competition is a more important source of price stickiness among firms that have implicit agreements with their customers not to raise prices when the market is tight (IMPLICIT), and among firms who think that their customers view price cuts as signals of deteriorating quality (QUALITY). It is less important for firms with a large fraction of sales going to regular customers (REGULARS). We also found a significant correlation with the stage of the business cycle, as measured by the index of coincident indicators—an unusual finding in this study. It suggests that firms might believe more in the nonprice competition theory at business cycle peaks than at troughs.

Chapter Summary

Prices may not move quickly to clear markets if other variables—such as delivery lags, promotional efforts, product quality, and service—are being used to clear markets as well. Carlton (1989) has argued that some degree of nonprice competition should be expected to be the norm, not the exception. In such cases, prices will appear "sticky" when viewed through the strict prism of the neoclassical paradigm.

To a considerable extent, the firms in our survey agree with Carlton—ranking this idea third among the twelve theories tested (and first in manufacturing). Roughly equal numbers of companies report that they often respond to higher demand not by raising price, but in one of the following four ways: by improving their service, by improving their product quality, by shortening delivery lags, or by making greater sales effort. Such nonprice responses in lieu of price increases are particularly likely if the surge in demand is perceived as transitory.

Nonprice competition seems to be especially prevalent where firms perceive implicit contracts with their customers to exist, and where firms believe that their customers judge quality by price. It is less common among firms which sell mainly to regular customers. And, over the one business cycle that occurred during the survey, nonprice competition appears to have intensified at the cyclical peak and weakened at the trough.

Part IV
Wrapping Up

Chapter 18

What Have We Learned?

The moving finger writes; and, having writ, moves on.
            —EDWARD FITZGERALD, *The Rubaiyat of Omar Khayyam*

Part III, one chapter for each theory, was tightly focused on the trees. It is now time to draw up a map of the forest—to put the research results into some perspective. In this concluding chapter, we highlight some things we have learned and mention some things we have not learned. We ask whether the highly unorthodox interview methodology delivered on its promises, and how it might be improved. Most important, we examine how the findings should change economists' views on price stickiness in the U.S. economy: What are the basic lessons for macroeconomics—or, for that matter, for microeconomics? Finally, what new questions have been raised? Where do we go from here?

Critical Aspects of the Methodology

Motivation and Research Strategy

Let us begin by recalling that the original motivation for choosing this highly unusual way to study price stickiness was grounded in three beliefs—and we choose the word beliefs advisedly.

First, the standard investigative tools of economics, theory and econometrics, had been unable to discriminate among alternative theories of price stickiness.

Second, this unsatisfactory state of affairs seemed likely to continue, largely because most of the competing theories predict nothing more than that prices are "sticky" relative to some unmea-sured—and perhaps unmeasurable—Walrasian norm.

And third, interviews might be a more promising route because real-world price setters, if confronted with plain-English versions of the thought processes that lead them to hold their prices fixed, should recognize and agree with these ideas.

This book is published nearly a decade after Blinder first con-ceived of this study, and the intervening years have strongly con-firmed the first two of these beliefs. During this time, theory and econometrics have continued to make little or no progress in dis-criminating among competing theories of price stickiness. Several new theories have cropped up, but none of the old ones appear to have been rejected empirically.[1]

The third belief was the leap of faith that rationalized the unorthodox research design. It has now been put to an empirical test and, in our judgment, survived rather well. With a few excep-tions (duly noted in earlier chapters), real-world decision makers could relate to the various theories and were able to offer coherent opinions on their validity. Out there in the real world, our inter-viewers encountered many more knowing nods than blank stares. Most respondents answered almost all the questions. Such obser-vations do not, of course, prove that the answers we were given were correct. But it certainly points in that direction and bolsters confidence in the interview methodology.

As noted in chapter 3, the major strategic choice in the research design was whether to gather data from a highly-structured survey instrument or through a more free-flowing "conversational" approach. We chose the former and, in retrospect, have no regrets whatsoever. Admittedly, a standardized questionnaire loses much of the richness and texture that can emerge from unstructured interviews that allow individual companies to tell their stories in their own words. And it surely misses many interesting nuances and details.[2] But, in our view, these shortcomings are more than compensated for by the great advantage of a structured survey: it gathers systematic data which have a legitimate claim to generaliz-ability and which are at least potentially replicable.[3] Findings that are neither systematic, nor generalizable, nor replicable may be use-ful in generating new ideas; but they are not very helpful in test-ing them. We do not denigrate this alternative style of research; we applaud and encourage it. But our interest was in testing theoretical hypotheses, and this requires systematic data.[4]

Micro Observations Versus Macro Theory

All of that said, we must acknowledge one weakness that is inherent in this methodology—at least in the way we executed it. From the outset, Blinder decided to limit the inquiry to questions that respondents could answer from their own firsthand knowledge— what happens inside their firms. So, for example, we did not ask respondents about the behavior patterns of other firms (although they sometimes told us). Nor did we quiz them on macroeconomic phenomena. We are convinced that this was a sound methodological precept. After all, our respondents spend their time running businesses, not studying macroeconomic interactions.

Nonetheless, macroeconomic interactions lie at the heart of several theories of sticky prices, and that creates some problems in interpreting the data. A good example is theory B6—cost-based pricing with lags. The central idea is that relatively short lags between cost changes and price changes at the level of the firm cumulate into large macroeconomic lags between, say, cost shocks and the eventual price responses. But we never asked our respondents what they thought about the cumulation idea. Thus the high rating attained by theory B6—second out of twelve theories—cannot be construed as a direct popular "vote" in favor of the cumulation hypothesis. The step from the microeconomic data provided by the firms to the macroeconomic cumulation hypothesis is an inference, not an observation.

Furthermore, the survey assesses each theory's *microeconomic* importance, which may not accurately reflect its *macroeconomic* importance. Aggregation is not a mechanical process of averaging survey responses, but an economic process that works through market interactions. As a simple illustration, imagine a stylized economy with one hundred manufacturing firms producing intermediate goods for sale to three hundred retail firms that sell final goods to consumers. Suppose all the manufacturers adhere closely to the menu cost theory, while the retailers simply mark up their costs immediately, with no lags. Then menu costs would be the sole cause of macroeconomic price stickiness, even though three-quarters of the sample would reject the theory outright.

A Portrait of Price Stickiness in the U.S. Economy: Facts

All these qualifications notwithstanding, what picture of price stickiness in the U.S. economy do the survey results paint?

Prices Are Sticky

First, the evidence gathered in this study emphatically supports the mainstream view that sticky prices are the rule, not the exception, in American industry. According to our respondents, the median number of price changes for a typical product in a typical year is just 1.4, and almost half of all prices change no more often than annually. Among firms reporting regular price reviews, annual reviews are by far the most common. At the other end of the spectrum, only about 10 percent of all prices change as often as once a week, and about 7 percent of all firms schedule price reviews at least weekly.[5]

Our respondents tell us that price adjustments typically lag about three months behind changes in either demand or cost. And, contrary to a common presumption, prices do not appear to respond more promptly to cost shocks than to demand shocks.[6] However, firms do report that their prices react more quickly to cost shocks that are permanent (rather than transitory), industry-wide (rather than idiosyncratic), and large (rather than small). All these are in accord with theoretical presumptions.

Using our constructed variable STICKY to measure the degree of price rigidity, and the orderly search procedure described in earlier chapters, we find that prices are stickier than average when firms:

(a)   enter into implicit contracts with their customers,

(b)   believe that their customers judge quality by price,

(c)   experience important hierarchical delays in changing prices,

(d)   have relatively high fixed costs (low marginal costs),

(e)   utilize inflation forecasts in setting prices,[7] and,

(f)   experience significant coordination failures in changing prices.

On the other hand, prices are less sticky than average among firms in the trade industries and whose businesses are more cyclically sensitive.

The following linear regression describes these correlations:

18.1 STICKY = .47 IMPLICIT + .44 QUALITY
    (n = 175) (.21)   (.25)

      + .32 HIERARCHY − .0071 MCPCT + .47 INFLATION
      (.12)   (.0040)   (.13)

      − .67 TRADE − .23 CYCLICAL + .15 COORD R^2 = .28
      (.28)   (.11)   (.08)

Prices Are Not More Rigid Downward

Many economists will be surprised to learn that the survey uncovered virtually no evidence in support of the characteristic Keynesian assumption that prices are stickier downward than upward.[8] Self-reported lags in reducing prices are no longer than those in raising prices. And the theories generally do a better job of explaining price stickiness in the upward direction than in the downward direction. Among the nine theories for which an asymmetry test could be conducted, only one appeared to do better at explaining downward price stickiness—the theory that markups are countercyclical because elasticity of demand is procyclical. By contrast, the answers to questions about four theories indicated a greater applicability to price stickiness in the upward direction.

The suggestion that prices may be stickier upward than downward raises a tantalizing possibility for future research. It has long been recognized that Keynesian models based on nominal wage rigidity imply that real wages should be countercyclical—a prediction not borne out by the data. Suppose that money wages are stickier downward than upward, while prices are stickier upward than downward.[9] Then a positive shock to aggregate demand might well boost wage growth by more than it boosts price growth, thereby raising real wages for a while. And a negative demand shock might reduce price inflation more than wage inflation, thereby once again *raising* real wages. This is a testable hypothesis that few theoretical models would generate.[10] However, Holmes and Hutton (1996) have recently reported some supporting evidence.

Business Executives Are Not Homo Economicus

Another surprise for theorists—and, in this case, a disconcerting one—is that relatively few firms make direct use of forecasts of economy-wide inflation in setting their nominal prices. Only about a quarter of firms told us that they do so often, while about half said they never use such information. Since most of these prices will be held fixed for some time (about eight and a half months in the median case), ignoring the aggregate inflation rate appears to be a blatant violation of rationality. It suggests—but certainly does not establish—the existence of money illusion.

Of course, it might be objected that inflation was low and stable during the time of this survey, making the economic value of inflation forecasts pretty small.[11] Perhaps. But such forecasts are publicly available at essentially zero cost. A rational cost-benefit calculus would certainly use relevant information that is costless and readily available.

Our interpretation of the survey data is different. It points to a world in which business executives are relatively uninterested in economy-wide inflation (as opposed, perhaps, to industry-specific inflation), do not price their goods and services in an anticipatory manner—as economic theory suggests they should—and may even have money illusion.

The view that pricing is not anticipatory is bolstered by another survey finding: While many firms report being able to "clearly foresee price increases for labor or other things [they] buy," less than half of these firms "raise [their] own prices in anticipation."[12] These responses evoke an image similar to Robert Gordon's (1990, 1151) metaphor: "the sensible firm just waits by the mailbox for news of cost increases and then, Okun-like, passes them on as price increases." Perhaps firms do not set prices on the basis of expectations because they view quantitative forecasts as unreliable and they dislike—or believe their customers dislike—price variability.

Time-Dependent Versus State-Dependent Pricing Rules

Contemporary theories of sluggish price adjustment can be divided into two camps: those based on "time-dependent" strategies which adjust prices only at fixed intervals (such as Blanchard 1983), and those based on "state-dependent" strategies, which are usually (S,s)-type models (such as Caplin and Spulber 1987). The implications of these two classes of models are quite distinct at the micro level, but can get blurred at the macro level by the process of aggregation. A survey may therefore be more promising than econometrics as a way to learn which type of strategy is more prevalent.

But the real world is a complicated place, and the survey responses paint a hybrid picture. A clear majority—perhaps as much as 70 percent of the sample—reports having "a customary time interval between price reviews."[13] That would seem to point clearly toward time-dependent rules as the norm. But a number of these firms report changing prices more often than they have price reviews! And most also report that their prices adjust in ways reminiscent of the (S,s) model. Specifically:

- An overwhelming majority tells us that they make price changes all at once, rather than in a series of small steps (question A10[b]).

- Among firms reporting significant adjustment costs (which are, however, only about 40 percent of all firms), a large majority attributes these costs to frequent price changes rather than to large ones (question B8[c]).

- When we ask about the nature of these adjustment costs, most companies give answers that sound like one or another variety of menu costs (question B8[b]).

In the end, the survey responses suggest a world in which firms deal with fixed costs of price adjustment not by adopting (S,s) strategies, as optimizing theory suggests, but by setting up a schedule of periodic—and not too frequent—price reviews, which they ignore whenever appropriate!

More Prolegomena to Any Future Theorizing

Finally, the survey unearthed a number of basic facts that ought to inform and color any future theorizing about pricing strategies in general and price stickiness in particular. We call the reader's attention to three specific areas.

First, about 85 percent of all the goods and services in the U.S. nonfarm business sector are sold to "regular customers" with whom sellers have an ongoing relationship (question A3). And about 70 percent of sales are business to business rather than from businesses to consumers (question A2). The pervasiveness of these regular business-to-business relationships casts serious doubts on the quantitative importance of theories based on psychological factors such as judging quality by price (theory B3) or pricing points (theory B4)—doubts which are deepened by the low scores received by these theories.

Second, and related, contractual rigidities—whether explicit or implicit—are extremely common in the U.S. economy. We estimate from the survey responses that about one-quarter of output is sold under contracts that fix nominal prices for a nontrivial period of time.[14] And it appears that discounts from contract prices are rare (question A8[d]). Roughly another 60 percent of output is covered by Okun-style implicit contracts which slow down price adjustments (question B2).

Third, firms typically report fixed costs that are quite high relative to variable costs (question A12). And they rarely report the upward-sloping marginal cost curves that are ubiquitous in economic theory. Indeed, downward-sloping marginal cost curves are more common, according to the survey responses (question B7[a]). If these answers are to be believed—and this is where we have the gravest doubts about the accuracy of the survey responses—then the whole presumption that prices should be strongly procyclical is called into question. But so, by the way, is a good deal of microeconomic theory. For example, price cannot approximate marginal cost in a competitive market if fixed costs are very high.

A Portrait of Price Stickiness in the U.S. Economy: Theories

The primary purpose of this study was not, of course, to establish that prices in the United States are sticky; we knew that already. Rather it was to try to discriminate among some of the many competing theoretical explanations for that stickiness—something that conventional theory and econometrics had failed to do. Did we succeed? Readers must judge for themselves. But our sense is that we had about as much success as should have been (and was) expected, though less than might have been (and was) hoped.

The Cellar Dwellers: Theories That Practitioners Reject

In formal hypothesis testing, statisticians can never "accept" a null hypothesis; they can only reject or fail to reject one. Similarly, it always seemed likely that the strongest results of our popularity poll among the twelve theories would be negative ones. That proved to be the case. In our view, four theories—two of which elicited a great deal of intellectual excitement during the last decade—can probably be dismissed on the basis of the survey evidence.

At the bottom of our hit parade, with an amazingly low average score of just 1.33 on the 1-to-4 scale, comes the idea that price cuts are often deterred because firms fear that their customers might interpret lower prices as signals of lower quality (theory B3). American businesses reject this theory with near unanimity. One reason may lie in two facts mentioned in the last section: Most sales are made to other businesses rather than to consumers and to regular rather than occasional customers. Such buyers are presumably more knowledgeable about product quality than are casual consumers. Despite its elegant theoretical roots in the economics of imperfect information, judging quality by price probably deserves to be dropped from further consideration as a theory of price rigidity.[15]

Similarly, the idea that hierarchical delays in large companies underlie sluggish price adjustment (theory B9), which was suggested by a businessman rather than an academic, is soundly rejected by our survey. Its average score is an abysmal 1.41, and only one firm out of seven (weighted by value added) regards the idea as a "moderately important" or "very important" source of price stickiness. However, five of the twelve "giant" corporations in our sample (the ones with sales above ten billion dollars) rate the theory this highly. So hierarchical delays should perhaps not be entirely dismissed.

Moving up the scale, two theories with considerable a priori appeal—inventories (theory B11) and constant marginal cost (theory B7)—obtain miserable, and almost identical, average scores (1.57 and 1.56).

The idea that the ability to vary inventories reduces both price and output variability follows from basic economic theory under extremely weak assumptions—provided the usual concavity conditions hold.[16] Nonetheless, the firms that hold inventories of finished goods—roughly half the sample—do not rate it an important source of price stickiness.[17] And, of course, about half of the U.S. economy, including virtually the entire service and construction sectors, cannot hold finished goods in inventory. Macro theorists had best look elsewhere.

Finally, Robert Hall (1986) popularized a simple and appealing theory of why prices might not move much over business cycles: If both marginal costs and markups are roughly constant over the cycle, then prices will be, too. This theory seems to make good sense, and about half the businesses we surveyed report having constant marginal cost. Within this sector, the theory scores modestly well (with a mean score of 2.19). But there are simply too few such firms to make this a major contending theory of macroeconomic price stickiness.

The Winners: Theories That Practitioners Believe

Turning now to the top-rated theories, we find coordination failure (B10), cost-based pricing with lags (B6), nonprice competition (B12), and Okun's implicit contract theory (B2) in the first division. The only other theory to earn an above-average score, ranking in fifth place, is explicit nominal contracts (B1). It is hard to resist the conclusion that these theories, as a group, have a distinctly Keynesian flavor.

Our specific version of the coordination failure idea—that firms hesitate to raise prices out of fear that their competitors will not follow suit—earned the highest average score among the twelve theories tested: 2.77. It also ranked no lower than third in any major sector. Firms in trade and service industries—which, by the way, set prices for a huge share of all the final goods and services in the U.S. economy—seem particularly enamored of the coordination failure theory. Also, unlike, say, inventories or constant marginal cost, this theory is at least potentially relevant to every sector of the economy. Note, by the way, that coordination failure is one theory that suggests greater price rigidity upward than downward on a priori grounds. This presumed asymmetry is borne out by the survey results.

Second on our list of success stories, with an average rating of 2.66, comes a theory based on the simple idea that prices react with a lag to changes in costs. The model holds that relatively short lags at each firm cumulate into sizable macroeconomic lags because goods must pass through several stages of production on their way to their ultimate users. Here we must repeat a caution issued earlier: Our respondents expressed agreement with the *microeconomic* notion that price increases wait for cost increases; we did not solicit their opinions on the *macroeconomic* cumulation hypothesis.

Ranking third overall, with a mean score of 2.58, is a theory that has garnered much less attention than it deserves: the idea that prices are sticky because firms have other ways to clear markets—such as varying delivery lags, sales effort, product quality, and quality of service. (Firms tell us, by the way, that these four aspects of nonprice competition are of roughly equal importance.) More than three-quarters of the companies in our sample accept the premise of this theory and, within this group, the theory earns a very high average score of 3.08. Nonprice competition is a popular theory across the board; looking across sectors, it ranks as high as first (in manufacturing) and never lower than fourth.

In a way, this finding illustrates the payoff to this kind of research: It focuses the spotlight on a sensible theory of price rigidity that has been all but invisible until now. However, one important caveat must be entered here. Some of our respondents may have been attracted to the theory because the elements of nonprice competition used as examples—such as shortening delivery lags, raising product quality, and improving service—all sound like "good things to do." If so, the ratings of theory B12 may have been boosted by a "motherhood effect." We have no way to assess this bias, if indeed it exists.

Rounding out the top four, with an average rating of 2.40, we find Okun's implicit contract theory (B2)—a model that seems pretty much untestable with conventional econometric methodology. As noted earlier, roughly two-thirds of American businesses perceive that they have tacit agreements with their customers not to raise prices when markets are tight. And, within this sector, the theory's average score is a remarkably high 3.16.

Surprisingly, the implicit contract theory is not more popular among firms that sell more of their output to repeat customers. This may suggest that building a reputation for "fairness," rather than economizing on search costs as emphasized by Okun, underpins implicit contracts. Remember, people leave tips in restaurants they never expect to patronize again. However, many of the other implications of Okun's model seem to be borne out by the survey results. For example, firms report that their customers will tolerate price increases if they are justified by higher costs (question B2[c]).

We close this brief section on the twelve theories with two other general impressions obtained from the survey data. First, differences in the rankings of the theories by industry and by firm size, while occasionally present, are typically not large. This finding offers a ray of hope to economists who seek a general theory of price stickiness. (We consider this idea further below.) Second, the grand average score across all twelve of the theories is a modest 2.00, which translates to "of minor importance"; and the top score is just 2.77, somewhat short of "moderately important." Theorists have a long way to go.

Implications for Macroeconomic Theory

The cornerstone of old-fashioned Keynesian macroeconomic theory was the existence of nominal price and/or wage rigidity—which essentially combined money illusion (the "nominal" part) with wage-price stickiness (the "rigidity"). Although in no way essential to any important conclusions, Keynesian economics often also assumes that this stickiness is strongly asymmetric, which is that prices or wages are significantly more rigid downward than upward.

Apart from the asymmetry, which real firms generally reject, the survey results bolster this basic view of the world. The evidence for price stickiness is, of course, overwhelming. The evidence for money illusion is far less clear. But the absence of anticipatory price increases and the failure to pay attention to economy-wide inflation forecasts at least point in this direction. The estimated mean lags in price adjustment—about three months—suggest that a simple macro model with a one-quarter lag in price-setting may serve as a baseline case.

What general picture of price stickiness emerges from the survey results? Clearly, no simple theory of price rigidity will do. But the theories are generally not mutually exclusive. So hybrid models, though theoretically inelegant, are quite acceptable. It seems to us that the survey responses suggest the following basic hybrid model of the causes and nature of price rigidity in U.S. industry.

First, price increases are explicitly prohibited by written contracts in a significant minority of cases (theory B1). Many firms that are not so constrained are nonetheless deterred from raising prices by concerns that competitors will not follow suit (theory B10). But cost increases are generally industry-wide rather than firm-specific (question B6[b]), so they can serve as convenient signals that other firms are probably under pressure to raise prices. Furthermore, quite a few firms have implicit contracts with their customers that deter price hikes when demand rises but permit them when costs rise (theory B2).

Firms typically delay price increases until some time elapses after costs have risen (theory B6). They do not practice anticipatory pricing—even when they can see cost increases coming (questions B6[d] and B6[f]). And rather than change prices in response to every fluctuation in costs (or, for that matter, in demand), many businesses prefer to hold their prices steady until the next regularly scheduled price review (question A9). But once firms decide to adjust their prices, they typically do so all at once—as suggested by menu cost models—rather than in a sequence of small steps (theory B8; question A10[b]).

Prices are also stabilized relative to the Walrasian benchmark because businesses employ various forms of nonprice competition to close gaps between supply and demand (theory B12). Among the prominent aspects of nonprice competition are variations in selling effort or service, changes in product quality, and shorter or longer delivery lags (question B12[b]).

Finally, and importantly, the survey results direct economists' attention toward a rationale for price stickiness that does not fit neatly into any of the conventional theoretical boxes—a reluctance to "antagonize" customers. Although we almost never prompted this response, firms offered it as an explanation for their behavior in a variety of contexts.[18] Consider the following points:

First, early in the questionnaire, before any of the theories had even been mentioned, we asked respondents an open-ended question: Why don't you change your prices more frequently than you do (question A10[a])? The most common answer was that more frequent price adjustments would "antagonize" or "cause difficulties for" their customers.

Second, when we asked firms why they do not raise prices in anticipation of predictable cost increases (question B6[g]), one of the two most common answers was that "it would antagonize or cause difficulties for our customers."

Third, firms that report costs of adjusting prices were asked to explain the nature of those costs (question B8[b]). The second most popular explanation was "loss of future sales by antagonizing customers."

Fourth, firms that saw some truth in the coordination failure theory were asked why they do not want to be the first to raise prices (question B10[a]). The second most common response was that they can raise prices "without antagonizing customers" only if other firms raise prices, too.

Fifth, although only a few firms viewed inventories as a source of price stickiness, we asked those that did why they prefer changing inventories to changing prices (question B11[d]). The second most popular reason was "it does not antagonize customers."

Sixth, and finally, the most frequent explanation for why firms prefer to change some nonprice attribute of their goods rather than change prices (question B12[e]) was that "it does not antagonize customers as much."

In total, 121 of the 200 firms offered this answer at least once—almost always without any prompting by the interviewers. It appears, in a word, that real-world companies were practically standing up and shouting that (what they view as) excessive price variability would "antagonize" or "cause difficulties for" their customers. But what exactly does that mean?

One interpretation was offered by Arthur Okun (1981), who argued that firms enter into implicit contracts that limit price variability in order to reduce customers' search and shopping costs. Forcing customers to incur more shopping costs certainly might "antagonize" them. But the survey finds no statistical association between the existence of implicit contracts and the share of output that is sold to repeat customers—which looks like bad news for this particular interpretation. Why would firms worry about reducing search costs for customers they do not expect to see again?

A second interpretation was suggested by Hugh Sibly (1995), in reaction to an early report on this research (Blinder 1994). His model posits that consumers care not only about the current price of a commodity, but also about the stock of goodwill that past price changes have created or destroyed. Goodwill, he assumes, accumulates when prices are cut and is drawn down by price hikes. Furthermore, consumers display "loss aversion," so price increases cost the firm more goodwill than price reductions gain for it. Sibly shows that these hypotheses about consumer behavior can lead to price rigidity.

Third, remember that most customers are other businesses, not consumers. If buyers have nonnegligible costs of adjusting prices, and if they generally change their prices only when their costs change, then frequent price adjustments by sellers will impose unwelcome costs on buyers. This explanation seems neat. But, unfortunately, less than half of all firms report nontrivial adjustment costs (question B8[a]).

Finally, there may be a "fairness" interpretation of these data which may or may not be consistent with neoclassical standards of rationality. Executives who say that frequent price adjustments would "antagonize" their customers may be telling us that buyers deem it "unfair" if prices rise too frequently. To the extent that frequent price hikes are needed just to keep pace with overall inflation, such a notion of fairness would imply money illusion. However, if customers are indeed "antagonized" by such price variability, it is rational for firms to take this into account in their pricing.

Implications for Macroeconomic Policy

Price stickiness is of interest to macroeconomists for many reasons, but the principal one is probably that sluggish price adjustment provides the lever by which monetary policy moves the real economy. If prices move less than proportionately to changes in money in the short run—an hypothesis that the survey evidence strongly supports—then monetary expansions and contractions are not neutral.[19]

But to understand why monetary policy has real effects, and to make judgments about whether countercyclical monetary policy is likely to improve social welfare, we need to know why prices adjust so slowly. What are the implications of our findings for these central questions of monetary theory and policy? Since the answers are certain to be theory-specific, we consider the leading theories one at a time.

Coordination Failure

Let us start with the most popular theory, coordination failure (theory B10), and imagine—unrealistically—that it was the only source of price rigidity. As Ball and Romer (1991) astutely observed, if uncoordinated behavior is the cause of the problem, then the obvious cure is greater coordination in wage and price setting, such as in the so-called Scandinavian model. But this "solution" is probably unattainable, and possibly illegal, in the American context. Failing that, the coordination failure model seems to open the door to a stabilizing monetary policy that mitigates recessions and limits inflations.

Note, however, that a large majority of the firms expressing belief in the coordination failure theory report that it deters price increases more than price decreases. If so, increases in the nominal money supply should be more effective at ending recessions than decreases are at causing them—just the opposite of old aphorisms like "pushing on a string" and "You can lead a horse to water, but you can't make it drink."[20]

Nonprice Competition

The survey results also highlight a theory of price rigidity that macroeconomists rarely discuss: the idea that markets clear along dimensions other than price (theory B12).[21] If that is so, short-run neutrality is no longer the central case from which deviations need to be explained. Instead, when the money supply (M)—and therefore aggregate demand—rises or falls, we would normally expect prices to move in the same direction as M but less than proportionately. The reason is simple: Other adjustment mechanisms which influence demand—such as delivery lags and quality of service—are also used to clear markets, leaving less of the burden on prices.

Both the positive and normative aspects of monetary policy need to be explored in this setting. And they may differ depending on the nature of the nonprice competition. We can do no more here than offer a few suggestive remarks and raise some questions for future research.

A little notation will help. Let P_i and Z_i denote the price of firm i and its choice of the nonprice competition variable (for example, the delivery lag), and let P be the economy-wide price level. Suppose demand for each firm's output is:

18.2 $q_i = D(P_i/P, M/P, Z_i)$.

To start on familiar ground, ignore the nonprice variable at first. If the money supply increases, creating excess demand in most (if not all) markets, prices begin to rise. If prices are sticky, they will not rise in proportion to money immediately; so money will not be neutral in the short run. But, presumably, prices will eventually rise in proportion to the money stock, leading to the classical equilibrium with unchanged relative prices and real balances. A stable dynamic adjustment process—which is often ignored in monetary theory—presumably takes us from the short-run sticky-price solution to the long-run equilibrium in which money is neutral.

Now bring nonprice competition into the picture. Once again, an increase in the money supply from M to, say, λM ($\lambda > 1$) creates excess demand in most markets. But now firms respond both by raising prices and by changing Z_i—to, say, αP_i ($1 < \alpha < \lambda$) and βZ_i. For example, after the central bank increases the money supply, delivery lags might lengthen across the economy, or product quality might deteriorate. Suppose these responses clear the market. The question is this: Are forces set in motion that will lead firms to raise their prices all the way to λP_i and to restore their nonprice variables Z_i to their original values? If so, what are they? If not, we appear to have multiple equilibria, with monetary policy able to move the economy from one equilibrium to another.[22]

The story is somewhat different if we suppose that demand for a firm's product depends not on, say, its own delivery lag, but rather on its delivery lag relative to those of competitors:

18.3 $q_i = D(P_i/P, M/P, Z_i/Z)$.

Then, say, a reduction in one firm's delivery lag attracts customers from another firm, but does not stimulate more total demand. Hence, individual firms' attempts to clear markets by nonprice methods will, on average, be frustrated by parallel actions by other firms. One firm will lose what the other firm gains. If all the Z_i/Z return to their original values, then presumably the classical equilibrium with prices λP_i obtains once more. But, in this case, there appear to be important externalities in a firm's choice of, say, delivery lag or product quality—with welfare implications that need to be explored.

Which case is more realistic, absolute or relative nonprice competition? Macroeconomists steeped in New Keynesian models of imperfect competition will naturally gravitate toward the relative version. But is it so unreasonable to assume that consumers might buy more goods and services if all firms shortened their delivery lags or improved product quality? Unlike price, it supposes no irrationality to assume that, say, waiting time or product quality enters consumers' utility functions directly. Similarly, unlike P_i, Z_i should enter firms' cost functions because nonprice competition has real resource costs that price competition does not.[23]

This last remark seems superficially at variance with the basic argument that Carlton (1989) invoked to support this theory: that it is costly to organize a market that clears on price alone. But there is no contradiction. Carlton emphasized the social costs of creating an organized market like a futures exchange, not the private costs of using such a market more intensively once it exists. Furthermore, his argument starts from the premise that, in the absence of a central auction market, it is privately costly for a firm to rely exclusively on price adjustments. Instead, profit-maximizing firms should use multiple methods to clear markets—just as we assume.

Implicit Contracts and Cost-Based Pricing

Finally, a few words on the implications of the other two theories that respondents ranked in the top four: cost-based pricing with lags (theory B6) and implicit contracts (theory B2). The former serves as a theory of price stickiness only if firms eschew anticipatory price increases—as real-world firms apparently do. But why don't companies raise (nominal) prices when they see (nominal) cost increases coming? The two most common explanations offered by our respondents are coordination failure and that (by now) old saw: "it would antagonize our customers." Similarly, the idea that customers object to ("are antagonized by") frequent price changes lies at the heart of the implicit contract theory.

If implicit contracts are derived from optimizing behavior, they should certainly apply to relative prices. There should be no money illusion. But, in fact, real-world implicit contracts (like most real-world explicit contracts) are nominal. Furthermore, firms rarely pay much attention to economy-wide inflation forecasts, even though expected inflation is positive and they expect to hold their nominal prices fixed for some time. This is yet another hint of money illusion.

Thus two unorthodox thoughts—money illusion and "antagonizing customers"—arise prominently in the context of both of these theories. These two thoughts may, in fact, be intertwined. If customers have money illusion, frequent adjustments of *nominal* prices to stabilize *real* prices might well "antagonize" them. In that not-quite-rational world, a firm that raises its nominal price might suffer a reduction in sales even if its real price falls.

It seems essential, therefore, to gain a better understanding of precisely what firms mean when they say that they hesitate to adjust prices for fear of "antagonizing" customers. Frankly, we are skeptical that conventional theoretical and econometric methods will take economists very far in answering this unconventional question. Instead—dare we say it?—a survey may hold more promise.

Looking Ahead

Social scientists in other disciplines often learn things by asking people questions, but economists do so rarely. So the survey reported in this book is, as far as we know, rather unique. We did not just gather a wealth of factual information, we used interviews to test theoretical hypotheses directly. And we did not just survey a random sample of people, we interviewed a random sample of American businesses—a far more difficult task. On balance, we judge the novel methodology a success, while admitting some of its weaknesses.

What new directions for research are suggested by these empirical results? Of the many that could be mentioned, two stand out.

First, firms often told us—in a variety of contexts—that they are loath to change prices because doing so would "antagonize" their customers. This imprecise thought does not fit neatly into any of economists' standard theoretical boxes, although it may be consistent with several. But it comes up so often that figuring out precisely what it means should be a high-priority item on any future research agenda.

Second, many firms appear to leave prices fixed in the face of shocks because they prefer to use one or more avenues of nonprice competition to adjust. Rather than cut prices in the face of sagging demand, firms can and do shorten delivery lags, raise product quality, improve terms of service, or make greater selling efforts. Nonprice competition raises both microeconomic and macroeconomic questions that have barely been addressed by theorists. Why do firms prefer nonprice competition to price competition even though the former appears to entail real resource costs that the latter avoids? What are the welfare implications of markets that clear along nonprice dimensions?

The answers to these and other questions must be left to future research. For now, we have made a landing on a heretofore unexplored planet—finding some things familiar and intelligible, and others puzzling and strange. But a single mission hardly constitutes thorough exploration, much less conquest and settlement. The climate appears hospitable. We invite others to come along.

Manufacturing Interview

Company name: _____

Company SIC code: _____

Main line of business: _____

Respondent's name: _____

    title:_____

    place of interview: _____

    telephone: _____

Answering for (check one):

                             _____whole company

                             _____division

                             (name)

                             _____other

                             (specify)

        Name of interviewer: _____

        Date:_____

The questionnaire is divided into two main parts.

The first part is a series of factual questions about your business.

The second part describes some ideas that economists have advanced to explain the way prices respond to changes in demand or costs. We are trying to find out what business people like yourself think of these ideas, and would like your opinions.

I will start with the factual questions.

PART A: DESCRIPTIVE QUESTIONS

A1.   Approximately what are the annual sales of the company/division for which you are answering the questions?

_____

A2.   Approximately what fraction of these sales go to consumers and what fraction to other businesses or other organizations?
- a.   CONSUMERS: _____   N
- b.   BUSINESSES:_____   Don't know or
                                             can't answer
- c.   OTHER (e.g., GOVERNMENTS): _____

_____

A3.   Approximately what fraction of your sales go to regular customers with whom you expect to do business again, as opposed to those you do not expect to be repeat customers?

                                             N
Percent to regular customers: _____ Don't know or
                                             can't answer

_____

A4.   If you cut your prices by, say, 10%, by what percent would you expect your unit sales to rise?

                                             N
_____percent   don't know or
                                             can't answer

_____

A5.   Do you ever put customers on allocation, that is, limit the amount they can buy?

1	2	3	4	N
no, never	rarely	sometimes	frequently, always	don't know or can't answer

_____

A6.   In some firms, sales rise and fall strongly with the ups and downs of the national economy. Sales in other firms are much less sensitive to the state of the economy. How would you characterize the sensitivity of *your* company's/division's sales to the state of the economy?

1	2	3	N
relatively insensitive	about average	relatively sensitive	don't know or can't answer

A7.   (a)   Do forecasts about the future outlook for the national economy ever *directly* affect the prices you set?

1	2	3	N
never	occasionally	often	don't know or can't answer

(b)   Do forecasts of future economy-wide inflation rates ever *directly* affect the prices you set?

1	2	3	N
never	occasionally	often	don't know or can't answer

A8.   What fraction of your sales is made under formal, written contracts that cover multiple sales?

1	2	3	4	5	N
none or almost none (under 10%)	a minority (10– 40%)	about half (40– 60%)	a majority (60– 90%)	almost all (over 90%)	don't know or can't answer
↓					
SKIP TO QUESTION A9					

(a)   Do these contracts normally set prices for a stated period of time?

1	2	3	4	N
rarely or never	sometimes	most of the time	always or almost always	don't know or can't answer
↓				↓
SKIP TO (c) BELOW.				SKIP TO (c) BELOW.

(b)   What is the typical duration over which prices are set in these contracts?

(c)   Do some contracts specify prices in some other way? If so, how? [EXAMPLES: TYING TO A PRICE INDEX OR TO COSTS.]

(d)   When prices are set by contracts, how often are discounts made off the contract price? (Exclude typical cash discounts for on-time payment.)

1	2	3	4	5	N
never or almost never (under 10%)	a minority of cases (10– 40%)	about half the time (40– 60%)	a majority of cases (60– 90%)	almost always (over 90%)	don't know or can't answer

A9.   Do you have a customary time interval—such as a week, a month, a quarter, or a year—between price reviews for your most important products?

1	2	3
NO	It varies by product	YES (specify interval)

A10.   How often do the prices of your most important products change in a typical year?

_____

_____

(a)   Why don't you change prices more frequently than that?

_____

_____

(b)   When you do raise or lower prices, do you normally do it all at once or in a series of smaller changes?

1	2	3	N
normally all at once	it varies	normally in small steps	don't know or can't answer

A11.   How accurately can you estimate how your costs will change when your sales change your level of production by, say, 5–10%?

1	2	3	N
not very well	moderately well	extremely well	don't know, can't answer

A12.   Roughly what fraction of your costs do you regard as *fixed*, that is, the same regardless of your level of production, and what fraction as *variable*, that is, costs that vary with the level of production?

			N
a.	percent fixed: _____%		don't know
			or
b.	percent variable: _____%		can't answer

A13.   Firms and industries differ in how rapidly their prices respond to changes in demand and costs.

(a)   How much time normally elapses after a significant increase in demand before you raise your prices?

_____   N
(numerical answer)   don't know or
                                  can't answer

(b)   What about when demand *declines* significantly? How much time normally elapses until you *reduce* your prices?

1   N

_____
(numerical answer)

we never   don't know or
reduce   can't answer
prices

(c)   Now let's turn to cost changes. How much time normally elapses after a significant increase in *costs* before you raise your prices?

_____   N
(numerical answer)   don't know or
                                  can't answer

(d)   What about when costs *decline*? How much time normally elapses until you *reduce* your prices?

1   N

_____
(numerical answer)

we never   don't know or
reduce   can't answer
prices

A14.   Are there any legal or regulatory restrictions on your ability to raise or lower prices?

1	2	N
		don't know or
No	Yes	can't answer
↓		↓
SKIP TO		SKIP TO
QUEST. A15		QUEST. A15

a.   What are the nature of these restrictions?

b.   What percentage of your sales are so restricted?

A15.   About what percentage of your output is produced to stock and what percentage is produced to order?
   a.   percent to stock: _____%
   b.   percent to order: _____%

A16.   About how many times per year does your inventory turn over?

PART B: THE MAIN THEORIES

Now we turn to the economic explanations of price changes. In each case, we would like to know how important or unimportant the idea is to pricing decisions in *your company*.

B1.   (NOTE: IF THE FIRM HAS NO CONTRACTS, SKIP TO QUESTION B2.)

One idea is that many goods are sold under explicit contractual agreements that set prices in advance, so firms are not free to raise prices while contracts remain in force.

How important is this idea in slowing down price adjustments in your company/division?

1	2	3	4	N
totally unimportant	of minor importance	moderately important	very important	don't know or can't answer

↓				↓
SKIP TO QUEST. B2				SKIP TO (b) BELOW

(a) Do contracts also prevent prices from *decreasing* when demand or costs *fall*?

1	2	3	4	N
no, totally inapplicable to price decreases	less applicable to price decreases	yes, just as applicable to price decreases	yes, even more applicable to price decreases	don't know or can't answer

---

(b) Do discounts become *more prevalent* when sales are weak? How much more? (ASK AS TWO QUESTIONS.)

1	2	3	N
no	yes, a little more	yes, much more	don't know or can't answer

---

(c) Do discounts become *deeper* when sales are weak? How much more? (ASK AS TWO QUESTIONS.)

1	2	3	N
no	yes, a little more	yes, much more	don't know or can't answer

---

(d) Do these contracts also prevent the volume of sales and/or production from changing in the short run?

1	2	3	4	N
rarely or never	in a minority of cases	in many cases	in most or all cases	don't know or can't answer

---

B2.   (NOTE: IF 100% OF SALES ARE UNDER WRITTEN CONTRACTS, SKIP TO QUESTION B3.)

Another idea has been suggested for cases in which price increases are not prohibited by explicit contracts. The idea is that firms have implicit understandings with their customers—who expect the firms not to take advantage of the situation by raising prices when the market is tight.

(a)   Is this idea true in your company/division?

1	2	N
no	yes	don't know or
		can't answer
↓		↓
SKIP TO		SKIP TO
QUEST. B3		(b) BELOW

How important is it in slowing down price adjustments in your company/division?

1	2	3	4	N
totally	of minor	moderately	very	don't
unimportant	importance	important	important	know
				or can't
				answer
↓				
SKIP TO				
QUEST. B3				

(b)   What about when the demand for your products is weak? Are your customers then willing to let you hold your prices, or do they insist on price reductions?

1	2	3	X	N
usually let	attitudes	usually insist	customers	don't
us hold	are	on price	don't	know
prices	mixed	reductions	know	or can't
			when	answer
			demand	
			slumps	

(c)   Does the understanding that prices should remain fixed hold when your *costs* increase, or do customers see price increases as justified when costs increase?

ANSWER: When costs increase, our customers normally . . .

1	2	3	X	N
still want us to hold our prices	attitudes are mixed	tolerate price increases	don't know what is happening to our costs	don't know or can't answer
↓	↓	↓	↓	↓
SKIP TO (e)			SKIP TO (e)	SKIP TO (e)

(d) Do customers normally tolerate full pass-through of costs, or only partial pass-through?

1	2	3
full	partial	don't know or can't answer

(e) What about when costs decline? Do customers then expect you to keep prices fixed or insist on pass-through of cost savings?

ANSWER: When our costs decline, our customers normally . . .

1	2	3	X	N
let us keep prices fixed	attitudes are mixed	insist on price decreases	don't know what is happening to our costs	don't know or can't answer
↓	↓	↓	↓	↓
SKIP TO QUEST. B3			SKIP TO QUEST. B3	SKIP TO QUEST. B3

(f) Do customers normally expect full or partial pass-through?

1	2	N
full	partial	don't know or can't answer

B3. Another idea is that firms hesitate to reduce their prices because they fear that customers will interpret a price cut as a signal that the *quality* of the product has been reduced.

(a)   Is this idea true in your company/division?

1	2	N
no	yes	don't know or can't answer
↓	↓	↓
SKIP TO (c) BELOW		SKIP TO (c) BELOW

How important is it in discouraging or delaying price decreases in your company/division?

1	2	3	4	N
totally unimportant	of minor importance	moderately important	very important	don't know or can't answer

↓
SKIP TO
(c) BELOW

(b)   Does this idea apply only when price cuts are indicated by *weak demand*, only when price cuts are indicated by *lower costs*, or in both cases?

1	2	3	N
applies only to weak demand	applies to both	applies only to lower costs	don't know or can't answer

(c)   What about applying this idea to price *increases*? That is, are you encouraged to *raise* prices because you think customers will interpret higher prices as an indication of higher quality?

1	2	3	4	N
rarely or never	sometimes	most of the time	always or almost always	don't know or can't answer

B4.   Another idea is that particular threshold prices are more attractive to customers than other prices. For example, a store might think that a shirt sells much better at $19.95 or $20 rather than $20.10.

(a)   Is this idea true in your company/division?

1	2	N
no	yes	don't know or
		can't answer
↓		↓
SKIP TO		SKIP TO
QUEST. B5		QUEST. B5

How important is it in deterring price increases in your company/division?

1	2	3	4	N
totally	of minor	moderately	very	don't
unimportant	importance	important	important	know
				or can't
				answer
↓				↓
SKIP TO				SKIP TO
QUEST. B5				QUEST. B5

(b)   Is the "barrier" broken once one firm raises its price above the critical threshold, so that other firms quickly follow suit?

1	2	3	N
rarely or	sometimes	usually	don't know or
never		or always	can't answer

(c)   Once the barrier is broken, do firms in your industry normally raise their prices all the way up to the next critical threshold (e.g., from $19.95 to $20.95), or are smaller increases typical?

1	2	3	N
rarely	sometimes	usually	don't know
up to next	up to next	up to next	or can't
threshold	threshold	threshold	answer

(d)   Do thresholds also deter small price *decreases* when demand or costs *fall*?

1	2	3	N
rarely or	sometimes	always or	don't know or
never		almost always	can't answer
↓			↓
SKIP TO			SKIP TO
QUEST. B5			QUEST. B5

(e)   In cases when prices do fall, do they normally fall all the way down to the next critical threshold (e.g., from $19.95 to $18.95), or are smaller decreases typical?

1	2	X	N
normally fall to next threshold	normally fall less than to next threshold	prices never fall	don't know or can't answer

---

B5.   It has been suggested that, when business turns down, a company loses its *least loyal* customers first and retains its *most loyal* ones. Since the remaining customers are not very sensitive to price, reducing markups will not stimulate sales very much.

(a)   Is this idea true in your company/division?

1	2	N
no	yes	don't know or can't answer
↓		↓
SKIP TO QUEST. B6		SKIP TO (c) BELOW

How important is it in explaining the speed of price adjustment in your company/division?

1	2	3	4	N
totally unimportant	of minor importance	moderately important	very important	don't know or can't answer
↓				
SKIP TO (c) BELOW				

(b)   In thinking about that, does it matter whether or not sales at competing firms are falling at the same time?

1	2	3	N
doesn't matter	matters a little	matters a lot	don't know or can't answer

---

(c)   How important is the effect in the opposite direction? That is, are you hesitant to raise markups when demand rises because you want to attract new customers, and you think these new customers will be quite price conscious?

1	2	3	4	N
totally unimportant	of minor importance	moderately important	very important	don't know or can't answer

---

B6.   A different idea holds that prices depend mainly on the *costs* of labor and of materials and supplies that companies buy from other companies. Firms are thought to delay price increases until their costs rise, which may take a while. But then they raise selling prices promptly.

How important is this idea in explaining the speed of price adjustment in your company/division?

1	2	3	4	N
totally unimportant	of minor importance	moderately important	very important	don't know or can't answer
↓				↓
SKIP TO QUEST. B7				SKIP TO (d) BELOW

(a)   Is the cost pass-through normally faster for *large* cost changes or for *small* cost changes?

1	2	3	N
faster for small cost changes	about the same	faster for large cost changes	don't know or can't answer

---

(b)   Is the cost pass-through normally faster for cost changes that are believed to be *industry-wide* or for cost changes that are believed to be *unique to your company*?

1	2	3	N
faster for unique cost changes	about the same	faster for industry-wide cost changes	don't know or can't answer

---

(c)   Is the cost pass-through normally faster for cost changes that are believed to be *permanent* or for cost changes that are believed to be *transitory*?

1	2	3	N
faster for	about the	faster for	don't know or
transitory	same	permanent	can't answer
cost changes		cost changes	

(d)   Are there times when you can clearly foresee price increases for labor or other things you buy?

1	2	3	N
no	sometimes	yes	don't know or
(rarely)		(often)	can't answer
↓			↓
SKIP TO			SKIP TO
QUEST. B7			QUEST. B7

(e)   In those instances, do you try to buy these things in advance of the price increases and store them in inventory?

1	2	N
no,	yes,	don't know or
or rarely	or often	can't answer

(f)   When you can see cost or wage increases coming, do you raise your own prices in anticipation?

1	2	N
no or	yes or	don't know
rarely	often	
↓		↓

SKIP TO QUESTION B7

(g)   If not, why not? (CHECK ALL APPLICABLE RESPONSES)

i)   _____   It would antagonize or cause difficulties for our customers.

ii)   _____   We are not confident in our cost estimates or forecasts.

iii)   _____   We are reluctant to take the lead because we worry that competing firms will not raise their prices.

iv)   _____   We do not need anticipatory price changes because, once costs rise, we can raise our prices promptly.

v)   _____   The people who have to sign off on a price increase may not agree.

vi)   _____   Other (SPECIFY)

B7. (a)   Some companies find that their *variable costs per unit* are roughly *constant* when production rises. Others incur either *higher* or *lower* variable costs of producing additional units when they raise production. How would you characterize the behavior of your own variable costs of producing additional units as production rises?

1	2	3	4	5	N
falling	mostly falling, but rising at certain discrete points	constant	constant, except for jumps at certain discrete points	rising	don't know or can't answer
↓	↓			↓	↓
SKIP TO QUEST. B8				SKIP TO QUEST. B8	

It has been suggested that many firms base prices on costs. Hence firms with constant variable costs per unit have no reason to change prices when production changes.

How important is this idea in explaining the speed of price adjustment in your company/division?

1	2	3	4	N
totally unimportant	of minor importance	moderately important	very important	don't know or can't answer

---

B8.   Another idea is that the act of changing prices entails special costs in itself, so firms hesitate to change prices too frequently or by too much. The costs we have in mind are *not* production costs, but costs like printing new catalogs, price lists, etc. or hidden costs like loss of future sales by antagonizing customers, decision making time of executives, problems with salespeople, and so on.

(a)   Does your firm incur such costs when it changes prices?

1	2	3	N
no	yes, but trivial	yes	don't know or can't answer
↓			↓
SKIP TO QUEST. B9			SKIP TO QUEST. B9

How important are these costs in slowing down price adjustments in your company/division?

1	2	3	4	N
totally unimportant	of minor importance	moderately important	very important	don't know or can't answer
↓				
SKIP TO QUEST. B9				

(b)   What is the nature of these costs in your company? (CHECK ALL APPLICABLE RESPONSES)

i)   _____ printing new catalogs, new price lists, new packaging, etc.
ii)   _____ informing salespeople and customers
iii)   _____ getting the sales force to cooperate
iv)   _____ decision making time of executives
v)   _____ loss of future sales by antagonizing customers
vi)   _____ other (SPECIFY)

c) Do these costs of changing prices come mainly from changing prices *often* or mainly from changing them by *large* amounts?

1	2	3	N
mainly from often	mainly from large amounts	both	don't know or can't answer

(d)   Do you incur these special costs of changing prices when you *decrease* prices as well?

1	2	3	4	N
no	yes, but smaller	yes (about equal)	yes, even larger	don't know or can't answer

(e)   If a company does *not* raise its prices when demand for its products increases, it is generally assumed that it will sell more. Is that true in your company/division?

1	2	N
no	yes	don't know or can't answer

↓
SKIP TO
QUEST. B9

(f)   When your demand rises, do you normally prefer to raise your production, increase your prices, or both?
ANSWER: Prefer to raise . . .

1	2	3	N
level of production	prices	both	don't know or can't answer

(g) Why is that? _____

(h)   When your demand falls, do you normally prefer to decrease your production, cut your prices, or both?
ANSWER: Prefer to decrease . . .

1	2	3	N
level of production	prices	both	don't know or can't answer

(i)   Why is that? _____

(j)   Do you incur special costs from the act of changing your production—analogous to the special costs you incur when you change prices? We have in mind things like temporary halts in production, expenses in recruiting new workers, etc.

1	2	3	N
no	yes, but minor	yes	don't know or can't answer

↓
SKIP TO
QUEST. B9

↓
SKIP TO
QUEST. B9

(k)   (ASK ONLY IF FIRM PREFERS TO CHANGE PRODUCTION.) Then why do you change production rather than change prices?

_____

_____

B9.   Some people think that price changes are slowed down by the difficulty of getting a large, hierarchical organization to take action.

How important is this idea in explaining the speed of price adjustment in your company/division?

1	2	3	4	N
totally unimportant	of minor importance	moderately important	very important	don't know or can't answer

↓				↓
SKIP TO QUEST. B10				SKIP TO QUEST. B10

(a)   What do you think causes these delays?
i)   _____ People worry about the public-relations aspects of price increases.
ii)   _____ Several/many people have to sign off on a price change.
iii)   _____ Hierarchical organizations tend to be cautious.
iv)   _____ Other (SPECIFY) _____

B10.   The next idea is that firms would often like to raise their prices, but are afraid to get out of line with what they expect competitors to charge. They do not want to be the first ones to raise prices. But, when competing goods rise in price, firms raise their own prices promptly.

How important is this idea in explaining the speed of price adjustment in your company/division?

1	2	3	4	N
totally unimportant	of minor importance	moderately important	very important	don't know or can't answer

↓				↓
SKIP TO (b) BELOW				SKIP TO (b) BELOW

(a)   Why is that? (CHECK ALL APPLICABLE RESPONSES)
i)   _____ We cannot sell anything at prices above those of our competitors.

ii) _____ If we raised our prices first, we would lose too much business to low-price competitors.

iii) _____ When other companies raise prices, we can raise ours without antagonizing our customers.

iv) _____ We worry that the need for a price rise is temporary.

v) _____ Other (SPECIFY) _____

(b) Do you also delay price *cuts* because you do not want to be among the first firms in the industry to *cut* prices?

1	2	3	X	N
rarely or never	sometimes	usually or always	we never cut prices	don't know or can't answer
↓			↓	↓
SKIP TO QUEST. B11			SKIP TO QUEST. B11	

(c) If so, why?

i) _____ If we cut prices first, we would get more business than we want or can handle.

ii) _____ Lower prices would hurt our profits.

iii) _____ We worry that the need for a price cut is temporary.

iv) _____ Other (SPECIFY) _____

B11. Still another idea has been suggested for firms that hold inventories of the goods they sell.

(a) Does your firm hold such inventories?

1	2	3	N
no	a little	yes	don't know or can't answer
↓	↓	↓	↓
SKIP TO QUEST. B12			SKIP TO QUEST. B12

According to this idea, a firm's initial response to fluctuations in demand is to let *inventory stocks,* rather than *prices,* vary. That is, when demand *rises,* they first let inventories fall rather than raise prices. And when demand *falls,* they first let inventories build up rather than reduce prices.

How important is this idea in explaining the speed of price adjustment in your company/division?

1	2	3	4	N
totally unimportant	of minor importance	moderately important	very important	don't know or can't answer
↓				↓
SKIP TO QUEST. B12				SKIP TO QUEST. B12

(b)   Is this idea more important for *decreases* in demand or for *increases* in demand?

1	2	3	N
more important for decreases	about equally important	more important for increases	don't know or can't answer

---

(c)   Suppose you thought a change in demand was transitory rather than permanent. Would that make you more likely to change prices or more likely to change *inventories*?

1	2	3	N
more likely to change inventories	about the same	more likely to change prices	don't know or can't answer

---

(d)   Why do you often/sometimes prefer changing your inventory to changing your prices? (CHECK ALL APPLICABLE RESPONSES)

i)   _____ It costs less to let inventories vary than to change prices.

ii)   _____ It does not antagonize customers.

iii)   _____ We like to delay price changes until we are confident that the increase or decrease in sales is permanent.

iv)   _____ Market forces may make it hard to make a price increase stick.

v)   _____ Other (SPECIFY) _____

B12.   According to the last idea we want to investigate, firms don't cut prices much when demand falls because price is just one of several elements that matter to buyers. More frequently, they shorten delivery lags, make greater selling efforts, improve service, or improve product quality.

(a)   Is this true of your company?

1	2	N
no	yes	don't know or can't answer
↓		↓
SKIP TO QUEST. B13		SKIP TO (c) BELOW

How important is this idea in slowing down price adjustments in your company/division?

1	2	3	4	N
totally unimportant	of minor importance	moderately important	very important	don't know or can't answer
↓				
SKIP TO QUEST. B13				

(b)   What nonprice elements are important in your case? (CHECK ALL APPLICABLE RESPONSES)

   i)   _____ Shortening delivery lags
   ii) _____ Greater selling efforts
   iii) _____ Improving service
   iv) _____ Improving product quality
   v)   _____ Offering some ancillary good or service at a low or zero price
   vi) _____ Other (SPECIFY) _____

(c)   Is the same idea applicable to increases in demand. That is, do you economize on some aspect of service rather than raise prices?

1	2	3	N
more applicable to increases in demand	about equally applicable	more applicable to decreases in demand	don't know or can't answer

(d)   Suppose you thought a change in demand was *transitory* rather than *permanent*. Would that make you more likely to change prices or more likely to change service?

1	2	3	N
more likely to change service	about the same	more likely to change prices	don't know or can't answer

(e)   Why do you sometimes/always prefer changing conditions of service to changing prices? (CHECK ALL APPLICABLE RESPONSES)

i)   _____ It costs less to vary service than to vary prices.

ii)   _____ It does not antagonize customers as much.

iii)   _____ We like to delay price changes until we are confident that the increase or decrease in sales is permanent.

iv)   _____ Changes in service are easier to reverse, should that prove necessary.

v)   _____ other (SPECIFY) _____

B13.   Are there any factors we left out that might bear directly on the speed with which you adjust prices?

List of Variable Names

Mnemonic	Description	Question
ACCURACY	How well can MC be measured	A11
ADJCOSTQ	Has costs of adjusting output	B8(j)
ADJCOSTS	Has costs of price adjustment	B8(a)
BUFFERS	Inventories slow price changes	B11
BUSINESS	Fraction of sales to businesses	A2(b)
CON	Construction/mining firm dummy	—
CONC	Concentration ratio	—
CONSUMER	Fraction of sales to consumers	A2(a)
COORD	Importance of coordination failures	B10
COSTS	Prices based on costs	B6
CYCLE	Index of coincidental indicators	—
CYCLICAL	Cyclically sensitive	A6
ELAST	Elasticity of demand	A4
FLATMC	Marginal cost	B7(a)
FORESEEN	Cost increases can be foreseen	B6(d)
FREQ	Frequency of price changes	A10
GOVT	Fraction of sales to others (gov't)	A2(c)
HIERARCHY	Hierarchy slows price decisions	B9
IMPLICIT	Implicit contracts	B2(a)
INDUSTRY	Industry	—
INFLATION	Inflation outlook affects prices	A7(b)
INTERVAL	Customary interval for price reviews	A9
INVENTORY	Firm holds inventories	B11(a)
LOYAL	Lose least loyal customers first?	B5(a)
MCPCT	Fraction of costs that are variable	A12(b)
MFG	Manufacturing firm dummy	—

NONPRICE	Firms adjust nonprice elements	B12(a)
OUTLOOK	Economic outlook affects prices	A7(a)
POINTS	Pricing points	B4(a)
QUALITY	Quality depends on price	B3(a)
RATION	Customers are put on allocation	A5
REGULATE	Some prices regulated	A14
REGULARS	Fraction sold to regular customers	A3
RETAIL	Retail trade firm dummy	—
SERV	Service firm dummy	—
S/I	Sales-inventory ratio	A16
SIZE	Log of firm's annual sales	A1
SIZE10B	Sales greater than $10 billion	A1
STICKY	Price stickiness (constructed)	A10, A13
STOCK	Fraction produced to stock	A15(a)
TCU	Transportation/communications/ utility firm dummy	—
TRADE	Retail and wholesale trade firm dummy	—
UNION	Unionization rate in industry	—
WHOLESALE	Wholesale trade firm dummy	—
WRITTEN	Fraction of sales under contract	A8

Notes

Chapter One

1. A reasonably comprehensive survey of theories of price stickiness is offered in chapter 2.
2. In fact, credit card interest rates are very sticky and many people actually do pay them. See Ausubel (1991).
3. The precise question was: "One theory on why wages do not fall states that workers do not like unpredictable changes in income. Therefore, workers and employers negotiate a stable wage that does not tend to fall during recessions or rise during booms. This steady wage acts as a type of wage insurance for the worker. How plausible or relevant does this seem as one reason why wages do not fall?"
4. Campbell and Kamlani's (1995) survey—with questions phrased somewhat differently than in the Blinder-Choi survey—also found mixed support for the theory.
5. Many Keynesians would answer that it is implausible that demand and cost curves could stay put for six or twelve months. So prices that remain fixed for that long must be "sticky." But true believers require more persuasive evidence.
6. See, for example, Stiglitz (1987). For more on this theory, see chapters 2 and 8.
7. See, for example, Mankiw (1985) and chapter 13.
8. One rare exception is the work of Levy et al. (1996), who actually produced direct measurements of sizable "menu costs" for supermarkets.
9. See, for example, Bils (1987) and Shapiro (1988).
10. For the reader's convenience, all questions discussed in the text are numbered as in the questionnaire, which is included as appendix A.

11. There were separate questionnaires for manufacturing, services, and (retail and wholesale) trade. The manufacturing questionnaire (used also for mining and construction firms) is given in the appendix because it was administered to the largest group. The other two questionnaires differed mainly in wording; for example, service companies were asked about their "sales" rather than their "production."

12. In fairness, the analogy applies better to questions about facts (as in part A of the questionnaire) than to questions about reasons (part B). The answers to these factual questions are mostly reported in chapter 4.

13. With one exception. Since one theory pertains to inventories, and thus applies only to firms that sell goods, it was omitted from the questionnaire administered to service companies.

14. The reality is a good deal more complicated than this simple statement. See chapter 3 for details.

15. Provided that there is no bias from differential response rates.

16. We have empirical evidence on the latter point. Academic economists are past masters at saying "I knew that" or "it's obvious." So, when giving seminars on these results, Blinder often insisted that people guess the answers before telling them the survey results. There were many wrong guesses (and, of course, some right ones).

Chapter Two

1. As noted in chapter 1, new theories pop up all the time. Our list was compiled in mid-1988, so theories developed later were necessarily excluded.

2. This is a big "if," to which we will pay much attention in this and subsequent chapters.

3. The quote is from Robert Gordon (1990, 1152), but the idea appears in his 1981 paper.

4. Blanchard (1987) and Mattey (1993) have shown that disaggregated price indexes adjust faster than more aggregated indexes. But this is not the same thing.

5. In fact, quadratic costs may not be a terribly reasonable assumption for quantity adjustments either. For criticisms, see Bar-Ilan and Blinder (1992).

6. Caplin and Spulber (1987), Caballero and Engel (1991), and Caballero (1992) provide examples and analyses of smoothing from aggregation.

7. Akerlof and Yellen refer to "near rationality" rather than to menu costs, by which they mean that firms are willing to drift away from their optimum price as long as the consequent sacrifice of profits is not too large. This is equivalent to conventional maximizing behavior in the presence of a fixed cost of adjusting price.

8. See, for example, Reagan (1982) and Blinder (1982).

9. These two papers study production of detailed goods for which physical product data exist. For broader groups of goods, a long history of studies show production to be *more* variable than sales, apparently contradicting the hypothesis that inventories help firms smooth production. See, for example, Blinder (1986).

10. This theory resembles the previous one if richer people have lower price elasticities of demand.

11. See Bils (1987), Domowitz, Hubbard, and Petersen (1988), and Rotemberg and Woodford (1991) for evidence on countercyclical markups. Shapiro (1988) estimates a procyclical elasticity of demand under the identifying restriction that market power is constant over the cycle.

12. Clear examples arise in regulated industries. For example, when air fares and bank interest rates were regulated, airlines and banks competed on the basis of quality of service rather than on price.

13. Several of the merchants with whom Kashyap (1995) discussed pricing suggested this theory to him.

14. See Friedman (1967).

15. See, for example, Phelps and Taylor (1977) and Fischer (1977a).

16. See Blinder (1977), Gray (1976), Fischer (1977b), and Card (1983).

17. See Kahneman, Knetsch, and Thaler (1986), Blinder and Choi (1990), and Shafir, Diamond, and Tversky (1995). The last of these papers emphasizes that money illusion may not be "irrational" if there are cognitive advantages of thinking in nominal terms.

18. See Tirole (1988), pages 83–85.

19. On the upside, price protection seems more innocuous. Continuing the example, if company A raised its price before it had delivered all two thousand drives to company B, it would guarantee to deliver the rest at the original price.

20. But see Maskin and Tirole (1988) for a repeated-game model that has the flavor of the kinked demand theory.

21. See Reid (1981).

22. The intra-industry coordination failure discussed here obviously is related to the more general-equilibrium sort of coordination failure in which there are multiple equilibria associated with different levels of product demand and labor demand. This latter approach has a long tradition in Keynesian economics—see Clower (1965) and Leijonhufvud (1968)—but could not be addressed directly in the survey.

23. See Scherer (1980) and Suslow (1988).

24. Warner and Barsky report that several store managers believe that price cutting is more profitable in high-volume periods.

25. We cannot name them here because each was promised confidentiality. But we owe them a special debt of gratitude. The subjects for the pretest were not chosen randomly; often, we got to them through

"connections." So these observations are not part of the data set used for statistical analysis.

26. Devoted taxonomists will note that this theory can, with some stretch, be considered a cost-based theory.

27. This question continued to be asked throughout the survey, but it turned up virtually no new suggestions.

28. It could be, however, that most executives are loath to admit that their firms are plagued by hierarchical delays, even if they are.

29. Three were retailers and two were builders.

30. This and subsequent page references are to Hall and Hitch (1939). A similar referencing style is used throughout this section.

31. "Emerged" may not be the appropriate verb. Since Hall and Hitch do not display the questionnaire, we cannot know to what extent the theories were spontaneously offered or prompted.

32. This adds up to ninty because two firms were in both the retail and service businesses.

33. At the time, worth about five million dollars. Nowotny and Walther state (without giving a source) that such firms produced two-thirds of Austrian industrial output. They do not give any information on their sample-selection technique nor response rate.

34. Attaining a target level of profit was second.

Chapter Three

1. We exclude, of course, such things as the Commerce Department's regular estimates of GDP and its components.

2. Indeed, while progress on this book was being delayed by Blinder's government service, researchers at the Bank of England conducted a similar study of the U.K. See Simon Hall, Mark Walsh, and Tony Yates (1996).

3. The word "almost" refers to hundreds of little judgment calls that had to be made along the way and would be too tedious to recount.

4. This is precisely the attitude that guided the studies by Kaplan et al. (1958), Fog (1960), Haynes (1962); and others summarized in chapter 2.

5. In fact, Oliver Blanchard (1994, 150–151) has already criticized the methodology on these grounds.

6. As Dillman (1978, 14) notes, "A questionnaire that looks formidable may be rejected simply because it looks like it will take a long time to complete." The British study referred to in note 2 used a mailed questionnaire, but it carried the imprimatur of the Bank of England—whose agents prescreened firms for their willingness to cooperate.

7. Hall, Walsh, and Yates (1996) present data on sample composition which suggest that this is so.

8. A number of the interviewers were given plant tours and/or offered lunch or souvenirs.

9. Here we are generalizing from personal reactions to both types of interviews. Pardon the amateur psychology. But Herbert Clark and Michael Schober (1992, 36), who are professionals, reach the same conclusion.

10. In this context, thanks go to George Akerlof, Laurence Ball, Olivier Blanchard, Dennis Carlton, Robert Gordon, Bruce Greenwald, Anil Kashyap, David Romer, Julio Rotemberg, Andrew Weiss, and Janet Yellen.

11. The phrase "conceptually correct" is a confession that there are surely measurement errors in the data.

12. A few variables were obtained from sources other than the interviews and adjoined to the data set, for example, the four-firm concentration ratio in the firm's four-digit industry. These will be explained as they are introduced.

13. There was also a code for "don't know or can't answer," but it was rarely used.

14. There are some minor exceptions to this rule. For example, if a theory was rated "totally unimportant" for price increases, we sometimes asked if it was any more important for price decreases. See the questionnaire.

15. For some examples, see the questionnaire (appendix A)—questions B6(g), B8(b), B10(a), B11(d), and B12(b).

16. The exceptions arose because some companies, wary about what we might ask, requested a copy of the survey in advance. We always complied with such requests rather than lose the interview.

17. Financial firms were omitted for two reasons. First, we were using Ward's business directory, which covers only nonfinancial companies. Second, we were going to stratify the sample by sales, which is not a terribly meaningful concept for, say, a bank. Since the full study did include financial firms, we will have more to say about banks later in this chapter.

18. Within each stratum, the sampling probability was equal for all firms. While this is not the right way to draw a truly representative sample, it seemed sufficient for the pilot study since our goal was only to estimate the response rate. The data gathered in the pilot were not used for any other purpose.

19. For one thing, we did not take advantage of any personal or Princeton connections in the pilot. For another, the pilot study taught us some things about how best to approach companies.

20. In 1991, government production accounted for about 12.5 percent of GDP; households and nonprofit institutions, about 4 percent; owners' equivalent rent, about 6 percent; regulated industries, about 4.5 percent; and farming, about 1.5 percent. Source: Survey of Current Business, October 1994.

21. For example, several (largely regulated) utilities fell into this category.

22. Again, a small number of exceptions were made. On several occasions, our database either gave the wrong address for the head office, or the company itself referred us to another office. In a few such cases, we wound up going outside the seventeen-state area to do the interview.

23. According to Commerce Department estimates of gross state product.

24. These were SIC codes 01, 02, 09, 43, and 83 to 86. We did not quite get what we asked for and so at times had to cull the sample by hand.

25. Data on value added by firm size are not available. The range cited in the text depends on whether we use sales or employment to proxy value added. Regarding employment, Ward's business directory for 1988 lists total employment of nonfinancial companies with sales over ten million dollars as fifty-six million—almost exactly half of total nonfinancial employment. It is typically assumed, however, that big companies have higher value added per worker. According to the IRS's Statistics of Income, in 1992 nonagricultural firms with less than ten million dollars in sales accounted for 26.4 percent of total sales. (See table 3.4.)

26. Across industries, the V/S ratio ranged from 0.21 in wholesale trade to 0.85 in legal services. Manufacturing ratios tended to be around 0.4.

27. This was done in 1988, years before Allen Berger, Anil Kashyap, and Joseph Scalise (1995) published comprehensive data of these and other aspects of the banking business.

28. We considered weighting by final sales rather than value added, on the grounds that we ultimately care about pricing to final customers. However, pricing of intermediate goods surely affects pricing of final sales, and it seemed unwise to ignore them. Further, weighting by final sales was not practical; the Trinet database only included total sales, and further information would have been needed to separate out intermediate goods.

29. Mechanically, the procedure was as follows. Suppose company 1 had 77 weighted employees; then it was assigned numbers 1 to 77. Suppose company 2 had 103 weighted employees; it was assigned numbers 78–180. And so on until all twenty-five thousand companies were assigned numbers. The result was a mapping of every integer from 1 to 16,984,726 (indicating that our sampling frame represented seventeen million weighted employees) to a company name. Random integers in this range were then drawn by computer, thereby selecting company names for the sample.

30. Duplicate names occurred since, as explained in the previous note, each company was assigned a range of numbers. Eliminating duplicate names made the experiment equivalent to sampling without replacement.

31. The firm was Drexel Burnham Lambert. Although Trinet was supposed to have eliminated government enterprises and nonprofits,

some slipped through. For example, most—but not all—hospitals are nonprofits, so SIC code 806 (hospitals) had to be left in. We drew over 50 hospitals randomly into the sample, but subsequently determined from the *American Hospital Association's Guide to the Health Care Field* that all but one of them were nonprofits. These were eliminated.

32. For reasons explained later in the chapter, an exception was made in the case of retailing.

33. As we explain later, requests for interviews were sent out in waves of (approximately) fifty.

34. We actually sent letters to 362 firms. Twenty-two of these turned out to be inappropriate for our study (such as nonprofits or regulated utilities) or to have disappeared for one reason or another (such as bankruptcy or reorganization). In the remaining ten cases, we failed to follow up after receiving no response to the first letter.

35. Missouri and South Carolina were not in our region, but one company listed as within our region turned out to be headquartered in each of those states.

36. Because of errors in the Trinet database, errors in reporting sales data to us, or recent declines in sales volume (sometimes due to business reorganizations), our sample actually included eleven firms with annual sales under ten million dollars.

37. Reassuringly, the correlation between sales as measured by the interviews (between 1990 and 1992) and as reported by Trinet (for 1986) was about 0.91 for the two hundred firms in the sample.

38. In the Trinet sample, the ratio of sales to employment is positively correlated with both sales ($p = .50$) and employment ($p = .09$). The correlation with employment is not statistically significant, but note that it is biased downward by measurement error (just as the correlation with sales is biased upward).

39. We actually asked for its reciprocal; see question A16.

40. Interviewers were instructed to read verbatim unless the situation clearly dictated otherwise—for example, if an earlier answer preempted the question.

41. For these training interviews, the "consensus" coding was entered into the database.

42. For a while we asked respondents if they were aware of the article. Virtually none were.

43. A few companies availed themselves of this privilege anyway by writing "no" on the reply card or sending us a short letter to that effect.

44. For example, some large corporations listed only the top officers (CEO, COO, CFO, and so on) and a large number of "vice-presidents" or "executive vice-presidents."

45. If this process moved us from one part of the company to another, we normally just accepted the company's decision rather than trying to fight it.

46. However, several companies sent more than one person to the interview.

47. Sometimes respondents offered different answers for different product lines. In such cases, we ascertained the relevant weights and coded appropriate weighted averages in the database.

48. Of course, there were exceptions. One particularly harried and uninterested owner of a small business zipped through the interview in twenty minutes. Another (only one, fortunately) decided the questions were irrelevant to him and actually threw our interviewer out of his office!

49. Of course, as noted earlier, considerable effort had been expended to guarantee the latter.

50. Interviewers probably got better at doing this as they gained experience. Such "learning by doing" probably introduced some noise—but no bias—into some of the results.

Chapter Four

1. Robert Gordon (1990, 1126ff) offers a useful summary.

2. The mean is meaningless because a few firms answered "we change prices all the time" or "several times a day" and were arbitrarily coded as changing prices one thousand times per year.

3. Ideally, firms should have abstracted from regular sales (such as Memorial Day sales) in answering this question, and interviewers were told to inform respondents to answer this way if asked. The reason for this is that such regular sales are not aimed at responding to demand or cost shocks, but can be thought of as part of a prevailing "seasonal" schedule of prices. The fact that about half the firms responded that prices change once a year or less suggests that many firms did abstract from such sales.

4. As usual, there were exceptions. Interviewers were told not to ask the follow-up question of respondents who reported extremely frequent price changes, such as daily or more often. Thus only 177 firms were asked the question.

5. A10 has the smallest loading, and the loadings of the four A13 variables are nearly equal.

6. The Goodman-Kruskal gamma statistic—a measure of association relevant for ordered categorical variables—is -0.59. The Goodman-Kruskal gamma is discussed in chapter 5.

7. Because firms are sampled with probability proportional to value added, the percentages cited in the text are appropriately interpreted as weighted by share of GDP.

8. We put the word "theories" in quotation marks because these are not really theories until the nature of the contract is explained.

9. The answers differ by sector. While the median (and mode) is one year in every sector, the mean contract length varies from twelve months in trade to twenty-four months in services and sixteen months in construction. The mean in manufacturing is eighteen months.

10. Note that these are discounts off contract prices, not discounts off list prices.

11. This does not mean that two-thirds of all output is sold under fixed-price implicit contracts because, unlike the case of explicit contracts, we did not ask firms for the fraction of sales covered by implicit contracts.

12. For the numbers in the "all" column to be consistent with our rough estimate that the ratio of sales to value added is two, 29 percent of the sales to other businesses must be final sales by National Income and Product Accounts (NIPA) definitions. This seems a bit high, but we have no number against which to check it. However, the trade sector, which sells relatively more of its output to consumers, is undersampled.

13. Here we omit the utilities and construction and mining sectors because the number of observations is so small. They are, however, included in the economy-wide totals.

14. According to a χ^2 test, however, the association between cyclical sensitivity and industrial sector is not significant at even the 10 percent level.

15. The χ_{16}^2 test of association between A7(b) and industrial sector yielded a test statistic of 29.3, which is significant at the 5 percent, but not the 1 percent, level.

16. T-statistics from ordered probits of question A7(b) on each of the five price stickiness variables are all statistically significant. (Ordered probits are discussed in chapter 6.)

17. While the questionnaire was being developed and tested, we also inquired about the relevance of forecasts of a variety of other macroeconomic variables—like the money supply and interest rates. The idea that such variables might matter seemed so foreign to firms that we dropped these other variables from further consideration.

18. On the other hand, one executive of a very large company, who had an MBA from a leading university, told us that their estimated product-line average elasticity of demand was −0.41!

19. We repeat, for the nth time, that the relevant prices referred to here are real prices. This still does not explain the reluctance of p_i to move with P.

20. In the case of a constant elasticity of demand and quadratic costs, it can be shown that the cost of holding a fixed price in the face of a

demand shock is declining in the level of marginal cost. See the mathematical appendix to chapter 6.

21. Sometimes, for example, the respondent thought we were referring to what accountants call "cost of goods sold" which excludes, among other things, labor costs.

22. These differences in means are all significant at the 10 percent level. Most are significant beyond that level as well.

23. With a very few exceptions, these questions were not posed to service companies nor to firms in the transportation, communications, and utilities sector (which are, after all, service companies).

24. These do not match the numbers given in the previous chapter exactly; the latter referred only to the manufacturing and trade sectors, whereas these include firms in construction and mining as well as a few firms in services and in transportation, communications, and utilities.

25. For trade firms, we asked what fraction of sales is sold directly from stock and what fraction is special ordered.

Chapter Five

1. To put the estimated standard errors into perspective, some benchmarks may be useful. The standard deviation of a multinomial distribution with four equally likely outcomes—1, 2, 3, and 4—is 1.11. If the four probabilities are (1/8, 3/8, 3/8, 1/8) instead, the standard deviation drops to 0.87; if they are (3/8, 1/8, 1/8, 3/8), the standard deviation rises to 1.32.

2. Readers puzzled about how a difference in means of, say, 0.29 can be significant when the standard deviations are in the 1.25 range should recall that we are testing the equality of the estimated means here. The estimated standard deviations for the means are in the .08 range.

3. Remember, there was some preselection: Blinder rejected theories that—in his judgment—seemed fanciful.

4. In a replication of this study on 654 U.K. companies, Hall et al. (1996) found that judging quality by price (theory B3) ranked tenth out of eleven theories tested. They did not test hierarchies (theory B9).

5. See Blinder (1982). We offer this as evidence that the election was not rigged.

6. This is true even if we ignore the difference between real marginal costs (to which the theory applies) and nominal marginal costs.

7. The average ranking across all theories and all respondents is exactly 2.0, which connotes "of minor importance." Economists obviously have a way to go!

8. Theory B11 (inventories) does not apply to services or to transportation, communications, and utilities (TCU).

9. In these calculations, theory B11 (inventories) is omitted from the list in the entries pertaining to services and TCU.
10. These are theories B1, B3, B6, B7, B8, and B9.
11. The measure of correlation used is the Goodman-Kruskal gamma statistic, which will be explained shortly.
12. Using standardized data, the equation is:

$$STICKY = -.28A10 + .44A13(a) + .47A13(b) + .49A13(c) + .52A13(d).$$

As observed in chapter 4, this principal component accounts for 56 percent of the variance. Unfortunately, this equation is based only on the subsample of sixty-four observations for which none of the five variables are missing. We imputed the value of STICKY for the remaining 136 observations, using whatever subset of the five variables is available for each observation and imputing the others. (Fortunately, we had at least three of the five variables in 98 of the 136 cases—and at least one of them in every case.) This yields a measure of price stickiness with a mean of about zero, a standard deviation of 1.6, and no missing data—though one that is presumably plagued by considerable measurement error. (Hence, its coefficient in regressions should be biased toward zero.)
13. If the two firms rated either (or both) theories the same, then the pair is neither concordant nor discordant, but tied. The Goodman-Kruskal gamma ignores ties.
14. The formula can be found in many textbooks and in the STATA manual.
15. The ordered probit model is discussed in detail in chapter 6.
16. The nonlinearity of the ordered probit model implies that it matters which variable is the dependent variable. The smaller of the two significance levels is shown in table 5.7; values marked with * indicate that the alternative ordering gives a significance level greater than .10.
17. Common alternatives to gamma—such as Kendall's tau-b, which adjusts the gamma statistic for the number of "tied" pairs— also agree in almost all cases. Interestingly, Pearson correlations give very similar results as well, suggesting that assuming cardinality in the responses would not be highly problematic. By contrast, χ^2 tests, which ignore order altogether, give very different results.
18. This point was noted as early as 1981 by Okun (1981, 165). However, it seems largely to have been ignored. Blinder was among the guilty parties—through many editions of Baumol and Blinder's *Economics: Principles and Policy*!
19. Actually, more than a quarter did so by giving response 1 or 2 (see later in this chapter) to question B12(c) (see the questionnaire). For

readers inclined to pay attention to the answers, the mean response (among the 138 respondents) was 2.69 on the following scale:

1 = more applicable to increases in demand
2 = about equally applicable
3 = more applicable to decreases in demand.

This is significantly above 2.0 at any conceivable significance level (*t*-ratio = 16.2), implying much more rigidity in the downward direction.

20. This is only about half the sample because only 114 firms accepted the factual premise that they had identifiable groups of "more loyal" and "less loyal" customers.

21. Formal hypothesis testing is easy once the hypothesis is specified. The mean response to B10(b) among the 106 firms just mentioned is only 1.76. This is not only significantly less than 3.0 but even significantly less than 2.0.

22. Wages are another matter. Survey evidence suggests that wage cuts will reduce morale and work effort more than wage increases will raise them (Carl Campbell and Kunal Kamlani 1995). The frequency of nominal wage cuts is in dispute. Kenneth McLaughlin (1994), David Lebow, David Stockton, and William Wascher (1995), and David Card and Dean Hyslop (1996) find that on average about 15 to 20 percent of individuals experience nominal wage cuts in a given year. But George Akerlof, William Dickens, and George Perry (1996) argue that this figure is exaggerated by measurement error. Five of the nineteen firms in Alan Blinder and Don Choi's (1990) small sample had recently cut nominal wages.

Chapter Six

1. Hence all the fuss over monetarism for decades was much ado about relatively little.

2. Fischer's model deals with nominal wage contracts. Edmund Phelps and John Taylor (1977) made the same point—that nominal rigidity gives anticipated money real effects—in the context of fixed nominal prices. But their model defies any short summary.

3. One important exception is the price-tag (or menu) case in which adjustment costs for "doing nothing" in nominal terms are zero while adjustment costs for "doing nothing" in real terms are positive.

4. See Alan Blinder (1977), Jo Anna Gray (1976), Stanley Fischer (1977b), and David Card (1983). Note, however, that the optimal degree of indexation can exceed 100 percent in some cases according to this analysis.

5. See Kahneman et al. (1986), Blinder and Choi (1990), and Eldar Shafir et al. (1995).

6. The reader is again reminded that respondents answered in their own words and interviewers coded the responses onto the four-point scale shown. Interviewers who were undecided were permitted to choose intermediate codes like 2.5 or 3.5. To keep the tables readable, these intermediate responses are not shown separately in this and other tables. Instead, for example, a 3.5 response is counted as a 50-50 weighted average of a 3 and a 4.

7. Actually, they ought to be more willing to hold their real price fixed. As already mentioned, economists do not fully understand the prevalence of contracting in nominal terms.

8. As discussed in chapter 4, many firms had trouble answering this question. The distinction between fixed and variable costs apparently is not natural for many businesses.

9. This question only applies to manufacturing and trade firms.

10. The ordered logit model is the same, except that the cumulative distribution function of u is assumed to be the logistic curve.

11. The precise model fit is known as the proportional odds model. It is programmed into the STATA package.

12. Owing to missing data, the sample size generally shrinks whenever a new independent variable is added.

13. These last two variables were not collected in the survey, but appended by us. Unionization rates were constructed by tabulating microdata in the 1990 and 1991 Current Population Surveys. Concentration ratios are for 1987 and were obtained from the Census Bureau's *Census of Manufactures, Census of Transportation, Census of Wholesale Trade, Census of Retail Trade, and Census of Service Industries.*

14. In a regression explaining STICKY with the ratings of theories B1 to B12 on the right (which is not strictly legitimate because it assumes cardinality of the ratings), nine theories have positive coefficients (four of which are statistically significant at the 10 percent confidence level). The R^2 is about 0.3.

15. Perhaps this strong asymmetry result is biased by the fact that we asked sellers rather than buyers. Presumably, a seller can violate a contract price unilaterally only by reducing price whereas a buyer can do so only by offering to pay a higher price. (If both parties agree, however, price can be adjusted in either direction.)

16. The Goodman-Kruskal gamma statistic has an exceptionally large value of $+.93$, with an asymptotic standard error of .03. (The simple correlation between the two variables is $+.82$.)

17. Remember, this statement only applies to prices written into contracts. Hence, it does not apply, for example, to retail items put "on sale."
18. The assumption of quadratic costs implies that marginal cost is increasing at a constant rate. All results in this appendix also hold in the case in which marginal cost is increasing at an increasing rate (that is, $C''' > 0$).

Chapter Seven

1. We mean that Okun does not offer it in this context. He does appeal to money illusion in rationalizing the Keynesian (nominal) wage floor.
2. One caveat, discussed in chapter 4, is appropriate here: The interviews were conducted during a period of fairly low inflation. At higher inflation rates, money illusion presumably withers away. Another caveat is that the economy-wide price index may not be the appropriate deflator for many companies.
3. This includes the eleven firms who responded that all their sales are made under written contracts. We did not ask question B2(a) of these firms, but simply coded them as having no implicit contracts, and as rating the theory "totally unimportant."
4. But the difference between the mean score in manufacturing and the mean score in construction is nearly significant at the 5 percent level.
5. However, given the skip pattern on the questionnaire, a firm that rejected the idea that implicit contracts slow down price responses to increases in demand (by answering "totally unimportant" to question B2) would not have been asked question B2(c).
6. To our regret, we did not specify whether we meant full percentage pass-through or full dollar pass-through.
7. The t-ratio is 2.94, which is significant at the .004 level.
8. Owing to the skip pattern, this question was asked of only fifty-eight firms; fifty-five answered.

Chapter Eight

1. Alternatively, even if firms can identify each worker's quality perfectly, notions of fairness that compress wage differentials relative to productivity differentials might generate similar results. A survey of one hundred and eighty firms by Campbell and Kamlani (1995) found considerable support for the notion that firms hesitate to cut wages for fear that the best employees will quit. Truman Bewley's (1995) survey of 334 firms also found support for adverse selection in labor markets.

2. See Allen (1988, 139). The data come from Means (1935, 8).
3. This question should have been asked of all firms. However, the interviewers misapplied the skip pattern in 28 cases, leading to a sample size of 172.
4. FREQ enters STICKY with a negative sign, indicating that more frequent price changes correspond to more flexible prices.

Chapter Nine

1. However, Huston and Kamdur (1996) offer an optimizing model based on the costs of processing information.
2. This statement presumes that money illusion is a psychological fact.
3. For a survey, see Monroe (1973).
4. A demand curve with more than one pricing point implies a marginal revenue curve that may not decline monotonically, as shown in figure 9.1. The reader will note that we could have drawn a marginal cost curve that would cross this complex marginal revenue at more than one level of output. This would imply more than one local profit maximum. Generally, however, only one of them will be a global maximum.
5. In interviews with companies for which a shirt was an especially inappropriate example, interviewers often substituted another product.
6. One firm gave an equivocal answer that we scored as halfway between yes and no.
7. Source: Department of Commerce, Bureau of the Census. If some of the output of the omitted categories of GDP are sold at retail outlets, this 74 percent figure could be a slight overestimate of the importance of retail firms in final sales.
8. This information is missing for four firms.
9. However, because of the skip pattern, we missed any firms that believed in pricing points only in the downward direction—if, indeed, there were any such firms.
10. Here, however, only thirty-three firms replied because the others either never cut prices or judged the theory inapplicable in the downward direction.
11. The service and retail industries are combined into a single dummy because separate dummies obtain almost the same coefficients.
12. As with the service and retail industries in equation 9.1, the wholesale, and construction and mining industries are combined into a single dummy because separate dummies obtain almost the same coefficients.

Chapter Ten

1. It is not clear that Ramey's claim is correct, however. In a private communication to the authors, Woodford indicates that a weakly countercyclical markup can be obtained from the Rotemberg-Woodford framework even assuming an average value-added markup as low as 10 percent. We do not presume to adjudicate this dispute here.
2. For example, we cannot expect truthful answers to a question about whether oligopolistic collusion—which is illegal—tends to break down at business cycle peaks.
3. As the industry approaches perfect competition, ϵ approaches infinity, so the markup approaches unity—that is, P = MC.
4. Bils (1989b) presents a related model in which monopolistic firms attempt to attract new, relatively price-sensitive customers who enter the market during booms.
5. It will be clear that the argument readily generalizes to any number of customer classes.
6. Five firms did not answer the question.
7. The Goodman-Kruskal gamma measure of association between CYCLICAL (question A6) and the answers to question B5(a) is -0.32 (p-value $= .00$); the t-statistic for testing the equality of the mean responses of the two groups is 3.0 (p-value $= .00$).

    It is possible that cyclically sensitive *firms* (as opposed to cyclically sensitive industries) are cyclically sensitive partly because their customers are less loyal.
8. It is not obvious, however, that *changes* in elasticity over the business cycle depend on how other firms react. If, for example, firms always (or never) match price cuts, regardless of the stage of the cycle, then elasticity might not be cyclical at all.
9. This is the recoded version of question B2(a) described in chapter 7.
10. We exclude a marginally significant interviewer dummy; including it changes the reported coefficients only slightly.
11. The indicator variable for manufacturing firms (MFG) is marginally significant (p $= .09$); excluding it from the regression has little effect on the reported coefficients.

Chapter Eleven

1. The quotation is actually from Gordon (1990, 1152), but the idea first appeared in his 1981 paper.
2. Blanchard motivates these equations by the requirement that expected profits must be zero. This is perfectly appropriate for the long

run, but it is not clear why such a condition should hold in every period during a dynamic adjustment process.

3. This version of the equation assumes that stage i producers adjust their prices in even periods t, t + 2, . . . while stage i−1 producers adjust at times t−1, t + 1, . . . A companion equation handles the opposite case.

4. There is no preliminary "factual" question for this theory because it seemed silly to ask firms whether they base prices on costs.

5. The Goodman-Kruskal gamma measure of association between CYCLICAL (question A6) and question B6 is −0.01 (*p*-value = .88).

6. We did not ask these questions of companies that rejected the cost-based pricing theory outright.

7. The sample is slightly smaller than for question B6(d) because firms that rarely or never see price increases coming were not asked question B6(f).

8. Gordon (1990, 1151).

9. See question B6(g) on the questionnaire for the exact wording of the five "stock" responses.

10. The two numbers add to sixty-three because nine firms gave both responses.

11. The average rating of theory B2 (implicit contracts) was 2.65 for those offering the "antagonize customers" explanation versus 2.08 for those citing "competition" as the reason. For theory B10, the corresponding average scores were 2.82 and 2.97.

12. The three firms which gave the hierarchy argument (number 5) all rate theory B9 a "very important" source of price stickiness.

13. Remember, these cost shocks could be wage changes or changes in materials costs. We did not distinguish among cost shocks from different sources.

14. The correlation between firms' ranking of the theory and their industry is slightly more significant when trade firms are separately categorized as retailers and wholesalers (p = .08).

15. The positive correlation with MCPCT is particularly reasonable for cost-based pricing, since it is presumably variable cost that is marked up by firms.

16. Strictly speaking, question A2(c) asks about the fraction of output that firms sell to "others," such as nonconsumer, nonbusiness units. We interpret this as primarily a measure of sales to government.

17. It is tempting to recode the inventory variables for service firms in order to enlarge the sample. For example, we might set INVENTORY (whether a firm holds inventories) equal to "no" for all service firms, or set the fraction produced to stock (STOCK) equal to zero for these firms. We resist this temptation because there is an important distinction between a manufacturing or trade firm which can hold

inventories but chooses not to, and a service firm (for which holding inventories is impossible).

18. Two interviewer dummies (not reported) also enter the regression.

19. Note that the sample is restricted to manufacturing and trade firms. One interviewer dummy (not reported) also enters the regression.

20. We also tried to include STOCK (question A15[a]), the fraction of output produced to stock, and firms' answers to questions B11(a) and B11 (which ask whether firms hold inventories and whether inventories slow price changes). These variables were not significant.

21. But see the caveat on pages 203–204.

Chapter Twelve

1. However, it does fall as output rises along a linear demand curve.

2. That is why the issue arises only in the short run. In the very long run, average and marginal costs are the same and, under constant returns to scale, are independent of the volume of output.

3. As quoted in Moggridge (1973).

4. There were a few notable exceptions. When we clumsily talked around the MC concept to an MBA-trained executive of one large company, he replied: "Oh, you mean marginal cost."

5. Apparently, this step proved to be easy for the interviewers. None of them selected either an intermediate choice or a "write in" candidate.

6. This confusion, in itself, may be bad news for the idea that prices are based on marginal cost.

7. The expected negative correlation of the elasticity of demand (ELAST) with any of the theories also holds only for rising marginal costs.

8. These variables are CYCLE (negatively correlated), REGULARS (negatively correlated), and ELAST (positively correlated).

9. There also was one significant interviewer dummy.

Chapter Thirteen

1. It is required, of course, in order to derive explicit solutions to rational expectations models.

2. See, for example, Sheshinski and Weiss (1983).

3. This is an example of a one-sided (S,s) rule. There are also two-sided rules, which are appropriate if the firm's real output price can rise as well as fall (as might be the case, for instance, if the aggregate price level can fall). Both classes of rules share the implication that firms' nominal prices will manifest discrete jumps.

4. Parkin (1986) and, in a different way, Akerlof and Yellen (1985) came up with the same insight at about the same time.

5. See, for example, Gordon (1990) and the references cited therein.

6. A χ^2 test rejects the hypothesis of independence at well beyond conventional levels (p = .00).

7. Specifically, we asked a firm this question if it did not answer 1 to question B8(a) and did not answer 1 to the main theory question, question B8.

8. One piece of evidence tempers this conclusion: namely, the answers to question B8(c) and A10(b) are essentially uncorrelated. For example, firms that change their prices all at once (that is, give response 1 to question A10[b]) should not report that adjustment costs attach mainly to large price changes (that is, give answer 2 to question B8[c]). In practice, 11 percent of them do. A chi-square test fails to reject the null hypothesis that the answers to A10(b) and B8(c) are independent (p = −.32).

9. See his table 3 on page 644.

10. Small price changes are not ruled out by an (S,s) rule—if the (S,s) bands are close together, then we will in fact observe small price changes. But these changes should not be frequent.

11. The average rating of the theory by the five retailers and five wholesalers who do report nontrivial adjustment costs (those that answer "yes" to question B8[a]) is 2.80.

12. For a discussion of the concept of loss aversion, see Kahneman, Knetsch, and Thaler (1991).

13. These last two sentences summarize four *t*-tests based on four different ways to dichotomize the sample. All are significant at the 5 percent level; all but one are significant beyond the 1 percent level.

14. For example, Gordon (1990, 1146) makes such an argument.

15. Not too much should be made of the value ½; it is an artifact of the linear specification.

16. In fact, seventy of these seventy-seven firms reported having nontrivial adjustment costs for prices (question B8[a] = 3).

17. Some companies did not make an explicit comparison, but simply said that the costs associated with adjusting output are very small.

18. Specifically, firms require an expectation of future values of p*, the price that equates marginal revenue with marginal production costs. See equation 13.2.

19. Technically, firms will condition their choice of the (S,s) bounds on certain characteristics of the inflation process—see Sheshinski and Weiss (1983). It might be a bit of a stretch to associate this with an answer to question A7(b), which asks whether forecasts of future economy-wide inflation rates ever directly affect firms' choice of prices.

20. Because question B8(j) was only asked of firms that reported adjustment costs for prices, we cannot determine whether the opposite statement—that firms with adjustment costs for output are more likely to have adjustment costs for prices—is also true.

21. One interviewer dummy (not reported) also entered the regression.

22. One interviewer dummy (not reported) also entered the regression.

23. The *t*-statistic from an ordered probit regression of question B8(a) on UNION equals 0.3 (p = .73). The gamma for question B8(a) and QUALITY is 0.06 (p = .63).

24. We combine the retail and wholesale indicators into the single indicator TRADE because the coefficients on these variables were not significantly different from each other.

Chapter Fourteen

1. For a classic reference on this point, see Robinson (1958). In their analysis of merger activity in the 1960s and early 1970s, Ravenscraft and Scherer (1987, 193) cite "slowed corrective responses" owing to more complex organizational structures as one reason why many acquisitions failed to prove successful. Similarly, Peters and Waterman (1982) report that the most successful companies keep decision making in small, decentralized groups.

2. In addition, three interviewer dummy variables remained statistically significant.

Chapter Fifteen

1. Twenty firms did not answer the question because they reported that they never cut prices. Another seventeen firms did not answer the question for other reasons.

2. In the Ball and Romer model, which is based on a monopolistically competitive market structure, the relationship of the elasticity of demand to the likelihood of coordination failure is somewhat ambiguous. Ball and Romer claim that the range of monetary policy shocks for which there may be multiple equilibria—and, hence, coordination problems—increases when demand becomes more elastic. But we argue in the appendix to this chapter that this claim is based on an inappropriate metric for the "range of monetary policy shocks." Using a metric that we believe is more reasonable, the scope for coordination failures in their model is largest for very inelastic demand.

3. But remember, we always asked such firms about their unregulated prices.

Chapter Sixteen

1. Much of this literature has revolved around the production-smoothing paradox; namely, that for broad groups of goods, production looks to be more variable than sales (such as Blinder, 1986). However, researchers who have examined production of specific goods for which there exist physical product data have found some evidence of production smoothing. See Fair (1989) and Krane and Braun (1991).

2. We also asked the question of seven firms that were classified in the services, construction and mining, or TCU sectors but that we suspected might hold inventories. These are all multiproduct firms—for example, an auto repair business that also sells cars and parts. In addition, two firms in the trade sector were mistakenly given the survey for service firms, and so were not asked any questions pertaining to inventories.

3. The score does not, however, include those service firms to which the question does not apply, even in principle.

Chapter Seventeen

1. Presumably, this response applies only to the case of an increase in demand that leads either to a higher price or to a reduction in service. It is hard to imagine that a customer would be antagonized by a price reduction or by an improvement in service.

Chapter Eighteen

1. For example, Warner and Barsky (1995).

2. In fact, many firms told us detailed and highly specific stories about their pricing strategies and other aspects of their businesses. But we neither coded not utilized this nonsystematic information.

3. Indeed, our study has already been (approximately) replicated once—by the Bank of England. See Hall, Walsh, and Yates (1996).

4. In criticizing our choice of a highly structured interview, Blanchard (1994) observed that the "picture which comes out" of free-form interviews like those conducted by Bewley (1995) "is both rich and confusing." That is precisely our point.

5. Table 4.7 showed that 11.6 percent of the 121 firms reporting regular price reviews do so weekly or daily. These 121 firms comprise 60.5 percent of the sample.

6. However, the firms that report having Okun-style implicit contracts with their customers do tell us that these contracts normally allow quicker reactions to cost shocks than to demand shocks. More on this later in the chapter.

7. In this case, the causation probably runs in the opposite direction: If a firm knows that its price will be fixed for a while, it has a greater incentive to pay attention to economy-wide inflation forecasts.

8. But students of empirical Phillips curves should not be surprised, for these equations do not display the convexity shown in Phillips' original work. See, for example, Gordon (1997).

9. For supporting evidence, at least at low inflation rates, see Akerlof, Dickens, and Perry (1996).

10. Care must be taken in testing. These are short-run implications about adjustment paths. Neither sort of shock should change real wages permanently.

11. In fact, CPI inflation was neither as low nor as stable during the interviewing period (April 1990 to March 1992) as it has been of late. Core CPI inflation rose from about 4.75 percent to about 5.5 percent, and then fell to below 4 percent.

12. The quotations are from questions B6(d) and B6(f). See chapter 11.

13. The precise percentage depends on how we classify firms that report strategies that "vary by product." See question A9 in appendix A.

14. The median is twelve months and the mean is twenty months.

15. These negative results cannot necessarily be extrapolated to the parallel theory of *wage* rigidity. As noted in chapter 8, at least some survey evidence supports the idea that fears of losing high-quality workers deter wage cuts.

16. See Blinder (1982, 1986).

17. Almost all of these firms are in manufacturing or trade.

18. The lone exception is the text of question B8. However, it also appeared on several lists of responses that interviewers could check if they heard something that sounded similar.

19. There are other routes to nonneutrality, but we believe that most economists would choose changes in the real money supply as the main one.

20. On these aphorisms, see Cover (1992). But Romer and Romer (1994) and Garcia and Schaller (1996) report evidence that monetary policy is effective at ending recessions.

21. We are grateful to Michael Woodford and Dennis Carlton for helpful discussions related to this section.

22. Of course, it could be argued that the unconventional equilibrium is an artifact of mismeasuring prices. On this view, once we convert any changes in nonprice variables into equivalent price increases, we would find that all "prices"—properly defined—had risen by a factor λ. But even then monetary policy would have some effects on the real allocation.

23. Here we are ignoring adjustment costs of changing prices. But such costs presumably apply to changing Z_i at least as much as to changing P_i.

Bibliography

Akerlof, George A., William T. Dickens, and George L. Perry. 1996. "The Macroeconomics of Low Inflation." *Brookings Papers on Economic Activity* (1): 1–76.

Akerlof, George A., and Janet L. Yellen. 1985. "A Near-Rational Model of the Business Cycle, with Wage and Price Inertia." *Quarterly Journal of Economics* 100(Supplement): 823–38.

Allen, Franklin. 1988. "A Theory of Price Rigidities When Quality Is Unobservable." *Review of Economic Studies* 55 (January): 139–51.

Ausubel, Lawrence. 1991. "The Failure of Competition in the Credit Card Market." *American Economic Review* 81 (March): 50–81.

Azariadis, Costas. 1975. "Implicit Contracts and Underemployment Equilibria." *Journal of Political Economy* 83 (December): 1183–202.

Baily, Martin N. 1974. "Wages and Employment Under Uncertain Demand." *Review of Economic Studies* 41 (January): 37–50.

———. 1978. "Stabilization Policy and Private Economic Behavior." *Brookings Papers on Economic Activity* (1): 11–59.

Ball, Laurence, and N. Gregory Mankiw. 1994 "Asymmetric Price Adjustment and Economic Fluctuations." *Economic Journal* 104 (March): 247–62.

Ball, Laurence, and David Romer. 1991. "Sticky Prices as Coordination Failure." *American Economic Review* 81 (June): 539–52.

Bar-Ilan, Avner, and Alan S. Blinder. 1992. "Consumer Durables: Evidence on the Optimality of Usually Doing Nothing." *Journal of Money, Credit and Banking* 24 (May): 258–72.

Barro, Robert. 1977. "Long–Term Contracting, Sticky Prices, and Monetary Policy." *Journal of Monetary Economics* 3 (July): 305–16.

Basu, Susanto, and John G. Fernald. 1994. "Constant Returns and Small Markups in U.S. Manufacturing." *Board of Governors of the Federal Reserve System International Finance Discussion Paper* 483.

Baumol, William J., and Alan S. Blinder. 1991. *Economics: Principles and Policy*, 5th ed. San Diego, Calif.: Harcourt Brace Jovanovich.

Berger, Allen N., Anil K. Kashyap, and Joseph M. Scalise. 1995. "The Transformation of the U.S. Banking Industry: What a Long, Strange Trip It's Been." *Brookings Papers on Economic Activity* (2): 55–218.

Bewley, Truman F. 1995. "A Depressed Labor Market, as Explained by Participants." *American Economic Review* 85 (May): 250–54.

Bils, Mark. 1987. "The Cyclical Behavior of Marginal Cost and Price." *American Economic Review* 77 (December): 838–55.

———. 1989a "Cyclical Pricing of Durable Goods." *National Bureau of Economic Research Working Paper* 3050.

———. 1989b. "Pricing in a Customer Market." *Quarterly Journal of Economics* 104 (November): 699–718.

Blanchard, Olivier J. 1983. "Price Asynchronization and Price Level Inertia." In *Inflation, Debt, and Indexation*, edited by R. Dornbusch and M. Simonsen. Cambridge, Mass.: Massachusetts Institute of Technology Press.

———. 1987. "Aggregate and Individual Price Adjustment." *Brookings Papers on Economic Activity* (1): 57–109.

———. 1990. "Why Does Money Affect Output? A Survey." In *Handbook of Monetary Economics*, edited by B.M. Friedman and F.H. Hahn. Amsterdam: North Holland.

———. 1994. "Comment on Sticky Prices: Academic Theories Meet the Real World." In *Monetary Policy*, edited by N.G. Mankiw. Chicago: University of Chicago Press.

Blanchard, Olivier J., and Nobuhiro Kiyotaki. 1987. "Monopolistic Competition and the Effects of Aggregate Demand." *American Economic Review* 77 (September): 647–66.

Blinder, Alan S. 1977. "Indexing the Economy Through Financial Intermediation." In *Stabilization of the Domestic and International Economy*, edited by K. Brunner and A. Meltzer. Carnegie–Rochester Conference Series 5 (January): 69–105.

———. 1981. "Retail Inventory Behavior and Business Fluctuations." *Brookings Papers on Economic Activity* (2): 443–505.

———. 1982. "Inventories and Sticky Prices: More on the Microfoundations of Macroeconomics." *American Economic Review* 72 (June): 334–48.

———. 1986. "Can the Production Smoothing Model of Inventory Behavior Be Saved?" *Quarterly Journal of Economics* 101 (August): 431–53.

———. 1991. "Why Are Prices Sticky?: Preliminary Results from an Interview Study." *American Economic Review* (May): 89–96.

———. 1994. "On Sticky Prices: Academic Theories Meet the Real World." In *Monetary Policy*, edited by N.G. Mankiw. Chicago: University of Chicago Press.

Blinder, Alan S., and Don Choi. 1990. "A Shred of Evidence on Theories of Wage Stickiness." *Quarterly Journal of Economics* 105 (November): 1003–15.

Bonoma, Thomas V., Victoria L. Crittenden, and Robert J. Dolan. 1988. "Can We Have Rigor and Relevance in Pricing Research?" In *Issues in*

Pricing: Theory & Research, edited by T.M. DeVinney. New York: Free Press.

Caballero, Ricardo J. 1992. "A Fallacy of Composition." *American Economic Review* 82(December): 1279–92.

Caballero, Ricardo J., and Eduardo M.R.A. Engel. 1991. "Dynamic (*S-s*) Economies." *Econometrica* 59 (November): 1659–86.

Campbell, Carl, and Kunal Kamlani. 1995. "The Reasons for Wage Rigidity: Evidence from a Survey of Firms." Mimeo, Colgate University.

Caplin, Andrew, and John Leahy. 1991. "State-Dependent Pricing and the Dynamics of Money and Output." *Quarterly Journal of Economics* 106 (August): 683–708.

Caplin, Andrew, and Daniel Spulber. 1987. "Menu Costs and the Neutrality of Money." *Quarterly Journal of Economics* 102 (November): 703–26.

Card, David. 1983. "Cost of Living Escalators in Major Union Contracts." *Industrial and Labor Relations Review* 37 (October): 34–48.

Card, David, and Dean Hyslop. 1996. "Does Inflation 'Grease the Wheels of the Labor Market'?" Paper prepared for National Bureau of Economic Research Conference on Monetary Policy and Low Inflation, 1996.

Carlton, Dennis W. 1984. "The Importance of Delivery Lags as a Determinant of Demand." Mimeo, University of Chicago Graduate School of Business.

———. 1986. "The Rigidity of Prices." *American Economic Review* 76 (September): 637–58.

———. 1989. "The Theory and Facts About How Markets Clear: Is Industrial Organization Valuable for Understanding Macroeconomics?" In *Handbook of Industrial Organization,* Vol. I., edited by R. Schmalensee and R.D. Willig. Amsterdam: North Holland.

Cecchetti, Stephen. 1986. "The Frequency of Price Adjustment: A Study of Newsstand Prices of Magazines, 1953 to 1979." *Journal of Econometrics* 31 (April): 255–74.

Chirinko, R.S., and S.M. Fazzari. 1994. "Economic Fluctuations, Market Power, and Returns to Scale: Evidence from Firm-Level Data." *Journal of Applied Econometrics* 9 (January): 47–69.

Clark, Herbert H., and Michael F. Schober. 1992. "Asking Questions and Influencing Answers." In *Questions About Questions: Inquiries into the Cognitive Bases of Surveys,* edited by J. Tanur. New York: Russell Sage Foundation.

Clower, Robert W. 1965. "The Keynesian Counterrevolution: A Theoretical Appraisal." In *The Theory of Interest Rates,* edited by F.H. Hahn and F. Brechling. London: Macmillan.

Cooper, Russell, and Andrew John. 1988. "Coordinating Coordination Failures in Keynesian Models." *Quarterly Journal of Economics* 103 (August): 441–63.

Cover, James P. 1992. "Asymmetric Effects of Positive and Negative Money-Supply Shocks." *Quarterly Journal of Economics* 107 (November): 1261–82.

Dillman, Don A. 1978. *Mail and Telephone Surveys: The Total Design Method.* New York: Wiley.

Domowitz, Ian, R. Glenn Hubbard, and Bruce Petersen. 1988. "Market Structure and Cyclical Fluctuations in U.S. Manufacturing." *Review of Economics and Statistics* 70 (February): 55–66.

Earley, James S. 1956. "Marginal Policies of 'Excellently Managed' Companies." *American Economic Review* 46: 44–70.

Estrella, Arturo. 1995. "Measures of Fit with Dichotomous Dependent Variables: Critical Review and a New Proposal." Mimeo, Federal Reserve Bank of New York.

Fair, Ray C. 1989. "The Production Smoothing Model Is Alive and Well." *Journal of Monetary Economics* 24 (November): 353–70.

Fellner, William. 1976. *Toward a Reconstruction of Macroeconomics.* Washington, D.C.: American Enterprise Institute.

Fischer, Stanley. 1997a. "Long-Term Contracts, Rational Expectations, and the Optimal Money Supply Rule." *Journal of Political Economy* 85 (February): 191–205.

———. 1997b. "Wage Indexation and Macroeconomic Stability," In *Stabilization of the Domestic and International Economy,* edited by K. Brunner and A. Meltzer. Carnegie-Rochester Conference Series 5 (January): 107–47.

Fog, Bjarke. 1960. *Industrial Pricing Policies: An Analysis of Pricing Policies of Danish Manufacturers.* Amsterdam: North Holland.

Friedman, L. 1967. "Psychological Pricing in the Food Industry." In *Prices: Issues in Theory, Practice, and Public Policy,* edited by A. Phillips and O. Williamson. Philadelphia, Pa.: University of Pennsylvania Press.

Garcia, René, and Huntley Schaller. 1996. "Are the Effects of Monetary Policy Asymmetric?" Mimeo, Carleton University.

Goodman, Leo A., and William H. Kruskal. 1954. "Measures of Association for Cross Classifications." *Journal of the American Statistical Association* 49 (December): 732–64.

Gordon, Donald F. 1974. "A Neoclassical Theory of Keynesian Unemployment." *Economic Inquiry* 12 (December): 431–59.

Gordon, Lawrence A., Robert Cooper, Haim Falk, and Danny Miller. 1981. *The Pricing Decision.* Canada: National Association of Accountants and The Society of Management Accountants of Canada.

Gordon, Robert J. 1981. "Output Fluctuations and Gradual Price Adjustment." *Journal of Economic Literature* 19 (June): 493–530.

———. 1990. "What Is New-Keynesian Economics?" *Journal of Economic Literature* 28 (September): 1115–71.

————. 1997 "The Time-Varying NAIRU and Its Implications for Economic Policy." *Journal of Economic Perspectives* 11 (Winter): 11–32.

Gray, Jo Anna. 1976. "Wage Indexation: A Macroeconomic Approach." *Journal of Monetary Economics* 2 (April): 221–35.

Greene, William H. 1993. *Econometric Analysis,* 2d ed. New York: Macmillan.

Greenwald, Bruce C., and Joseph E. Stiglitz. 1988. "Money, Imperfect Information, and Economic Fluctuations." In *Finance Constraints, Expectations, and Macroeconomics,* edited by M. Kohn and S. Tsiang. Oxford, England: Oxford University Press.

————. 1989. "Toward a Theory of Rigidities." *American Economic Review* 79 (May): 364–69.

Groves, Robert M., Nancy H. Fultz, and Elizabeth Martin. 1992. "Direct Questioning About Comprehension in a Direct Survey." In *Questions About Questions: Inquiries into the Cognitive Bases of Surveys,* edited by J. Tanur. New York: Russell Sage Foundation.

Hall, Robert E. 1986. "Market Structure and Macroeconomic Fluctuations." *Brookings Papers on Economic Activity* (2): 285–322.

————. 1988. "The Relation Between Price and Marginal Cost in U.S. Industry." *Journal of Political Economy* 96 (October): 921–48.

Hall, R.L., and C.J. Hitch. 1939. "Price Theory and Business Behavior." *Oxford Economic Papers* (May): 12–45.

Hall, Simon, Mark Walsh, and Tony Yates. 1996. "How Do U.K. Companies Set Prices?" Unpublished manuscript, Bank of England.

Haltiwanger, John, and Joseph E. Harrington, Jr. 1991. "The Impact of Cyclical Demand Movements on Collusive Behavior." *RAND Journal of Economics* 22 (Spring): 89–106.

Haynes, W. Warren. 1973. *Pricing Decisions in Small Business.* Westport, Conn.: Greenwood Press (Originally published in 1962 by University of Kentucky Press).

Holmes, James M., and Patricia A. Hutton. 1996. "Keynesian Involuntary Unemployment and Sticky Nominal Wages." *Economic Journal* 106 (November): 1564–85.

Huston, John, and Nipoli Kamdur. 1996. "$9.99: Can 'Just Below' Pricing be Reconciled with Rationality?" *Eastern Economic Journal* 22 (Spring): 137–45.

Jobber, D., and Graham Hooley. 1987. "Pricing Behavior in U.K. Manufacturing and Service Industries." *Managerial and Decision Economics*: 167–71.

Kahneman, Daniel, Jack Knetsch, and Richard Thaler. 1986. "Fairness as a Constraint on Profit: Seeking Entitlements in the Market." *American Economic Review* 76 (September): 728–41.

————. 1991. "Anomalies: The Endowment Effect, Loss Aversion, and Status Quo Bias." *Journal of Economic Perspectives* 5 (Winter): 193–206.

Kandori, Michihiro. 1991. "Correlated Demand Shocks and Price Wars During Booms." *Review of Economic Studies* 58 (January): 171–80.

Kaplan, A.D.H., Joel B. Dirlam, and Robert F. Lanzillotti. 1958. *Pricing in Big Business: A Case Approach*. Washington, D.C.: The Brookings Institution.

Kashyap, Anil K. 1995. "Sticky Prices: New Evidence from Retail Catalogs." *Quarterly Journal of Economics* 110 (February): 245–74.

Keynes, John Maynard. 1939a. *The General Theory of Employment, Interest, and Money*. New York: Harcourt, Brace & World.

———. 1939b. "Relative Movements of Real Wages and Output." *Economic Journal* 49 (March): 34–51.

Krane, Spencer D., and Steven N. Braun. 1991. "Production Smoothing Evidence from Physical-Product Data." *Journal of Political Economy* 99 (June): 558–81.

Lanzillotti, Robert F. 1964. *Pricing, Production, and Marketing Policies of Small Manufacturers*. Pullman, Wash.: University of Washington Press.

Lebow, David E., David J. Stockton, and William L. Wascher. 1995. "Inflation, Nominal Wage Rigidity, and the Efficiency of Labor Markets." Mimeo, Federal Reserve Board.

Leijonhufvud, Axel. 1968. *On Keynesian Economics and the Economics of Keynes*. New York: Oxford University Press.

Levy, Daniel, Mark Bergen, Shantanu Dutta, and Robert Venable. 1996 "On the Magnitude of Menu Costs: Direct Evidence from Large U.S. Supermarket Chains." Paper prepared for National Bureau of Economic Research's Economic Fluctuations conference.

Maccini, Louis J. 1973. "On Optimal Delivery Lags." *Journal of Economic Theory* 5 (April): 107–25.

Mankiw, N. Gregory. 1985. "Small Menu Costs and Large Business Cycles: A Macroeconomic Model of Monopoly." *Quarterly Journal of Economics* 100 (May): 529–38.

Maskin, Eric, and Jean Tirole. 1988. "A Theory of Dynamic Oligopoly II: Price Competition, Kinked Demand Curves, and Edgeworth Cycles." *Econometrica* 56 (May): 571–99.

Mattey, Joe P. 1993. "Cumulation of Individual Responses to Input Price Changes: Estimates from an Input-Output System with Distributed Activities." *Economic Systems Research* 5: 17–40.

McFadden, Daniel. 1974. "Conditional Logit Analysis of Qualitative Choice Behavior." In *Frontiers in Econometrics*, edited by P. Zarembka. New York: Academic Press.

McLaughlin, Kenneth J. 1994. "Rigid Wages?" *Journal of Monetary Economics* 34 (December): 383–414.

Means, Gardner C. 1935. "Industrial Prices and Their Relative Inflexibility." U.S. Senate Document 13, 74th Congress, 1st Session, Washington.

Moggridge, Donald, ed. 1973. *The Collected Writings of John Maynard Keynes*, vol. XIV. London: Macmillan.

Monroe, Kent B. 1973. "Buyers' Subjective Perceptions of Price." *Journal of Marketing Research* X (February): 70–80.

Nowotny, Ewald, and Herbert Walther. 1978. "The Kinked Demand Curve—Some Empirical Observations." *Kyklos* 31: 53–67.

Okun, Arthur. 1981. *Prices and Quantities: A Macroeconomic Analysis.* Washington, D.C.: The Brookings Institution.

Parkin, Michael. 1986. "The Output-Inflation Tradeoff When Prices Are Costly to Change." *Journal of Political Economy* 94 (February): 200–24.

Peters, Thomas J., and Robert H. Waterman, Jr. 1982. *In Search of Excellence.* New York: Harper & Row.

Phelps, Edmund S., and John Taylor. 1977. "Stabilizing Powers of Monetary Policy Under Rational Expectations." *Journal of Political Economy* 85 (February): 163–90.

Phelps, Edmund S., and Sidney G. Winter. 1970. "Optimal Price Policy Under Atomistic Competition." In *Microeconomic Foundations of Employment and Inflation Theory*, edited by E.S. Phelps. New York: Norton.

Ramey, Valerie A. 1991a. "Nonconvex Costs and the Behavior of Inventories" *Journal of Political Economy* 99 (April): 306–34.

———. 1991b. "Comment." *National Bureau of Economic Research Macroeconomics Annual*, 134–39.

Ravenscraft, David J., and F.M. Scherer. 1987. *Mergers, Sell-offs, and Economic Efficiency.* Washington, D.C.: The Brookings Institution.

Reagan, Patricia. 1982. "Price and Inventory Behavior." *Review of Economic Studies* 49 (January): 137–42.

Reid, Gavin C. 1981. *The Kinked Demand Curve Analysis of Oligopoly.* Edinburgh, Scotland: Edinburgh University Press.

Robinson, E.A.G. 1958. *The Structure of Competitive Industry.* Chicago: University of Chicago Press.

Romer, David, and Christina D. Romer. 1994. "What Ends Recessions?" *National Bureau of Economic Research Macroeconomics Annual.*

Rotemberg, Julio J. 1982. "Sticky Prices in the United States." *Journal of Political Economy* 90 (December): 1187–211.

Rotemberg, Julio J., and Garth Saloner. 1986. "A Supergame-Theoretic Model of Price Wars During Booms." *American Economic Review* 76 (June): 390–407.

Rotemberg, Julio J., and Michael Woodford 1991. "Cyclical Markups: Theories and Evidence." *National Bureau of Economic Research Macroeconomics Annual.*

Samiee, Saeed. 1987. "Pricing in Marketing Strategies of U.S.- and Foreign-Based Companies." *Journal of Business Research.*

Sargent, Thomas J. 1971. "A Note on the 'Accelerationist' Controversy." *Journal of Money, Credit, and Banking* 3 (August): 721–25.

Scherer, Frederick M. 1980. *Industrial Market Structure and Economic Performance*, 2d ed. Chicago: Rand McNally.

Shafir, Eldar, Peter Diamond, and Amos Tversky. 1995. "On Money Illusion." Mimeo, Priceton University.

Shapiro, Matthew D. 1988. "The Cyclical Behavior of Price-Cost Margins: Demand Elasticity and Marginal Cost." Mimeo, Yale University.

Sheshinski, Eytan, and Yoram Weiss. 1983. "Optimum Pricing Policy Under Stochastic Inflation." *Review of Economic Studies* 50 (July): 513–29.

Sibly, Hugh. 1995. "Customer Disenchantment, Loss Aversion, and Price Rigidity." Mimeo, University of Tasmania.

Smiley, Robert. 1988. "Empirical Evidence on Strategic Entry Deterrence." *International Journal of Industrial Organization* 6 (June): 167–80.

Stigler, George J., and James K. Kindahl. 1970. *The Behavior of Industrial Prices*. New York: Columbia University Press.

Stiglitz, Joseph E. 1979. "Equilibrium in Product Markets with Imperfect Information." *American Economic Review* 69 (May): 339–45.

———. 1987. "The Causes and Consequences of the Dependence of Quality on Price." *Journal of Economic Literature* 25 (March): 1–48.

Stiglitz, Joseph E., and Andrew Weiss. 1981. "Credit Rationing in Markets with Imperfect Information." *American Economic Review* 71 (June): 393–410.

Suchman, Lucy, and Brigitte Jordan. 1992. "Validity and the Collaborative Construction of Meaning in Face-to-Face Surveys." In *Questions About Questions: Inquiries into the Cognitive Bases of Surveys*, edited by J. Tanur. New York: Russell Sage Foundation.

Suslow, Valerie Y. 1988. "Stability in International Cartels: An Empirical Survey." Mimeo, Hoover Institution.

Sweezy, Paul M. 1939. "Demand Under Conditions of Oligopoly." *Journal of Political Economy* 47 (August): 568–73.

Taylor, John B. 1980. "Aggregate Dynamics and Staggered Contracts." *Journal of Political Economy* 88 (February): 1–23.

Tirole, Jean. 1988. *The Theory of Industrial Organization*. Cambridge, Mass.: Massachusetts Institute of Technology Press.

U.S. Bureau of the Census. 1989. *1987 Census of Manufactures, Subject Series.* Washington: U.S. Government Printing Office.

———. 1990a. *1987 Census of Retail Trade, Subject Series*. Washington: U.S. Government Printing Office.

———. 1990b. *1987 Census of Wholesale Trade, Subject Series*. Washington: U.S. Government Printing Office.

———. 1991a. *1987 Census of Service Industries, Subject Series*. Washington: U.S. Government Printing Office.

———. 1991b. *1987 Census of Transportation, Subject Series*. Washington: U.S. Government Printing Office.

Warner, Elizabeth J., and Robert B. Barsky. 1995. "The Timing and Magnitude of Retail Store Markdowns with Reference to Weekends, Holidays, and Business Cycle Fluctuations." *Quarterly Journal of Economics* 110 (May): 321–52.

Weiss, Andrew. 1980. "Job Queues and Layoffs in Labor Markets with Flexible Wages." *Journal of Political Economy* 88 (June): 526–38.

Weiss, Yoram. 1993. "Inflation and Price Adjustment: A Survey of Findings from Micro Data." In *Optimal Pricing, Inflation, and the Cost of Price Adjustment*, edited by E. Sheshinski and Y. Weiss. Cambridge, Mass.: Massachusetts Institute of Technology Press.

Wessel, David. 1991. "The Price Is Wrong, and Economists Are in an Uproar." *Wall Street Journal*, January 2, 1991.

Woglom, Geoffrey. 1982. "Underemployment Equilibrium with Rational Expectations." *Quarterly Journal of Economics* 97 (February): 89–107.

Zarnowitz, Victor. 1973. *Orders, Production, and Investment—A Cyclical and Structural Analysis*. New York: National Bureau of Economic Research, distributed by Columbia University Press.

Index

Main entries to the questions on the manufacturing interview are indexed alphabetically by primary concept.

adverse selection theory applied to
    price rigidity (Allen), 125, 165–67,
    173–74
  in judging quality by price, 167–73
  in market clearing, 165
Akerlof, George, 21
Allen, Franklin, 166, 173
asymmetry in price adjustment
  coordination failure question
    (B10[b]), 264–65
  in costs of adjusting prices, 240–41
  downward Keynesian wage-price
    stickiness, 306
  of imperfect information, 165
  in nominal contract (B1), 121, 144
  Okun's prediction, 156–59
  price adjustment with nominal con-
    tracts, 144–45
  in pricing point theory (B4), 180
  procyclical elasticity of demand, 196
  test conducted for, 299
  testing price/quality theory for,
    169–70
  of upward and downward price stick-
    iness, 119–25
  See also symmetry
asymmetry questions, 120–24, 180
Azaraidis, Costas, 28, 149

Baily, Martin N., 35, 149
Ball, Laurence, 33, 238, 261, 270–73,
    310
Barro, Robert, 5
Barsky, Robert, 35

Basu, Susanto, 187
Bils, Mark, 24, 186
Blanchard, Olivier, 20, 198, 203, 270,
    301
Blinder, Alan, 29, 230, 274, 276, 282
Braun, Steven N., 23
business cycle
  correlation of nonprice competition
    with, 291
  discounts during, 143
  firms' sensitivity to, 189–90, 193
  marginal cost function, 18
  theory of price rigidity over, 8
  See also variable correlations

Caballero, Ricardo, 230
Canetti, Elie, xi-xii
Caplin, Andrew, 230, 301
Carlton, Dennis, 21, 25, 231, 235,
    283–84, 291, 312
Cecchetti, Stephen, 83, 215
Chirinko, Robert, 187
Choi, Don, 5
Clower, Robert, 260
collusion, 32–34
complementarity, strategic, 261
constant marginal cost (B7)
  correlation with other theories,
    116–19
  firms' ranking and rating of, 108–15
  of price stickiness, 18–19, 70, 102,
    108, 112, 216–20, 225, 303–4
  (B7[a]) variable costs per unit, 77,
    102, 216–25, 302

consumers
  significance of pricing points for,
    25–26, 179, 185
  See also sales to consumers and busi-
    ness (A2)
contracts
  implicit, 151–52
  indexation of, 132
  price stickiness theories based on,
    27–30, 92–95
  questions related to explicit and
    implicit, 92–95
  See also implicit contracts (B2); nomi-
    nal contracts (B1)
contracts with customers (A8)
  as source of price stickiness, 93
  (A8[a]) price setting in, 94
  (A8[d]) discounting, 143, 302
Cooper, Russell, 33, 261
coordination failure (B10)
  asymmetry question related to,
    123–24
  Ball-Romer model, 261, 270–73
  correlation of variables related to,
    265, 304
  correlation with other theories,
    116–19
  firms' ranking and rating of theory,
    108–15, 265–70
  implications for macroeconomic pol-
    icy, 310
  in price stickiness theories, 32–33,
    86, 108, 111, 260–69, 304, 307
  (B10[a]) firms' raising prices first, 58,
    263, 308
  (B10[b]) price cutting delays,
    123–24, 264–65
  (B10[c]) reasons for delays in price
    cutting, 265–66
cost-based pricing (B6), 19–20, 69, 72,
    85, 108, 111, 197–210, 297,
    304–5, 307, 312–13
  correlates of importance of, 207–10,
    304–5
  correlation with other theories, 116–19
  firms' ranking and rating of, 108–15,
    200–202, 218–20
  implications for macroeconomic pol-
    icy, 312–13
  (B6[a,b,c]) speed of change of price,
    205–7, 307

(B6[d]) foreseeing of price increases,
    202–3, 280, 307
  (B6[e]) stockpiling in advance of
    price increases, 203
  (B6[f]) circumstances for raising
    prices, 203, 307
  (B6[g]) circumstances for not raising
    prices, 204–5, 308
costs
  to maintain fixed price, 145–48
  price stickiness theories based on,
    18–22
  questions related to, 100–104
  summary of firms' part A responses,
    106
costs of price adjustment (B8)
  asymmetry question related to, 123
  correlation with other theories,
    116–19
  firms' ranking and rating of, 108–15
  price stickiness related to, 70–71,
    112, 226–31, 236–37, 242, 244
  (B8[a]) special or hidden costs,
    91–92, 161, 231–33, 244, 248,
    250, 266, 309
  (B8[b]) sources of adjustment costs,
    233, 301, 308
  (B8[c]) costs related to frequency of
    price change, 91–92, 234, 301
  (B8[d]) effect of decreased price on
    costs, 123, 237–38
  (B8[f]) effect of demand on produc-
    tion and prices, 239–42
  (B8[h]) firms' response to declining
    demand, 242
  (B8[j]) costs related to change in
    production, 161, 242–43
  (B8[k]) production change as alter-
    native to price change, 243
cost structure (A11)
  costs related to change in production
    level, 100, 207
cost structure (A12)
  fixed and variable costs, 100–101,
    135, 302
  marginal cost concept, 100–104, 112,
    135
customers
  differentiation among, 24
  elasticity of demand, 188–91, 196
  firms' concern with response of, 85,
    263, 287

firms' sales to, 96–97
implicit contract theory (B2), 152–58
in Okun's product market theory,
    149–51
perception of pricing points, 179, 185
rationing of products sold to, 95
reaction to cost-based price rise,
    204–5
regular, 302
See also consumers; contracts with
    customers (A8); sales to customers
    (A3)

data
    availability of study data, xiv
demand
    change in price or output with
        changes in, 239
    kinked demand curve of oligopoly
        theory, 30–32
    met out of inventory, 22–23
    price stickiness theories based on,
        23–26
    questions related to firms' response
        to, 96–99
    See also procyclical demand elasticity
        (B5)
demand elasticity
    in implicit contracts, 159–60
    procyclical, 188–89
    See also procyclical demand elasticity
        (B5)
Dillman, Don, 51
Dirlam, Joel, 40
discounts from contract price, 143, 302
Domowitz, Ian, 187

Earley, James, 42
economic conditions
    (A6) firm's sensitivity to, 97, 102,
        114
    (A7) influence of forecasts, 97–98
    See also business cycle
Engel, Eduardo, 230
Estrella, Arturo, 141, 163, 173
expectations with price cuts (A4), 99,
    135

Fair, Ray, 23
fairness
    money illusion in concept of, 27–28

in Okun's implicit contract theory of
    prices, 28, 150–51, 164
Fazzari, Steven, 187
Fernald, John, 187
firm characteristics
    application of sticky price theories to,
        109–15
    correlated with cost-based pricing
        theory, 207–10
    correlated with importance of coordi-
        nation failure theory, 269–70
    correlated with nonprice competition,
        289–91
    differences in MC curve, 220–25
    maintenance of fixed price, 145–48
firms
    conditions for price stickiness,
        298–99
    costs of price adjustment, 231–36
    differentiation among, 48, 53
    excluded from study, 95
    following (S,s) rule pricing strategy,
        89–92, 227–28, 230–32, 235,
        300–301
    menu costs of adjustment, 90–92,
        227–30, 233–34, 236, 238, 261
    random sample of GDP, 60–68
    rating importance of implicit con-
        tracts, 152, 159–64
    rating of importance of judging qual-
        ity by price, 167–74
    rating of nominal contract theory
        (B1), 134–39, 144
    reasons for and timing of price
        adjustment, 85–92
    response to change in demand,
        239–42
    response to cost shocks, 205–7
    sampling method for choosing, 13,
        60–68
    sensitive to business cycles, 189–90,
        193
    sensitivity to price, 159
    threshold prices of, 177–78, 180–81,
        185
    using implicit contracts, 153–55
    See also hierarchy in large firms (B9)
firms: factual questions
    (A1) firm's annual sales, 162, 316
    (A2, A3, A4, A6) on customer base,
        50, 56, 76, 97, 102, 114, 135, 155

firms: factual questions (*continued*)
  (A5, A8) contracts with customers,
    56, 95
  (A9, A10, A13) pricing practices, 56,
    84, 86, 92, 115, 161, 245, 307
  (A7) attention to forecasts, 97–99, 153
  (A11, A12) cost structure, 56, 77, 135
  (A13) time lag related to price
    change, 56, 86
Fischer, Stanley, 131
flat marginal cost
  firms with, 135
  theory, 112, 220–25
Fog, Bjarke, 41–42
forecasts (A7)
  effect on prices set, 97–98
  (A7[a,b]) influence of forecasts on
    price, 97–99, 153
Fultz, Nancy, 51

Goodman, Leo, 116
Goodman-Kruskal gamma, 116–17,
  125, 133, 137, 143, 162, 280
Gordon, Donald, 149
Gordon, Lawrence, 43
Gordon, Robert J., 4, 20, 36, 197, 203,
  300
Greene, William H., 140
Greenwald, Bruce, 37, 38, 54, 165
Groves, Robert, 51

Hall, R. L., 31, 39–40, 215
Hall, Robert E., 18, 187, 212–15, 218,
  304
Hall, Simon, 51
Haltiwanger, John, 34
Harrington, Joseph, 34
Hart's Law, 92–93
Haynes, Warren, 42
hierarchy in large firms (B9)
  correlates of importance of hierarchy,
    257–59
  correlation with other theories,
    116–19
  firms' ranking and rating of, 108–15,
    255–56
  menu costs, 245
  in price stickiness theories, 38–39, 69,
    71, 108, 111–12, 253–56, 303
  (B9[a]) cause of delays in price
    adjustment, 255–56

Hitch, C. J., 31, 39–40, 215
Holmes, James M., 300
Hooley, Graham, 43–44
Hubbard, Glenn, 187
Hutton, Patricia A., 300

implicit contracts (B2)
  applied to prices, 149–50
  asymmetry question, 119–20
  correlates of existence and impor-
    tance of, 159–64
  correlation with other theories,
    116–19
  to explain wage rigidity, 149
  firms' ranking and rating of, 108–15
  implications for macroeconomic
    policy, 312–13
  influence of, 5–6
  in price stickiness theories, 28, 79,
    86, 95, 108, 111, 153–59, 161–62,
    245, 302, 304–8, 312–13
  tests of, 151–53
  (B2[a]) countercyclical markup the-
    ory, 9–10, 95, 153–55, 159,
    161–62, 193, 196, 207, 261, 266,
    299
  (B2[b]) price level with weak
    demand, 120, 156
  (B2[c]) customers response to cost
    increase, 156–58
  (B2[e]) customer response to declin-
    ing costs, 157–58
inflation
  effect on pricing decisions, 153
  firms' use of forecasts of, 300
information
  asymmetrically imperfect, 165
  price stickiness theories based on
    imperfect, 36–39
interview technique
  as alternative to econometric
    method, 10–12
  as data collection method, 7–10
  design of, 48–53
  Fog survey, 41–42
  Hall-Hitch survey, 39
  idea and efficacy of, 7–12
  interviewers, timing, and problems,
    68–79
  Kaplan survey, 40
  L. Gordon survey, 43

questionnaire design and testing,
12–13
See also manufacturing interview
(Appendix)
inventories (B11)
asymmetry question related to, 124
correlates of importance of, 279–82,
303–4
correlation with other theories,
116–19
costs to hold, 245
firms' ranking and rating of theory,
108–15, 278
price stickiness theories related to,
22–23, 108, 274–82, 303–4
(B11[a]) costs to hold stocks, 245
(B11[a]) firms' holding of inventories, 276–78
(B11[b]) inventory changes related
to levels of demand, 124, 279
(B11[c]) firms' circumstances for
changing inventories, 278
(B11[d]) changing inventory as alternative to price adjustment, 278–79,
308
inventory turnover (A16), 104, 162,
277–78
invisible handshake theory.
See implicit contracts (B2).

Jobber, D., 43–44
John, Andrew, 33, 261
Jordan, Brigitte, 51, 53

Kahneman, Daniel, 150
Kandori, Michihiro, 34
Kaplan, A. D. H., 40, 42, 48, 215
Kashyap, Anil, 21, 176–77, 231, 215,
235
Keynes, John Maynard, 129, 215
Keynesian economics
coordination failure, 260–61
downward sticky prices of, 119–20,
125, 299, 306
lag in price response to costs, 20
neo-Keynesian customer and auction
markets, 164
neo-Keynesian menu costs of price
adjustment, 21, 261
nominal contracts of macro models,
27

predetermined price level, 129–30
real wage countercyclicality, 299
wage-price stickiness of, 3–4
Kindahl, James, 143
Kiyotaki, Nobuhiro, 270
Krane, Spencer D., 23
Kruskal, William, 116

Lanzillotti, Robert, 40, 41
Leahy, John, 230
Lebow, David, xii
Leijonhufvud, Axel, 260
Levy, Daniel, 231
limits on customers (A5), 95

Maccini, Louis, 283
McFadden, Daniel, 141, 163, 173
macroeconomic policy
implications for, 309–13
questions related to, 35–36
macroeconomic theory
implications for, 306–13
wage-price stickiness, 4
Mankiw, N. Gregory, 21, 90, 228, 238
manufacturing interview (Appendix A)
part A questions, 316–20
part B questions, 320–36
marginal cost
firm's MC curve, 216–25
firms with high level of, 135
Hall's analysis, 212–15, 221, 223, 225
procyclical, 186
See also constant marginal cost (B7);
flat marginal cost
marginal revenue
compared to shadow value of inventories, 275
with downward sloping demand
curve, 24
relation to price, 188
with kinked demand curve, 31–32
related to pricing points, 26
markets
nonprice methods of clearing, 25,
283–84
Okun's implicit contract theory,
149–51, 164
price stickiness theories based on
actions in, 30–36
Martin, Elizabeth, 51

money illusion
in concept of fairness, 27–28
evidence for, 153
in implicit contracts, 151, 164
possibility of, 132, 300
proscribed in rational behavior
models, 19

neoclassical economic theory
conditions for firm to raise prices,
283
marginal cost curve, 218
nominal price contracts, 27
nominal contracts (B1)
asymmetry question, 120–21
correlates of importance of, 137–39
correlations with other theories,
116–19
discounting in nominal contracts, 143
firms' ranking and rating of, 108–15,
133–34
as source of price stickiness, 70–72,
111–12, 132–34, 307
(B1[a]) role in price decreases,
142–43
(B1[d]) effect on volume of sales
and/or production, 144
nonprice competition (B12)
correlates of importance to firms of,
288–91
correlation with other theories,
116–19
firms' ranking and rating of theory,
108–15, 284–85
implications for macroeconomic policy, 310–12
in price stickiness theories, 25, 78,
108, 111, 162, 283–92, 304–5,
307, 310–12
(B12[a]), 267–68, 284
(B12[b]) important nonprice elements, 285–86, 307
(B12[c,e]) changing services as alternative to changing price, 78,
287–88, 308
(B12[d]) price change to meet temporary change in demand, 287
Nowotny, Ewald, 43

Okun, Arthur, 9, 28, 94–95, 105,
149–51, 161, 164, 207, 308

oligopoly theory
kinked demand curve of, 30–32
Rotemberg-Saloner model, 33–34
output production
as alternative to price change, 239–44
costs to change, 239–40, 242–44
percent to stock and to order (A15),
104, 245, 277–78

Parkin, Michael, 21
Part A questions. *See* firms: factual
questions; manufacturing interview
(Appendix A).
Petersen, Bruce, 187
Phelps, Edmund, 38
price adjustment
Blanchard's production model,
198–200, 202–3
econometric testing of, 6–9
Gordon's theory of sticky, 197–99,
203
mean lags, 202
price adjustment lags (A13), 85–89
price adjustment review (A9), 89–90,
92, 161, 245, 301, 307
related to cost-based price, 218–20
related to hierarchy in the firm (B9),
254–55
price adjustment costs of changing
prices, 231–36
convex and quadratic, 226–30, 234–35
correlates of existence and importance of, 244–51
Mankiw model, 228
menu costs, 90–92, 227–28, 233–34,
236, 238, 261
for quantity change, 239–40
Rotemberg model, 226–27, 230
price change (A10), 84–86, 90–92, 115
(A10[a]) frequency of price change,
84–85, 88, 307–8
(A10[b]) incremental or all- at-once,
90–91, 234–35, 301, 307
price change (A13)
(A13[a,b,c,d]) timing of price adjustment, 86–88, 115
(A13[a,b,c,d]) timing of price change,
158
price elasticity
downward rigidity, 196
procyclical, 186–89; 189

price in judging quality (B3)
asymmetry question related to, 121–22
correlation with other theories, 116–19
firms' ranking and rating of, 108–15, 168, 170–73
importance to firms interviewed, 111–12, 167–74, 303
as price stickiness theory, 302
variable correlations, 170–73
(B3[a]) hesitation to reduce price, 57–58
(B3[b]) conditions for price cuts, 169–70
price rigidity
basic model of, 307
constant marginal cost theory of (B7), 112, 216–20, 303–4
contracts as source of, 92–95
coordination failure as source of, 262–63, 269
with kinked demand curve, 175–76
Mankiw's model of price adjustment cost, 228
theory, 211–12
unobserved variation in cost of capital, 38
prices
absolute and relative, 18–19
based on historic costs (Okun), 150–52
countercyclical markup, 186–88, 216
in implicit contract theory, 149–53, 164
maintaining fixed, 145–48
pro- and countercyclical, 186–88, 299
pro- and countercyclical markups, 23–24
sticky, 4–5
threshold prices, 177–78, 180–81, 185
time in contracts for set price, 94–95
Walrasian market-clearing, 4, 6
price setting
of final price, 34
firms' agreements with customers, 94–95
under imperfect competition (Ball/Romer), 261, 270–73
under nominal contracts, 94, 132–34, 144

related to coordination failure, 260
summary of firms' part A responses, 106
price stickiness
in American industry, 298
conditions for, 298–99
costs and benefits to firms of, 134–39
direct measures of, 84–89
flat marginal cost theory, 112, 220–25
on frequency of price change (A10), 84–85, 88, 115
nominal, 176
over business cycles, 196
questions A10 and A13, 85–89
questions related to, 83–89
selection of theories used, 12–13, 17–18
theories of, 7
upward, 299
price stickiness theories
correlations among, 116–19
cost of capital variations, 38
criteria in selection and categories of, 17–18, 45–46
by name and number, 108, 321–38
nominal contracts (A8), 27
oligopoly theory kinked demand curve, 30–32
price protection (B13), 29–30
ranking and ratings of, 107–15
resale price maintenance, 34–35
"thick markets" theory, 35
uncertainties in price versus quantity changes, 37
(B1) nominal contracts, 27, 57, 70–72, 86, 93, 108, 111–12, 132–34, 307
(B2) implicit contracts, 28, 79, 86, 95, 108, 111, 153–59, 245, 304–5, 307–8, 312–13
(B3) price in judging quality, 36–37, 57–58, 108, 111–12, 167–74, 303
(B4) pricing points, 25–26, 108, 175–77
(B5) procyclical demand elasticity, 9, 23–25, 79, 108, 195
(B6) cost-based pricing, 19–20, 69–70, 72, 85, 108, 111, 197–210, 297, 304–5, 307, 312–13

price stickiness theories (*continued*)
  (B7) constant marginal cost theory,
    18–19, 70, 102, 108, 112, 216–20,
    303–4
  (B8) costs of price adjustment,
    21–22, 70, 85, 91–92, 108, 112
  (B9) hierarchy in large firms, 38–39,
    69, 71, 108, 111–12, 253–56, 303
  (B10) coordination failure, 32–33,
    86, 108, 111, 304, 307, 310
  (B11) inventories, 22–23, 108,
    274–82, 303–4
  (B12) nonprice competition, 25, 78,
    108, 111, 162, 283–92, 304–5,
    307, 310–12
pricing
  earlier survey research, 39–46
  relation of demand to, 96–99
  theories derived from interviews,
    surveys, and questionnaires, 39–45
  See also cost-based pricing (B6)
pricing points (B4)
  asymmetry question related to, 122
  correlates of existence and impor-
    tance of, 181–85
  correlation with other theories,
    116–19
  firms' ranking and rating of, 108–15,
    181–85
  in price stickiness theories, 25–26,
    108, 175–77, 302
  (B4[a]) breaking through, 177–78,
    179, 244
  (B4[b]) point at which barrier is
    broken, 179–80
  (B4[c,d]) price levels after price
    barrier is broken, 180–81
probit model
  nominal contracts, 139–42
  procyclical elasticity of demand,
    195–96
procyclical demand elasticity (B5)
  asymmetry question related to,
    122–23
  correlation with other theories,
    116–19
  firms' ranking and rating of, 108–15,
    190–96
  in price stickiness theory, 24–25, 79,
    186–88, 195–96
  (B5[a]) loyal customers sensitivity to
    price, 9, 77, 161, 193, 195
  (B5[b,c]) relevance of pricing by
    other firms, 122–23, 192
production
  production allocation (A15), 104,
    245, 277
productivity, procyclical Hall's analysis,
    212–15
psychological pricing points.
  See pricing points (B4).

quality
  customer inferences about, 165–67
  observable and unobservable differ-
    ences, 7, 37, 166–67
  See also price in judging quality (B3)
quantities
  cyclical behavior of (R. E. Hall),
    212–13
  nominal contract effect on, 145
  varying delivery of, 25
quantity theory of money, 3–4
questionnaire
  asymmetry questions, 120
  coding of responses, 108–9
  design and testing of, 12–13, 48–55
  Earley survey, 42
  Hall-Hitch survey, 39
  Jobber-Hooley, 43–44
  Kaplan survey, 40–41
  Lanzillotti survey, 4
  for manufacturing, services, and
    trade, 342–11
  part A design, use, and findings,
    13–14, 56, 83, 315–21
  part B questions and follow- up
    questions, 12–13, 56–58, 321–38
  respondents' understanding of, 75–79
  Samiee survey, 44
  section A factual questions, 50, 56,
    316–21

Ramey, Valerie, 102, 187, 215, 218
rationing. *See* limits on customers (A5).
Reagan, Patricia, 274
restrictions, legal or regulatory (A14),
    245
Romer, David, 33, 261, 270–73, 310
Rotemberg, Julio, 21, 33, 34, 90, 187,
    196, 226, 261
Rudd, Jeremy, xii

sales (summary of firms' part A responses), 106
sales to consumers and business (A2), 161, 302
  (A2[a]) fraction sold to consumers, 245
  (A2[c]) sales to governments, 207, 245
sales to customers (A3), 96–97, 155, 302
Saloner, Garth, 33, 196
Samiee, Saeed, 44
sampling method and size, 13, 49–50, 52, 60–68
Sargent, Thomas, 230
Shapiro, Matthew, 189
Sibly, Hugh, 237
Smiley, Robert, 44
Solow residual, 212–13
Spulber, Daniel, 230, 301
(S,s) rule, 89–92, 227–28, 230–31, 235, 300–301
state-dependent pricing rules, 89–92, 300–301
Stigler, George, 143
Stiglitz, Joseph, 32, 37, 38, 54, 165
Suchman, Lucy, 51, 53
survey instrument
  part A in Appendix A, 50, 56, 316–20
  part B in Appendix A, 56–58, 320–36
surveys
  design of Blinder survey, 17–18
  L. Gordon, 43
  Nowotny-Walther, 43
  pilot study of Blinder survey, 58–60
  random sampling of firms, 60–68
  response rate for sticky price survey, 58–60, 72–75
  Samiee, 44
  Smiley, 44
  See also interview technique; questionnaire; sampling method and size
Sweezy, Paul, 31
symmetry
  of constant marginal cost theory (B7), 119
  in nominal contract (B1) responses, 121
  of price stickiness related to inventories, 282
  in procyclical demand elasticity, 192

of stickiness in implicit contract theory, 152
testing in price adjustment cost theory, 237–38
testing price/quality theory for, 169–70
See also asymmetry

Taylor, John, 198
Theory B1. *See* nominal contracts (B1).
Theory B2. *See* implicit contracts (B2).
Theory B3. *See* price in judging quality (B3).
Theory B4. *See* pricing points (B4).
Theory B5. *See* procyclical demand elasticity (B5).
Theory B6. *See* cost-based pricing (B6).
Theory B7. *See* constant marginal cost (B7).
Theory B8. *See* costs of price adjustment (B8).
Theory B9. *See* hierarchy in large firms (B9).
Theory B10. *See* coordination failure (B10).
Theory B11. *See* inventories (B11).
Theory B12. *See* nonprice competition (B12).
time-dependent pricing rules, 89–92, 300–301
Tirole, Jean, 34

user's guide, xiii-xiv

variables: Appendix B list, 337–38
variable correlations
  price stickiness theories, 134–39
  (B1) nominal contracts, 134–42
  (B2) implicit contracts, 159–64
  (B3) price in judging quality, 170–73
  (B4) pricing points, 181–85
  (B5) procyclical demand elasticity, 193–96
  (B6) cost-based pricing, 207–10
  (B7) constant marginal cost, 220–25
  (B8) costs of price adjustment, 244–51
  (B9) hierarchy in large firms, 256–59
  (B10) coordination failure, 265–70
  (B11) inventories, 279–82
  (B12) nonprice competition, 288–91

wage-price stickiness
  allocative significance, 4–5
  Keynesian economics, 3–4, 306
  measuring, 6–7
  using interview method to collect
    data, 7–10
wages
  implicit contract theory of, 149–50
  Keynesian countercyclical, 299
  sticky, 4–6
Walther, Herbert, 43

Wanner, Eric, xi, 59
Warner, Elizabeth, 35
Weiss, Yoram, 4, 165
Wessel, David, 29
Winter, Sidney, 38
Woglom, Geoffrey, 32
Woodford, Michael, 33, 34, 187, 261

Yellen, Janet, 21

Zarnowitz, Victor, 104